1950. 6. 25～1953. 7. 27

Korean War 1129

Abridgment

Woojung Books

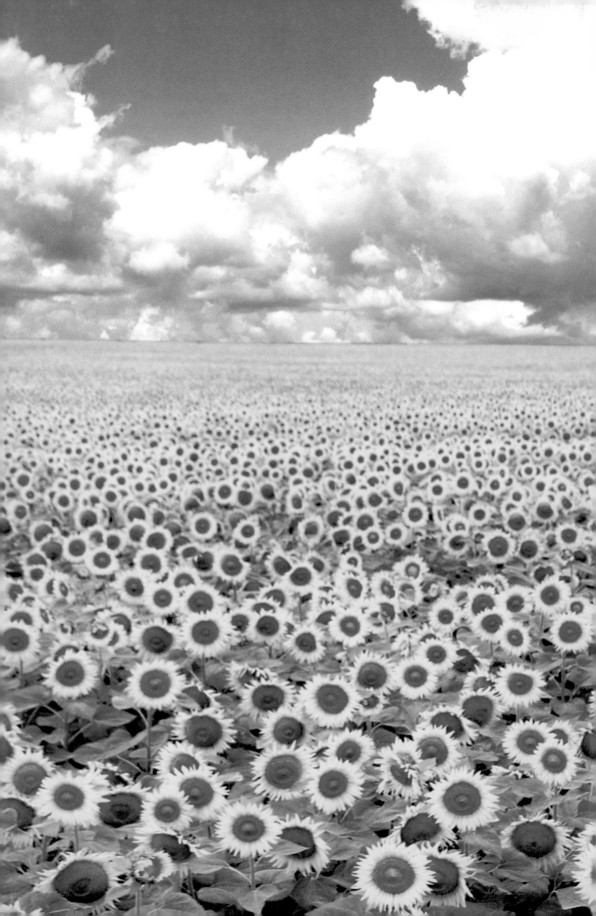

Lee, Joong Keun (李重根)

Lee, Joong Keun is the founder of Booyoung Group which is specialized in constructing houses for rent, having greatly contributed to the developmet of the Korean housing culture, as one of the pioneers in that area. His pen-name is Woojung.

With a strong belief that "investment in educational infrastructure is important for the future," he began his donation work from 1991 with the construction of the Booyoung elementary school in Suncheon. Thereafter, he has donated a total of 140 educational facilities covering dormitories, libraries, gymnasiums, and other educational welfare facilities across the country.

Since 2003, his contribution activities expanded to the Asia-Pacific and African regions. So far, in 16 countries 60,000 digital pianos, 600,000 blackboards and 600 school buildings have been donated.

He also tried to spread Korean favorite folk songs such as "Arirang" and "Graduation Song" to those countries.

In addition, he has contributed financially to the various international organizations; among others, US $3 million to "the UN Habitat" and US $10 million to "the World Taekwondo Federation".

With his interest in the academic community, he has served as chairman of the board of directors of many educational institutions and foundations. He received Ph.D degree in public administration from Korea University, and honorary doctorate degrees from four universities.

He serves now as Chairman of ROKAFIS(ROK Air Force Internet Society), Vice-Chairman of the Korea Senior Citizens Association, and Vice-Chairman of the National Unification Advisory Council, Seoul Branch. All of his public contributions as such have been recognized with many merits of honor received.

Among many of his publications, some significant writing include "Public Policy on Rental Housing." "History of Korean Housing" "1,775 Days from the Day of Liberation" and many other articles.

This book is published to help the post-war generation to correct their distorted views on the Korean War.

1950. 6. 25~1953. 7. 27

Korean War 1129

Edited by Lee, Joong Keun

Woojung Books

Prelude

Lee, Joong Keun 李重根

The Korean War, which broke out in the mid-20th century, was equivalent to a Third World War, except that nuclear weapons were not used.

In human history, the Korean War stands out as a most unique civil war. Nearly two million soldiers representing countries from all over the world fought for the freedom of South Korea. At the time of the war, 63 of the 93 independent countries in the world provided South Korea with troops and war supplies. On the other hand, only the Soviet Union and Communist China provided North Korea with air force and ground troops support – while Bulgaria, Czechoslovakia, Hungary, Poland, and Romania provided medical assistance. Mongolia and East Germany provided additional aid.

The Korean War was a turning point in the process of achieving the current economic success of South Korea. All of these unique factors make it necessary to look at the Korean War from a broad objective perspective. This is my duty, to hand down the facts about the Korean War "as it happened," while avoiding the prejudices that might warp narration of the events that unfolded.

"The Korean War 1129 Days" is the first project published by "Woojung Books."
This publication collected and recorded what happened on the Korean Peninsula relative to the international community starting with the North Korea Forces' launch of a full-scale invasion of a defenseless South Korea, with about 242 tanks and 170 combat planes at 4 a.m. on June 25, 1950, and going all the way through to the Armistice agreement between the UN and North Korea at 10 a.m. on July 27, 1953.

South Korea today is a shining example of a great historical triumph, recovering from the devastation of war and a hopeless situation to become a modern, advanced society.
In this 21st century era, there is a need to reveal the realities of the unfinished war and reflect on that "forgotten war." It would be wise to learn lessons from the bloody war and reflect on them in the light of today's culture, since culture is a reflection of economic achievement. It is the author's wish that this book serves as a mirror of history to reveal the realities of the Korean War so that it can be used as a primary source for studies on the Korean War.
I dedicate this book to my beloved wife, Na, Kil Soon (羅 吉 順).

4, May 2015

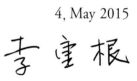

Korea's Long-Existing Military Demarcation Line
Becomes Increasingly Fortified · 568

1952

The Year of Black Dragon
Dangi 4285

1953

The Year of Black Snake
Dangi 4286

From the Yalta Conference to the Korean War

Lee, Joong Keun 李重根

Until the official documents pertaining to Korean War were released, it was a common belief that the top-level leaders of the United States (USA), the United Kingdom (UK), and the Soviet Union came to an agreement over a trusteeship plan regarding the 38th parallel at the Yalta Conference in February of 1945. According to the document numbered "319-ABC File 1942~1948, No. 387" held by the U.S. National Archives and Records Administration and "As I Saw It," the Cold War memoirs written by Dean Rusk, Secretary of State in the Kennedy administration, the 38th parallel was a military border set up to block a Soviet occupation of the entire Korean Peninsula. Dean Rusk and Charles Bonesteel, the chief of policy division at the Department of War urgently drew a border at the 38th parallel on a 1942 National Geographic Map of the Korean Peninsula at midnight when Japan proposed an unconditional surrender on August 10, 1945. The Soviet Union conceded to the American plan and halted their troops' advance at the 38th parallel.

The 38th parallel was accepted as inevitable by the Korean people who had just been liberated from 36 years of Japanese colonization and became a practical fixed line. As a matter of fact, the division of the Korean Peninsula at the 38th parallel was not a subject of discussion at the Cairo, Yalta, and Potsdam Conferences held before the end of World War II.

"Korea's freedom and independence through appropriate procedure" was promised at the Cairo Conference on November 23, 1943 and was reconfirmed later;

The United States and the Soviet Union Forces that were stationed to neutralize the Japanese Forces in the south and the north of the 38th parallel established military administrations.

On August 25, the division of North and South Korea was further solidified when inter-Korean civilian crossings, telephone calls, postal exchanges and railroad connections were prohibited. Soviet troops took initial steps starting with the occupation of each provincial capital of the North, leading to eventual complete occupation of North Korea (August 29).

On September 6, the long distance telephone line between Haeju and Seoul was disconnected and the division of South and North Korea at the 38th parallel became complete.

Despite the fact that the 38th parallel became a fixed divider of demarcation, Soviet troops arbitrarily moved south across the 38th parallel.

There is proof that Soviet troops often stayed in Kaesong before it became a station for U.S. forces. Soviet political officers had even appeared at the banquet for the provincial government executives on the day when U.S. troops were dispatched to Chuncheon on September 20.

The Soviet military administration disbanded the "Korean Country Founding

Commission (建國準備委員會)", which was intended to establish a unified Korean government. As a substitute, the Soviets supported the establishment of a Granzhdanskia Administration (literally meaning "civilian government") by the 25th Army Commander, Gen Ivan Chitiakove.

Soviet military administration inaugurated the "Temporary Council of People's Commissars (臨時人民委員會)" led by Kim Il Sung and carried out socialism rapidly. More than 90% of the industrial base in North Korea was nationalized. In February of 1947, the "Temporary Council of People's Commissars" was revamped as the "Council of People's Commissars of North Korea (北朝鮮人民委員會)" and began to prepare for the establishment of a legitimate government.

On the other hand, South Korea was experiencing social upheaval caused by reaction to international talks regarding trusteeship. Unlike the Soviet forces that rapidly moved to occupy stations in North Korea, U.S. troops were methodically slow to move, respecting the prearranged 38th parallel borderline between the Soviet Union and the United States. The United States did not even send troops to Korea from Okinawa until September 3.

U.S. troops established the Occupation Forces Headquarters on September 9 after their entry to Seoul and conducted a signing ceremony for the Japanese surrender at 4 p.m. on that day at the colonial Japanese authorities' building (which was later renamed the South Korean Capitol Building upon the establishment of the Korean Government). Three days later, on September 12, the U.S. Army military administration was established and started military rule. The U.S. administration advocated political neutrality within South Korea and supported freedom of thought. South Korea was free under the U.S. administration. Unlike centralization led by Kim Il Sung in North Korea, it was not easy to rally and form political alliances in South Korea.

The United States, British, and Soviet trusteeship plan agreed to in Moscow in December 1945 became a major point of political contention, causing social unrest throughout South Korea. This decision caused severe left-right ideological conflicts in South Korea. The U.S.-Soviet Joint Talks aimed at producing conditions for a provisional government for Korea failed to bring forth any tangible results after two years of back and forth meetings. The United States proclaimed its abandonment of the trusteeship plan and transferred authority to the U.N.

On November 14, 1947, the UN made a decision to hold general elections in both South and North Korea. The UN dispatched a UN Temporary Commission for Korea to administer general elections in both South and North Korea. The Soviet Union opposed the elections and denied the UN representatives' entry into North Korea. The UN thus decided to execute the general election only in South Korea where the commission activities were allowed.

On May 10, 1948, a general election was carried out in South Korea, with 198 members of the National Assembly elected and the first National Assembly formed; despite strong objections from Leftists and sabotage by the South Korea Labor Party (南勞党).

Four days after the election, at noon on May 14, North Korea cut off electricity supply to South Korea without pre-notification and South Korea abruptly became a nation without electric power. On July 17, the Constitution of the Republic of Korea (ROK, (大韓民國)) and the National Government Organization Act were proclaimed. On August 15, 1948, the ROK Government was finally established three years after gaining independence from Japanese colonialism.

Shortly after the ROK Government was established, North Korea named Kim Il Sung Prime Minister and Pak Hon-yong the Deputy Prime Minister and established the Democratic Peoples' Republic of Korea (DPRK (朝鮮人民共和國) on September 9, 1948. North Korean central authorities created the opportunity for communization of North Korea and disregarded any opportunity to hold a general election under UN jurisdiction.

On July 29, 1949, U.S. Forces stationed in Korea withdrew their troops, a move that was followed by a Soviet announcement of its forces withdrawal plan on September 19, 1949. By the time the U.S. forces stationed in Korea withdrew, there had been frequent armed clashes near the 38th parallel.

At 4 a.m. on June 25, 1950, North Korean troops launched a full scale invasion with an attack order named "Pok Poong" (literal meaning is "storm," or 暴風 in Korean), with frontal force advancements near the 38th parallel border line ranging from the Ongjin Peninsula in the western region to Kaesong, Pocheon, Chuncheon, and Yangyang (four axes with 11 attachment points). North Korea was equipped with 242 of its T-34 Soviet tanks and approximately 200 aircraft, which included 170 combat planes. The North Korean troops were estimated at more than 200,000. By contrast, the ROK military did not have any tanks or combat planes at all, with a mere 20 training-purpose planes and liaison aircrafts

At midnight on June 24, 1950, the South Korean Armed Forces lifted the emergency alert which had been in effect for some time and sent soldiers home with two weeks special leave to help rice planting in farming areas. Also, of particular note, the day of June 25, was a weekend so almost half of the South Korean military was on leave or off their positions. The Army Chief of Staff, Chae Byeong Deok (蔡秉德) and high-ranking officials had attended the Army Club inauguration ceremony on the night of June 24 and they had only just gotten to bed, inebriated from a night of celebration, before being woken up by the nation's most dire emergency alert.

The United States called upon the UN Security Council and demanded an immediate debate on the conflict that had broken out on the Korean Peninsula. A session of the UN Security Council was held at 2 p.m. on June 25 (Korea time 4 a.m). The UN Security Council passed a resolution calling for the immediate cessation of combat action by the North Korean forces and the withdrawal of invading North Korean forces back to north of the 38th parallel .

On June 29, U.S. President Harry Truman called upon General Douglas MacArthur, Commander of the Allied Forces in the Far East, to lead the deployment of ground forces and prosecute airstrikes on military targets north of the 38th parallel. The units under MacArthur's command were deployed directly to the frontlines. The U.S. Army 24th Infantry Division's Task Force Smith arrived in Busan on July 1 as an advance element and engaged in the first exchange of fire with North Korean forces in the vicinity of Osan(Jukmiryeong) on July 5. The U.S. Forces were immediately stunned by the high-level artillery tactics displayed by the North Koreans.

On July 7, the UN made a decision to establish a U.S.-led UN Forces Command with primary military support coming from the United States.

This decision served as a lever to draw in countries such as Australia, Belgium, Canada, Columbia, France, Greece, Ethiopia, Luxembourg, The Netherlands, The Philippines, Thailand, Turkey, UK, and South Africa to provide military support for a UN Forces contingency effort in Korea.

A fierce battle erupted between UN and North Korean forces near the Nakdong River defense line. Fighting on the Nakdong River defense line was deadlocked and lasted until the Incheon Amphibious Operation (Incheon Landing) on September 15. The Incheon Landing served as a major turning point for the UN forces, who were able to use the operation to cut off North Korea's supply lines and disrupt North Korean forces' rear area operations. ROK Armed Forces and UN forces used the momentum created by the Incheon landing to perform a successful counter-offensive on the Nakdong River defense line, defeat North Korean forces below the 38th parallel and eventually to recapture Seoul. The pre-Korean War conditions were successfully restored.

However, the battlefield successes sparked controversial debates regarding a military push north beyond the 38th parallel. The side supporting a push north insisted on executing war criminals and reunifying Korea as a fulfillment of the original UN objective for the Korean Peninsula. On the other hand, the side opposing the push north worried that it would bring about direct intervention from the Soviet Union and Communist China. President Syngman Rhee (李承晩) ordered a march north and ROK Armed Forces breached the 38th parallel on October 1. The UN passed a resolution for the "incapacitation of the North Korea military force" in order to uphold the goal "to resolve the division of the Korean Peninsula and establish the authority of the UN."

President Truman approved the UN plan of sending MacArthur's UN Command to continue marching north.

The speed of advance north was faster than the speed of the advance south that the North Koreans had achieved in the first stage of the war. On October 1, the ROK 1st Corps broke through the 38th parallel and advanced north at a rate of 26km per day and pushed through to occupy the port of Wonsan, which was designated the most important military strategic location on October 10. The U.S. 1st Corps (U.S. First Calvary Division, U.S. 24th Division, ROK 1st Division) and ROK 2nd Corps (ROK 6th Division, 8th Division) were the first forces to occupy North Korea's capital city, Pyongyang. By the end of October 1950, the atmosphere of victory was prevailing. ROK Forces and UN Forces anticipated that the war would end by Thanksgiving, November 23. It seemed like the dream of reunification had come true.

However, Mao Zedong (毛澤東) was sent a telegram by Kim Il Sung requesting military aid at the first founding anniversary ceremony of the People's Republic of China at Tiananmen (天安門) Square.

Mao already had prepared military armed support foreseeing that this event could happen and he dispatched the "Peoples' Volunteer Forces (人民志願軍)" under the slogan of the "war to resist US aggression, to aid North Korea and defend our homeland (抗美援助, 保家衛國)." On October 19, 18 divisions (approximately 180,000 soldiers) of the Chinese 13th Group Army crossed the Yalu River from the Andong, Changdian, and Jian areas. The war had now entered a new phase.

Chinese Communist Forces attacked from the west line Jekyuryong Mountains, south of the Unsan-Huicheon positions, and east along the line north of Changjin Lake in order to block the advance of ROK and UN Forces. Most of the UN Forces were destroyed or isolated by the first wave of the Chinese Communist Forces' attacks. The Chinese second round of attacks was also fierce. The U.S. 2nd Infantry Division was annihilated at Gunu-ri and the U.S. Marines were isolated at Changjin Lake. The U.S. 1st Marine Division desperately attempted a breakout. On December 11, the U.S. 1st Marine Division fought desperately and broke through the siege, overcoming severe weather and rugged terrain.

Right after that, the United States deployed its 3rd and 7th Infantry Divisions and the ROK 1st Corps to Hamheung, established a beachhead and then proceeded with Hamheung evacuation operations. It was the largest humanitarian evacuation operation recorded in human history, in that more than 100,000 troops, 91,000 refugees, 17,500 vehicles, and 350,000 tons of war supplies were transported. The last outgoing vessel, the SS Meredith Victory, had 14,000 refugees, which was more than 230 times more than its rated capacity. Refugees had to stand and were jammed like sardines in a can for 3 days on a winter voyage destined for Geoje Island. This was just one example of a dramatic exodus that resulted from the Korean War. As a result of the Chinese Communist Army entry into the war, the frontline now became the 37th parallel.

However, the Communist Chinese troops ceased their full force attacks on all frontlines on about January 8, 1951 allowing ROK and UN Forces to recapture Seoul.

Although the UN Forces were able to successfully repel several massive Chinese Army offenses, the UN Forces were reaching the conclusion that complete victory would be difficult. The Chinese Communist Army's attempt at a massive spring offensive failed and both sides decided to seek a ceasefire instead of attempting to secure a complete victory, and so started the truce agreement talks.

The frontline was locked in a stalemate around the 38th parallel after one year of long, arduous battles, and debates regarding Armistice talks were started. Neither side was assured of victory; therefore the prevailing atmosphere was one supporting an Armistice agreement. UN Forces and the Communist Party opened ceasefire talks with behind-the-scenes contact.

On June 23, 1951, the Soviet Union Ambassador to the UN, Yakov Malik, positively responded to the motion to "restore peace through a ceasefire and the restoration of pre-war conditions." This was merely the start of a two-year-long negotiation that lasted from July 10, 1951 until the Armistice was signed on July 27, 1953.

Talks entered into genuine discussion and negotiations and started with setting up a Military Demarcation Line for establishment of the Demilitarized Zone. Despite objections from South Korea, UN Forces gave consideration to domestic and international public opinion and established a Military Demarcation Line. However, it took more than one year and eight months of negotiations to reach a complete Armistice agreement.

Negotiations over prisoner of war (POW) exchanges were an unexpected variable that prolonged the talks. Negotiations over POW exchanges started in 1951 right after the issue of setting up a Military Demarcation Line went to the subcommittee. UN Forces suggested the exchange of information regarding a roster of POWs and camp locations at the joint subcommittee and a mutual exchange took place. However, the roster that the Communist Party turned in was very different from what the UN negotiators had expected. The POW exchange issue led to a standstill in talks until mid-January 1952.

On March 5, 1953, when Joseph Stalin abruptly died of cerebral hemorrhage, war was coming to a conclusion and all the issues were concentrated on progress toward an Armistice. However, public sentiment in South Korea was different. People were outraged by the fact that negotiations were set to put the Korean Peninsula back to the prewar conditions after their huge sacrifices and bloodshed. President Syngman Rhee opposed the Armistice; public demonstrations and mass rallies against Armistice were held every day nationwide.

On May 1953, General Mark W. Clark, UN Forces Commander, visited President Rhee in Seoul and he explained the stance the UN forces took on the ultimatum regarding the POWs who refused repatriation. He pledged America's political, economic, and military support if President Rhee would cooperate with the ceasefire agreement; but President Rhee would not agree.

On June 8, 1953 a POW repatriation agreement was signed without South Korean consent. Signing a POW repatriation agreement crossed a major hurdle toward the Armistice. President Rhee made a political decision and took a stance to express South Korea's public furor over the exclusion of their opinion on the POW issue. He authorized the release of anti-Communist POWs without prior consultation with the United States and at midnight on June 18, 1953, as many as 27,389 anti- Communist POWs who were confined in concentration camps in Busan, Gwangju, Nonsan, Masan, Yeongcheon, Bupyong, and Daegu were released.

In order to rectify the situation, Assistant Undersecretary of Defense W.S. Robertson visited Korea and on July 12, 1953, Robertson agreed to sign an ROK-U.S. Mutual Defense Treaty after 14 rounds of negotiation with the ROK Government. This accelerated the Armistice talks.

At 10 a.m. on July 27, the ceasefire agreement was signed at the signing ceremony hall in Panmunjom. The representatives of both sides did not even greet each other. They signed at their seats, exchanged the documents through their senior officers and then left.

Although gunfire stopped on the frontlines, several issues still remained to be resolved. Most importantly, the boundary line for the sea was not clear. Regarding the maritime border, the UN insisted that three nautical miles from the land should belong to the respective countries while the Communists insisted on 12 nautical miles. So they could not reach an agreement. The control authority for the "islands of coastal waters and level of sea" followed the same criteria used before June 24, 1950. But there were no specific rules. The jurisdiction of the Commander in Chief of UN forces (CINC) was set as a proviso stipulation to be the only available ruling authority to govern the management of the five disputed islands in the West Sea (Baengnyeong, Daecheong, Socheong, Yeonpyeong, and Udo Islands).

On August 30, one month after the Armistice agreement, General Clark, CINC UNC unilaterally established the Northern Limit Line (NLL) between the province of Hwanghae-do in North Korea and the five Northwest Islands in the west sea, which are south of the 38th parallel, with the intent of avoiding any military conflicts and maintaining the ceasefire agreement. The establishment of the NLL was notified only to the ROK Navy as one of the UNC's mandated navy regulations. After the Korean War, the NLL was maintained without any practical difficulties and North Korea did not present any specific objections until 1973. However, North Korea has since brought this issue up as a major area of dispute between South and North Korea since the 1990s.

Even after the Armistice agreement, the POW repatriation was continued. On January 28, 1954, a total of 347 remaining Communist POWs were handed over to the North and on February 8, 1954, POWs numbering 88 chose to be sent to neutral nations left for India with an Indian military convoy at Incheon harbor. Following these exchanges, POW repatriation was closed.

Attack of North Korean People's Army(NKPA) on the South(1950. 6. 25～9.15)

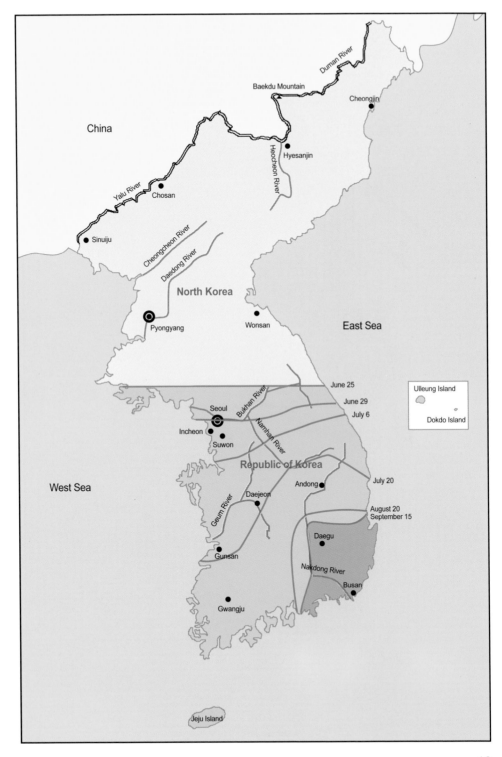

Advancement of UN forces and the ROK army to the North(1950. 9. 15～11. 30)

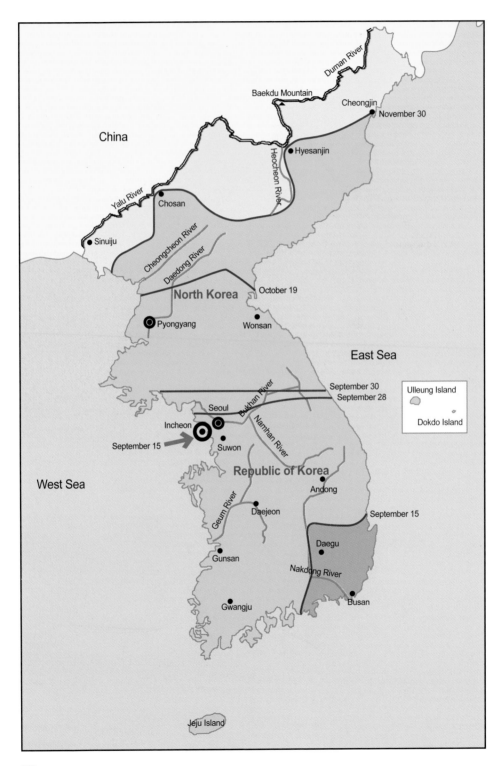

Military Demarcation Line (MDL) and Northern Limit Line (NLL) due to the Cease-fire Agreement(1953. 7. 27~)

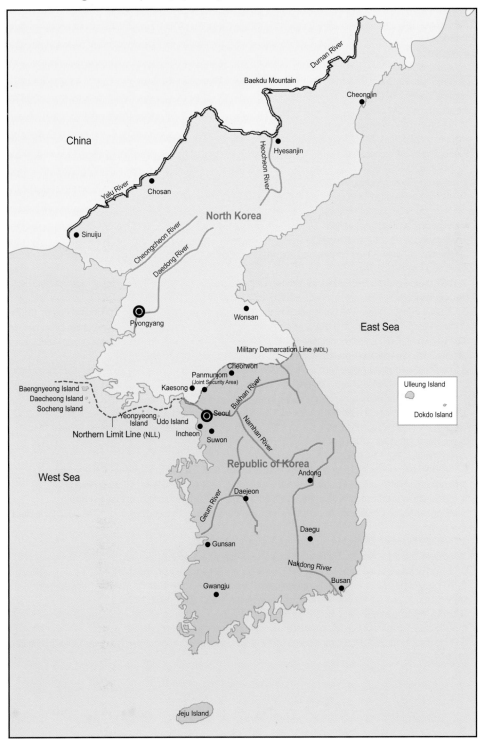

Note

1. This narrative spans the period from the outbreak of the Korean War (June 25, 1950) to the signing of the Armistice agreement (July 27, 1953). It covers the war situation, international politics, socio-cultural situations, and the daily lives of the common people.

2. In order to deliver the vividness of the historical facts, present tense is used throughout this book.

3. Presentation of materials is based on the date of occurrence of the event. Some are based on the date when an event was announced in the media, or at a press conference. The following are the standards for content selection.

① War Situation: General situation of the frontline. Combat situation of UN forces, ROK military, North Korean soldiers, Communist Chinese or Soviet soldiers. Deployment or order of command that might influence the frontline, the situation of POW camps.

② At Home: General situation of domestic politics, economy, and society. Situation of major personnel who may affect national politics. Situation of support from UN related NGOs. Major situational changes in North Korea and Pyongyang media broadcasts.

③ Overseas: Major events in Asia, Australia, America, Western Europe, Africa, Eastern Europe.

4. The new English terminology translated from Korean is registered on the online Naver Dictionary.

5. The South Korea system of Romanizing Korean is used to transliterate the names of individuals and for geographic locations in the South Korea. However, the names of individuals linked to a specific historical or personal preference for transliteration are kept unchanged.

6. The following terms are interchangeable:

① Republic of Korea Armed Forces, also known as the ROK Armed Forces, refers to the armed forces of South Korea. (Source: Wikipedia)

② The Korean People's Army (KPA), also known as the People's Army, refers to the military forces of North Korea. (Source: Wikipedia)

③ Chinese military forces who participated in the Korean War are called Chinese Communist Forces (CCF) or Chinese People's Volunteer Army (PVA), which is different from the Chinese regular army, People's Liberation Army (PLA); however, PVA is mostly composed of PLA especially from Manchuria. The Chinese government takes an official stance that volunteers participated in the Korean War. (Source: Wikipedia)

④ The Korean Armistice Agreement, a.k.a. Korean Armistice Negotiation was signed between the United Nations Command and the Chinese-North Korean Command on July 27, 1953. (Source: Wikipedia)

7. The following are the main resources consulted in researching this book:

① Korean War (Ministry of National Defense War History Compiling Board, 1952 ~ 1954)
- Korean War I, (1950.5.1 ~ 1951.6.30)
- Korean War II, (1951.7.1 ~1952.6.30)
- Korean War III, (1952.7.1 ~1953.7.27)

② The Chronological Table of Korean History (First) (1984 printing, The National Institute of Korean History)

③ Materials for History of the Republic of Korea v. 17~v. 29 (The National Institute of Korean History)

④ The Chronological Table for Korean History (2008 printing, The National Institute of Korean History)

⑤ Military Armistice Conference Record of Events and Transcripts of Proceedings 1~10 (The National Institute of Korean History)

⑥ The Chronological Table for National Defense History (1945~1990)

⑦ The Daily Log of the Korean War (Korea Institute for Military Affairs, 1991)

⑧ Foreign Relations of the United States 1~7 (The National Institute of Korean History)

⑨ The documents related to the UN Korea temporary delegation 1~7 (The National Institute of Korean History)

⑩ The Chronology of the People's Republic of China History (1950. 1951. 1952. 1953)

⑪ Xinhua News Agency (Beijing, Reference Room)

⑫ Photo data: Korean War I. II (Nunbit, 2010)

⑬ Photo data: 1950 0625: Photograph collection for 60th Anniversary of Korean War (Gyeonggi Cultural Foundation, 2010)

"The June 25 War was provoked illegally by the North Korean Communists aiming at communizing South Korea by Force"

-President Trueman

1950

The Year of White Tiger Dangi 4283

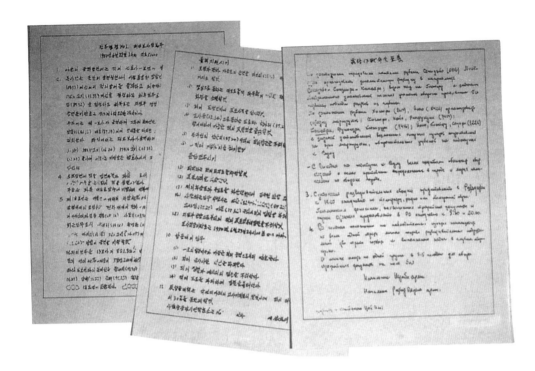

Operation No. 1 of North Korean Army 4th Infantry Division (1950. 6. 22)

North Korean Army Motorcycle Unit is moving to the south through Uijeongbu.

June 25, Sunday (May 10, by lunar calendar, 辛卯日 White Rabbit) Rainy and Very clear
1 Day of the War

War Situation
- The North Korean People's Army(North Korean Army) launches an all-out attack on the South.
- At 4 a.m. the secret code "Storm" for attack was issued to all the North Korean Units. Along the 38th parallel, the 1st, 2nd, 3rd, 4th, 5th, 6th and 12th Divisions and the 105th tank brigade crossed the border at 11 points and invaded South Korea.
- An North Korean advance unit crosses the Imjin River.
- The ROK Army Chief of Staff, Chae Byung-duk, announces that 40,000 to 50,000 North Korean troops and 94 tanks have begun invading South Korea.

At Home
- President Syngman Rhee holds an emergency meeting with the UN Commission on Korea and express his hope for a peaceful resolution. All Government agencies are put on alert. Acting Prime Minister and Defense Minister, Shin Sung-mo requests that the United States supply arms to South Korea.
- The UN Commission on Korea proposes an immediate ceasefire to North Korea by broadcast and to hold a peace conference for resolution of the situation.
- The Government proclaims a special presidential decree to punish crimes under the state of emergency (Presidential emergency decree No.1).

Overseas
- The UN Security Council holds a special session and adopts a resolution proposed by the United States, calling for an immediate ceasefire and withdrawal of the North Korean Forces to the 38th parallel (voting at 9 a.m., Soviet Union absent, Yugoslavia abstains).
- The Supreme Commander of the Allied Powers (SCAP) conducts urgent airlift operation of transporting arms to Korea.
- President Truman authorizes the U.S. Air Force and the U.S. Navy to operate only within the area south of the 38th parallel.

June 26, Monday (May 11, by lunar calendar, 壬辰日 Black Dragon) Clear
2 Day of the War

War Situation
- Two airplanes of North Korean Army again bomb Gimpo and Yeouido Airports.
- A U.S. Mustang fighter (F-80) engages in its first air scramble with a Soviet-made Yak in

President Syngman Rhee, together with Brigadier General Church(first, left), Counselor Drumright of U.S. Embassy (second, left) and U.S. Ambassador, John Mucho(first, right). At this meeting, Daejeon was decided as a provisional capitol.

the skies over Seoul.

At Home
- The Plenary Session of the National Assembly approves a message to be sent to the United Nations, the United States Congress and the United States President.
- North Korea establishes the Defense Commission (Prime Minister: Kim Il Sung, members: Park Hon-young, Hong Myung-hee, Kim Chaek, Choi Yong-gun, Park Il-woo, and Chung Joon-taek).

Overseas
- General of the Army Douglas MacArthur requests the Japanese Government to suspend the publication of the Communist "Red Flag."
- The UN Commission on Korea reports to the UN Secretary-General that the North Korean aggression was a deliberate, all-out invasion of the Republic of Korea.

June 27, Tuesday (May 12, by lunar calendar, 癸巳日 Black Snake) Cloudy
3 Day of the War

War Situation
- U.S. Far East Command establishes an Advance Defense Command (ADCOM) at Suwon.

• The North Korean Forces occupy Chuncheon and cross the Soyang River.

At Home

• The Government moves its capital to Daejeon.

Overseas

• The UN Commission on Korea moves to Tokyo.
• Truman announces, "The June 25 war was provoked illegally by the North Korean Communists aiming at communizing South Korea by Force."
• The State Department announces the appointment of General of the Army MacArthur as the highest Commander over military operations in Korea.

June 28, Wednesday (May 13, by lunar calendar 甲午日 Blue Horse) Cloudy
4 Day of the War

War Situation

• The North Korean Forces start entering Seoul early morning. The North Korean Army Forces occupy Hongcheon.

At Home

• The Government proclaims a "special decree on the proclamation of emergency laws" and "a special measure to punish crimes under the state of emergency."
• The Government announces a "special measure to regulate deposits and withdrawals from banks" (President's Urgent Decree No. 2).

Overseas

• Britain's deputy representative to the UN notifies the UNSC president that Britain has decided to have its naval forces stationed near Japanese waters participate in the war.
• The Philippines informs the UN of its intent to dispatch troops to Korea.

June 29, Thursday (May 14, by lunar calendar, 乙未日 Blue Horse) Clear
5 Day of the War

War Situation

• General MacArthur flies to Korea, assesses the war situation, and inspects the defense posture

General MacArthur arrives at Seoul by private plane to assess the war situation. (1950. 6. 29)

of the ROK Forces, and the U.S. Air Force and the Navy extend their areas of operation beyond the 38th parallel.

At Home
- President Rhee meets with General MacArthur visiting Korea.
- Financial organizations in Daegu start imposing limits on deposit withdrawals.

Overseas
- UNSC adopts a resolution of military support for South Korea.
- The Government of India supports the UN resolution on Korea.

June 30, Friday (May 15, by lunar calendar, 丙申日 Red Monkey) Rainy
6 Day of the War

War Situation
- The U.S. Advance Command and Liaison Group(ADCOM) in Korea moves its post from Suwon to Daejeon.

At Home
- Major General Chung Il-kwon is appointed as Commander-in-Chief of the ROK Army, Navy and Air Forces, and concurrently as the ROK Army Chief of Staff.
- 500 students organize an "Emergency Students Volunteers Unit" at Suwon.

Overseas
- Thirty-two member states express support for the UNSC resolution calling for military assistance to South Korea.
- General MacArthur, Commander of the Far East Command, receives full authorization to mobilize the 24th Division stationed in Japan and to launch attacks against the North beyond the 38th parallel.

July 1, Saturday (May 16, by lunar calendar, 丁酉日 Red Rooster) Cloudy
7 Day of the War

War Situation
- Major General William Dean, Commander of the 24th Infantry Division, is appointed as the Commander-in-Chief of the U.S. Forces in Korea.
- Advance U.S. Ground troops arrive in Busan; the United States and the ROK discuss combined operation plans (between Chung Il-kwon and General John Church).

At Home
- Banks in Busan restricts the weekly amount of deposit withdrawal to 10,000 won.
- The North Gyeongsang Province starts food distribution by ration.
- The Busan Railroad authorities announce the suspension of freight service.
- Foreign news services report that Chinese troops were assembling near the Yalu River.

Overseas
- India's representative to UN proposes a U.S.-Soviet meeting to seek a peaceful resolution to the Korean issue.
- The Taiwan Government's proposal to dispatch troops to Korea (three ground forces divisions and 20 airplanes) is turned down by the UNSC.

July 2, Sunday (May 17, by lunar calendar, 戊戌日 Yellow Dog) Clear
8 Day of the War

War Situation
- The North Korean Forces occupy Yongin, and the North Korean Army's Air Force increase their combat air power from 100 Units to 110.
- U.S. bombers and fighters strike North Korean Army's assembly areas and Units, pontoon bridges, transportation equipment, and warehouses.

At Home
- The ROK and the U.S. Air and Navy Forces establish the Busan Port Defense Command.
- The Daegu tax office starts to punish illegal brewers of alcoholic beverages.
- The ROK Air Force receives 10 F-51 fighters from the United States.

Overseas
- The United States ECA (Economic Cooperation Agency) resumes the supply of aid materials (petroleum and food).
- The United States State Department refutes the Soviet's allegation that the UNSC resolution to support South Korea was illegal.

July 3, Monday (May 18 by lunar calendar, 己亥日 Yellow Pig) Clear
9 Day of the War

War Situation
- North Korean tanks cross the Han River.
- The U.S. and British Fleets perform their operations in the coastal waters of the East Sea.
- Night bombing begins on Pyongyang.
- The ROK Army Headquarters move to Pyongtaek.

At Home
- The Busan Postal Office limits an individual's weekly deposit disbursement to 10,000 won.
- Korean patriot Kim Hong-ryang dies.

Overseas
- Chiang Kai-shek of Taiwan severely denounces the Soviet Union as the instigator and mastermind to have provoked the war.
- 200,000 Chinese troops move to the borders with French-controlled Indochina.

July 4, Tuesday (May 19, by lunar calendar, 庚子日 White Rat) Clear and Cloudy
10 Day of the War

War Situation
- General MacArthur establishes the headquarters of the U.S. Forces Command in Korea at Daejeon and the Busan U.S. Forces Command.
- The ROK Army headquarters moves to Daejeon.
- Pyongyang radio broadcasts that Kim Il Sung has assumed the post of the Supreme Commander of the North Korean Forces.

At Home
- The National Assembly decides to reinforce its emergency committee, by selecting committee members (Shin Ik-hee, Chang Taek-sang, Cho Bong-am, Chung Il-hyung, Ji Dae-hyung, Kim Dong-sun, Lee Jong-hyun, Chung Hun-gwon, and Hwang Sung-soo).
- North Korea appoints Kim Il Sung as Supreme Commander of the Korean People's Army (North Korean Army) and announces Reform Plan for the Liberated South."

Overseas
- India expresses its willingness to the United States and the Soviet Union to play a role in mediation of the war.
- The Canadian Government plans to provide Air Force support and to send two destroyers to Korea.
- The U.S. Navy notifies the Soviets of its blockade of the Korean coasts.
- Soviet Vice-Foreign Minister Gromyko issues a statement demanding American troop withdrawal from Korea.

Major General Patridge (left) of U.S. 5th Tactical Air Force, Lieutenant General Walker, Lieutenant General Jimmy Doolittle discuss on future air operations (1950. 7)

July 5, Wednesday (May 20, by lunar calendar, 辛丑日 White Ox) Rainy
11 Day of the War

War Situation
- U.S. Artillery Unit engages in its first contact with the North Korean Forces on the west front at 11 a.m. The Task Force Smith fought the first battle of Osan(Jungmiryeong).
- General Dean moves out to the frontline.
- The ROK and U.S. Forces start a combined operation forming a joint frontline, sharing responsibility – the United States for the west sector, and the ROK for the east sector.

At Home
- The ROK Army headquarters orders the troops not to destroy any bridges whatsoever.
- Busan Prosecution Office plans to investigate excessive buying and holding of grains.

Overseas
- The United States sends UN member states a draft resolution for establishing the United Nations Command and appointing General MacArthur as its Commander.

July 6, Thursday (May 21, by lunar calendar, 壬寅日 Black Tiger) Cloudy and Clear
12 Day of the War

War Situation
- At 6 p.m., the North Korean Forces occupy Pyongtaek.

- The UN Air Forces bomb the Daedong River bridge, Pyongyang and Haeju.

At Home
- The United States and the ROK establish the Joint Navy Defense Command in Busan.
- A signed agreement allows advance payments in Korean currency issued by the Bank of Korea to American personnel: "The agreement between the Republic of Korea and the United States military personnel in Korea concerning payment of expenses."
- The governor of the North Gyeongsang Province issues a public statement to ban forced donations.

July 7, , Friday (May 22, by lunar calendar, 癸卯日 Black Rabbit) Clear
13 Day of the War

War Situation
- The 24th Infantry Division builds the defense line at Pyongtaek along the 37th parallel.
- On the east coast, the North Korean Forces move from Samcheok and Pohang toward the southwest, getting ready to advance south.
- The ROK Army establishes the Ordinance Management Command at Busan Base Command.

At Home
- President Rhee orders humanitarian treatment of the North Korean prisoners of war.
- The Currency Adjustment Committee complements the shortage of cash bills by issuing bank cashiers' checks.

Overseas
- The UNSC adopts the resolution to establish the United Nations Command and request that the United States appoint its Commander.
- The Supreme Commander of the Allied Powers (SCAP) is established and General MacArthur is appointed as Commander of the UN Forces.

July 8, Saturday (May 23, by lunar calendar 甲辰日 Blue Dragon) Cloudy and Rainy
14 Day of the War

War Situation
- Due to the North Korean Army tanks' fierce shelling, the U.S. Forces retreat from Cheonan, about 57 kilometers northeast of Daejeon.
- Two North Korean Army Divisions assemble at Wonju aiming to encircle the Daejon area and to cut off north-south traffic, and the North Korean Forces assemble on the east coast to attempt to advance south.
- B-29s bomb the military installations and facilities between Goseong and Heungnam, the North Korean Navy bases at Wonsan, and the Heungnam fertilizer plant.

At home
- Jong Il-kwon, the Martial Law Commander, issues Martial Law Proclamation No. 1.
- A UN Tank Unit arrives in Korea.

Overseas
- The use of UN flag is limited to Korea only.
- The Chinese Army augments its forces in Hwabuk and Manchuria and their Units stationed in the south move to the north.

July 9, Sunday (May 24, by lunar calendar, 乙巳日 Blue Snake) Rainy and Cloudy
15 Day of the War

War Situation
- The UN Forces complete combat deployment.
- The main Forces of North Korea head for Daejeon.
- Lieutenant General Walker, after inspecting the frontline the day before, comments, "The North Korean command and combat capabilities are excellent."
- From July 8, more than 100 combat airplanes of the Far East Command strike major targets in the rear areas of the North Korean Forces.

At Home
- The ROK Army headquarters establishes the Office of Civil Affairs and declares Martial Law throughout the country.
- The Eighth U.S. Army sets up its headquarters at Daegu.

July 10, Monday (May 25, by lunar calendar, 丙午日 Red Horse) Very clear
16 Day of the War

War Situation
- The 25th U.S. Army Division arrives in Busan and the 5th U.S. Air Force moves to South Korea.
- Three hundred UN Air Force fighters strike hard in the western area of Korea and disrupt the transportation routes connecting Jeonui, Suwon, and Chungju.
- UN Secretary-General says world peace must be achieved with the strength of the United Nations.

At Home
- President Rhee argues the 38th parallel has lost its legitimacy due to the North Korean provocation of the war.
- The Busan City limits power supply to general households.
- In Cheongwon County, detainees at the Ochang police branch and the Ochang rice warehouse are found dead.

General MacArthur receives the UN flag from General Collins to carry out his mission for the Korean War. (1950. 7. 13)

July 11, Tuesday (May 26, by lunar calendar, 丁未日 Red Sheep) Clear
17 Day of the War

War Situation
- The UN Forces recapture Chungju and Danyang.
- The North Korean Forces approach Daejeon from two directions.
- B-29s bomb Wonju and Jincheon. B-26s strike Jochiwon and Jincheon.

At Home
- With the improved battle situation, the delegation of the Economic Cooperation Agency announces plans to return to Korea soon.
- The Office of Foreign Capital Management announces abolition of the fertilizer ration system to replace it with a direct purchase system.
- The Bank of Korea suspends currency exchange between the won and the dollar.

Overseas
- General MacArthur requests the UN flag.
- UN Secretary-General says world peace must be achieved with the strength of the United Nations.
- A British aircraft carrier anchors at Singapore on the way to join the UN operations in Korean waters.

• The French Far East fleet joins the UN Forces under American command.

July 12, Wednesday (May 27, by lunar calendar, 戊申日 Yellow Monkey) Cloudy and Rainy
18 Day of the War

War Situation
• The UN Forces in the Daejeon area make a strategic retreat from the south bank of the Geum Rivier.
• B-29s (about 50 of them) drop 500 tons of bombs on major North Korean military targets.

At Home
• Chief of the police bureau of the South Gyeongsang Province Lee Dong-cheol announces a plan to organize "Tongs" on the basis of every 10 households.
• The Busan Branch of the Bank of Korea limits daily deposit withdrawal to 5,000 won per person.

July 13, Thursday (May 28, by lunar calendar, 己酉日 Yellow Rooster). Cloudy and Rainy
19 Day of the War

War Situation
• Lt. Gen. Walker, Commander of the Eighth U.S. Army, is designated as Commander of the UN Forces in Korea.
• North Korean Forces occupy Cheongju.

At Home
• The Education Department of the Busan City implements summer vacation for elementary schools. The rice price drastically falls in the Daegu area.
• 50 B-29s drop 500 ton bombs on various military targets.
• The U.S. Army establishes the Busan Logistics Support Command at Busan.

July 14, Friday (May 29, by lunar calendar, 庚戌日 White Dog). Cloudy
20 Day of the War

War Situation
• Operational control of the ROK Armed Forces is transfered to the Commander of the United Nations Command.
• The British Navy participates in operations along the west coast and bombards North Korean military targets.

At Home
• President Rhee tells in a press conference that the UN Forces will march north beyond the 38th parallel to achieve national unification.
• President Rhee sends General MacArthur a signed letter transfering the operational

command authority of the ROK Forces (the Daejeon Agreement).
- The ROK Government moves from Daejeon to Daegu.

Overseas
- The UN Secretary-General, Trygve Lie requests the UN member countries to send their Ground Forces.
- The Yugoslavian Government protests the Bulgarian military invasion of, and firing in, the Yugoslavian territory.

July 15, Saturday (June 1, by lunar calendar, 辛亥日 White Pig). Cloudy
21 Day of the War

War Situation
- The 2nd ROK Army Corps is founded at Hamchang (Sangju, North Gyeongsang Province).
- The North Korean Forces secure a beachhead early on, at a location south of the Geum River and 32 km east of Daejeon.

At Home
- Minister of Home Affairs Baek Sung-uk resigns, and Cho Byung-ok replaces him.

Overseas
- UN Secretary-General Lie sends letters to member states, requesting that they dispatch ground Forces to Korea.
- American volunteers aviators joint the British pilots task force team (F-51 fighter unit) in the Philippines to be deployed in Korea.
- Soviet Forces assemble at the Iranian border.

July 16, Sunday (June 2, by lunar calendar, 壬子日 Black Rat). Cloudy and Clear
22 Day of the War

War Situation
- The 21st Regiment of the 8th ROK Army Division, with support of U.S. Artillery fire, attacks the numerically superior North Korean Forces.
- The North Korean Forces occupy Mungyeong.
- The Australian Air Force raids the North Korean troops concentrated near the Geumgang river.

At Home
- The Government moves from Daejon to Daegu (to the office building of North Gyeongsang Province).
- President Rhee issues a statement on the ROK's accession to the International Red Cross.

July 17, Monday (June 3, by lunar calendar, 癸丑日 Black Ox) Cloudy and Clear
23 Day of the War

War Situation

- The 19th and 34th Regiments of the 24th U.S. Division completely retreat to new bases.
- A portion of the North Korean Forces advances to Yeongyang.
- The U.N. Air Force initiates more than 230 consecutive sorties.

At Home

- The Defense Ministry's Public Information Chief, Lee Sun-geun issues a statement of warning against those attempting to flee from the country and against those rich people who do not cooperate with the Government.

Overseas

- Soviet Vice Foreign Minister Gromyko comments on Britain's peace proposal, saying, "The best path to a peaceful resolution is to call for a UNSC meeting with China's participation."

July 18, Tuesday (June 4, by lunar calendar, 甲寅日 Blue Tiger) Very Clear
24 Day of the War

War Situation

- Reconnaissance troops of the 19th and 34th U.S. Regiments continue reconnoitering the North Korean Forces , while the UN Forces repel the advance of the North Korean elements.
- Deck airplane fighters from the aircraft carrier of the Far East Air Force, the Australian Air Force and the British Air Force launch air raids on the logistic facilities of communication and transportation as well as the concentrated areas of the North Korean Forces throughout the battles in support of the UN Forces advancing north.

At Home

- President Rhee issues a statement concerning the implementation of Martial Law, requisition and conscription.
- The association of Dong administrative offices of the Busan City delivers a letter of recommendation that the price of rice released by the Government be reduced and people be allowed to purchase such rice with bank cashier's checks.
- The UN flag is delivered to Lt. General Walker.

July 19, Wednesday (June 5, by lunar calendar, 乙卯日 Blue Rabbit) Rainy and Cloudy
25 Day of the War

War Situation

- The North Korea Forces occupy Iri and Youngdeok.
- The UN Navy continues striking the North Korean military target on the east coast.

- The New Zealand Navy joins the UN Forces in the war.

At Home
- "Special Measures Decree on Payment for Financial Deposits" is issued (Presidential Emergency Order No. 4).
- The Busan branch of the South Korean Power Company "Namseon Electricity" cancels the all-time electric supply schedule except for major organizations.

Overseas
- The Calcutta Times reports that Chinese troops have invaded Tibet.
- President Truman issues a special State of the Union message on the Korean War to Congress (The measures included implementation of conscription, mobilization of the reservists, and conversion of four Divisions of State National Guards to active duty).

July 20, Thursday (June 6, by lunar calendar, 丙辰日 Red Dragon) Cloudy and Rainy
26 Day of the War

War Situation
- The UN Forces fired the newly developed rockets at Daejeon airport to destroy seven North Korean Army tanks.
- Daejeon falls to the North Korean Forces, Major General Dean, Commander of the 24th Division, is reported missing.
- Kim Il Sung issues an order from his war command at Suanbo to the North Korean Forces to "Occupy Busan by August 15."

At Home
- The ROK Student Volunteers' Corps holds a patriotic students rally in Busan.
- The new currency notes of 1,000 won and 100 won are issued for circulation.

July 21, Friday (June 7, by lunar calendar, 丁巳日 Red Snake) Cloudy and Rainy
27 Day of the War

War Situation
- A fierce battle of a large scale takes place north of the adjacent area of Daejeon. ROK Army occupies Yecheon.
- The North Korean Forces while pressing on Daejeon advance to Jeonju and Wonju. The North Korean Army troops enter Yeongdeok.
- The 24th U.S. Division retreats from the Daejeon defense line, but stops North Korean Forces from marching from the east of Daejeon.

At Home
- The Speaker of the National Assembly, Shin Ik-hee calls for an emergency meeting of lawmakers.

- Both chambers of U.S. Congress passed a bill proposed by President Truman that would extend the service term of the 300,000 troops and remove the ceiling of strength at 2 million troops.

July 22, Saturday (June 8, by lunar calendar, 戊午日 Yellow Horse) Rainy
28 Day of the War

War Situation
- Major General Dean has been missing since July 20 in the Daejeon area (press reports).
- The UN Navy Force strikes Yeongdeok, and the ROK Forces recaptures Yeongdeok in the afternoon. The 7th Regiment of the 1st U.S. Cavalry Division lands in Pohang.
- The 6th North Korean Army Division occupies Jeongup.

At Home
- The Emergency Decree on homeland defense is issued (Presidential Emergency Decree No.7).
- Ku Yong-seo, Governor of the Bank of Korea, holds a press conference on the issue of new currencies.

Overseas
- The French Navy ship La Grandiere, leaves the port of Singapore for Korea to join the UN Forces.
- War correspondents, Wilson and Hilder of Time-Life are killed during the retreat operations at Daejeon.
- Bolivia and Belgium decide to provide assistance to the ROK. Bolivia dispatches 30 military officers to the UNC and Belgium commits to playing a role in air transportation.

July 23, Sunday (June 9, by lunar calendar, 己未日 Yellow Sheep) Cloudy and Clear
29 Day of the War

War Situation
- A fierce battle erupts in the area of Daejeon and Yeongdong.
- The UN Air Force flies 165 mission fighters in a series of sorties.
- B-29s bomb the railroads in the areas of Chungju including the bridges and the roads of Youngsari, southwest of Chungju and near Gongju.
- The North Korean Forces occupy Gwangju and advance toward Sooncheon.

At Home
- The Seoul City establishes "the Liaison Office for the war refugees and victims." in Busan.
- The Association of Nationwide Cultural Organizations holds a "Save-the-Nation Rally by the People of Culture." and recruits volunteers for the Second Peoples' Force.

Overseas

U.S. Corps of Engineering dredges stones up from the river. (1950. 7. 24)

- Twelve South American countries express absolute support for the UNSC resolutions.

July 24, Monday (June 10, by lunar calendar, 庚申日 White Monkey) Very Clear
30 Day of the War

War Situation
- The North Korean Army troops advance to the area of Yeongdong, pressing the 25th U.S. Division.
- The UN Forces establish the Air Force Command of the Far East in Korea.
- The 29th U.S. Regiment arrives in Busan.

At Home
- Minister of Social Affairs, Lee Yoon-young holds a press conference on the status of refugees and relief work.

July 25, Tuesday (June 11, by lunar calendar, 辛酉日 White Rooster) Very Clear
31 Day of the War

War Situation
- The 1st U.S. Cavalry Division still holds its positions at a location 12 kilometers northwest of Yeongdong.
- The Cavalry Regiment of the ROK Capital Division begins combat engagement at Chongsong.
- The North Korea Forces occupy Mokpo, and breach the U.S. defense line of Daejeon and

Yeongdong.

At Home

- The ROK Army headquarters decides that simplified trials would be held by squad leaders and higher officers to punish deserters from their Units.

Overseas

- General MacArthur submits his first report to the United Nations, stating, "The enemy has lost its opportunity to take advantage of a favorable situation."
- The United Nations Command is officially established in Tokyo.

July 26, Wednesday (June 12, by lunar calendar, 壬戌日 Black Dog) Very Clear
32 Day of the War

War Situation

- The 24th U.S. Infantry Division establishes its headquarters at Hapcheon.
- In support of the UN ground forces, the UN Navy Forces bombard the North Korean military targets in the Yeongdeok area.
- The 6th North Korean Army Division penetrates into Hadong.

At Home

- "Special measures on military trials under the Martial Law" is proclaimed by the Emergency Presidential Order No. 5.
- "The special measures order on requisition" is proclaimed by the Emergency Presidential Order No. 6.

North Korean Forces congratulate their victory. (1950. 7. 27)
On the end of July 1950, North Korean Forces occupied 90 % of South Korea except Nakdong Defense Line.

- "Implementation regulations of the special measures order on requisition" is announced (Defense ministry's temporary order No. 1).

July 27, Thursday (June 13, by lunar calendar, 癸亥日 Black Pig) Clear and Cloudy
33 Day of the War

War Situation
- U.S. Forces strike and destroy the Yeongdong tunnel, killing a large number of North Korean troops.
- Major General Chae Byung-duk dies in battle at Hadong.
- The 4th Infantry Division of North Korean Army occupies Anui.
- In the southwest sector, the North Korean Forces continue to advance south to the road between Jeonju and Hamyang.
- Three North Korean Army Divisions wage a massive offensive on the east of Yeongdong.

At Home
- The 8th National Assembly convenes in Daegu.
- The National Assembly adopts a resolution of appreciation to be delivered to the United Nations.
- Disagreement and confusion rise among the policymakers over the issue of rice prices due to paying wages in goods (rice) instead of cash.

July 28, Friday (June 14, by lunar calendar, 甲子日 Blue Rat) Rainy
34 Day of the War

War Situation
- In the Yeongdong area, the UN Forces launch fierce repelling operations.
- The 1st U.S. Cavalry Division successfully defends the Hwanggan area against the North Korean Forces.
- The UN Navy Force sinks a group of 12 North Korean transport ships in the West Sea.
- The Canadian Air Force participates in the war.

At Home
- President Rhee issues a statement of appeal to defend Daegu at all costs.
- The United States and the ROK sign an agreement on payment of expenses for the UN Forces.
- Railroad operation is withdrawn beyond the northern areas of Chupungryeong.
- The Government announces "Measures for supply and exchange of Bank of Korea notes" (Emergency presidential decree No. 10).

ROK Army is on the freight-train car to move up to the front. (1950. 7)

July 29, Saturday (June 15, by lunar calendar, 乙丑日 Blue Ox) Rainy and Cloudy
35 Day of the War

War Situation
- Lt. General Walker orders the 25th U.S. Division to defend Sangju at all costs.
- The 1st U.S. Cavalry Division retreats from Hwanggan to Kimcheon.
- The U.S. Air Force launches a sortie to resist the North Korean Army Forces near Geochang and Aneui.

At Home
- The Busan Volunteers Security Organization is established and holds its launching rally.

Overseas
- Special Envoy of the UN Secretary-General reports that there are about one million refugees fleeing from the war in Korea.
- India announces its plan to send a field hospital unit to Korea.
- Washington excludes Chiang Kai-shek's Taiwan from foreign assistance.
- Belgium recalls troops home from West Germany to put down the strikers protesting the King's coronation.

July 30, Sunday (June 16, by lunar calendar, 丙寅日 Red Tiger) Rainy
36 Day of the War

War Situation

- B-29s conduct three sorties to bomb the major logistic facilities in Pyongyang, Wonsan and Hamheung.
- The 8th North Korean Army Division occupies Yecheon, and the 4th North Korean Army Division occupies Geochang.
- The Canadian Navy participates in the war.

At Home
- Andong Railroad Station and Daejeon Railroad Station withdraw from Hwabon and Gimcheon respectively.

Overseas
- The UN Commission on Korea holds its first open plenary session at Daegu.
- British Prime Minister Atlee describes the North Korean invasion as a part of an international Communist plot.

July 31, Monday (June 17, by lunar calendar, 丁卯日 Red Rabbit) Rainy and Cloudy
37 Day of the War

War Situation
- The 1st and the 6th ROK Divisions retreat from Hamchang.
- U.S. reinforcement troops arrive in Busan to be assigned to the 2nd U.S. Infantry Division, the 1st U.S. Cavalry Division and the 5th U.S. combat brigade.

At Home
- The Incheon Supply Depot and the Busan Supply Depot are incorporated into the Busan Base Supply Depot.
- The Daejeon Broadcast Station submits to the cabinet conference a secret monitoring report covering the broadcast contents of Japanese Broadcasting Stations, the Voice of America and the North Korean Radio Station.

Overseas
- The UN Commission on Korea holds an open plenary meeting.
- The UNSC passes a resolution on " Emergency aid and relief assistance to Koreans."
- General MacArthur opposes the Taiwan Government's dispatch of troops to Korea.
- In accordance with President Truman's instruction, General MacArthur leaves for Taiwan on a mission on June 27, and General MacArthur begins a meeting with Chiang Kai-shek.
- AP correspondent William Moore is killed while taking care of a wounded tank crew member.

August 1, Tuesday (June 18, by lunar calendar, 戊辰日 Yellow Dragon) Cloudy and Rainy
38 Day of the War

War Situation
- ROK and UN Forces join Forces to build the Nakdong Defense Line. The 1st U.S. Marine brigade arrives in Korea, getting ready for combat.
- The 12th North Korean Army Division occupies Andong and begins crossing the Nakdong River. The 1st North Korean Division occupies Hamchang.
- Lt. General Walker, Commander of the Eighth Army, orders the units to build the Nakdong Defense Line (called the Busan beachhead).

At Home
- The National Assembly approves an emergency budget in total amount of KRW 4.348 billion.
- The Ministry of Finance doubles the price of tobacco (The price of a pack of Kongjak doubles, from 300 to 600 won).
- The health Division of Busan City administers immunization shots for smallpox.
- The Korea Youth Corps and the Cultural Enlightenment Corps of North Gyeongsang Province merge into the Daehan (Korean) Young Mens' National Salvation Corps of North Gyeongsang Province.

The newly-recruited soldiers are marching to the training center in Busan. (1950. 8. 1)

The U.S. Forces move to Nakdong Defense Line. (1950. 8)

Overseas
• Australian Prime Minister, Robert Menzies, mentions the dispatch of Australian combat forces to Korea.
• New Zealand Air Force Commander says New Zealand will send ground troops to Korea.

August 2, Wednesday (June 19, by lunar calendar, 己巳日 Yellow Snake) Cloudy and Clear
39 Day of the War

War Situation
• The 5th U.S. Marine Regiment arrives in Busan and moves to Masan.
• With the fire support in the night from the UN Artillery Force, the 3rd ROK Division recaptures Yeongdeok and advances.
• The 7th North Korean Division confronts the ROK Forces near Andong.
• The 8th North Korean Army Infantry Division attempts to cross the Nakdong River.
• The UN Air Force completely destroys the Wonsan oil refinery by continuous daily bombing.

At Home
• President Syngman Rhee visits the Daegu ROK Army Hospital.

Overseas
• Filipino President Quirino announces that Filipino troops are ready to leave for Korea.
• A spokesman of the U.S. Defense Department reports on the improvement of the Korean

War situation and predicts a victory in two weeks.
- Liberia provides rubber worth $10,000 for military supplies of South Korean Army.

August 3, Thursday (June 20, by lunar calendar, 庚午日 White Horse) Clear
40 Day of the War

War Situation
- The UN Forces form a new defense line (the Walker Line) linking Masan, Waegwan, and Yeongdeok, (later Pohang). They blow up the railroad bridge of the Nakdong River.
- The North Korean Forces cross the Nakdong River to start their August offensive.
- The 12th ROK Army Regiment destroys an advance unit of the 13th North Korean Army Division at the Nakdong River.

At Home
- Kim Hoon, Minister of Commerce and Industry, states that Korea's trade is being handled through Japan since the outbreak of the war.
- The Daegu Defense Command conducts a siren signal as the war situation deteriorates.
- North Korea have organized 18,000 units of the Farmers Committee in the area of their occupation in South Korea.

Overseas
- UNSC disapproves the Soviet proposal for reviewing the agenda of China's admission first and approves the United States proposal on the Korean issue.
- Japan (a postal ship company) provides the United Nations Forces with five cargo ships
- The Philippines dispatches one Infantry Regiment with 17 tanks.

August 4, Friday (June 21, by lunar calendar, 辛未日 White Sheep) Clear
41 Day of the War

War Situation
- The Busan beachhead is defended by 141,808 soldiers in total, (including 82,000 ROK troops, 47,000 U.S. troops, and 12,808 other nationals).
- The North Korean Forces occupy Cheongsong, Inhwadong, Wonri, Dono and Gumi.
- The UN Navy Force shells military targets in the areas of Yangyang and Jumunjin.
- B-26s bomb Incheon, sinking a 10,000-ton cargo ship.

At Home
- Proclamation of "the law on temporary measures for accommodation of refugees" (Law No. 145) is issued.
- The Emergency Measures Committee of South Gyeongsang Province holds a patriotic women's rally.

August 5, Saturday (June 22, by lunar calendar, 壬申日 Black Monkey) Cloudy and Rainy
42 Day of the War

War Situation

- North Korean Forces occupy Gunwi, Euiseong, and Sangju.
- UN Forces hold off the August offensives of the North Korean Forces at the Nakdong River defense line, a ROK Division repels the North Korean Forces.
- UN Navy Force shells the North Korean Army Forces in the northern area of Youngduk all day. The UN Air Force strikes Gimpo Airport in Seoul, destroying 27 North Korean Air

The U.S. Forces arrive at Pusan Port, unloading. (1950. 8. 6)

48

Force Yak fighters.
- The 5th US Air Force launches sorties with 400 fighter/bombers.
- B-26 fighter/bombers of the 5th US Air Force drop incendiary bombs at night over the cities of Gimcheon, Daejeon, Suwon, Seoul and Incheon.

At Home
- Foreign Minister Lim Byung-jik makes a statement to denounce the Soviet proposal to the UNSC.
- President Rhee orders a special promotion by one step in rank to all members of the 1st ROK Marine Battalion, including its Commander, in recognition of their combat achievement.
- Mao Zedong orders the Northeast Peripheral Command to complete its operations plan by the end of the month.
- Korean residents in Japan organize a volunteer military group.

Overseas
- 4,500 Turkish troops are ready to leave for Korea.
- The U.S. Senate approves $266 million to support the occupation of Japan, Australia, and Okinawa.
- In the Republic of South Africa, many volunteers join the UN Forces in Korea.

August 6, Sunday (June 23, by lunar calendar, 癸酉日 Black Rooster) Cloudy and Clear
43 Day of the War

War Situation
- The UN Air Force has made 530 sorties.
- The ROK Forces kill more than 1,000 of North Korean Army troops in the north area of Euisung.

At Home
- The Youth Defense Corps summons its officers urgently.

Overseas
- The UN Commission on Korea holds its 2nd open session in Busan.
- UN Secretary-General Lie reminds all member states of their obligations to assist Korea.
- An Australian destroyer leaves for Korea.
- The Air Force of the Taiwan Nationalist Government bombs the coastal waters of Quemoy (金門島), destroying 134 Chinese boats.
- India notifies the UN Forces of its shipment of medical supplies and relief goods.

August 7, Monday (June 24, by lunar calendar, 甲戌日 Blue Dog) Rainy and Cloudy
44 Day of the War

War Situation

- The ROK Forces annihilate the North Korean troops crossing the Nakdong River. Near Yangjidong, the ROK Forces repel the North Korean Army troops' offensive.
- At 6:30 a.m. UN Forces and ROK Forces launch their biggest offensive operations since the start of the war.
- The US Task Force called "Kin" (which is provisionally organized by the 25th U.S. Division, the 5th Regiment combat group and the 1st Marine brigade) launches operations to recapture Jinju.

At Home

- President Rhee has a meeting with Averell Harriman, Special Envoy of the U.S. President.
- The Agriculture Division of Busan carries out a special rice distribution for the refugee Government workers and their families.
- The Mokpo Radio Station operates a mobile broadcasting boat, which is loaded with broadcasting equipment, for the coastal area of the West Sea (Output 50 W, with Lee Tae-gu in charge).

August 8, Tuesday (June 25, by lunar calendar, 乙亥日 Blue Pig) Rainy and Cloudy
45 Day of the War

War Situation

- The North Korean Forces' offensive forces the 8th ROK Army Division to retreat to the south of Andong.
- The 19th ROK Regiment destroys one North Korean Army Regiment and captures Hill 36 at Sukjumak.

At Home

- All students of the Gunwi Agricultural Middle School volunteer to join the ROK Forces to fight alongside them.
- Minister of Health and Social Welfare, Koo Young-suk, holds a press conference on immunization against contagious diseases.

Overseas

- The World Health Organization (WHO) dispatches five health specialists and five sanitation specialists to Korea.
- The Lower House of the Philippines unanimously approves the dispatch of troops to Korea.

August 9, Wednesday (June 26, by lunar calendar, 丙子日 Red Rat) Cloudy and Rainy
46 Day of the War

War Situation

- The 7th Cavalry Regiment of the 1st U.S. Cavalry Division engages in Geumubong

Combat (August 9 -11).
- B-26s and F-82s launch night sorties to bomb Geumsan, Jaecheon, Yeosu, Gwangju, Daejon, the North Korean Army supply vehicles in Gunsan. B-29s bomb the communication networks at Heungnam and Youngheung.

At Home
- Director of the Public Information Office, Lee Chul-won announces the merger of four news agencies into the Daehan News Agency.
- The Martial Law Command of the South Gyeongsang Province announces tighter ID checking and searches in Busan. The Korea Youth Volunteers Corps recruits new members.

August 10, Thursday (Lunar June 27, by lunar calendar, 丁丑日 Red Ox) Clear
47 Day of the War

War Situation
- The 24th U.S. Division attacks the beachhead and other positions of the North Korean Forces, and at 9 a.m., the North Korean Forces are beginning to retreat from the Nakdong River.
- The Task Force, Kin continues fighting to march to Daecheonri, and captures a hill east of Jinju, destroying the North Korean Army Forces (at 2 p.m. the task Force recaptures Jinju).

At Home
- Medical teams of the Health Ministry conduct immunization injections to 12,000 residents in the Wolbae area.
- The Martial Law Command declares that all doctors and nurses should register at the Government.

Overseas
- The UNSC discusses the representation issue for the Republic of Korea and North Korea.
- The U.S. Commerce Department announces a ban on the export of strategic materials from Japan to Communist countries.

August 11, Friday (June 28, by lunar calendar, 戊寅日 Yellow Tiger) Clear
48 Day of the War

War Situation
- The ROK Forces destroy the North Korean Forces at Duidong. A street battle is fought in the center of Pohang City. The ROK Forces attack the main Unit of the North Korean Forces in the direction of Gigae. The special Forces Unit of the 2nd ROK Army destroys three of the North Korean Army's tanks.

At Home

- In Seoul, the North Korean Army launches an ambitious, coercive recruiting effort for 100,000 men.
- The Government announces implementation regulations for "the Emergency Homeland Defense Law."
- The Office of Public Information proclaims the laws on "the provisional measures for the accommodation of refugees" and "the special measures for wartime requisition."

August 12, Saturday (June 29, by lunar calendar, 己卯日 Yellow Rabbit) Cloudy
49 Day of the War

War Situation
- The UN Forces' tank unit repels the North Korean troops and begins mopping them up from Pohang.
- The ROK Forces annihilate the North Korean Army troops positioned 10 km north of Doiwon.
- The 1st ROK Army guerrilla unit captures Hill 434 and Hill 564 and destroys the North Korean Army's battalion troops moving southward.
- The North Korean Forces occupy Hyeonpung and Goseong.

At Home
- Lee Sun-geun, Director-General for the Public Information Bureau of the Defense Ministry,

A bridge on a northern region of Gilju was destroyed by bombing. (1950. 8. 13)

issues a warning that his Ministry will treat those who hoard rice for profits the same as the Communist troops.
- The ROK Army headquarters assigns call signals to its major units for aviation and communication.
- Two British war correspondents have been killed on duty in the Nakdong battle: Ian Morris of The Times (London) and Christopher Buckley of The Daily Telegraph (London).

Overseas
- The UN Command announces Operations Plan 100-B, planning landing operations and designating the landing units.
- Colonel Naal, the Indian representative to the UN Commission on Korea, is killed while inspecting the Nakdong defense line.
- China begins to support the Ho Chi Minh regime.
- The U.S. Air Force calls up 1,762 reserve officers in the ranks of captain and lieutenant and 1,532 military doctors/veterinaries back to active duty.

August 13, Sunday (June 30, by lunar calendar, 庚辰日 White Dragon) Cloudy
50 Day of the War

War Situation
- The ROK Forces readjust the Nakdong defense line, linking with Waegwan, Dabudong, Gunwi, Bohyeonsan and the south of the river entrance.
- Three U.S. Army units defeat two North Korean Army battalions near the North Korean beachhead of Changryung. The 24th U.S. Division kills 125 enemy troops and captures 13 prisoners of war of the North Korean Army troops who were crossing the river. The 5th U.S. Marine Regiment advances to an area 5 kilometers from Sacheon. The 5th U.S. Marine Regiment advances to an area 5 kilometers from Sacheon.
- Student fighters repel 300 North Korea invading troops from the Nakdong defense line.

At Home
- The Seoul Broadcasting Station is hit by air raids and fire breaks out.
- Busan City holds a national rally to overcome the national difficulties.
- A protective facility is set up in Daegu for refugee livestock.

August 14, Monday (July 1, by lunar calendar, 辛巳日 White Snake) Rainy and Cloudy
51 Day of the War

War Situation
- A U.S. Armed Unit engages in combat in the area of Pohang.
- ROK Forces recapture Hill 328 in the area of the Nakdong River. ROK Forces kill 30 North Korean troops at Hill 300. The 18th ROK Regiment and an ROK Armored Unit capture

State Council held at temporary war-time camp. (1950. 8. 15)

Ipam.
- The 24th US Division advances 90 meters in its tough battle with North Korean Forces.

At Home
- Busan City holds an organization ceremony of the Self Defense Corps.
- The Military Academy and the Infantry School are consolidated into the ROK Army Infantry School (at Dongrae).

Overseas
- The UN Economic and Social Council approves a relief program for the Korean refugees.
- The United States representative to the UN sends a letter to UN Secretary-General Lie to request that the UN dispatch a Red Cross team to North Korea to investigate the treatment of POWs and other detainees in North Korea.

August 15, Tuesday (July 2, by lunar calendar, 壬午日 Black Horse) Cloudy and Rainy,
52 Day of the War

War Situation
- A UN Artillery Unit shells three North Korean Army battalions positioned at a new beachhead near the east bank of the Nakdong River 32 kilometers southwest of Daegu.
- Kim Il Sung orders: "Send everything to the frontline!"
- Ground combat troops of the UN Navy Force land at an area near Cheongjin, and destroy a tunnel and return safely to their Unit.
- An anti-Communist oratory contest is held at the Busan Citizens' Hall.
- A massive rally to overcome the national crisis is held in Busan.

At Home
- President Rhee appoints Kim Hwal-lan as the Director of the Office of Public Information.
- The 2nd anniversary ceremony of August 15 Liberation is held at the Daegu Culture Theater.

Overseas
- General MacArthur, UNC Commander, submits a report to UNSC requesting an immediate increase of ground forces.

Flag bearers at the welcoming ceremony for the U.S. Marines at Busan Port. (1950. 8. 15)

- Kim Il Sung meets Nizturyang, China's ambassador to North Korea, for the first time since his assignment to the post.

August 16, Wednesday (July 3, by lunar calendar, 癸未日 Black Sheep) Cloudy and Rainy
53 Day of the War

War Situation
- The 17th ROK Regiment advances 1.6 kilometers in the Pohang area, and the 12th ROK Regiment captures Hill 837.
- The 1st U.S. Cavalry Division repels 200 North Korean Army troops from the Nakdong River northwest of Daegu.

At Home
- President Rhee accepts the American advice that the Korean Government move to Busan.
- "The Students Alliance to Save the Nation" issues a statement urging all students to rally for the protection of the nation.

August 17, Thursday (July 4, by lunar calendar, 甲申日 Blue Monkey) Clear
54 Day of the War

War Situation
- The North Korean Forces reorganize their 40,000 to 60,000 troops after being bombed at the Waegwan area.
- The 24th U.S. Division strikes and destroys the beachhead and positions of the North Korean Forces in the Youngduk area.

At Home
- The External Relations Department of the Bureau of Public Information and Education, Ministry of Defense, recruits female volunteers.
- Han Pyo-uk, secretary of the Korean Embassy in Washington requests the Assistant Undersecretary of State, Dean Rusk to provide an additional supply of arms to Korea.

Overseas
- General MacArthur, UNC Commander, files a report to the UNSC, with a request for an increased number of ground Forces.
- The UN accepts the Philippines' dispatch of troops to Korea.

August 18, Friday, (July 5, by lunar calendar, 乙酉日 Blue Rooster) Very Clear
55 Day of the War

War Situation
- The 1st ROK Corps captures Pohang and Gigae completely.
- Four (4) North Korean Divisions approach the northern area of Daegu, after they began an

offensive on August 17, and citizens are told to evacuate from the area.
- The 1st ROK Division and the 27th U.S. Regiment resist the North Korean Army Forces in the northern area of Daegu.
- The ROK Marines annihilate the main elements of the North Korean Army Forces that invaded Tongyoung. The ROK Navy lands on Dukjok-do Island.

At Home
- The Government moves from Daegu to Busan.
- Number of railroad cars used for the relocation: 3,354 passenger cars and 11,755 freight cars.

August 19, Saturday (July 6, by lunar calendar, 丙戌日 Blue Monkey) Clear
56 Day of the War

War Situation
- The ROK military unit under the command of Col. Lee Jeong-il destroys the main force of the North Korean Army in the Pohang area.
- The ROK Army ruptures the North Korean Army's elements at Hill 549 and engages in fierce battles at Samdong and Yeosandong.
- The transport aircraft of the U.S. Air Force transport a total 4,535,900 kg of military supplies and 6,000 persons from Japan since the outbreak of the war.

At Home
- Fourteen civilians of the village of Geumseong-myeon are killed in the valley of Hwarim-ri, Geumseong-myun of Geumseong-gu.
- The North Korea regime proclaims "Labor Laws" in the South Korean areas occupied by them.
- General MacArthur, General Lawton J. Collins, the U.S. Army Chief of Staff, Admiral Forrest D. Sherman, Chief of Naval Operations discuss, at the military strategic conference in Tokyo, the Incheon landing operation and a possibility of advancing north of the 38th parallel.

August 20, Sunday (July 7 by lunar calendar, 丁亥日 Blue Monkey) Clear
57 Day of the War

War Situation
- The ROK Army advances 26 km from Pohang, and repels 3,000 North Korean troops, the greatest victory recorded since the outbreak of the war.
- A military unit of the ROK Army under the command of Ham Byung-seon beat a regimental unit of the North Korean Army and kills the commander of its division in Changnyeong, north of Wiseong.

At Home

- Kim Hoon, Minister of Commence and Industry makes a statement on "the counter-measures on electricity supply, planning for war-time economic reconstruction and development of Jeju Island, etc.
- A delegation of the U.S. House of Representatives visits Korea to observe the war situation.

Overseas

- General MacArthur, Commander of the UN Allied Forces sternly warns Kim Il Sung by radio broadcasting and leaflets not to commit any more atrocities.
- Jang Myeon, Korean Ambassador to the USA refutes the trusteeship of North Korea.

August 21, Monday (July 8, by lunar calendar, 戊子日 Yellow Rat) Clear
58 Day of the War

War Situation

- The ROK 2ⁿᵈ Division repels a Regiment of the North Korean Army at Yeongchon area.
- The ROK Army takes a hill located 5km north of Waegan.
- The ROK Marines capture Seo-eo Island, 72km southwest of Incheon and Seongap Island 40 km from Incheon.

At Home

- The Government proclaims "The Regulations on Requisition" (Presidential Decree No. 381).
- The Counter-Intelligence Unit of South Gyeongsang Province arrests Kim Dong San, former chairman of the South Gyeongsang committee of the North Korean Peoples' Republican Party.

Overseas

- A plenary session of the U.S. Senate passes a bill on "the Laws for War-time Economic Management."
- The British Government decides an urgent dispatch of the British troops stationed in Hong Kong.

August 22, Tuesday (July 9, by lunar calendar, 己丑日 Yellow Ox) Cloudy
59 Day of the War

War Situation

- The ROK Forces advance to a point 28 km north of Pohang.
- Seventy B-29 bombers of the U.S. Far East Air Forces drop 700 tons of bombs (each bomb weighing 227 kg) on North Korean military facilities.

At Home

- Yoon Yong-seon, Minister of Agriculture and Forestry holds a press briefing on food distribution and purchase of autumn crops.

- Kim Tae-seon, Police Chief issues a warning to the merchants and medical doctors who grossly neglect or refuse their own professional services.

Overseas

- The U.S. begins to deploy its largest kind of atomic bombs.
- Israel offers medical supplies worth US$63,000.

August 23, Wednesday (July 10, by lunar calendar, 庚寅日 Blue Monkey) Cloudy and Rainy
60 Day of the War

War Situation

- The ROK Capital Division repels the North Korean Army troops northward, and defeats their military elements in the north of Waegwan.
- UN naval destroyers fire their guns toward the Cheongjin area.

At Home

- The Martial Law Commander of Busan district, Yoo Seung-yeol makes a statement on the issues related to "recruitment of soldiers."
- The ROK Naval Operation Command permits fishing in some areas that have been restricted since the war broke out.

August 24, Thursday (July 11, by lunar calendar, 辛卯日 Blue Monkey) Clear
61 Day of the War

War Situation

- All elements of the North Korean Forces retreat in the north and west of Daegu. Six islands off Incheon are retaken.
- The U.S. Marines support the ground Forces in the western front lines.

At Home

- The Cabinet Meeting determines five principles to support the relief measures for refugees.
- The Central and Provincial Governments hold an urgent conference to decide on the establishment of provisional refugee camps and free distribution of food rations.

August 25, Friday (July 12 by lunar calendar, 壬申日 Blue Monkey) Cloudy and Clear
62 Day of the War

War Situation

- The UN and ROK Forces initiate their offensive and the North Korean Army counter-attack with their tanks (30 Units).
- A large assembly of the North Korean Army troops is seen near Hayang.
- The U.S. 2nd Division completely encircles a battalion of the North Korean Army Forces at

a point 25km southwest of Daegu.

At Home
- Kim Jong-won, Provost Martial issues a statement on illegal conscription of automobiles.
- The ROK Navy establishes the Jangchoongdan altar in Jinhae to enshrine the fallen spirits.

Overseas
- New Zealand decides to send its Infantry and Artillery troops to Korea.
- The Washington Post stresses that Korean unification is the UN's ultimate purpose justifying the advance north beyond the 38th parallel.

August 26, Saturday (July 13, by lunar calendar, 癸巳日 Blue Monkey) Cloudy
63 Day of the War

War Situation
- The ROK Army repels the North Korean troops that have attempted to attack Pohang including the Gigye zone.
- B-26 bombers begin to destroy the bridges in the Seoul area and B-29 bombers destroy the main railroads of mid-north areas and a switchyard of Giljoo.

At Home
- Yang Seong-bong, Governor of South Gyeongsang Province makes a statement to encourage enlistment.
- The Counter-Intelligence Corps (CIC) of South Gyeongsang Province arrests a ring of espionage agents under feigned names of CIC.
- A field hospitals unit of Sweden leaves for Korea.

August 27, Sunday (July 14, by lunar calendar, 甲午日 Blue Monkey) Cloudy
64 Day of the War

War Situation
- The North Korean troops continue reconnaissance and attacks in most of the frontline areas, capturing Euheung.
- The special task unit, "Jackson," is deployed in the Gyeongju area.

At Home
- Koo Young-suk, Minister of Health holds a press interview regarding a visit of the UN's medical unit and an issue related to medical doctors in the Daegu area.
- The UN Commission on Korea holds its third open conference in Jinhae and Masan.

August 28, Monday (July 15, by lunar calendar, 乙未日 Blue Monkey) Clear
65 Day of the War

War Situation

- The U.S. Air Force drops 326 tons of bombs on a metal working factory and 284 tons of bombs on the North Korean military facilities as well.
- The 550 squadron of the U.S. Far East Air Force dropped 500 tons of bombs on the military bases of the North Korean Communist troops
- The Australian Air Force and the U.S. 5th Far East Air Forces fly 250 sorties bombing Pyongyang airport and other facilities.

At Home
- The Presidential Decree no. 382 "The Order for the ROK Army Supplementary Officers" is proclaimed.
- The Presidential Emergency Decree no. 10 is proclaimed in connection with "the matters related to the Circulation and Exchange of Joseon Bank Notes"
- Col. Kim Jong-won is appointed as the Martial Law Commander in Busan area.

Overseas
- The UN Secretary-General's Office deals with an appeal from China in regard to the bombing of Manchuria.
- The UN Security Council holds a secret meeting and discusses matters related to the yearly report to be submitted to the UN General Assembly.

August 29, Tuesday (July 16, by lunar calendar, 丙申日 Blue Monkey) Clear
66 Day of the War

War Situation
- The North Korean Forces attempt to cross the river in the areas of Bugok-ri, Chilhyeon-ri, and Dugok-ri.
- The ROK Navy destroys two propelled-boats carrying enemy soldiers.
- The British 27th Infantry Regiment arrives in Busan.

At Home
- The ROK Army Headquarters issues warnings that there will be degradations for all the military personnel involved and an immediate court-martial will be held for the military leaders on the charges of a surprise strike being made by the enemy troops or degradation.
- The Martial Law Commands of Masan and Busan are integrated into the Martial Law Command of South Gyeongsang District.

August 30, Wednesday (July 17 by lunar calendar, 丁酉日 Blue Monkey) Very clear
67 Day of the War

War Situation
- The ROK Forces engage in battle with the North Korean troops which penetrate into the

north of Sinnyeong.
- The U.S. 2nd and 25th Divisions attack the enemy's reconnaissance.
- The UN 77th Mobile Cruiser initiates an all-out attack at Jinnampo.

At Home
- Minister of Education, Paik Nak-joon announces counter-measures to operate "the war-time schools."

Overseas
- United States Secretary of State, Acheson states that the UN would not attempt to advance north beyond the 38th parallel if the Communist Forces withdraw.
- United States Defense Secretary Johnson says that the Communists' attack of South Korea is a clear sign of the intention to communize the entire free world.

August 31, Thursday (July 18 by lunar calendar 戊戌日Yellow Dog) Cloudy
68 Day of the War

War Situation
- A second battle is fought in the area of the Nakdong River and Yeongsan (up to September 1).
- B-29 bombers drop 600 tons of explosives on a chemical plant, a steel mill and the railroad yard in Jinnampo.

At Home
- The Government issues a statement of opposition to any international conference that discusses the Korean issue without the participation of South Korea.
- The Government designates Suyoung airport as the temporary Busan International Airport.

Overseas
- UNSC debates the American warplanes' bombing in the border area of Manchuria.

September 1, Friday (July 19, by lunar calendar, 己亥日 Yellow Pig) Cloudy
69 Day of the War

War Situation
- The 9th Regiment and the 72nd tank battalion of the 2nd U.S. Infantry Division clash with the North Korean Forces in the Yeongsan battle (through August 5).
- The North Korean Forces continue offensives at the confluence of the Nakdong River and the Namgang River.
- The UN Forces recapture Haman

At Home
- President Rhee issues a statement on the implementation of the Military Conscription Law and the registration of the "The Second Peoples' Force.
- The Ministry of National Defense activates the Women's Volunteers Corps for Training (the Defense Ministry's General Order No. 58)

September 2, Saturday (July 20, by lunar calendar, 庚子日 White Rat) Very Clear
70 Day of the War

War Situation
- The North Korean Forces start an all-out attack at the Nakdong River
- The U.S. Forces begin to deploy new Patton-type tanks to the battlefields in Korea.
- The Commander of the Far East Air Force Command mentions the halt of railroad operations to the north beyond the 37th parallel.

At Home
- The plenary session of the National Assembly adopts a resolution calling for an all- out offensive by the UN Forces.
- Martial Law Commander Chung Il-kwon orders business stores that were closed deliberately by the owners in Daegu to reopen.

Overseas
- General MacArthur, UNC Commander, reports to the UN for the third time on the indications that China recruits Koreans living in Manchuria to forcefully conscript them for the purpose of joining the Chinese Military Forces.

September 3, Sunday (July 21, by lunar calendar, 辛丑日 White Ox) Cloudy and Rainy
71 Day of the War

War Situation

- The North Korean Forces penetrate the Geongju area. The North Korean troops wage the last of the all-out offensives to the north of Daegu.
- The UN troop advance to Nakdong River. UN fighters from the aircraft carrier protect the ground forces in the Masan area.
- B-29 bombers drop 480 tons of bombs on the North Korean military targets west of the Nakdong River.

At Home
- President Syngman Rhee encourages the youth to rally for national defense.
- Minister of Home Affairs Cho Byung-ok states on the ban of the illegal transactions of United States products.
- The director of military conscription for the Busan area urges all eligible personnel to return to their registered resident addresses.
- Lee Yun-young, Provost Marshal of the Busan military police command, announces a statement of the Martial Law Commander regarding vehicle registration.

September 4, Monday (July 22, by lunar calendar, 壬寅日 Black Tiger) Cloudy and Rainy
72 Day of the War

War Situation
- The North Korean Forces occupy Andong.
- At Gigae, 24 kilometers northeast of Waegwan, ROK Forces engage in a fierce battle with

U.S. Marines are searching Jongno area to sweep the remaining enemy troops. (1950. 9)

North Korean Forces.
- The UN and ROK Naval Forces annihilate the North Korean troops around the Jindo Island.
- Female volunteers join the military for the first time. A Cemetery Registration Unit is set up under the ROK Army logistics command.

At Home
- The 14th meeting of the 8th National Assembly Sessions elects members and judges of the Constitutional Court.
- The monthly morning meeting of the Government for September takes place at the office building of South Gyeongsang Province.

September 5, Tuesday (July 23, by lunar calendar, 癸卯 Black Rabbit) Rainy
73 Day of the War

War Situation
- The headquarters of the Eighth U.S. Army, the ROK Defense Ministry, and the ROK Army headquarters move to Busan from Daegu which has been isolated due to the September offensives of the North Korean Forces.
- B-29 bombers drop bombs, despite rain storms, on the fertilizer plant at Haeju and the railroad yard in Pyongyang.
- The 2nd ROK Corps resists, encircles and destroys the 15th North Korean Army Division in the Yeongcheon area.

At Home
- The National Assembly selects ROK representatives to the UN (Shin Ik-hi, Chang Taek-sang, Chung Il-hyung, Hwang Sung-su, Kim Dong-sung, and Suh Min-ho)
- The United States ECA determines a new allotment of assistance to Korea for $9, 634,000.

Overseas
- France applies to UNSC for the dispatch of Infantry troops to Korea.
- Zhou Enlai, Chinese Foreign Minister, announces the Chinese position to intervene in the Korean War if the UN Forces cross the 38th parallel into the north

September 6, Wednesday (July 24, by lunar calendar, 甲辰日 Blue Dragon) Cloudy and Rainy
74 Day of the War

War Situation
- The 1st US Cavalry Division stops the North Korean Army Forces from advancing to Daegu.
- The ROK Forces block the North Korean Forces from advancing to Gyeongju.
  The 8th ROK Division engages in the Yeongcheon battle.

- More than 360 UN airplanes attack the eastern frontline, destroying 41 North Korean Army tanks

At Home
- Chang Taek-sang, as the senior representative of the ROK delegation to the United States, reports on his visit to the U.S.
- Director of Government properties Shin Gui-shik announces a requisition policy on "reverted housing properties."
- The Women Volunteers Army is established.

Overseas
- The UN representatives of the United States, Britain, and France discuss the measures to take on the Korean issue at the UNSC and the UN General Assembly.
- The U.S. representative denounces North Korea as the aggressor, and the Soviet Union exercises its 44th veto.

September 7, Thursday (July 25, by lunar calendar, 乙巳日 blue snake) Cloudy and Rainy
75 Day of the War

War Situation
- B-29s bomb the steel mill in Cheongjin.
- B-26s carry out night raids bombing the North Korean Forces 20 km north of Daegu.

U.S. LST unloads troops and gears onto the coast.

- The 25th U.S. Division repels one North Korean Army battalion attacking the Haman area.

At Home
- The plenary session of the National Assembly passes a resolution calling for an all-out attack by the UN Forces
- Frank Emory, a war correspondent of INS, dies in the crash of a transport plane.

September 8, Friday (July 26, by lunar calendar, 丙午日 Red Horse) Rainy
76 Day of the War

War Situation
- A Regiment of the 5th North Korean Army Division occupies Wunjaesan.
- The ROK Forces capture the town of Yeongcheon and secure the road between Yeongcheon and Gyeongju. The ROK Marines occupy the Daeyeonpyong-do Island in Haeju Bay.

At Home
- The National Assembly passes a motion for the legislation of a relief law for wounded soldiers and police officers.
- The ROK Navy resettles refugees from Busan to the Gadukdo Island.

September 9, Saturday (July 27, by lunar calendar, 丁未日 Red Sheep) Rainy
77 Day of the War

War Situation
- UN Naval Forces strike the North Korean Forces in the areas of Pohang and Jinhae.
- The Task Force Davidson is deployed to the eastern sector of the battlefront.

At Home
- President Rhee and the National Assembly dispute over the dispatch of a National Assembly delegation to the United Nations.
- The National Assembly passes an emergency expenditure budget for September to take care of the aftermath of the Korean War.
- President Truman broadcasts to the Americans to increase the production of war materials.

September 10, Sunday (July 28, by lunar calendar, 戊申日 Yellow Monkey) Rainy
78 Day of the War

War Situation
- The 1st ROK Division repulses the 1st North Korean Army Division from Palgongsan Mountain.
- 227 UN aircraft planes attack the North Korean Forces in the front of the Daegu defense line.

- The ROK Army Artillery Command is established in Busan incorporating the officers and equipments of the 1st Artillery Corps.

At Home

- The UN Commission on Korea sends four members to the United States for the UN General Assembly.
- A group of civilians are sacrificed in the United States bombing on a village of the Wolmido Island near Incheon.

September 11, Monday (July 29, by lunar calendar, 己酉日 Yellow Rooster) Cloudy and Clear
79 Day of the War

War Situation

- The UN and ROK Forces begin advancing with the fire support of tanks and artillery in the area of Pohang.
- The United States appoints Major General John Coulter, former Commander of the 24th U.S. Army Infantry Division, to assume command of the 9th U.S. Army Corps.

General MacArthur receives reports on the operational situations on USS fleet McKinley, a command ship of Incheon Landing Operations. (1950. 9. 15)

U.S. Army watching at bridgeheads of North Korean Army on the front line of Nakdong River (1950. 9. 12)

- The 7th ROK Army Training Center opens in Jinhae, South Gyeongsang Province.

At Home
- The National Assembly holds a closed session to discuss the accommodation of refugees.
- Minister of Social Affairs, Lee Yun-young issues a statement on registration of buildings.
- The South Gyeongsang Province adopts "the regulation on consumption of grains" and sends it to cities and counties for implementation.

September 12, Tuesday (August 1, by lunar calendar, 庚戌日White Dog) Cloudy and Clear
80 Day of the War

War Situation
- A group of marine transport boats leaves Busan port.
- According to the Marine headquarters, the 1st Marine Regiment armed completely with new weapons left Busan port to participate in the Incheon landing operations.
- The 1st U.S. Army Corps is reorganized into the 1st Cavalry Division, the 24th Infantry Division and the 1st ROK Army Division.

At Home
- The plenary session of the National Assembly passes "a bill of recommendation on refugee relief."
- The Foreign Ministry begins the registration of the Japanese who desire to return to Japan.

September 13, Wednesday (August 2, by lunar calendar, 辛亥日 White Pig) Cloudy and Rainy
81 Day of the War

War Situation
- The UN and ROK Forces capture a North Korean position 8 km southwest of Pohang.
- The ROK Forces' utmost frontline is located 20 km east of Yeongdong.

At Home
- President Rhee comments that the 38th parallel has perished by itself.
- The plenary session of the National Assembly decides to return the "Waste Cleaning Bill" to the Government.

Overseas
- The Australian Foreign Minister requests that the United States and South American countries join a Pacific Alliance.
- The Council on Foreign Affairs of the U.S. Congress suggests to consult with General MacArthur to seek other countries' views on the peace treaty with Japan.

September 14, Thursday (August 3, by lunar calendar, 壬子日 Black Rat) Rainy and Cloudy
82 Day of the War

War Situation
- U.S . Forces cross the Nakdong River and advance 1 km north by noon.
- The ROK Forces begin offensives at 8.5 km west of Andong and B-29s bomb the railroad.

At Home
- Finance Minister Choi Sun-ju makes an announcement on the exchange of the 100 won notes with the new notes of the Bank of Korea to prohibit the use of the old notes.

September 15, Friday (August 4, by lunar calendar, 癸丑日 Black Ox) Rainy and Cloudy
83 Day of the War

War Situation
- UN Marines start landing at Incheon from early morning.
- UN Marines capture Wolmido Island, beginning the main thrust of the offensive at 17:30 hours.
- The 1st U.S. Marines Division and the 10th U.S. Army Corps which are the main offensive forces participate in the landing at Wolmido under the command of Rear Admiral, James Doyle and General MacArthur in the front.
- 70,000 UN troops and 260 combat vessels participate in the landing with air support.
- In a joint landing operation on the West and East Coast, the ROK Forces land on Jangsadong, south of Yeongdeok, early in the morning.

At Home

- The National Assembly reviews a bill to organize a comfort group of national lawmakers and to activate para-military combat organizations.
- The ROK Marines participate in the successful Incheon landing operations and penetrate onto the shore.

September 16, Saturday (August 5, by lunar calendar, 甲寅日 Blue Tiger) Rainy
84 Day of the War

War Situation
- The UN Forces expands its beachhead toward a wider sector to breach the North Korean Army's first frontline of defense set up 6 km east of Incheon.
- The UN Forces including the 8th Army begin an all out counter offensive from the Nakdong River battle line.

At Home
- Mayor of Incheon returns to normal duty.
- President Rhee issues a stern warning against illegal disposition of relief goods and materials.
- The Government proclaims "Instructions on temporary ranking system for the ROK Forces (Presidential decree 384).

September 17, Sunday (August 6, by lunar calendar, 乙卯日 Blue Rabbit) Rainy and Cloudy
85 Day of the War

War Situation
- At 8:00 p.m., the 5th Marine Regiment of the 1st U.S. Marine Division completely occupies Gimpo Airport and arrives at the southwestern part of the Han River.
- The UN Forces approach near Waegwan and an North Korean Army Division Commander flees from the battle.

At Home
- The National Assembly deliberates on the special bills of the special law on the "screening the collaborators during the war" and the law on the "elimination of death penalty."
- Minister of Home Affairs, Cho Byung-ok issues a statement of compassion for the people in the areas under Communist guerillas' control. Korean patriot Han Hoon dies.

Overseas
- The United States proposes that the UN Economic and Social Council establish the Korean Economic Reconstruction Commission.
- Jang Myeon, ROK Ambassador to the United States, speaks before an audience of the American Bar Association on "Korea and Law Enforcement."

September 18, Monday (August 7, by lunar calendar, 丙辰日 Red Dragon) Cloudy
86 Day of the War

War Situation
- The UN Forces destroy 16 North Korean Army tanks in Seoul, and an advance ROK Unit enters Yeongdeungpo.
- The UN Marines march from the northwest of the Han River, while other UN marines advance along the Incheon-Seoul road.

At Home
- The Government establishes a war criminal court in Incheon.
- The National Assembly passes a law prohibiting private punishment.

Overseas
- Ho Chi Minh's Forces occupy Tomkei near the Chinese border in Indochina.
- The NATO Board of Directors meeting approves the establishment of a NATO Force.
- The Colombian Embassy minister to the United States announces that Colombia will provide a battle cruiser of the 2,000 ton class to assist the UN Forces in Korea.

September 19, Tuesday (August 8, by lunar calendar, 丁巳日 Red Snake) Cloudy
87 Day of the War

War Situation
- A Marine search units cross the Han River from four locations. An advance marine Unit arrives at a location 3 km southwest of Seoul.
- The ROK and the UN Forces cross the Han River and start using Gimpo Airport.

At Home
- President Rhee attends a successful Incheon landing ceremony and states that he would not permit interferences with Korean unification, ordering the ROK Forces to advance to the Korea-Manchuria border.
- The Government joins the International Telecommunications Agreement.

Overseas
- The 5th UN General Assembly convenes. Rau, the Indian representative, proposes at the beginning of the General Assembly that a Chinese representative be invited; Dean Acheson, senior U.S. representative, objects; the Soviet Union supports their view of China's representation; at the end the proposal is rejected.
- The French Forces recapture Luong Khe in Vietnam.
- West Germany announces the trilateral Foreign Ministerial meeting's communiqué.

September 20, Wednesday (August 9, by lunar calendar, 戊午日 Yellow Horse) Cloudy
88 Day of the War

War Situation
- Marine search units cross the Han River to begin an offensive on the North Korean Army troops in Seoul, followed by the river crossing of the main forces.
- The ROK Marines and the 5th U.S. Marine Regiment cross the Han River and march forward to Susaek.

At Home
- The National Assemblymen's comfort team departs for their destinations to meet the soldiers, police officers and refugees.
- President Rhee announces that he will follow the decision of United Nations on the issue of going beyond the 38th parallel.

September 21, Thursday (August 10, by lunar calendar, 己未日 Yellow Sheep) Clear
89 Day of the War

War Situation
- The 5th U.S. Marine Regiment arrives at a position 6 km west of Seoul.
- The UN Forces destroy a large supply center of the North Korean Forces in Yeongdungpo leaving it in flames, while carrying out mop-up operations throughout the Seoul area.

At Home
- The defeated Communists flee from Seoul.
- The Central Military High Court delivers a death sentence to Colonel Choi Chang- shik, Chief of the ROK Army Corp of Engineers, holding him responsible for the destruction of the Han River Bridge (his family asked for a retrial and the judges found him not guilty on November 14, 1964).

September 22, Friday (August 11, by lunar calendar, 庚申日 White Monkey) Clear
90 Day of the War

War Situation
- The 7th U.S. Division which landed at Incheon goes down south to enter Suwon.
- The ROK Marine penetrates into the old streets of Seodaemoon.

At Home
- Police stations reopened at Uiseong, Gunwi, Cheongsong, and Chilgok.
- President Rhee holds a press conference on issues arising after the recapture of the capital city.
- In Yangpyoung, 33 men have been taken by the Communist agents and shot to death.

September 23, Saturday (August 12, by lunar calendar 辛酉日 White Rooster) Very Clear
91 Day of the War

War Situation

- Kim Il Sung issues an order of the total retreat of the North Korean Army Forces.
- The UN Marines occupy a Hill behind the Ewha Woman's University

At Home

- The Martial Law Command for the South Gyeongsang Province, which had been suspended, reopens with Colonel Kim Jong-won as its Commander.
- Finance Minister, Choi Sun-ju speaks of the measures to control inflation and monetary supply.
- Restoration work of the railroad between Seoul and Busan begins, and the construction of a temporary bridge over the Nakdong River is undertaken.

Overseas

- The General Assembly adopts a United States proposal for creating a UN Force for the prevention of invasion.
- Britain conveys to the United States its position on the issues of crossing the 38th parallel and establishing a unified Government in Korea.

September 24, Sunday (August 13, by lunar calendar, 壬戌日 Black Dog) Very Clear
92 Day of the War

War Situation

- The 1st U.S. Marine Division enters the southern suburbs of Seoul.
- The 7th U.S. Division marches eastward from Youngdeungpo and occupies a Hill 11 km out of Seoul, and takes control of the road to the south.

At Home

- The Government sets up a temporary liaison office in Incheon.
- The Director of the Tax Service in Busan announces imposition of income taxes on the salaries of refugee Government workers and employees of private companies.

Overseas

- Italy establishes a three-year-plan for the rearmament.

September 25, Monday (August 14, by lunar calendar, 癸亥日 Black Pig) Clear and Cloudy
93 Day of the War

War Situation

- The North Korean Forces wage determined resistance operations against the UN Forces in the Seoul area, the strongest since the beginning of the war. The Marine advances about 670 m.
- The 1st U.S. Cavalry Division enters Jochiwon and captures Cheonan.

At Home

The soldiers of ROK Army are hoisting the Korean flag in front of the Capitol Building (1950. 9. 26)

- The Government proclaims an amendment to "the temporary law for accommodation of refugees" (Law No. 146)
- The ROK Army headquarters issues an order to refrain from inflicting damage on civilians.

September 26, Tuesday (August 15, by lunar calendar, 甲子日 Blue Rat) Rainy
94 Day of the War

War Situation
- The Task Force Lynch of the 1st U.S Cavalry Division initiates a link-up operation and finally meets the 31st Regiment of the 7th U.S. Division under the 10th U.S. Army Corps at a location north of Osan.

At Home
- Minister of Home Affairs, Cho Byung-ok issues a statement on the restoration of law and order.
- Commerce and Industry Minister, Kim Hoon makes a statement on the promotion of free trade.
- Koo Yong-seo, Governor of the Bank of Korea, issues a statement on the completion of exchanges of the old notes issued by the Bank of Joseon.
- Kim Jong-won, Martial Law Commander for South Gyeongsang Province, extends curfew hours.

September 27, Wednesday (August 16, by lunar calendar, 乙丑日 Blue Ox) Cloudy
95 Day of the War

War Situation
- The U.S. Marines occupy two-thirds of the Seoul area, and hoist the American flag at the U.S. Embassy at 3 p.m.
- The ROK Capital Division and the 3rd ROK Division capture Wooljin and Chunyang.

At Home
- The Ministry of Finance proclaims "the Ministry's Special Order no. 3 on the Government funds in the disaster areas affected by the war."
- Martial Law Commander for the South Gyeongsang Province Kim Jong-won makes a statement on the return of war refugees to their areas of residence.

September 28, Thursday (August 17, by lunar calendar, 丙寅日 Red Tiger) Cloudy and Clear
96 Day of the War

War Situation
- The ROK Capital Division enters Yeongweol and the 6th ROK Division captures Chungju.
- The 2nd US Division enters Cheongju.

At Home

- President Rhee issues an instruction forbidding reprisals, retention, or beating and battery out of personal resentments in the recaptured areas.
- The ROK Army Headquarters prohibits the troops from requisitioning, or plundering of properties or foodstuff, and from abusing women.
- Kim Il Sung holds an emergency meeting of the Central Political Committee of the Workers' Party of Korea, which decides to request direct military assistance from China and the Soviet Union.

Overseas

- Indonesia joins the United Nations as its 60th member state.
- General MacArthur gives a report on an outline of his plan to advance to the north.
- President Truman declares that the UN should decide on the issue of crossing the 38th parallel.

September 29, Friday (August 18, by lunar calendar, 丁卯日 Red Rabbit) Clear
97 Day of the War

War Situation

- The 3rd ROK Division occupies Samcheok and the 8th ROK Division captures Danyang.
- The UN Forces advance to Gwangju, after capturing Namwon and Damyang.

At Home

- President Syngman Rhee, accompanied by General MacArthur, returns to Seoul by air and issues a special statement on the capture of Seoul.

Overseas

- Eight member states recommend that the United Nations authorize General MacArthur to decide whether or not to cross the 38th parallel.
- The United States authorizes the UN Forces' plan to advance north. The British Foreign Minister advocates crossing the 38th parallel.

September 30, Saturday (August 19, by lunar calendar, 戊辰日 Yellow Dragon) Very Clear
98 Day of the War

War Situation

- Parachute troops (of the 187th Airborne Regiment Combat Group) land on the Gimpo Peninsula.
- The 3rd ROK Division at Inguri near the 38th parallel awaits an order to attack beyond the border.

At Home

- Lt. General Walker, Commander of the Eighth U.S. Army, orders the ROK Forces to cross the 38th parallel.

- The plenary session of the National Assembly decides to send a message to the UN General Assembly concerning the crossing of the 38th parallel.

Overseas

- China and the Soviet Union exchange documents of ratification on the Treaty of Friendship and Alliance for Mutual Assistance and five other agreements.
- Indian Prime Minister Nehru opposes the crossing of the 38th parallel.

October 1, Sunday (August 20, by lunar calendar, 己巳日 Yellow Snake) Very Clear
99 Day of the War

War Situation

- General MacArthur, UNC Commander, urges North Korea (Kim Il Sung) to surrender.
- The ROK Forces (the 3rd and the Capital Divisions) cross the 38th parallel.
- The North Korean Forces concentrate on the defense of the 38th parallel.
- Kim Il Sung calls on Mao to dispatch Chinese troops to Korea.

At Home

- The National Assembly passes the wartime emergency budget for October.
- The Martial Law Commander for the South Gyeongsang Province, Minister of Social Affairs and Governor of South Gyeongsang Province issue a joint statement on refugees' return to their homes.
- The Government increases the Police Force by a large scale up to 15,417 to secure law

The British Common Royal Marines and Special Forces are discussing operations while examining at the map. They were one of the strongest military Units the U. K. On October 1950, many countries joined with the UN Forces. (1950. 10)

and order for the North Korean areas captured by the UN Forces and to facilitate the supply of military materials between the front and rear areas.

Overseas
- United States representative, Austin assumes the Presidency of the UNSC.
- General MacArthur demands Kim Il Sung to surrender.

October 2, Monday (August 21, by lunar calendar, 庚午日 White Horse)Very Clear
100 Day of the War

War Situation
- The 3rd ROK Division occupies Yangyang after crossing the 38th parallel.
- The 6th ROK Division captures Chuncheon, and the 8th ROK Division captures Yangpyeong.
- The 7th UN Marines launch a fierce attack on Chuncheon.

At Home
- Shin Ik-hi, Speaker of the National Assembly, speaks about the National Assembly's return to Seoul.
- Lee Ki-bung, Mayor of Seoul City, issues a proclamation concerning the returning of public properties and the reporting of "collaborators" with the Communists.
- Jeong Il-kwon, Martial Law Commander, issues a proclamation to prohibit the illegal occupation or destruction of Government properties, following the return to Seoul.

October 3, Tuesday (August 22, by lunar calendar, 辛未일 White Sheep) Cloudy
101 Day of the War

War Situation
- An advance unit of the 3rd ROK Division arrives at Goseong.
- The 1st US. Cavalry Division penetrates into Uijeongbu.
- The 6th ROK Division advances north from the southern area of Chuncheon, preparing to cross the 38th parallel.
- The 2nd Corps of the ROK Army enters Seoul.

At Home
- All banks in Seoul reopen for business: commercial banks and banking cooperatives restore their business.
- The railroad agencies return to work in the Wonju area.
- Lee Jun-shik, Martial Law Commander of the Seoul-Incheon area, issues a proclamation to punish wartime crimes.

October 4, Wednesday (August 23, by lunar calendar, 壬申日 Black Monkey) Cloudy

War Situation
- The 3rd ROK Division occupies Goseong north of the 38th parallel.

At Home
- Kim Wan-yong, Director of Civil Affairs of the Martial Law Command, warns against illegal occupation of Communist-related houses.

Overseas
- The UN political committee adopts a resolution proposed by eight Western nations for marching north beyond the 38th parallel and holding free elections in all areas of the entire Korean Peninsula.
- A spokesman for the headquarters of the allied forces announces that the 3rd U.S. Division has departed the west coast of the USA for Korea.
- India provides 400,000 gunny bags to Korea.

October 5, Thursday (August 24, by lunar calendar, 癸酉日 Black Rooster) Very Clear
103 Day of the War

War Situation
- The ROK Forces capture the Gumalri power plant and take captive 200 North Korean Army POWs.
- The UN Naval Forces concentrate on demolition of floating mines in the Korean straits.

On 5th October 1950, Peng Dehuai(standing) insisted on sending troops to Korean peninsula at the Enlarged Meeting of Political Bureau of the CPC Central Committee. Mao Zedong (left, 5th) didn't allow recording, and thus the artist Gao Chuan reproduced the scenes of that meeting based on testimonies of the participants.

At Home
- The budget and accounts committee of the National Assembly approves the Government's special financial account for transportation (up to 23 million won) without change to the original bill.

Overseas
- The steering committee of the UN General Assembly approves a United States proposal for referring the issue of Taiwan's future to the General Assembly.
- North Korea and the Soviet Union conclude an agreement on mutual trade terms and delivery conditions.

October 6, Friday (August 25, by lunar calendar, 甲戌日 Blue Dog) Very Clear
104 Day of the War

War Situation
- The 2nd ROK Army Corps begins marching north in the middle sector of the frontlines.
- The 2nd North Korean Corps forms a second front in the Iron Triangle area.

At Home
- Seoul City implements the distribution of a free daily food ration (1.4 hop per head per day/ 1 hop is equivalent to 1.18 liters). Seoul City starts supplying tap water.
- The price of rice and food items falls.

ROK Army crosses the 38th Parallel, advancing to the north(1950. 10. 8)

October 7, Saturday (August 26, by lunar calendar, 乙亥日 Blue Pig) Clear
105 Day of the War

War Situation
- Four ROK Divisions have crossed the 38th parallel and keep advancing north.
- The U.S. Forces cross the 38th parallel at 17:14 p.m. for the first time to advance north.
- The 1st U.S. Cavalry Division captures Kaesong.

Overseas
- The UN General Assembly passes the proposal submitted by eight Western nations for crossing the 38th parallel (October 7).
- The Indian Government decides not to participate in the seven-member commission on Korea.

October 8, Sunday (August 27, by lunar calendar, 丙子日 Red Rat) Cloudy and Rainy
106 Day of the War

War Situation
- The 3rd ROK Division arrives at Sangeumri, 12 kilometers south of Wonsan
- The 6th ROK Division advances to Hwacheon.
- The 6th and the 7th Divisions of the ROK Forces keep advancing north, and some elements of the Divisions cut off the Pyongyang-Wonsan railroad line.

At Home
- The plenary session of the National Assembly decides to turn down the resignation of Speaker Shin Ik-hee.
- The Government issues a statement to the people explaining the situation in which the Government's relocation was carried out on June 28.

Overseas
- The Chinese Forces reorganize the Northeast Peripheral Army as the People's Volunteers Army and order it to depart for Korea.

October 9, Monday (August 28, by lunar calendar, 丁丑日 Red Ox) Clear
107 Day of the War

War Situation
- The UN Forces begin operations to advance further north.
- The ROK Forces arrive at the southern tip of Wonsan at 23:00 hours.
- The ROK Capital Division occupies the southern part of Mt. Shingosan.

At Home
- The Ministry of Education establishes a temporary committee for the local educational reconstruction in all of the provinces.

• The Busan Wireless Communication Bureau reopens wireless committee with Seoul.

October 10, Tuesday (August 29, by lunar calendar, 戊寅日 Yellow Tiger) Clear
108 Day of the War

War Situation
• The 3rd ROK Division occupies Wonsan and Myungsashimni airport in the morning.
• The 1st Ground Combat Unit of the ROK Marines occupies Suncheon, the second ROK Marines ground combat unit occupies Goheung.

At Home
• The Cabinet Meeting endorses the October 7 resolution on Korea of the UN General Assembly.
• The Government of the Republic of Korea requests the assistance of American experts for the restoration of administration service.

Overseas
• China and the Soviet Union discuss Soviet air support for the Chinese Forces to be dispatched to Korea.
• Prior to the meeting with General MacArthur, President Truman issues a statement on his intention to build "a unified Government in Korea."
• The French Government sends a federal minister and the Generalissimo of Morocco to Indochina to exercise necessary administrative authority.

October 11, Wednesday (September 1, by lunar calendar, 己卯日 Yellow Rabbit) Cloudy and Rainy
109 Day of the War

War Situation
• Kim Il Sung issues an order to the North Korean Army Forces to fight and resist the enemy until the last minute.
• The 6th, 7th and 8th Divisions of the ROK enter Pyeonggang.

At Home
• The Education Ministry convenes a secretariat chiefs' conference of the five provinces in the North to discuss assignment of education administrators to those areas.
• Minister of Agriculture Yoon Young-sun reports to the National Assembly on the Government's policy measures on grain demand and supply.

October 12, Thursday (September 2, by lunar calendar, 庚辰日 White Dragon) Clear
110 Day of the War

War Situation
• The 1st ROK Division captures Sakju and the ROK Forces occupy Haeju.

• The 1st U.S. Cavalry Division enters Hanpori.

At Home
• Over 20,000 books belonging to the Central National Library, which were hidden by the Communists, are found in Wuidong.

Overseas
• Zhou Enlai reports to Mao Zedong on his meeting with Stalin.
• "The Korea-Japan Navigation Agreement" goes into effect.

October 13, Friday (September 3, by lunar calendar, 辛巳日 White Snake) Cloudy and Rainy
111 Day of the War

War Situation
• The UN Forces capture Haeju and Cheorwon.
• The 3rd ROK Division captures Muncheon.
• The 1st U.S. Cavalry Division captures Kimcheon.
• A fleet of 37 battleships, including the Missouri, launches a fierce shelling toward the coast of the Hambuk Province.

At Home
• The National Assembly passes the "collaborators treatment law."
• President Rhee and the Cabinet reject UNCURK's plan for nationwide general elections.

October 14, Saturday (September 4, by lunar calendar, 壬午日 White Snake) Clear
112 Day of the War

War Situation
• The ROK 1st Division occupies Singye, Gowon and Goksan.
• The ROK 3rd Division approaches Yongheung.
• 30 B-29s concentrate on bombing the key points of traffic facilities between Pyongyang and Sinuiju.

At Home
• The Korean Government rejects the proposal for a nationwide general election suggested by the UN Commission on Korea.
• Vice-Minister of Foreign Affairs Cho Jeong Hwan, raises objection against the decision of the UN Commission on Korea to attribute the North Korean administration under the UN authority.

October 15, Sunday (September 5, by lunar calendar, 癸未日 White Snake) Cloudy
113 Day of the War

War Situation

- The ROK Capital Division and the ROK 8th Division approach Yongheung and Goksan respectively.
- The U.S. 1st Cavalry occupies Namcheonjeom.

At Home
- The Government proclaims "the Law on the provisional registration of Government Officials"(Law No. 148)
- Minister of Home Affairs Cho Byung-ok and Justice Minister Kim Joon-yeon give stern warnings against plundering of private properties.

October 16, Monday (September 6, by lunar calendar, 甲申日 White Snake) Cloudy and Rainy
114 Day of the War

War Situation
- An Advance Unit of the Chinese Forces crosses the Yalu River.
- The U.S. Forces occupy Jeongpyeong, and start to exert pressure by encircling the Pyongyang defense lines.
- The British and Australian troops sweep 8,000-10,000 troops of the North Korean Forces.

At Home
- The Government offices hold their first morning conferences at the Capitol Building since returning to Seoul.
- The organization of the Ministry of Transportation is converted to the pre-war system.
- Elementary schools in Seoul reopen.

October 17, Tuesday (September 7, by lunar calendar, 乙酉日 Blue Rooster) Clear
115 Day of the War

War Situation
- The main Forces of the Chinese volunteer army again delay the crossing of the Yalu river.
- The ROK Capital Division captures Hamheung and Heungnam.
- An advance north limit line has been set along the Seoncheon and Seungjin line.

At Home
- The Government publishes proof of the Chinese intervention in the Korean War.
- President Rhee speaks of sending his own administrators to the occupied areas of North Korea in response to the UN resolution regarding administration of the same areas.

Overseas
- At the UN Economic and Social Council, the United States representative submits a proposal for establishment of a Korean reconstruction agency.
- United States representative Dulles requests that the seven-state proposal be discussed for the purpose of establishing a strong international organization free from vetoes to build peace.

October 18, Wednesday (September 8, by lunar calendar, 丙戌日 Red Rooster) Cloudy
116 Day of the War

War Situation
- The 24th U.S. Division and one British brigade march toward Jinnampo.
- Three thousand defeated North Korean Army troops occupy Gangneung to commit atrocities, then retreat toward Jumunjin.

At Home
- The Decrees on Honorary Combat Medal have been proclaimed. (Presidential Decree No. 385)
- The National Assembly decides to use the National Theater for its assembly hall.

October 19, Thursday (September 9, by lunar calendar, 丁亥日 Red Pig) Cloudy and Rainy
117 Day of the War

War Situation
- The main Forces of the Chinese Volunteer Army begin crossing the Yalu River.
- The UN and the ROK Forces (the 1st ROK Division and the 1st U.S. Cavalry Division) occupy Pyongyang, and open the airport.
- The ROK Capital Division captures Hongwon.

At Home
- Agriculture Minister Yoon Young-sun confirms that the land reform will continue.
- The Monetary Policy Committee approves the establishment of a temporary reconstruction headquaters.
- A ceremony for the completion of a temporary Han River bridge is held and the bridge is open for traffic.

Overseas
- The Soviet Union supports India's proposal regarding the election of a new UN Secretary-General to replace Trygve Lie.
- The UN political committee approves the proposal on cooperation for peace.

President Truman(left) flew to Wake Island and met with General MacArthur. They discussed what effects would their future policies have on Korean War. (1950. 10. 15)

October 20, Friday (September 10, by lunar calendar, 戊子日 (Yellow Rat) Rainy
118 Day of the War

War Situation
- Three Divisions of the UN Forces cross the Daedong River to march north.
- U.S. Major General Almond, Commander of the 10th Corps, has been made responsible for the areas above the latitude 38 degree and 10 minute line.

At Home
- President Rhee expresses his congratulations on the capture of Pyongyang.
- Agriculture Minister Yoon Young-sun comments that the land reform would be carried out according to the law.

October 21, Saturday (September 11, by lunar calendar, 己丑日 Yellow Ox) Rainy and Cloudy
119 Day of the War

War Situation
- The ROK Capital Division breaches the 40th parallel.
- The 1st U.S. Cavalry Division begins to carry out a joint operation with the 187th U.S. Airborne Regiment in the Suncheon area.
- The U.S. 1st Corps conducts military administration in Pyongyang.
- The military administration headquarters of the 1st Corps is established in Pyongyang.

At Home
- Three American prisoners of war rescued from Pyongyang arrive at Gimpo.
- Pyongyang radio broadcasts that the North Korean capital has moved to Shinuiju.
- The Seoul Military Service Command announces the beginning of registration of "the Second Peoples' Force."

October 22, Sunday (September 12, by lunar calendar, 庚寅日 White Tiger) Clear
120 Day of the War

War Situation
- The ROK Capital Division occupies Bukcheong, Jungyangri, Majondong and Shinheung
- The bodies of 68 American prisoners of war are discovered in the area of Suncheon.

At Home
- The Government begins transporting food by air to Pyongyang, and appoints a new mayor of Pyongyang.
- The telephone lines open between Seoul and Pyongyang.

October 23, Monday (September 13, by lunar calendar, 辛卯日 White Rabbit) Clear
121 Day of the War

War Situation
- The U.S. 1st Corps arrives at the Cheongcheon River.
- The 1st U.S. Cavalry Division headquarters appoints Colonel Elmoves as the new military administrator of Pyongyang City.

At Home
- At an interview with the foreign press, President Rhee says that the Republic of Korea starts to govern North Korea.
- The temporary Lane A of the Han River Bridge is open for public traffic.
- The Joseon Ilbo daily continues to publish two-page morning newspapers of tabloid size at 30 won per copy.

October 24, Tuesday (September 14, by lunar calendar, 壬辰日 Black Dragon) Clear
122 Day of the War

War Situation
- The UN Forces launch an all-out offensive (the Thanksgiving offensive).
- The 27th British Commonwealth brigade crosses the Cheongcheon river.

At Home
- The Decree on Meritorious Badge for Wounded Soldiers is proclaimed (Presidential Decree No. 389).
- The Decree on Meritorious Badge for the 6.25 war participants is proclaimed (Presidential Decree No. 390).

Overseas
- The French Air Force bombs the positions of the Ho Chi Minh Forces at Langson, which was previously lost.
- President Truman emphasizes the possibility of avoiding war and maintaining peace at a UN commemorating lecture.

October 25, Wednesday (September 15, by lunar calendar, 癸巳日 Black Snake) Clear
123 Day of the War

War Situation
- The 8th ROK Division enters Gujangdong. The ROK Forces occupy Bakcheon and Seocheon.
- The 27th British Commonwealth brigade completes the crossing of the Chungcheon River.

At Home
- A citizens' rally to welcome President Rhee's visit to Pyongyang is held. The President does not attend the rally.
- Due to the war, the population of Seoul decreases by 243,532 (17%) persons, and 62,987

households.
- A liaison office of the Transportation Ministry is set up in Pyongyang.

October 26, Thursday (September 16, by lunar calendar, 甲午日 Blue Horse) Clear
124 Day of the War

War Situation
- Additional Chinese Forces (the 50th and the 66th) Armies) begin crossing the Yalu River.
- ROK and UN Forces advance up to the areas of Bakcheon, Daecheon, Wunsan, Onjongri, Hoicheon and Iwon.

At Home
- The Government determines the requirements for the supply and demand of emergency relief materials and establishes the central, comprehensive reconstruction research headquarters.
- A special decree is proclaimed on the "Special Order for Bank Deposit Within the Penetrated Areas"
- Civilian passenger trains begins to run on the Gyeongbu line
- Uruguay provides 70,000 sheets of blanket.

October 27, Friday (September 17, by lunar calendar, 乙未日 Blue Sheep) Very Clear
125 Day of the War

War Situation
- The ROK Capital Division occupies Hwangsuwonri.
- Some troops of the 24th U.S. Division advance to Taecheon the 1st U.S. Cavalry Regiment occupies Macheonryoung.
- The UN Forces cross the Daeryoung River at Bakcheon, 80 kilometers north of Pyongyang.
- Chinese prisoners captured by the ROK Forces at Anju say that 20,000 Chinese troops have entered North Korea.

At Home
- The administrative organizations of the Government return to Seoul. Celebration for retaking Pyongyang takes place.

Overseas
- The United Nations Command announces that the UN Forces would advance to all necessary areas to mop up the North Korean Forces.
- Mao Zedong approves the deployment of the 9th Chinese Army Corps into the Korean war.
- A spokesman of the U.S. Government announces that the United States and the Soviet Union would meet again after the Soviet Union reviews the proposed peace treaty with

Japan.

October 28, Saturday (September 18, by lunar calendar, 丙申日 Red Monkey) Clear
126 Day of the War

War Situation
- The ROK Forces enter and secure Seongjin. The ROK Capital Division captures Samsu, 13 kilometers from the border.
- The 3rd ROK Division engages in a fierce battle with the Chinese troops.

At Home
- The plenary session of the National Assembly fails to meet due to the lack of quorum.
- The joint investigation headquarters review more than 10,000 cases of potential collaborators with the Communists.

October 29, Sunday (September 19, by lunar calendar, 丁酉日 Red Rooster) Clear
127 Day of the War

War Situation
- The 7th U.S. Division lands at Iwon, 280 kilometers north of Wonsan.
- The U.S. Marines occupy Gojeo, 48 kilometers south of Wonsan.

At Home
- President Rhee visits Pyongyang.
- With the power plants at Youngwol and Danginri undamaged and the Hwacheon plant secured, there is no problem to meet the demand for power supply.

October 30, Monday (September 20, by lunar calendar, 戊戌日 Yellow Dog) Clear
128 Day of the War

War Situation
- The 7th ROK Division captures Changdong, east of Taecheon.
- The 6th ROK Division retreats from the areas of Onjeong and Unsan because of strong resistance by a Infantry Division of the North Korean Army.

At Home
- An estimated 4,500 people are massacred in Ongjin area by the troops and regime of North Korea.

October 31, Tuesday (September 21, by lunar calendar, 己亥日 Yellow Pig) Very Clear
129 Day of the War

War Situation
- The Communist Chinese Forces invade Youngwon.

- The ROK Army occupy Goseongri.

At Home
- Finance Minister Choi Sun-ju speaks of reforming the tax system at a province governors' conference.
- Industry and Commerce Minister Kim Hoon announces complete restoration of the Cheongpyong power plant.

11 NOVEMBER 1950

November 1, Wednesday (September 22, by lunar calendar, 庚子日 White Rat) Clear
130 Day of the War

War Situation
- The 10th Corps Units and the 7th U.S. Division Units continue mop-up operations and march north, arriving at a point 61 km from the border.
- The U.S. Advance Units repel the North Korean Army Forces that are under the air cover protection of Soviet aircraft, and arrive at a location 30 kilometers to the border.

At Home
- The 41st plenary session of the National Assembly convenes.
  The bill on lifting Martial Law is suspended during the committee deliberation.
- Cigarette prices are raised to 500 won for Baekhak, and 300 won for Gongjak.

Overseas
- The UN General Assembly resolves to extend the tenure of Secretary General Lie by three years, as proposed by 15 member states.
- The French Forces continue holding the isolated positions in Lauke, near the China-Vietnam border, after withstanding the heavy pressure of the Ho Chi Minh Forces.

November 2, Thursday (September 23, by lunar calendar, 辛丑日 White Ox) Very Clear
131 Day of the War

War Situation
- The 3rd ROK Division replaces the 1st U.S. Marine Division at Sudong.
- The U.S. 1st Corps and the 7th U.S. Division conduct mop-up operations, marching toward Pungsan.

At Home
- The National Assembly lifts, by voting, the Martial Law for all areas of South Korea. The National Assembly approves the dispatch of a fact-finding team to survey the North Korean situation.
- Chang Chang-kuk, Provost Marshal of the Seoul Military Police Command, issues a statement concerning the defense of the Capital and night traffic.

November 3, Friday (September 24, by lunar calendar, 壬寅日 Black Tiger) Very Clear and Cloudy
132 Day of the War

War Situation
- The ROK Forces resist the Chinese Forces moving along the Manpo line and reorganize to

form a defense line of Youngbyon, Gujang and Youngwon.
- The U.S. 9th Corps moves to Suncheon to engage in the western frontline.

At Home
- The funeral is held for the former ROK Army Chief of staff, Chae Byung-duk.
- The three-fold increase of Government workers' salaries goes into effect retroactively from the month of October.

November 4, Saturday (September 25, by lunar calendar, 癸卯日 Black Rabbit) Rainy and Cloudy
133 Day of the War

War Situation
- The ROK Forces continue to crush the North Korean Forces along a defensive line from Yeongbyon, to Gujang, Dukcheon and Yeongwon and reinforce their defense positions.
- One battalion of the 24th U.S. Infantry Division advances along the northern bank of the Cheongcheon River 8 km south of Yeongbyon, repelling the resistance of the North Korean troops.

At Home
- The UNC Civil Affairs Director for the South Pyongan Province comments that the administrative formula in the Pyongyang area does not represent military rule.

November 5, Sunday (September 26, by lunar calendar, 甲辰日 Blue Dragon) Cloudy
134 Day of the War

War Situation
- The ROK Forces capture Myungcheon and Gilju, breaching the 41st parallel.
- The 3rd U.S. Division makes an administrative landing at Wonsan.

At Home
- The Eighth U.S. Army officially confirms the Chinese intervention in the war with two Divisions.
- Total damage to the industrial facilities by a joint assessment of the United States ECA and the ROK Ministry of Commerce and Industry amounts to KRW 76 billion.
- Colonel Manski, Civil Affairs Director of the UN Forces for the South Pyongan Province, says that the administration for the South Pyongan Province is not of military rule.

November 6, Monday (September 27, by lunar calendar, 乙巳日 Blue Snake) Very Clear
135 Day of the War

War Situation
- The ROK Forces arrive at Myungju.

- The newest Soviet-made aircraft cross the border to participate in the war for the first time.
- The 7th Regiment of the 6th ROK Division completes a retreat to Gaecheon from Chosan.

At Home
- President Rhee comments at a press conference that the Chinese intervention was instigated by the Soviet Union.
- Kim Chang-ryong, chief of the joint military, police and prosecution investigation headquarters, holds a press conference for discussion with reporters.

Overseas
- Austin, United States representative to the UN, officially notifies the United Nations of the Chinese intervention in the Korean War.
- The United Kingdom denies the rumor on the withdrawal of its recognition of China.

November 7, Tuesday (September 28, by lunar calendar, 丙午日 Red Horse) Clear
136 Day of the War

War Situation
- The UN Forces secure a beachhead at the Cheongcheon River.
- Canadian troops being dispatched to Korea arrive at Busan.

At Home
- About 20,000 war refugees are on the run from the Cheongcheon river area.
- The Martial Law Command executes 23 traitors convicted of collaboration with the Communists who were sentenced to death by court martial
- Belgium provides Korea with 400 tons of sugar.

November 8, Wednesday (September 29, by lunar calendar, 丁未日 Red Sheep) Very Clear
137 Day of the War

War Situation
- The ROK Army advances 20km from the north of Myeongchon.
- The 27th Infantry Regiment of the 24th U.S. Division advances to Bakcheon.
- The 2nd U.S. Division occupies Deokcheon.

At Home
- President Rhee issues a statement to the people calling for their unity in national spirit.
- Chang Du-kwan, Director of the Civil Affairs Division of the Martial Law Command for the South Gyeongsang Province, warns against illegal possession of arms.

Overseas
- The UN Economic and Social Council approves a proposal for land improvement in underdeveloped areas.

- The UNSC votes in favor of Britain's proposal to hear a Chinese representative speak about China's intervention in the war in Korea.
- James Byrnes, former United States Secretary of State, is elected as Governor of California.
- The mid-term congressional elections show a decline in support of the Democratic Party.

November 9, Thursday (September 30, by lunar calendar, 戊申日 Yellow Monkey) Very Clear
138 Day of the War

War Situation
- The ROK Forces advance to Yongcheon-dong north of Myungcheon.
- A spokesman of the UN Command under General MacArthur reveals that 50 Chinese Army Divisions are assemblying and stand by in Manchuria.
- The UN member states participating in the Korean War issue a joint statement demanding the withdrawal of the Chinese troops and promising that the UN Forces would not invade Manchuria.

At Home
- Chief Prosecutor, Suh Sang Wan states that collaborators would be humanely treated.
- The Government spokesman emphasizes that all-out resistance and actions should be shown by the Korean people to confront the Chinese participation.

November 10, Friday (October 1, by lunar calendar, 己酉日 Yellow Rooster) Clear
139 Day of the War

War Situation
- The ROK Army advances to Youngcheon-dong, north of Myeongchon, and 10km southeast of Hapsu.
- The U.S. Fleet air wing bombs Sinuiju destroying the bridge, direct hitting six bombings.

At Home
- A general rally by the Korean Youth League takes place.
- Dr. Burns of the UN Economic Commission for Korea leaves for Thailand to take up his new assignment.

November 11, Saturday (October 2, by lunar calendar, 庚戌日 White Dog) Very Clear
140 Day of the War

War Situation
- The remnants of the defeated North Korean troops penetrate into Hwacheon and Yanggu.
- The U.S. Air Force drops 1,092 bombs on Cheongjin and Eujoo.

At Home

- The Government proclaims "The Special order to punish collaborators by single trial system."
- The Governor of Gyeonggi province speaks about the relocation of the provincial main office to Suwon.

November 12, Sunday (October 3, by lunar calendar, 辛亥日 White Pig) Very Clear
141 Day of the War

War Situation

- The ROK Army repels the regiments of the defeated North Korea troops at Cheorwon and Gimhwa.
- Brigadier General Park Beom Joon, Chief of Staff, ROK Air Force, dies during his air battle operational mission in Hamheung.

At Home

- The railroad service for Seoul and Daidonggang River reopens.
- Chang Chang-guk, Provost Marshal takes an additional position as the Commander of the combined military polices (provost marshal office).
- The railroad service for Seoul and Pyongnam Daidong reopens.

Overseas

- Henry A. Wallace, former United States Vice President makes a statement that the United States should continue to strengthen its military power until the USSR and China begin to show their practical actions and commitment to world peace.

November 13, Monday (October 4, by lunar calendar, 壬子日 Black Rat) Clear
142 Day of the War

War Situation

- The ROK Army confronts the North Korean troops face to face in the areas of Yongcheon-dong north of Myungcheon.
- The U.S. 1st Cavalry Division captures three hills in the Youngbyeon area.

At Home

- The National Assembly finally passes the bill on "the special law on the punishment of collaborators."
- President Syngman Rhee asks all engineers and technicians to exert their utmost efforts to ensure the reconstruction of war damages.

Overseas

- Tibet makes a direct appeal to the UN to activate its role of mediation on the Chinese invasion of Tibet.

- Taiwan Government reveals a report on the meetings among Mao Zedong, Kim Il Sung and the Soviet Ambassador Stikov at Shenyang.
- The United States Government states that their proposed draft on "the economic policy for the underdeveloped countries" is intended mainly to halt the Soviets' aggression.

November 14, Tuesday (October 5, by lunar calendar, 癸丑日 Black Ox) Very Clear
143 Day of the War

War Situation
- The U.S. 1st Corps confronts the 90,000 Chinese troops.
- The Eighth U.S. Army confronts the Chinese troops on the frontlines despite the freezing weather.
- The 7th Regiment of the U.S. Marine approaches Hagalwoori.

At Home
- The National Assembly passes a bill related to "the Special committee on the national reconstruction and unification."
- The Ministry of Transportation revises the form of passenger ticket of the national railroad.

November 15, Wednesday (October 6, by lunar calendar, 甲寅日 Blue Tiger) Clear and Cloudy
144 Day of the War

War Situation
- A Reconnaissance Unit of the 1st U.S. Cavalry Division enters Yongpyon.
- The UN Forces confront a strong resistance from the North Korean Forces in the east of the Cheongcheon River.
- The North Korean Forces break through the central, strategic part of the UN Forces' frontline to advance 6km.

At Home
- Chang Du-kwan, chief of civil affairs of the Martial Law command for South Gyeongsang Province, says that implementation of the land reform will be continued.
- Senator Knowland inspects the frontline in Korea.

November 16, Thursday (October 7, by lunar calendar, 乙卯日 Blue Rabbit) Cloudy
145 Day of the War

War Situation
- The UN Forces, in the cold weather, launch an attack on the Chinese Forces, forcing them to retreat to the Korea-Manchuria border.

At Home

- The National Assembly approves a bill for the Government to purchase 1,800,000 bags of rice, at a price of 8,000 won per bag.
- Army Chief of Staff Chung Il-kwon states in relation with the "Box of People's Voices."
- Partial street car operation begins in Seoul from Dongdaemun to the crossroads of Jongno in front of the Hwashin Department Store.

Overseas
- President Truman issues a statement that the United States has no intention of war, and that peace in the Far East depends on China's attitude.

November 17, Friday (October 8, by lunar calendar, 丙辰日 Red Dragon) Cloudy
146 Day of the War

War Situation
- The ROK Forces in the northeast sector of the frontline prepare their battle line in the northeast direction of Myungcheon and near Yongju-dong and Hapsu.
- The ROK Forces secure the positions of frontlines at Wonri, Deokcheon and Young won.

At Home
- President Rhee requests that the National Assembly reconsider the nomination of Paik Nak-joon for the post of Prime Minister.
- The Education Ministry demands a fair but stern review of student collaborators.

November 18, Saturday (October 9, by lunar calendar, 丁巳日 Red Snake) Rainy and Clear
147 Day of the War

War Situation
- North Korean guerrillas enter the Chuncheon area to cause trouble.
- The U.S. Air Force makes about 100 sorties; Navy aircraft take off in 241 sorties, protecting the 7th Division and destroying a bridge at Hyaesanjin.

At Home
- President Rhee speaks at a ceremony for the establishment of the Homeland Defense Force (35,000 men).
- Defense Minister Shin Sung-mo calls for establishment of a buffer zone in Manchuria.

November 19, Sunday (October 10, by lunar calendar, 戊午日 Yellow Horse) Very Clear
148 Day of the War

War Situation
- The ROK Capital Division advances to the Korea-Soviet border along the east coast.
- The 7th U.S. Division passes through Gapsan to approach a location 20 km from the border.

At Home
- The Government proclaims an order to protect the forest.
- "The Special measures for deposit payment by financial organizations" is proclaimed and implemented (Emergency Presidential Order No, 4).
- Defense Minister Shin Sung-mo returns home from Tokyo where he welcomed the new UN Commission on Korea.

Overseas
- The representative of El Salvador requests that the UN condemn the Chinese invasion of Tibet.
- The British Red Cross decides to dispatch a Red Cross Crusade to Korea for civilian relief assistance.

November 20, Monday (October 11, by lunar calendar, 己未日 Yellow Sheep) Clear and Cloudy
149 Day of the War

War Situation
- The 7th Division of the U.S. 10th Corps arrives at a location 3 km from the Korea-Manchuria border.
- The ROK Forces arrive at a location 25 km north of Myungcheon, 33 km short of reaching the Cheongjin Port, the largest port on the east coast of Korea.
- The 1st U.S. Marine Division encircles the Jangjin(Chosin) Reservoir power plant and crushes the positions of the Communist Chinese Artillery guns in the west of Jangjin(Chosin) Reservoir.

At Home
- Registration for the Second Peoples' Force is carried out across the country.
- The Seoul metropolitan police arrests 14,000 collaborators.
- No Bang-ju and 248 other residents have been executed by the 5th Company, the 2nd Battalion, the 20th Regiment of the 11th ROK Army Division.

November 21, Tuesday (October 12, by lunar calendar, 庚申日 White Monkey) Clear
150 Day of the War

War Situation
- The Advance Unit (the 17th Regiment) of the 7th U.S. Infantry Division occupies Hyesanjin, a border city of Manchuria.
- The ROK Capital Division, moving fast along the east coast line, advances to a location 24 km south of Cheongjin.
- Some troops of the 1st U.S. Cavalry Division retreat from near Yongbyon due to the pressure of the Communist Forces.

At Home

- The Government appoints Lee Goo-ha as civil administrator of Hamgyung-namdo Province.
- The Civil Affairs Division of the Martial Law Command for South Gyeongsang Province announces implementation of ID checks on the street.

November 22, Wednesday (October 13, by lunar calendar, 辛酉日 White Rooster) Very Clear
151 Day of the War

War Situation
- The 7th U.S. Division, in snowstorms, advances toward Samsu, 16 kilometers south- west of Haesanjin.
- The ROK Forces capture Youngwon on the western front, while another Division of the 2nd ROK Corps builds positions at a location 8–10 kilometers north of Dukcheon.

At Home
- President Rhee inspects Hamheung (for a second time) and returns to Seoul.
- President Rhee nominates Ambassador Jang Myeon as new Prime Minister and asks for approval by the National Assembly.
- The war damage in total: 470,000 people killed and KRW 27.1184 trillion lost in property damage.

November 23, Thursday (October 14, by lunar calendar, 壬戌日 Black Dog) Clear
152 Day of the War

War Situation
- The ROK Police Force conducts a "guerilla mop-up operation" in the areas of Wicheon, Puksan, and Geochang County, killing 119 North Korean troops and capturing seven.
- The Thai Amy joins the UN Forces to fight in Korea.

At Home
- President Rhee issues a Thanksgiving Day message.
- The National Assembly approves the nomination of Jang Myeon as Prime Minister.

Overseas
- The UN decides to refer Taiwan's proposal to denounce the Soviet Union to the UN Interim Committee.
- The ECA administrator comments that ECA assistance will help protect Asia from the threat of Communist invasion.
- British Foreign Secretary Bevin sends a message to Zhou Enlai that the Chinese Forces of aggression should withdraw from Korea as soon as possible, since the UN Forces would assure the security of the Chinese regime.

November 24, Friday (October 15, by lunar calendar, 癸亥日 Black Pig) Very Clear
153 Day of the War

War Situation
- The ROK Capital Division closes in – 11 kilometers from Cheongjin.
- The ROK Forces, responsible for the left wing of the western sector, advance toward Taecheon, an assembly point for the Communist Forces.

At Home
- President Rhee speaks out against the UN's interference in the internal affairs of Korea.
- The Government submits a bill to the National Assembly to establish the National Defense Corps.
- Lee Kwang-sun, Provost Marshal for the Busan Military Police, warns against illegal transaction of military materials.

Overseas
- The political department of the Chinese Support Forces distributes its second political combat publication.
- A senior United States diplomat comments that the UN Forces' general offensive is an expression of the firm UN resolve and he expects "the show of force to bring a peaceful resolution"
- The Soviet Union takes issue with the United States proposal for a peace treaty with Japan, opposing United States control of the Ryukyu Islands.

November 25, Saturday (October 16, by lunar calendar, 甲子日 Blue Rat) Very Clear
154 Day of the War

War Situation
- On the eastern front, the ROK Capital Division occupies Cheongjin, and the 3rd ROK Division occupies Baekam.
- The 3rd U.S. Division on the eastern frontlines engages in a battle with the 126 Chinese Division.
- The Communist Chinese Forces counterattack with "a sea of humans strategy" deploying 600,000 troops against the general offensive of the Eighth U.S. Army.

At Home
- "Rules for review of prisoners of war" is proclaimed (Presidential Decree No, 486).
- The Government's revised supplementary budget (the fifth revision) is passed by the National Assembly: total amount 243.8 billion won.
- Ziauddin of Pakistan has been appointed as the representative of the UNCURK.

November 26, Sunday (October 17, by lunar calendar, 乙丑日 Blue Ox) Clear
155 Day of the War

War Situation
- The ROK Forces enter Cheongjin and advance 12 km north from the city, while other ROK Forces arrive at Hapsu.
- The Communist Forces occupy Deokcheon.

At Home
- The National Assembly passes the additional budget plan. The Korean Government announces the purchase prices of grains. The Munhwashibo(Munhwa Daily News) publishes its first issue.

Overseas
- The 12 members of the UNCURK arrive in Seoul and their senior commissioner makes an arrival statement.
- A surgery team of the People's Assistance Organization of Beijing departs for the Korean front.

November 27, Monday (October 18, by lunar calendar, 丙寅日 Red Tiger) Clear
156 Day of the War

War Situation
- The 25th and the 2nd U.S. Divisions crush the counter-attacks of the Chinese Communist Forces against the Eighth U.S. Army on the western front.
- The Communist Forces occupy Youngwon, after defeating the Youngwon defense line of the Second ROK Army Corps.

At Home
- President Rhee appoints Oh Han-young as Minister of Health and Lee Chul-won as Director of the Office of Public Information.
- A war relief service organization provides used clothes worth U.S$1 million.

November 28, Tuesday (October 19, by lunar calendar, 丁卯日 Red Rabbit) Clear and Cloudy
157 Day of the War

War Situation
- The ROK Forces capture Cheongjin and continue marching north. The ROK Forces kill 600 North Korean troops in the Yeoncheon area during mop-up operations.
- On the eastern front, the ROK Forces face no enemy resistance to their advance north of Cheongjin; while on the western front, the ROK Forces are forced to retreat by the overwhelming pressure of the Communist Chinese and North Korean Forces.

At Home

- The joint investigation headquarters (commanded by Colonel Kim Chang-ryong) announces the capture of 240 Communist guerillas and more than 80 rifles and machine guns during a mop-up operation at Mount Bukaksan.

November 29, Wednesday (October 20, by lunar calendar, 戊辰日 Yellow Dragon) Snowy and Clear
158 Day of the War

War Situation
- The Communist Chinese Forces launch a failed night attack on the U.S. Marines near the Anbyun area of Jangjin(Chosin) Reservoir.
- UN Forces participating in the Korean War: Ground Forces from 13 countries, Naval Forces from 10 countries, Aviation Forces from four countries and Transportation Units from seven countries.

At Home
- Minister of Home Affairs, Cho Byung-ok announces that the topic of discussion at the UNCURK was "restoration of Korea's sovereignty."

Overseas
- Director of the UNC economic assistance to Korea says that assistance materials are being transported to Korea to help eliminate disease, hunger and insecurity.
- Present at the UNSC meeting, ROK Foreign Minister Lim Byung-jik says that Chinese intervention is an act of mad aggression, demanding withdrawal of the Chinese Forces.
- Austin, United States representative to the UN, requests discussion of the six member states' resolution.
- The UK decides to make efforts to resolve the Korean question in cooperation with the United States and France.

November 30, Thursday (October 21, by lunar calendar, 己巳日 Yellow Snake) Clear
159 Day of the War

War Situation
- The 3rd Company, the 22nd Regiment, the 3st ROK Division, advances to Haesanjin.
- The UN Forces retreat from Shinanju airport.
- In the areas of Cheorwon and Gapyong, the North Korean Army remnants have been defeated by the ROK Army and the police Forces.

At Home
- "Temporary Tax Increase Law" (Law No. 154) is proclaimed
- Average monthly retail price index for Seoul: 860.3 (1947=100). 720.1 for Busan.

Overseas

- The Soviet Union vetoes a proposed resolution by six member states of the UN Security Council calling for withdrawal of the Chinese Forces from Korea.
- The United States considers embargos on the export of strategic goods to the Soviet Union and its satellite countries.
- American public opinion prevails in favor of the use of atomic weapons in a critical situation, but opposes it in the present situation.

December 1, Friday (October 22, by lunar calendar, 庚午日 White Horse) Very Clear
160 Day of the War

War Situation
- On the northeastern front, the U.S. 10th Corps (the 7th U.S. Division and the 1st U.S. Marine Division) begins to retreat from the Chinese Communist Forces at Jangjin(Chosin) Reservoir.
- The 8th U.S. Army retreats from its beachhead at the Cheongcheon River with support of the 5th Regiment of the 24th U.S. Division and one British Commonwealth battalion.
- The ROK military police members arrest 500 suspects for spreading rumors in Pyongyang.

At Home
- "The order to prohibit private punishment" is proclaimed (Law No. 156).
- Streetcar fare goes up from 20 to 50 won.

Overseas
- Responding to President Truman's mention of the potential use of atomic weapons, representatives of the UN member states propose a peaceful withdrawal of the Chinese Forces from Korea.

December 2, Saturday (October 23, by lunar calendar, 辛未日 White Sheep) Very Clear
161 Day of the War

War Situation

The 1st U.S. Marine Division is embarking at Heungnam Port (1950. 12). They managed to evacuate by a close call from Jangjin(Chosin) Reservoir.

- At Jangjin(Chosin) Reservoir, the Communist Chinese Forces build pressure to engage the U.S. Marines in a fierce battle.
- The 31st and the 32nd Regiments of the 7th U.S. Division retreat to Hagalwuri.

At Home
- President Rhee requests special cooperation for the implementation of taxation on temporary land use and tax payment in kind.
- Normal operations of the Seoul-Busan railroad line are restored.

December 3, Sunday (October 23, by lunar calendar, 壬申日 Black Monkey) Snowy and Cloudy
162 Day of the War

War Situation
- On the eastern front, about six Chinese Divisions surround and attack the resisting U.S. Marine and Infantry Units.
- In the vicinity of Jangjin(Chosin) Reservoir, the Communist Chinese Forces release 27 American POWs.
- On the western front, the UN Forces retreat from Suncheon and Sukcheon, while the Chinese Forces prepare to move down south to Pyongyang.

At Home
- President Rhee issues a special statement on payment of land tax in kind, saying that payment of tax in cash causes a problem to the Government's grain purchase policy.
- President Rhee announces a message to the people, urging them to arm themselves on a village basis throughout the country.
- Minister of Defense Shin Sung-mo requests that the UN authorize the use of atomic bombs.

December 4, Monday (October 25, by lunar calendar, 癸酉日 Black Rooster) Very clear
163 Day of the War

War Situation
- General MacArthur, UNC Commander, warns that one million Chinese troops are assembling in North Korea.
- The Chinese Forces continue to penetrate the right flank of the northwestern front.
- B-26s protect the retreating UN Forces by bombing the Communist Forces.

At Home
- The UN Commission on Korea holds an informal meeting with the representatives of the ROK Government.
- Relief food unloaded at the Incheon harbor: 2,519 tons of foreign rice and 1,358 tons of pressed barley stored in warehouses; and 3,152 tons kept in outdoor facilities.

Overseas

According to the evacuation order of Lt. General Walker, commander of the Eighth U.S. Army, the UN Forces are moving to the south by crossing Daedong River. (1950. 12. 4)

- The representatives of India and China continue their meeting while others are waiting anxiously for the results.
- The Canadian representative distributes copies of the Canadian Foreign Minister's address to member states at the UN headquarters.
- Yoshida, Prime Minister of Japan, mentions that Japan will not allow volunteers for South Korea.

December 5, Tuesday (October 26, by lunar calendar, 甲戌日 Blue Dog) Clear
164 Day of the War

War Situation
- The 7th U.S. Division completes operations to retreat to Shinheungri from Hyesanjin.
- The 5th U.S. Air Force strikes the Communist Forces for 24 hours, killing 2,500 Chinese troops.

At Home
- Representative Pendayston, new chairman of the UN Commission on Korea, pledges to Seoul citizens a maximum degree of assistance to Korea.
- The National Museum decides to ship important items to Busan, and actual shipping begins.

December 6, Wednesday (October 27, by lunar calendar, 乙亥日 Blue Pig) Clear
165 Day of the War

War Situation
- The UN Forces near Jangjin(Chosin) Reservoir break through the Chinese Forces' encirclement and succeed to connect with other Units in the rear area.
- UN Forces recapture Goksan.

At Home
- Government resumes payments to the bereaved families of the patriots who sacrificed their lives for the country.
- General Collins, U.S. Army Chief of Staff, visits President Syngman Rhee.

Overseas
- The representatives of the United States and other nations condemn China's illegal invasion, with severe cross-fire arguments.
- The UN political committee decides to discuss the six-state proposal on the Korean issue including China's immediate withdrawal as its priority agenda.
- Essam Pasha, Secretary-General of the Council of Europe requests to the UN Secretary-General to declare an immediate cease-fire of the Korean War.
- The Truman-Atlee summit reconfirms no appeasement policy to China firmly denouncing the Chinese invasion of Korea, and fully agrees on the strengthening of the European countries Defense Forces including NATO.

December 7, Thursday (October 28, by lunar calendar, 丙子日 Red Rat) Snowy and Cloudy
166 Day of the War

War Situation
- The UN Air Force strikes hard on the left side of Jangjin(Chosin) Reservoir, and helps the rescue operations of the Ground Forces on the northeast front.
- The UN Naval Force bombards the Wonsan area with Artillery, while the British and Dutch Fleets conduct their operations on the west coast.

At Home
- Minister of Social Affairs, Huh Chung announces a plan to organize his Ministry to meet wartime requirements.

December 8, Friday (October 29, by lunar calendar, 丁丑日 Red Ox) Cloudy
167 Day of the War

War Situation
- The U.S. Forces fight a fierce battle to find an exit to safety at Jangjin(Chosin) Reservoir; the U.S. Marine and the troops of the 7th U.S. Division succeed to exit to Gotori.

- The UN and ROK Forces form a defense line in the areas of Gyumipo, Chunghwa, Suan, Goksan and Shingae.
- Fierce battle takes place with the Chinese Forces at a point 80 km south of Gotori.

At Home
- President Rhee requests that the United States arm 500,000 Korean troops.
- The Martial Law Commander comments that women and children are free to seek refuge.

December 9, Saturday (November 1, by lunar calendar, 戊寅日 Yellow Tiger) Clear
168 Day of the War

War Situation
- General MacArthur, UNC Commander, orders the U.S. 10th Corps Units to withdraw from Heungnam by sea to Busan, Masan and Ulsan for integration under the command of the Eighth US Army.
- The 17th Regiment of the 7th U.S. Division and the ROK Units that entered Haesanjin are surrounded by the Chinese Forces.

At Home
- The Seoul Police Bureau puts a state of emergency into effect.
- For the limited areas under the Martial Law, no warrant is required for arrest or detention.
- Lt. General Walker, Commander of the Eighth U.S. Army, commits to the defense of Seoul, saying, "We will not give up Seoul."

Overseas
- A meeting takes place among the 13 countries that have appealed to China to stop at the 38th parallel.
- ROK Foreign Minister Lim Byung-jik, speaking at the UN political committee, points out that any appeasement or submission to China by the UN would be unacceptable.

December 10, Sunday (November 2, by lunar calendar, 己卯日 Yellow Rabbit)Very Clear
169 Day of the War

War Situation
- On the northeast front, the UN Forces have broken through the Chinese Forces' encirclements from Jangjin(Chosin) Reservoir and elsewhere and withdrawn to Heungnam.
- The remnants of dispersed North Korean Army troops in the area of Hwanghaedo reassemble at Anak.

At Home
- 500,000 North Korean compatriots escape from the North as refugees to the free South.
- The North Korean refugees are accommodated at refugee camps in Yeonbaek.

Overseas

- UN Secretary-General Lie mentions his hope for a possible compromise with China.
- The British and Canadian summit agrees on views of world affairs.

December 11, Monday (November 3, by lunar calendar, 庚辰日 White Dragon) Clear and Cloudy, 170 Day of the War

War Situation
- Retreat operations from Jangjin(Chosin) Reservoir have been completed, defeating three Chinese Divisions.
- The 1st U.S. Marine Division completes withdrawal operations from Yudamri to Heungnam.
- The Communist Chinese Forces arrive at Goksan, Suan and Shingae.

At Home
- President Rhee assures the defense of the capital city of Seoul.
- The first temporary session of the National Assembly confirms that the legislature has 178 members, except for the missing members.

December 12, Tuesday (November 4, by lunar calendar, 辛巳日 White Snake) Cloudy 171 Day of the War

War Situation
- The Eighth U.S. Army announces that the UN Forces are carrying out combat operations to the north of the 38th parallel.
- The UN Forces begin retreat operations from Heungnam.
- The ROK Forces fight a fierce battle with the North Korean Forces advancing south from Yeoncheon to Pocheon.

At Home
- President Rhee makes clear to the press corps that South Korea would not compromise with China.
- The Children's Relief Organization provides new and used clothes worth $5,033.

December 13, Wednesday (November 5, by lunar calendar, 壬午日 Black Horse) Cloudy 172 Day of the War

War Situation
- The Communist Forces in the area of Yicheon and Shingae have been joined by the guerillas, and they are attempting to march down south.
- The ROK Forces resist the advance of the 25th, the 27th and the 35th Communist Regiments in the areas of Hwacheon, Sachangri and Yanggu.
- B-29s bomb Pyongyang.

At Home

- The Ministry of Commerce and Industry exempts or reduces electricity fees for the occupied areas.
- The Ministry of Social Affairs announces a policy for non-combatant citizens to leave as refugees.

Overseas
- The UN General Assembly passes a resolution to establish a management organization for South West Africa.
- Mao Zedong sends a reply to Peng Dehuai telling him to make sure that the People's Support Forces advance to the south of the 38th parallel.
- President Truman and his administration reach an agreement with the leaders of both parties on the strengthening of the U.S. military power.

December 14, Thursday (November 6, by lunar calendar, 癸未日 Black Sheep) Clear
173 Day of the War

War Situation
- Twenty-five thousand troops of the U.S. Marine Corps and the 7th U.S. Infantry Division who had broken through the encirclement by the Chinese Forces retreat to a beachhead at Heungnam.
- The ROK Forces in the mountainous area of Yiheon and Chulwon confront and fight in combat with the North Korean Forces at Sachnagni, Hwacheon and Yanggu.

At Home
- The Government announces the quantity of grains stored at the Incheon harbor: 22,857 tons of foreign rice and wheat flour.

Overseas
- The UN General Assembly adopts the resolution on Korean ceasefire proposed by 13 states to establish a three-person committee and approves the appointment of the three members.

December 15, Friday (November 7, by lunar calendar, 甲申日 Blue Monkey) Very Clear and Cloudy
174 Day of the War

War Situation
- The Communist Chinese Forces wage a collective offensive on the beachhead of the UN Forces on the east frontline, but the U.S. 10th Corps defeats them.
- A large Communist Chinese Unit moves from the area south of Pyongyang toward the southeast.

At Home
- President Rhee issues a statement asking the people to rally in total unity.

- The Government submits a bill to revise the special law to dispose acts of collaboration.

December 16, Saturday (November 8, by lunar calendar, 乙酉日 Blue Rooster) Snowy and Cloudy
175 Day of the War

War Situation
- The U.S. 10th Corps carries out defense operations to protect the Heungnam beachhead and to withdraw by sea.
- On the western front, the UN Forces engage the North Korean Forces in combat.

At Home
- An amendment to the National Defense Corps Law passes the National Assembly.
- The National Assembly adopts a message to support the UN proposal of a Korean War ceasefire.
- Nicaragua provides 100 tons of rice and 5,000 kilograms of alcohol.

December 17, Sunday (November 9, by lunar calendar, 丙戌日 Red Dog) Very Clear
176 Day of the War

War Situation
- The Communist Chinese Forces in the area of Pyongyang make no special movement.
- The North Korean Forces keep advancing south through the vacant areas to approach the new positions of the UN Forces.

At Home
- Chang Du-kwan, Civil Affairs Director of the Martial Law Command for the South Gyeongsang Province, issues a warning on the treatment of firearms.

Overseas
- The UN three-person committee meets for a meeting.
- Secretary Acheson departs for Brussels.

December 18, Monday (November 10, by lunar calendar, 丁亥日 Red Pig) Clear and Snowy
177 Day of the War

War Situation
- Some of the enemy elements operating in the north of Heungnam are confirmed to be the troops of North Korea.
- The ROK 1st Corps retreat from Heungnam by sea and land on Mukho.
- B-29s bomb the field camps in the night at Jinanmpo and Sinanjoo areas causing severe damage.

At Home

- The United States Department of State calls the Korean Government's attention to the treatment of collaborators with the communists.
- An Advance Unit of New Zealand's field Artillery enters Busan port.

December 19, Tuesday (November 11, by lunar calendar, 戌子日 Yellow Rat) Cloudy and Snowy
178 Day of the War

War Situation
- The UN Forces strengthen the defense lines of Heungnam beachhead and resist the increasing pressure by the Communist troops by firing back.
- The whole defense lines between the west coast and Yangyang is completely set up
- The U.S. Navy and Air Force block the advancing troops with participation by the U.S. battleships of Missouri, Renshaw, Rochester.

At Home
- Minister of Home Affairs Cho Byung-ok requests all walks of life to participate in air-defense exercise. (ADE).
- On Geoje Island, refugee camps are established. Smallpox breaks out in Busan.

Overseas
- Ambassador Grosse is appointed as the U.S. representative on the UN Peacekeeping Commission.

The refugees are swarming at a wharf of Heungnam Port(1950. 12. 19)

- General MacArthur endorses the dispatch of Columbia's Infantry battalion to Korea.

December 20, Wednesday (November 12, by lunar calendar, 己丑日 Yellow Ox) Cloudy
179 Day of the War

War Situation
- Increasing offensives by the Communist troops intensity the war of attrition.
- No particular activities are noted on the western frontlines, but some elements of the North Korean troops are detected at a point 11km from Imjin River.

At Home
- The ROK Army promises to take action upon the accusation made by the British Army on the way of execution of death penalty.
- The Civil Affairs Bureau of the Gyeongsang Province makes a special announcement on the severe punishment against the violation of curfew hours.

December 21, Thursday (November 13, by lunar calendar, 庚寅日 White Tiger) Snowy and Clear
180 Day of the War

War Situation
- Three battalions of North Korean troops attack from the north of Chuncheon.
- The U.S. Navy rocket battleship starts to perform its debut operation.
- Along the UN beachheads of the eastern front, two divisions of North Korean forces continue to attack UN forces. The division of Chinese forces are behind the North Korean forces.

At Home
- The Government proclaims on "the special law on the number of seats for the National Assembly. (Law No. 173)
- The Command of South Gyeongsang Province Military Affairs Bureau states that there would be no forced draft or recruitment of refugees from North Korea.
- The North Korean Army begins to operate Radio Pyongyang.

Overseas
- Lee Bum-suck, Korean Ambassador to Taiwan leaves for Taipei.
- Mao Zedong sends telegrams to Peng Dehuai concerning the overall war situation and troops operation.

December 22, Friday (November 14, by lunar calendar, 辛卯日 White Rabbit) Snowy and Cloudy
181 Day of the War

War Situation
- Considerable numbers of Chinese troops assemble in the areas of Yeonchon-Gimhwa and

Gimhwa-Hwacheon.

- Results of the 5th U.S. Air Force: 250 sorties per annum, killing 250 enemy troops and destruction of 102 buildings.

At Home   (

- According to the Communication Decrees No. 13, open "the Central Military Postal Office (within the premises of the ROK Army headquarters)" and "the Central Navy Post Office (within the premises of the ROK Navy headquarters)."

December 23, Saturday (November 15, by lunar calendar, 壬辰日Black Dragon) Cloudy
182 Day of the War

War Situation

- Commander of the Eighth U.S. Army, Lt. General Walton Walker is killed in a jeep accident at the south of Uijeongbu while inspecting the frontlines.
- Considerable numbers of Chinese troops assemble at the areas of Yeoncheon, Gimhwa and Hwacheon.

At Home

- President Syngman Rhee expresses his gratitude to the UN troops in Korea.
- The Commander of the Civil Affairs of North Gyeongsang Province Martial Law states that the Korean Military Police would treat the criminal cases of the civilian employees and translators attached to the U.S. Army.

Overseas

- In Beijing, the Literary Contest of "Resist America and Assist Korea" takes place.
- The United States signs agreements with Vietnam, Laos and Cambodia for military aid and alliance.

December 24, Sunday (November 16, by lunar calendar, 癸巳日 Black Snake) Cloudy and Snowy
183 Day of the War

War Situation

- 105,000 UN troops including the ROK troops and 91,000 refugees succeed to evacuate from Heungnam port. The retreating operation is completed by mobilizing 132 marine transporters.
- The Chinese troops attempt to advance to the south from northeast of Chuncheon but are repelled.

At Home

- President Syngman Rhee orders Seoul citizens to evacuate due to Chinese engagement in the Korean War.
- Fire breaks out at Sinchandong Kukje market in Busan burning down 65 shops.

Overseas
- The UN Three Members' Committee for a Korean War Ceasefire holds a conference.
- Twelve nations' representative hold an urgent meeting. (The Philippines is not present among 13 nations from Asia and the Arab world.)

December 25, Monday (November 17, by lunar calendar, 甲午日 Blue Horse) Cloudy and Snowy
184 Day of the War

War Situation
- The 3rd ROK Division engages in offensive and defensive operations with the North Korean Forces near Hongcheon.
- The 9th ROK Division fights the North Korean Army troops near the Hyunri area.

At Home
- The Korea teachers' association and cultural organizations sponsor a people's rally for spiritual armament at the Chungmuro Plaza, Busan.

December 26, Tuesday (November 18, by lunar calendar, 乙未日 Blue Sheep) Clear and Cloudy
185 Day of the War

War Situation
- Communist Chinese troops assemble near Yuncheon.
  The UN Forces fight the North Korean Forces in the area of Chuncheon.
- The Eighth U.S. Army reports: The Communist Chinese Forces are poised to advance toward Seoul from the 38th parallel.

At Home
- President Rhee denies the reports on the relocation of the Government. President Rhee decorates the soldiers of the 1st ROK Division for their meritorious combat achievements.
- Lt. General Ridgway, new Commander of the Eighth U.S. Army, arrives in Seoul.

December 27, Wednesday (November 19, by lunar calendar, 丙申日 Red Monkey) Very Clear
186 Day of the War

War Situation
- The UN Forces retreat from Kaesong.
- The UN troops initiate the fierce battles to prevent a penetration by the Chinese troops between Gwandaeri, northeast of Chuncheon, and Napyeongri. The Communist Forces in the direction of Gorangpo have been dispersed by the Artillery fire of the UN Forces.

At Home
- Lt. General Ridgway holds meetings with Defense Minister Shin Sung-mo and the representatives to the new UN Commission on Korea.

- North Korea purges Kim Mu-jeong for the failure in the war.

Overseas
- The UN Korean ceasefire committee writes a draft report on the failure of its efforts.
- A communiqué of the Supreme Allied Command ascertains the reinforcement of the North Korean military strength.

December 28, Thursday (November 20, by lunar calendar, 丁酉日 Red Rooster) Very Clear
187 Day of the War

War Situation
- The UN Forces launch a fierce attack on the North Korean Forces near Naepyeong-ri, northeast of Chuncheon.
- On the line of west sea coast- Gorangpo, the 39th, the 50th and the 66th Chinese Armies are assembled for deployment.

At Home
- Busan City opens luxurious restaurants and hotels to accommodate the families of the soldiers and police officers.
- The new UN Commission on Korea submits a report to its headquarters on relief assistance to refugees.

Overseas
- The UN representatives of 12 Arab and Asian countries call for an urgent meeting.
- The Ho Chi Minh troops wage a strong offensive on the French Forces at a location 64 km north of Hanoi.
- The United Nations Command announces that the Chinese Forces have deployed 4 Armies and 19 Divisions in the north of Seoul and are getting ready to launch a general offensive.

December 29, Friday (November 21, by lunar calendar, 戊戌日 Yellow Dog) Cloudy and Rainy
188 Day of the War

War Situation
- Defeated Communist troops reassemble in the northeast of Chuncheon; an advance UN Unit marches 8 km to the north of the 38th parallel.
- On the eastern front, the UN Forces launch a strategic advance, while the Communist Chinese Forces begin moving to the east.
- The Communist Chinese Forces try to build a temporary bridge over the Imjin River.

At Home
- Prime Minister, Jang Myeon conveys a message to UN Secretary-General Lie.
- The UNCURK moves to Busan.

December 30, Saturday (November 22, by lunar calendar, 己亥日 Yellow Pig) Very Clear
189 Day of the War

War Situation
- The UN Forces retreat from all sectors of the frontline 16 km south of the 38th parallel.
- 35 to 40 MIG-15s attack 15 U.S. Saber jets, and one Communist plane is shot down.

At Home
- Up to 840,000 people are to be evacuated from Seoul (49% of the population).

December 31, Sunday (November 23, by lunar calendar, 庚子日 White Rat) Very Clear
190 Day of the War

War Situation
- The Communist Chinese Forces begin serious attacks in night
- The Communist Forces begin their third general offense and reinforced at the 38th parallel.
- The 6th ROK Division retreats from the northern area of Dongducheon, after fighting a fierce battle with three Communist Chinese Divisions.

At Home
- President Rhee urges the people to repair the roads in an all-out nationwide effort.
- Film makers who had remained in Seoul (Choi In-gyu, Lee Myung-woo, Hong Gae-myung, Park Ki-chae, Bang Han-jun, Ahn Chul-young and others) are taken to North Korea.

"As an alternative solution instead of all-out withdrawal from the battle line, should we seek an expansion of the War against China or shall we give up Korean peninsula!"

- General MacArthur, UNC Commander

1951

The Year of White Rabbit *Dangi* 4284

January 1, Monday (November 24, by lunar calendar, 辛丑日 White Ox) Very Clear and Clear
191 Day of the War

War Situation
- Six Chinese Armies are in an all-out offensive from across the 38th parallel.
- From the northwest area of Chuncheon, the Chinese and North Korean Forces advance south under the protection of heavy artillery guns, mortars and rockets.

At Home
- President Syngman Rhee addresses a New Year's message.
- President Syngman Rhee awards a medal to the Commander of the 5th U.S. Air Force.
- The Martial Law Command issues a directive on price control and prevention of undue profiteering activities.

January 2, Tuesday (November 25, by lunar calendar, 壬寅日 Black Tiger) Cloudy and Clear
192 Day of the War

War Situation
- From the western front, the UN Forces retreat to a new defense line north of Seoul.
- The 1st and the 6th ROK Divisions retreat to south of the Han river.

At Home
- The Director of the Seoul Metropolitan Police Bureau announces that it will issue permits to barber shops and public bathhouses.
- The Civil Affairs Division of the Martial Law Command for the South Gyeongsang Province holds the 3rd law and order conference with the participation of heads of various organizations. This conference discusses the accommodation of refugees and decide to set up checkpoints and their operation manual.

Overseas
- *Beijing Broadcasts* reports that three Chinese Regiments inflict great damage on the heavy Tank Unit of the 29th British Infantry Brigade at Uijeongbu.

January 3, Wednesday (November 26, by lunar calendar, 癸卯日 Black Rabbit) Very Clear
193 Day of the War

War Situation
- The Chinese Communist Forces breach the frontline defense of the 24th U.S. Division and arrive at a location 11 km north of Seoul.

The refugees at the time of the January 4th Retreat

At Home
- Top leaders of the Government and the military move to Busan.
- The Government chooses Busan as s temporary capital city.
- In the last group of evacuees from Seoul, 300,000 refugees leave homes to cross the frozen Han River on foot.

January 4, Thursday (November 27, by lunar calendar, 甲辰日 Blue Dragon) Very Clear and Cloudy
194 Day of the War

War Situation
- Advancing on the roads between Kaesong and Seoul and between Yeoncheon and Seoul, the Chinese Communist Forces approach the UN Forces.
- The ROK and UN Forces withdraw from Seoul.
- A Patrol Unit of Chinese Communist crosses the Han River from southwest of Seoul but is repelled by the UN Forces.

At Home
- The Martial Law is proclaimed for all areas of the country.
- The Government and other organizations move to Busan.
- The Seoul Central Broadcast Station organizes a withdrawal team and takes measures to disenable the transmission facilities at Yunhee station.

January 5, Friday (November 28, by lunar calendar, 乙巳日 Blue Snake) Clear and Cloudy
195 Day of the War

War Situation
- The 1st and the 3rd ROK Corps retreat to the line of Wonju and Samcheok.
- The Communist Chinese Forces approach to Wonju.

At Home
- A public relations diplomacy league is created:
  Chair: Kim Hwal-ran; members: Kim dong-sung and Oh Wi-young.
- The Dalseong Tax office announces a stronger income tax collection plan.
- National Patriot Suh Jae-pil dies.

January 6, Saturday (November 29, by lunar calendar, 丙午日 Red Horse) Cloudy and Rainy
196 Day of the War

War Situation
- The Communist Chinese Forces occupy Hongcheon.
- The 1st ROK Division encounters the Communist Chinese Forces in combat near Anyang.

At Home
- The Busan Branch of the Information and Education Bureau of the Ministry of National Defense publishes a statement on the withdrawal from Seoul.
- At Gochang Country, 10 residents have been killed on an empty ground near a school.

January 7, Sunday (November 30, by lunar calendar, 丁未日 Red Sheep) Cloudy and Rainy
197 Day of the War

War Situation
- The Communist Chinese Forces advance to a location 32 km from Chungju.
- The ROK and UN Forces block the Communist Forces' advance to the Chungju-Samcheok line.

At Home
- President Rhee states that he has asked the United States to provide firearms for 500 thousand young Koreans.
- Minister of Social Affairs, Huh Chung explains relief programs for refugees.
- Prices of residential homes in Busan rise due to increasing number of refugees.

January 8, Monday (December 1, by lunar calendar, 戊申日 Yellow Monkey) Cloudy and Clear
198 Day of the War

War Situation
- Fierce battles continue on the middle front.

The U.S. troops and ROK Army are chasing the Communist guerillas with the police guidance in Jinju(1951. 1. 7)

• The Communist Forces occupy Osan.

At Home

• President Rhee says, "'Human sea warfare' should be fought by 'human sea warfare.'"

• President Rhee appeals to the patriotic rich businessmen and their wives to rise up in a rally.

January 9, Tuesday (December 2, by lunar calendar, 己酉日 Yellow Rooster) Cloudy and Rainy
199 Day of the War

War Situation

• The UN Forces, waging a small counter attack, turn around the battle situation from retreat to resistance.

• 300 aircraft fighter bombers, including B-29 strategic bombers, from the 5th U.S. Air Force strike Pyongyang and other areas.

At Home
- President Rhee issues a statement of encouragement to the people.
- The Government develops plans for the accommodation of POWs and refugees: refugees would be dispersed to various locations and the Government determines measures to dispose of groundless rumors.

January 10, Wednesday (December 3, by lunar calendar, 庚戌日 White Dog) Rainy and Cloudy
200 Day of the War

War Situation
- The reconnaissance unit of the 2nd U.S. Division enters Wonju and returns to its home base.
- An estimated strength of 280,000 men of the Communist Chinese Forces is deployed along the battle line stretching 120 kilometers between Osan and Wonju.

At Home
- The Ministry of Social Affairs sets up a milk distribution center in Busan to provide free milk porridge to the aged and the undernourished people.
- The Minister and Vice Minister of Transportation meet with the Commander of the Railroad Transportation Office of the UN Forces and agree on food transportation.

January 11, Thursday (December 4, by lunar calendar, 申亥日 White Pig) Cloudy and Clear
201 Day of the War

War Situation
- U.S. 2nd Division consisted of U.S., French and Dutch troops fight a fierce battle with 7,000 Communist troops in the Wonju area, crushing 3,000 of them and protecting their positions.
- The UN Air Force attacks 5,000 Chinese troops who were marching south on the road between Osan and Daegu.

At Home
- 70 members of the National Assembly meet in an emergency meeting.
- Jean-Marie de Prémonville de Maisonthou, an AFP war correspondent, is killed while covering a reconnaissance platoon at a location northeast of Seoul.

Overseas
- The Defense Department of the Taiwan Government announces that a partial withdrawal of the Chinese troops from Korea indicates China's advancement to Indochina.

January 12, Friday (December 5, by lunar calendar, 壬子日 Black Rat) Cloudy and Clear
202 Day of the War

War Situation
- The UN Forces engage two North Korean Divisions in combat in the direction of Wonju, capturing a strategic hill.
- B-29s and other combat airplanes bomb Wonju.

At Home
- North Gyeongsang Province announces a plan of relief food distribution.
- The first discharge ceremony for wounded soldiers takes place at Unit 839.
- Representative of the Netherlands to the UN commission on Korea arrives.

January 13, Saturday (December 6, by lunar calendar, 癸丑日 Black Ox) Very Clear
203 Day of the War

War Situation
- The Communist Forces occupy Yeongwol.
- The UN Air Force flies 640 sorties.

At Home
- The National Assembly sends a representative to General MacArthur to request assistance for a total armament of the nation.
- Huh Chung, Minister of Social Affairs, completes an inspection tour of Jeju Island, decides that peace and order are perfect on Jeju Island, and announces that 40,000 refugees would be sent to the island.

January 14, Sunday (December 7, by lunar calendar, 甲寅日 Blue Tiger) Very Clear
204 Day of the War

War Situation
- The Communist Forces of 300,000 troops begin offensives on the middle and western fronts.
- The ROK and UN Forces build defense positions along the axis of Pyongtaek and Samcheok.
- The UN Forces resist the Communist Chinese Forces of 300,000 troops on the middle and western fronts.

At Home
- Cho Byung-ok, Minister of Home Affairs, announces the decision through the Office of Public Information that the Government would disperse the refugees assembled in Busan and Daegu to other regions of the country.
- The Government submits to the National Assembly a supplementary budget bill of 50.7 billion won for the projects of the Ministries of National Defense and Home Affairs.
- The Government carries out its first relocation of refugees to Jeju Island.

Overseas

- U.S. Army Chief of Staff, General Collins and three other top U.S. military leaders meet with General MacArthur in Tokyo to review actions of the Communist Chinese Forces.
- A Foreign War Veterans organization in the southern U.S demands the arrests of 5,500 Communists in the United States.

January 15, Monday (December 8, by lunar calendar, 乙卯日 Blue Rabbit) Very Clear
205 Day of the War

War Situation

- Quiet situation is noted all day on the eastern front.
- About 4,000 Communist troops invade Yeongwol, but are repelled by the UN Forces.

At Home

- While visiting and inspecting Jinhae and Daegu, President Syngman Rhee meets with General Collins to discuss important issues.
- The National Assembly again passes a resolution calling for General MacArthur's assistance in armament.
- The 6th plenary session of the National Assembly resolves to write a bill to improve the treatment of servicemen in the Second Peoples' Force.

January 16, Tuesday (December 9, by lunar calendar, 丙辰日 Red Dragon) Very Clear
206 Day of the War

War Situation

- The 2nd U.S. Division retreats from Wonju to a new defense line
- The 5th U.S. Air Force bombs the airports of Pyongyang and Wonsan.

At Home

- The UN Commission on Korea says, "It is not scientific to counter a human sea strategy with a human sea strategy."
- The Director of the Military Service Command for the South Gyeongsang Province denies to the press that there has been an illegal coercive administration of military conscription.
- The Government submits a 6th supplementary budget for 58.7 billion won to the National Assembly.

January 17, Wednesday (December 10, by lunar calendar, 丁巳日 Red Snake) Very Clear
207 Day of the War

War Situation

- A reconnaissance unit of the UN Forces enters Wonju.
- The 77th mobile Navy fleet conducts air raids by its deck planes to attack a group of 3,000

Communist troops found in a valley near Danyang, killing 2,200 of them.
- The UN Air Force kills or injures 562 Communist soldiers.

At Home
- President Syngman Rhee has a meeting with General Collins in Daegu.
- The plenary session of the National Assembly discusses the issue of refugees.
- The ROK Army headquarters orders a strong defense posture against the enemy guerrilla operations including airborne penetration.

January 18, Thursday (December 11, by lunar calendar, 戊午日 Yellow Horse) Cloudy
208 Day of the War

War Situation
- A battle breaks out at a location 16 km northeast of Yeongwol.
- A UN Search Unit fights a ferocious city battle at Yeongwol and retreats from there.

At Home
- The revised law of the special disposition law for collaborators is proclaimed.
- Members of the review committee of petitions on reverted properties selected: Kim Hyung-duk and Kim Su-hak.
- The National Assembly passes for the second time the special measures law to punish crimes under the state of emergency as proposed by the Government.

Grains for the emergency relief being unloaded at Busan Port(1951. 1. 18)

January 19, Friday (December 12, by lunar calendar, 己未日 Yellow Sheep) Cloudy and Clear
209 Day of the War

War Situation
- The UN Forces recapture Wonju.
- The UN Cavalry Unit enters Pyeongcheon 3 kilometers north of Osan.
- The UN Air Force kills or injures 300 Communist troops.

At Home
- The National Assembly resolves to mourn the death of Dr. Suh Jae-pil.
- The appointment of administration officials in the North Korean regions by the Government and the United Nations causes confusion.
- The Ministry of Social Affairs holds a relief conference for refugees.
- The Ministry of Education organizes a wartime measures committee.

January 20, Saturday (December 13, by lunar calendar, 庚申日 White Monkey) Clear
210 Day of the War

War Situation
- The Communist Forces occupy Gangneung.
- The Communist Forces attack from three directions and wage a city battle with the strength of one regiment.
- General MacArthur takes his 8th inspection tour to the front line, saying, "Nobody can drive us out to the middle of the sea."

At Home
- The restoration work of the Waegwan railroad bridge is carried out for the second time.
- The Director of Public Information Office goes on radio to call for the people to support the soldiers on the front.
- The National Assembly passes a resolution defining China as an aggressor.
- The plenary session of the National Assembly criticizes the Government's unreasonable policy on the conscription of the members for the Second Peoples' Force and on the evacuation of refugees.

Overseas
- The United States submits to the UN a proposal to define China as the aggressor.

January 21, Sunday (December 14, by lunar calendar, 辛酉日 White Rooster) Very Clear
211 Day of the War

War Situation
- The UN Forces recapture Wonju with the combat support of tanks and artillery.
- The ROK Navy receives four of the newest Navy vessels from the United States.

At Home
- The Government submits a temporary land tax bill to the National Assembly.
- The ROK Army headquarters instructs integration of all the police troops in South Jeolla Province with the 11ᵗʰ ROK Infantry Division.
- ROK Ambassador to Washington, Jang Myeon delivers a four-point message in a meeting with President Truman.

January 22, Monday (December 15, by lunar calendar, 壬戌日 Black Dog) Very Clear
212 Day of the War

War Situation
- The North Korean Forces suddenly attack the UN Forces near Andong.
- The first ROK Army training center moves from Daegu to Mosulpo on Jeju Island: the training center was first established under the direct command of the ROK Army headquarters (July 11, 1950) and then reorganized as a part of the Central Army Training Center(August 14, 1950).

At Home
- The Government establishes a medical care committee for wounded soldiers (Presidential decree No. 444).
- The Government announces an organization for nursing homes for the wounded soldiers (Presidential decree No. 445).
- The Government raises the price of grain distribution, 278 won for rice per kilogram, 299 won for sticky rice per kilogram, 251 won for barley per kilogram, and 330 won for wheat flour per kilogram.

January 23, Tuesday (December 16, by lunar calendar, 癸亥日 Black Pig) Very Clear
213 Day of the War

War Situation
- The UN Forces fight a ferocious battle at the city of Yeongwol.
- The UN Air Force sinks 23 small enemy vessels in Asan Bay.
- Admiral Arthur W. Radford, Commander of the Pacific Fleet, and Vice Admiral Turner Joy, Commander of the Naval Forces Far East, meet with Commander of the Eight U.S. Army Lt. General Ridgway.

At Home
- The National Assembly holds a hearing on problems with the treatment of the Second Peoples' Force from the Vice Minister of National Defense.
- The Government submits an amendment bill to the organization law for the Armed Forces to the National Assembly:

(1) Each service of the Armed Forces would have its own Chief of Staff.

(2) A Joint Chiefs of Staff would be established.

(3) The previous separate law for the Air Force would be incorporated in the revised law.

January 24, Wednesday (December 17, by lunar calendar, 甲子日 Blue Rat) Cloudy
214 Day of the War

War Situation
- The UN Forces re-enter Yeongwol.

At Home
- The National Assembly passes a bill related to "The Special Tax Law."
- Huh Jeong, the Minister of Social Affairs makes an announcement warning to those who would not respond to the accommodation of the refugees.
- Busan City announces the special measures on disposal of the Government bonds for nation building.

Overseas
- The United States and China show sharp conflicts of opinion over the cease fire of the Korean War.

January 25, Thursday (December 18, by lunar calendar, 乙丑日 Blue Ox) Very Clear
215 Day of the War

War Situation
- The UN and ROK Forces begin their intensive reconnaissance operation in the south of the Han River.

At Home
- The Government disbands the Special Committee of Emergency Relief for the War Victims and Refugees, and establishes "The Special Committee on War Relief and Aid."
- Jeongyangwon (The Recuperation/Convalescence Center operated by the Ministry of Social Affairs) for the disabled soldiers and veterans opens at Donrae hot spring.

January 26, Friday (December 19, by lunar calendar, 丙寅日 Red Tiger) Very Clear
216 Day of the War

War Situation
- The UN Forces advance to the 24 km point of Seoul killing 477 Chinese soldiers by bayonet fighting.
- The UN Forces capture Suwon and Kimyangjang.

At Home
- President Syngman Rhee gives a news briefing to support the U.S.'s "Peace Treaty Policy

for Japan.
- Suh Min-ho, president of the Joseon Electricity Corporation expresses his resignation from his post.
- UNICEF donates clothes worth U.S.$ 200,000.

January 27, Saturday (December 20, by lunar calendar, 丁卯日 Red Rabbit) Very Clear
217 Day of the War

War Situation
- The UN Forces advance toward a point 16 km from Seoul.
- The ROK Navy attempts a four-hour landing operation at Incheon port.

At Home
- The plenary session of the National Assembly deals with the bills related to "the Anti-Communists laws," "the Pacific Alliance Treaty," and "the message to denounce Nehru's proposal."
- The National Assembly postpones the sending of a message to the UN to denounce Nehru's proposal ignoring the Korean peoples' sovereignty until the U.S. decides its position.
- "An urgent bill for Pacific Alliance Treaty" proposed by Park Young-chul and others is submitted to the Committee of Defense and Foreign Affairs of the National Assembly.
- Kim Chong-won, Director of the Civil Affairs of South Gyeongsang Province made a statement on "evacuation plan and its necessary registration for military families and registration."

January 28, Sunday (December 21, by lunar calendar, 戊辰日 Yellow Dragon) Very Clear
218 Day of the War

War Situation
- The UN Forces begin to penetrate 16 kilometers south of Seoul.
- The 2nd Army Corps of the North Korean Army is repelled at Yeongwol and Danyang.

At Home
- Provost Martial and Brig. General, Choi Keong-rok issues a warning statement to "the war profiteers and dishonest merchants."
- The Military and Police joint investigation team arrests a North Korean agent who is ex-security leader of Hamheung and actively operates in Busan.
- Epidemics such as smallpox, typhoid fever and typhus fever prevail in North Gyeongsang Province.

Overseas
- The Australian Government accepts the visit of U.S. Secretary of State Dulles.

- Minister of Foreign Affairs, Lim Byung-jik strongly denounces the Soviet Union's policy in an article contributed to the *New York Times*.

January 29, Monday (December 22, by lunar calendar, 己巳日 Blue Snake) Very Clear
219 Day of the War

War Situation
- The UN Armored Reconnaissance Unit re-penetrates into Hoengseong.
- A battalion of the Chinese Army begins to attack at the point of 18km south of Seoul.
- The U.S. battleship *U.S.S Missouri* launches fierce bombing in the area of Ganseong.

At Home
- The plenary session of the National Assembly has an interpellation on various pressing issues such as "purchase of clothes," "combating guerilla operations," "excessive issue of proclamation or decrees," etc.
- The Industrial Committee of the National Assembly rejects again the proposed bill related to "the temporary laws on land price."
- The teletype operation with the United States (Busan-San Francisco) and the teletype and wireless system with Japan (Busan-Tokyo)reopen.

January 30, Tuesday (December 23, by lunar calendar, 更午日 White Horse) Very Clear
220 Day of the War

War Situation
- A company of the UN Forces engages in a combat with a company of the Communist Army 1.6km south of Gangneung, and kills 200 with 15 captured.
- The UN Forces recapture Gangneung.

At Home
- The National Assembly (concerned with the two Committees, namely, of the Home Affairs and the National Defense) passes the budget to cover war damages in amount of 58,745,393,300 won.
- The Government proclaims a revised "special presidential decree to punish crimes under the state of emergency."
- Prime Minister, Jang Myeon gives a report to the National Assembly to emphasize the reinforcement of foreign diplomatic relations.

January 31, Wednesday (December 24, by lunar calendar, 辛未日 White Sheep) Very Clear
221 Day of the War

War Situation
- General Ridgway, Commander of the Eighth U.S. Army visits the military Units of the

frontlines including the command of the Puerto Rican Army.
- The UN Forces advance 457 meters in the eastern front line.
- The Greek Army successfully defeats about 3,000 Chinese troops in the battle between Suwon and Icheon.

At Home
- The Government issues a public announcement on the trial of drivers involved in the traffic accident death of General Walker: three years imprisonment on the charged drivers while the others were acquitted of the charge.
- The plenary session of the National Assembly deals with the issues concerned with "how to help refugees," "the revision of Governmental organizations," and others.
- Kwon Oh-hun, a National Assembly lawmaker who was attacked by an American soldier is in a critical condition.
- The Joint Investigation Team arrests the alleged pro-Communists at the refugees' camp of Goejedo Island.
- Kim Chaek, Vice-Prime Minister and Industrial Minister of North Korea dies in action.

Overseas
- The UN Security Council convenes a meeting for the first time after November 13, 1950, and accepts a proposal made by the U.K. to exclude the Korean issue from its agenda.
- The UN's Preliminary Committee for Freedom of Information passes a bill "the exceptional clauses related to "the limit of freedom of press and broadcasting concerned with national security, etc.

The Chinese troops are attempting to advance to the frontline at the Battle of Hoengseong district (1951. 2).

General Ridgway inspects the frontline after being appointed as Commander of the Eighth U.S. Army. (1951. 2)

The U.N. Forces recovered the lost region by a counter-attack on 25th January, they faced difficulties again due to 4th offensive by the Chinese Army. U.S. troops are on the march. (1951. 2)

February 1, Thursday (December 25, by lunar calendar, 壬申日 Black Monkey) Very Clear
222 Day of the War

War Situation
- The UN Forces repel the sudden attacks by the Communist Forces from three different directions in the Jipeong area.
- Three regiments of the Communist Army are defeated with hand-to-hand combat in the north of Yeoju.

At Home
- President Syngman Rhee visits the headquarters of Defense Command and the 10th Corps of the U.S. Army.
- Prime Minister Jang Myeon meets with the National Assemblymen to discuss various war situations.
- Kim Joon-yeon, the Minister of Justice, announces "the severe punishment measures related to stealing and embezzling of military supplies, relief and aid goods."
- The U.S. Economic Cooperation Agency decides to send 70 pontoons.

February 2, Friday (December 26, by lunar calendar, 癸酉日 Black Rooster) Very Clear
223 Day of the War

War Situation
- The National Assembly adopts a resolution to promote and encourage the agreement on "the Pacific Treaty."
- The UN Forces attacks the Communist Army in the north of Suwon by long-range artillery.
- The UN Forces close in within firing range of Seoul.

At Home
- Government begins to execute "the war-time administrative procedures."
- The National Assembly rejects a bill related to the cooperative organization linking the legislation and administration bodies, and passes the bill for the resolution to support "the Pacific Treaty."

Overseas
- At the political committee of the UN, the British representative, Austin flatly rejects the Soviet allegation that U.S. and Taiwan invaded Korean peninsula.
- The UN decides the extension of the tenure of Secretary-General Trygve Lie.

February 3, Saturday (December 27, by lunar calendar, 甲戌日 Blue Dog) Very Clear

War Situation

- The U.S. Army captures Pyeongchang.
- The Turkish Army retakes a hill 27 km from the south of Seoul.

At Home

- President Syngman Rhee awards a silver medal to Vice Admiral, Arthur D. Struble, the U.S. 7th Fleet.
- The National Assembly passes a bill to lift the law on punishment of antinational activity.
- Busan branch of AFIED("Armed Forces Information and Education Division") opens its consulting center for military servicemen and civilians.
- Yoon Chi-young, minister of the Korean Embassy in France is recalled during his stay in the U.S. due to desertion from his duty posting in Paris.
- Daegu establishes a vaccination plan due to prevailing smallpox.

February 4, Sunday (December 28, by lunar calendar, 乙亥日 Blue Pig) Clear and Cloudy
225 Day of the War

War Situation

- The ROK Army repels a counter-attack by the Communist Army in the areas of

Korean Laborers are carrying military supplies by A-frame (1951. 2. 4)

Kimyanhjang and Icheon, and takes the 383 Hill in the northwest of Suwon.
- Hand-to-hand combat between the UN and Communist Forces takes place in the mountains located in the south of Seoul.

At Home
- Minister of Foreign Affairs, Lim Byung-jik, opposes the idea to halt the further advance of the UN Forces beyond the north of the 38th parallel.
- The civilian Air Defense Control Center has its first meeting.
- Col. Kim Chong Won, Commander of the Military Affairs of South Gyeongsang Province Area announces the call-up of reserve forces (soldiers).

February 5, Monday (December 29, by lunar calendar, 丙子日 Black Rat) Clear and Cloudy
226 Day of the War

War Situation
- The largest Tank Units start to operate and penetrate into the Communist Forces' zone, 8km south of Seoul.
- A minesweeping boat sinks by the contact with a mine at the coastline of Gangneung with four dead, four missing and nine wounded.
- The ROK 3rd Corps and the 10th Corps of the U.S. Army begin to encircle the battle lines of Hongcheon.

February 6, Tuesday (January 1, by lunar calendar. 丁丑日 Red Ox) Very Clear
227 Day of the War

War Situation
- On the central frontlines, the UN Forces approach a point 40 km from the 38th parallel.
- General Ridgway, Commander of the Eighth U.S. Army makes a statement that the casualty ratio of the Communist Army and the UN Forces stands at 100 to one.

At Home
- Minister of Industry and Trade, Kim Hoon makes an announcement on the renewal of the "Korea-Japan Trade Agreement" focused on imports.
- Commander of the National Defense Corps, Kim Yoon-geun makes a statement on the status of the Corps.
- Police Chief Kim Tae-seon has a press briefing on the preventive measures against prevailing epidemics.

February 7, Wednesday (January 2, by lunar calendar, 戊寅日 Yellow Tiger) Clear
228 Day of the War

War Situation

- The ROK Marines begin to secure the islands on the East coast.
- Communist Forces numbering 250,000 assemble in the northeast of Icheon.
- Major general of the 7th Infantry Division of the U.S. Army says that the moral of the U.S. military Units is high enough.

At Home

- The Ministry of Foreign Affairs plans to prohibit Koreans' visits to Japan upon invitation of their relatives or associates by the request of the Allied Forces Supreme Command.
- The Ministry of Social Affairs, Gyeonggi provincial Government and Seoul City jointly establishes the emergency relief and aid task force center for refugees.
- The Students Volunteers Corps of North Gyeongsang Province begins the military training for female students.

February 8, Thursday (January 3, by lunar calendar, 己卯日 Blue Rabbit) Cloudy and Rainy
229 Day of the War

War Situation

- The ROK and U.S. Forces advance 8 kilometers to the north of Hoengseong, and take Changpyeong in the northeast of Pyeongchang.
- The U.S. Tank Units bomb Seoul.

At Home

- Col. Lee Sun-young, Chief Director of Civilian Affairs Bureau of Kyongbuk Province Area Martial Law Command makes a public announcement on the enforcement of rigid control against illegal restaurant business and other entertainment houses.
- Food distribution commences: 1.5 hop (1 hop is equivalent to 5.54 liters) for the general public, 2.5 hops for Government officials and 5 hops for other officials with special missions.
- Kim Il Sung sends a nationwide appeal in writing to the military Units to commemorate the 3rd anniversary of the national foundation.

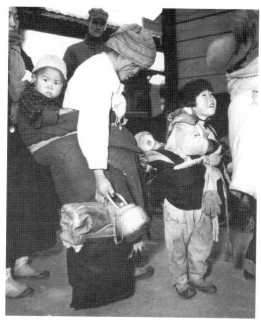

Refugees are waiting for the ship to go to Geoje Island from Busan(1951. 2. 8)

- A plenary session of the UN General Assembly rejects a resolution to bomb the mainland China.
- The military leader of Amboy Island accepts sending their two battalions to Korea.

February 9, Friday (January 4, by lunar calendar, 庚辰日 White Dragon) Rainy and Cloudy
230 Day of the War

War Situation
- ROK soldiers assigned to the U.S. 25th Infantry Division engages in street fighting with the Chinese Army after penetration into Seoul.
- Seoul City stops communication between Seoul and Incheon at a point 17.7 km south of Seoul.

At Home
- President Syngman Rhee, in a press interview, comments on the revision of the Constitution for direct election of the president.
- The Government decides the rice pricing rate applicable to the land tax based on the year 1950 standard land price: 16,000 won per seok (180 geun: one geun is equivalent to 600 gram.)
- The Ministry of Social Affairs announces payments to support living expenses according to the Veterans Administration laws.

February 10, Saturday (January 5, by lunar calendar, 辛巳日 White Snake) Clear and Cloudy
231 Day of the War

War Situation
- The ROK 1st Infantry Division advances toward the Han River.
  Takes Yeongdeungpo at 09:30 hours, complete control of Gimpo Airport at 16:30 hours and reach the Han River.

At Home
- Prime Minister, Jang Myeon urges through urgent written messages the strict abiding of working hours by the Government officials.
- Col. Kim Chong-won, Commander of the Military Affairs of Martial Laws Command in the South Gyeongsang Province Area gives a warning to military personnel to strictly respect and maintain public morality.
- The UN Relief Center for Civilians begins inoculation against smallpox and typhoid fever for all South Korean people.
- Reconstruction works for Gimpo Airport and Incheon Port begin.

Overseas

• The Prime Minister of New Zealand departs Washington for his home country.

February 11, Sunday (January 6, by lunar calendar, 壬午日 Black Horse) Very Clear
232 Day of the War

War Situation

• The ROK Capitol Infantry Division crosses the 38th parallel, and retakes Yangyang.
• About 2,000 Communist troops start maneuvering in the north of Seoul.

At Home

• President Syngman Rhee makes a statement on the prevalence of epidemics.
• The Headquarters of the ROK Navy announces on the landing of Incheon by its Marines.
• The "Geochang Massacre of Civilians'" erupts, and about 500 unarmed civilians are killed due to their alleged charges involved with the Communist guerilla.

February 12, Monday (January 7, by lunar calendar, 癸未日 Black Sheep) Very Clear
233 Day of the War

War Situation

• The spokesperson of the Eighth U.S. Army reports on the safe return of its military Unit after capturing Yangyang.

At Home

• Prime Minister Jang Myeon holds his first press interview after taking office.
• The Martial Law Commander, General Chung Il-kwon issues a proclamation on the lifting of goods registration.
• Mayor of Daegu, Huh Eok announces the provisional admission of refugee children into elementary schools.

February 13, Tuesday (January 8, by lunar calendar, 甲申日 Blue Monkey) Very Clear and Cloudy
234 Day of the War

War Situation

• The three units of the U.S. Army including the 23rd Regiment of the 2nd Infantry Division start to engage in bloody combats over the human sea and firing strategy attempted by the Chinese Forces. Enormous results are recorded.

At Home

• The plenary session of the National Assembly decides on sending of the delegation to Japan and on other issues.
• The National Assembly decides to send the assemblymen, Chang Taek-sang and Ji Cheong-cheon to General MacArthur to negotiate supporting the armament of one million

Korean youth.
- The Chief of Staff, Eighth U.S. Army issues a warning to delay the homecoming of refugees until further notice.
- KBS (Korean Broadcasting Station) starts to broadcast a song titled "Let's crush China!" produced by the Public Information Office.

Overseas
- The combined fleets of the United States and Britain complete their exercises in the Mediterranean Sea.

February 14, Wednesday (January 9, by lunar calendar, 乙酉日 Blue Rooster) Rainy and Cloudy
235 Day of the War

War Situation
- The Eighth U.S. Army confirms that the ROK Marines and the U.S. Marines successfully landed at Wonsan port and captured two islands (namely Hodo Island and Yeodo Island).
- The Communist Army encircles Jipeong in the early morning launching an attack with tanks and automatic weapons.

At Home
- The Vice Speaker of the National Assembly states that breaching the 38th parallel is a pre-determined matter.
- The Government proclaims "the laws on the lifting of punishment laws related to anti-nation movements." (The Laws No. 176)
- Daegu allocates the national bonds to the entertainment business places and citizens.

February 15, Thursday (January 10, by lunar calendar, 丙戌日 Red Dog) Clear and Cloudy
236 Day of the War

War Situation
- Most of the central frontlines engage in reconnaissance and patrol.
- Air sorties amount to 1,025 times which is the largest number of missions since the onset of the war.

At Home
- Vice-President Lee Shi-young makes statements that he will withdraw from any organization which uses his name illegally.
- The Martial Law Commander, General Chung Il-kwon issues a warning to those who are involved in exclusive or monopolistic purchases of rice.
- Minister of Foreign Affairs, Lim Byung-jik expresses his condolences on the death of Lt. Col. Omen, Commander-in-Chief of the Dutch Forces in Korea.
- The Government designates Sunday and Thursday as "No meat days."

February 16, Friday (January 11, by lunar calendar, 丁亥日 Red Pig) Cloudy and Clear
237 Day of the War

War Situation
- 1,000 Chinese troops attack 248 Hill east of Jipyeong, but defeated by the UN Forces.
- B-29 fighters drop 120 tons of bombs on Hamheung and Wonsan.

At Home
- The number of refugees fleeing to the South is estimated about two million.
- The Government designates the 25th day of every month as "A day to overcome national hardships."
- The Government makes an announcement on the decree, "The Regulations on the gradual decrease rate on the compensation for the purchased land."
- The Intelligence department of the National Police arrests a ring of illegal opium traffickers.

February 17, Saturday (January 12, by lunar calendar, 戊子日 Yellow Rat) Very Clear
238 Day of the War

War Situation
- The 5th Corps of the Communist Army sends an advance unit up to a point 4.8 km from Jecheon.

At Home
- The plenary session of the National Assembly has a hearing from the Ministers and Vice-ministers of Defense, Social Affairs, Education and Finance.
- The Government makes an announcement on "Suspension of telephone communication under an emergency."
- Minister of Social Affairs, Huh Jeong states that food would be distributed to the refugees staying beyond the north of the Kumgang River,

February 18, Sunday (January 13, by lunar calendar, 己丑日 Blue Ox) Very Clear
239 Day of the War

War Situation
- Little confrontation is evident in the eastern frontlines. The UN Forces take Jumunjin.
- North Korean Infantry Division attacks the perimeter of 6.4 km in the area of Jecheon.
- The Communist Forces begin to retreat on the central frontlines.

At Home
- Jang Myeon, Prime Minister has a press interview at Daegu:
  1) Korea is now kept absolutely safe.
  2) The UN resolution passed in October 1950 to permit attack north of the 38th parallel is still valid.

3) The Republic of Korea has resourceful manpower.

The 110,000-strong ROK Army is not well-equipped with sufficient amount of armament to cope with the Communist Forces.

Overseas
- The ROK Army retreats from Gangneung for the purpose of strategic rearrangement of the battle lines.
- The UN Forces repel the three infantry Divisions of the Chinese Forces.

February 19, Monday (January 14, by lunar calendar, 庚寅日 White Tiger) Very Clear
240 Day of the War

War Situation
- The UN Forces advance 1.8 km at the central frontlines amid the general retreat of the Communist Forces.
- The UN Forces defeat three infantry Divisions of the Chinese Army at the southeast of Wonju.

Overseas
- Prime Minister Jang Myeon, and Minister of Defense Shin Seung-mo carry out a tour of the western frontlines.
- A national rally takes place in Busan to oppose the reported stoppage at the 38th parallel.
- The UN Navy issues an announcement to handle military goods and supplies for 24 hours at the Incheon port.

February 20, Tuesday (January 15, by lunar calendar, 辛卯日 White Rabbit) Very Clear
241 Day of the War

War Situation
- A Reconnaissance Unit of the UN Forces crosses the river from the point 8 km from the south of Seoul and battles with 30 Communist soldiers.
- The Communist Forces begin to retreat from Seoul.

At Home
- The plenary session of the National Assembly passes a bill on the revised laws related to education.
- Prime Minister Jang Myeon makes an announcement to abolish the chief clerk (called "Gyejang' in Korean) system to ensure more effective and simplified administration procedures.
- Kim Yoon-geun, Commander of "the National Defense Corps," has a press interview on the public accusations regarding the Corps.
- Direct wireless cable system opened between Busan and Tokyo.

General MacArthur is visiting the frontlines near Han River(1951. 2. 20)

February 21, Wednesday (January 16, by lunar calendar, 壬辰日 Black Dragon) Cloudy
242 Day of the War

War Situation

- Under the commandership of General Ridgway, the Eighth U.S. Army initiates an all-out offensive in the central frontlines.
- The U.S. 9th and 10th Corps launch "Killer Operation," with all-out attacks targeting Yangpyeong, Hoengseong and Pyeongchang from the two frontlines including the central frontline.
- Odnill, Inspector-general for military training of the U.S. Army visits the frontlines. He said," The Command of the Communist Forces is just nothing more than Stalin himself and his political bureau."

At Home

- The National Assembly passes a bill to shorten the term of office of the Assembly's Speaker and Vice-Speaker for up to two years, and rejects the secretarial service system for the assemblymen.
- The Director General of the Armed Forces Information and Education Bureau of the Ministry of Defense announces that a total of 180,000 volunteers are mobilized for "the Students' Volunteers Army Corps."
- The import amount for imported relief goods stands at 32,000 tons and the total amount of

foreign exchange collected amounts to 76 billion won.

Overseas
- The UN Security Council begins to discuss the issue on Kashmir, and the United States and Britain submit their resolution bill.
- Italy receives a seat on the UN Trusteeship Committee, and asks for voting rights.

February 22, Thursday (January 17, by lunar calendar, 癸巳日 Black Snake) Cloudy and Clear
243 Day of the War

War Situation
- Defense Minister Shin Seong-mo visits the central frontlines.
- A large-scale military element of the Communist Forces establishes fighting foxholes at the point 9.7 km in the north of Wonju.
- One hundred thousand UN Forces advance 19.3 km from the central frontlines and approach Heongseong and Pyeongchang.

At Home
- The Ministry of Social Affairs pays 20,000 won to every wounded soldier to support their job seeking.
- The rice price is readjusted to two hops per head.
- The Emergency Order by Martial Law is lifted on Jeju Island

February 23, Friday (January 18, by lunar calendar, 甲午日 Blue Horse) Cloudy and Clear
244 Day of the War

War Situation
- The Chinese Forces begin to retreat from Seoul and a small number of the North Korean troops remains.
- The U.S. cruiser, *SS Manchester*, bombs the mainland of Wonsan area and Sindo.
- The U.S. 5th Tactical Air Force launches 300 sorties.

At Home
- The National Assembly deliberates on the amendment bill of the Commodity Tax Law.
- The National Assembly passes the bill for new committees (Steering, Agriculture and Forestry, Industry, and Foreign Affairs).

Overseas
- The UN Economic Council rejects a hearing of appeals made by the World Labor Association toward the French Government.
- Shanghai citizens deliver the relief fund (in amount of 11,478,240,000 won) for North Korean refugees to North Korea.

February 24, Saturday (January 19, by lunar calendar, 乙未日 Blue Sheep) Cloudy
245 Day of the War

War Situation

- The ROK and UN Forces advance to south of the Han River.
- Major General Bryant E. Moore of the U.S. 9th Corps dies after a helicopter crash near the Han River.

At Home

- The bill for the war budget (in the amount of 726.8 billion won) is submitted to the National Assembly.
- The National Assembly decides to send an inspection team to examine "the status on war-victims and necessary relief measures." in the eight cities in Jeolla Provinces.
- The Police Chief of Gangwon Province gives a briefing about the overall situation on epidemics and food needs.

February 25, Sunday (January 20, by lunar calendar, 丙申日 Red Monkey) Cloudy
246 Day of the War

War Situation

- The ROK Marines lands on Sindo and Jindo in the Wonsan area.
- The ROK Navy repels the advancing Communist Forces which attempt to take Yonghodo Island of Jinnampo port.

At Home

- The Government decides the buying price of gold at 32 Won per 1 gram.
- The Martial Laws Command (Bureau of Civilian Affairs) of North Gyeongsang Province extends the curfew hours in the areas of Daegu, Pohang, and Gimcheon.
- The National Police registers "the Police Bulletin (represented by the Police Chief of the South Gyeongsang Province Police."

February 26, Monday (January 21, by lunar calendar, 丁酉日 Red Rooster) Cloudy
247 Day of the War

War Situation

- A slight confrontation takes place during reconnaissance activities in the northwest and northeast of Yangpyeong.
- The Communist Forces show a strong resistance in the west and northern zones of Banglim-ri.
- The reconnaissance team of the U.S. 25th Infantry Division cross the Han River and safely returns after penetration in the southeast of Seoul.

At Home

- The business license system is adopted for the electrical works businesses beginning March 1.
- Commander of the Military Affairs, South Gyeongsang District Office, Col. Kim Jong-won announces the physical competency examination for drafted soldiers, saying that those candidates aged over 36 would be returned home.

February 27, Tuesday (January 22, by lunar calendar, 戊戌日 Yellow Dog) Rainy
248 Day of the War

War Situation
- An offensive attempted by the Communist Forces is completely repelled in the central frontlines.
- The U.S. 1st Marine Division captures the Dongbang hill and penetrates into Hoengseong.
- The U.S. 7th Infantry Division breaches the defense line of the North Korean Forces in the central frontlines.

At Home
- The National Assembly passes a bill related to "The Anti-Communist Law."
- The Ministry of Social Affairs makes an announcement to help the refugees to learn "how to safely return home". (With "the ID Certificate of refugees" and "The Certificate for Returning Home").
- Minister of Social Affairs, Huh Jeong makes an announcement on precautions for the refugees when they return home.
- The U.S. Army gives a briefing to the ambassadors of the Korean War-participating countries about the war situation.

February 28, Wednesday (January 23, by lunar calendar, 己亥日 Yellow Pig) Cloudy and Rainy
249 Day of the War

War Situation
- The U.S. Forces bombard the beachheads of the Communist Forces and their elements between Jumunjin and Gangneung.
- The friendly forces and the enemy engage aggressive reconnaissance missions.

At Home
- The Government announces "the regulations on compensation for the wounded war veterans."
- Chung Il-kwon, Martial Law Commander announces on the release of commandeered vehicles."
- Vice Minister of Social Affairs makes a presentation on his investigation results about war damages and refuges situation in Seoul and Gyeonggi-do regions.

150

An anti-aircraft Unit of the Chinese Army is protecting the trains carrying the war supplies

The war supplies being dropped from the sky by parachutes (1951. 3)

March 1, Thursday (January 24, by lunar calendar, 庚子日 White Rat) Clear
250 Day of the War

War Situation
- The U.S. 1st Marine Division kills 88 Chinese troops in hand-in-hand combat in the east of Heongseong.
- The U.S. Defense Ministry announces that the total loss of American casualties stands at 50,765 (7,636 killed).

At Home
- Ceremony for 3.1 Independence Movement Day takes place at each Ministry concerned.
- President Syngman Rhee visits the Rehabilitation Center for the Wounded Veteran Soldiers at Dongrae.
- *Daedong Shinmun* newspaper reopens in Busan.
- The Government decides the price of seed grains (13,000 won per tong / box)
- The Bank of Korea initiates the national treasure management by its branch system.

March 2, Friday (January 25, by lunar calendar, 辛丑日 White Ox) Clear and Cloudy
251 Day of the War

War Situation
- The U.S. 1st Marine Division completes its penetration into Heongseong.
- The Communist Forces strongly resist the UN Forces near the north of Anheung.
- The POWs of the ROK Army and Kang Tae-mu who defected to North Korea (ex-ROK major and commander of an NKPA regiment) hold an interview about witnessing the war casualties.

At Home
- The National Assembly passes a bill to abrogate the laws on the anti-nationalistic activities.
- Minister of Social Affairs Huh Jeong gives a press briefing on the matters related to the job-seeking assistance for the wounded veterans.
- General Chung Il-kwon makes an announcement on the release of commandeered vehicles (100 Units).

March 3, Saturday (January 26, by lunar calendar, 壬寅日 Black Tiger) Very Clear
252 Day of the War

War Situation
- U.S. Marines attacks the entrenchment of the Communist Forces at the 321 Hill north of

Heongseong.
- UN Forces bomb Seoul.
- UN ground Forces mark military achievement causing 2,371 casualties and capturing 40.

At Home
- The delegation of the electrical specialists of the Ministry of Industry reports on the status of damage incurred to Yeongwol Thermal Power Plant.
- The Ministry of Education makes a public notice on "the regulations on the qualification test for admission to high schools."
- North Gyeongsang Province issues a statement urging the people not to use the Japanese musical albums and songs.
- The Association of briquette manufacturers in Busan asks the Ministry of Industry for a price increase and that results in decrease of the overall production level.

March 4, Sunday (January 27, by lunar calendar, 癸卯日 Black Rabbit) Clear
253 Day of the War

War Situation
- The U.S. Marines approach a point 14.4 km from Hongcheon.
- The ROK 3rd Division engages in a 10-hour battle and captures the Hill 14.4km from the southeast of Heongseong.

The UN Forces are looking at the collapsed bridge of Han River (1951. 3. 3)

- The UN Forces penetrate into Soksari.

At Home
- President Syngman Rhee visits the Central Research Institute for Livestock Chemical Treatment.
- The National Assembly prepares to consider a bill to lift the emergency Martial Law in four provinces: South Gyeongsang, North Gyeongang, South Jeolla and North Jeolla.
- The Ministry of Health succeeds in producing medicines for anti-rabies inoculation.

Overseas
- About 660,000 workers in Shanghai, China, hold a rally to protest against the U.S. decision to permit Japan's re-armament.
- The United States sends a field inspection team consisting of five specialists to investigate the epidemics prevailing in Korea and Japan.

March 5, Monday (January 28, by lunar calendar, 甲辰日 Blue Dragon) Very Clear
254 Day of the War

War Situation
- The ROK 7th Division approaches Hajinbu 40 km from the 38th parallel.
- The U.S. 2nd and 7th Divisions including the French Forces pursue 6,000 Communist troops in the mountain terrain of the central frontlines.

At Home
- The Government announces that the lands are distributed to 12 million tenant farmers in accordance with the Land Reform Law.
- The National Assembly proposes a bill related to "revision of education laws.
- According to the law on "the National Defense Corps," the Corps is organized in the form of a standing Army in compliance with the regular Army system.
- Six staffs of the UN enter Korea to seek aid and relief programs for Korean War victims and refugees.

March 6, Tuesday (January 29, by lunar calendar, 乙巳日 Yellow Snake) Rainy and Cloudy
255 Day of the War

War Situation
- The ROK Army and the UN Forces complete their annihilation operation.
- The U.S. 2nd Division takes Jangpyeong.

At Home
- President Syngman Rhee give a presidential citation to the Commander of the U.S. 5th Tactical Air Team.
- Minister of Home Affairs, Cho Byung-ok gives permission to the farmland refugees to

return to their recovered hometowns.
- The American Women's Association for the War Relief and Aid send relief goods worth U.S$5,000.
- The representative of UNICEF finishes the necessary purchase of clothes for Korean children.

Overseas
- General MacArthur says that many of the new military units of the Communist Forces, up to 9-12 Division levels, appeared in the central frontlines.
- U.S. Undersecretary of State, McKee, arrives in India to discuss food matters.
- The court trial on espionage involved in atomic bomb begins for the first time in American history.

March 7, Wednesday (January 30, by lunar calendar, 丙午日 Red Horse) Very Clear
256 Day of the War

War Situation
- The ROK 7th Division retreats near Amidong due to heavy pressure from the Communist Forces.
- The U.S. 25th Division crosses the Han River from the southeast of Seoul, and establishes a bridgehead.
- The U.S. 24th Division repels the enemy troops at 153 Hill north of Yangpyeong with fierce hand-to-hand combat,

At Home
- The plenary session of the National Assembly discusses the issue of collaboration with the Communists by some of the assemblymen and the revision of the Educational Law.
- The National Assembly passes a bill revising the laws on education. (6-3-3-4 year system), and abolishes the "September Semester' system.
- President Truman awards the highest Medal of Honor to General Baik Seon-youp.

March 8, Thursday (February 1, by lunar calendar, 丁未日 Red Sheep) Very Clear
257 Day of the War

War Situation
- The Communist troops launch a frontal attack against the four Divisions of the UN Forces engaging in a fierce battle overnight.
- The U.S. cruiser SS Manchester and three destroyers combined with other battleships launch an attack into Seungjin Bay, bombing main military facilities.

At Home
- President Syngman Rhee has an interview with NBC.

- The plenary session of the National Assembly discusses a bill of special law on the requisition of school buildings and the Government-vested lands.
- The amendment bill of the education laws is reviewed, and the National Assembly passes the bill for the educational system on three-year middle school and two-year junior college (for high school graduates.).
- Yoon Ik-hyun, deputy Commander-In-Chief of the National Defense Corps makes an announcement on the homecoming of the soldiers aged over 31 years.
- Both North and South Gyeongsang Provinces agree to lift the Emergency Martial Law and submit the bill to the National Assembly.

March 9, Friday (February 2, by lunar calendar, 戊申日 Yellow Monkey) Cloudy and Rainy
258 Day of the War

War Situation
- The U.S. 7th Division retreats from Daemi after a fierce hand-to-hand battle with the North Korean troops.
- The U.S. 25th and 24th Divisions succeed in conducting a link-up operation at Yangpyeong zone.

At Home
- The National Assembly passes the bill related to "the special law on the Government-vested farmlands."
- Prime Minister Jang Myeon sends a notification about the reduction of the Government officials assigned to South Gyeongsang Province.
- The Association of Busan City's Dongs (*A dong is a smallest administrative Unit) appeal to the President and the National Assembly about the urgent counter-measures on distribution of charcoal and food.

March 10, Saturday (February 3, by lunar calendar, 己酉日 Yellow Rooster) Cloudy and Clear
259 Day of the War

War Situation
- The U.S. 25th Division advances 1-4km from a point 24 km east of Seoul.
- The U.S. 24th Division captures Hill 880, northwest of Yangpyeong.
- U.S. Air Force airplanes drop 2,400 empty beer bottles on the Communist troops near the north of Heongseong.

At Home
- The Ministry of Agriculture announces its plan to mine 400,000 tons of peat in the areas of Milyang and Cheonan.
- The Government submits its bill to propose the issue of "the national reconstruction

Government bonds worth 50 billion won.
- The whole sale index stands at 1,938 (compared with the year 1947 = 100).

March 11, Sunday (February 4, by lunar calendar, 庚戌日 White Dog) Cloudy
260 Day of the War

War Situation
- The Chinese troops strongly resist the attacks in the Banglim area.
- The Chinese troops retreat from Hongcheon zone due to the attack by the UN Forces.
- The U.S. cruiser *SS Manchester* bombs Seongjin.

At Home
- President Syngman Rhee urges that repair works for the roads and bridges be completed and says that the traffic regulations should be obeyed by the people.
- The Government issues lottery to help the refugees.
- The Commander of the U.S. War Veterans Corps, General Cork and the U.S. presidential envoy, Major General Duwoo visit the front lines and return to Tokyo.
- A Danish hospital ship anchors in Busan port.

Overseas
- Red China executes 45 former-officials of the Taiwan Peoples' Government (including military officers).
- It is rumored that China would send the reinforcement troops numbering 200,000 to the Korean frontlines: the 2nd Field Army under command of Ryu Bo-cheong.

March 12, Monday (February 5, by lunar calendar, 辛亥日 White Pig) Very Clear
261 Day of the War

War Situation
- An advance unit of the U.S. Forces approaches 8 km from Hongcheon.
- The Chinese troops begin to retreat from Seoul.

At Home
- President Syngman Rhee visits the frontlines near Yeongwol.
- Huh Jeong, Minister of Social Affairs, makes an announcement on the imminent transportation of relief grains and support programs for home-returning refugees.
- ROK Navy permits free fishing and free sailing in the West Sea except for a specific zone.

March 13, Tuesday (February 6, by lunar calendar, 壬子日 Black Rat) Cloudy and Clear
262 Day of the War

War Situation
- The Communist troops stop their engagement with the UN troops and start to retreat from

UN Forces are hearing about the enemy's movements from villagers in Chuncheon (1951. 3. 13)

the frontlines.
- The Communist troops in the eastern frontlines commence full-scale retreat.
- Commander-in-chief of the U.S. 10th Corps awards a silver medal to Brig. General Choi Young-hee.

At Home
- The Ministry of Defense announces on the regulations on audit of accounting.
- The relief grains, 37,000 bags sent by the UN, arrive in Busan port.

Overseas
- The U.S. Far East Air announces the use of Razon bombs (radio-guided bomb).
- The 150,000 Chinese troops under the command of Lin Biao and 20,000 Chinese soldiers stationed in the south-west border are reported to be ready to advance to North Korea.

March 14, Wednesday (February 7, by lunar calendar, 癸丑日 Black Ox) Clear
263 Day of the War

War Situation
- ROK Marines and 10th Infantry Division of the North Korean Army engaged in battles.
- The U.S. Armored Units passes Hongcheon advancing 29 km from the 38th parallel.

At Home

- President Syngman Rhee issues a special statement on the open bidding on Government-vested properties.
- The Government establishes a five-item plan for economic stability and inflation control.
- The Office of Publicity makes an announcement on "the status of overseas relief goods received."
- UN-supplied medicines for 8,800,000 persons arrive.

March 15, Thursday (February 8, by lunar calendar, 甲寅日 Blue Tiger) Very Clear
264 Day of the War

War Situation
- The U.S. 2nd Division engages in hand-to-hand combat with North Korean troops in the north of Yongduri killing 600, with eight captured.
- U.S. Tank Units capture Hongcheon.

At Home
- "The Amendment of the national assembly laws" is proclaimed.
- President Syngman Rhee sends his message about the recovery of the capital to General MacArthur and U.S. President Truman.
- A part of the Government offices (the Ministry of Social Affairs and Ministry of Health) leaves for Seoul.
- Minister of Defense, Shin Sung-mo speaks about the abolition of the 38th parallel.

March 16, Friday (February 9, by lunar calendar, 乙卯日 Blue Rabbit) Very Clear and Cloudy
265 Day of the War

War Situation
- The U.S. Marines engage in combat to secure Hongcheon.
- The ROK 1st Infantry Division continues to penetrate into Seoul.
- The National Police launches an operation to mop up isolated Communist guerillas killing 194 and capturing 61, with 51 rifles seized.

At Home
- General MacArthur sends a letter to President Syngman Rhee and asks him to withhold the return of the Government office to Seoul.
- Shin Sung-mo, Minister of Defense makes a statement about the crossing of the 38th parallel.

Overseas
- The UN Deputy Representative of the U.S. reports to the U.S. Secretary of State about the direct negotiations with North Korea.
- The 3rd Corps of Chinese Army is organized and begins its operation in North Korea.

March 17, Saturday (February 10, by lunar calendar, 丙辰日 Red Dragon) Cloudy and Clear
266 Day of the War

War Situation
- Greek troops repel the attack by the Chinese troops three times in the Chuncheon area.
- UN Forces advance 1 km to the suburban area north of Seoul.

At Home
- The military police of the ROK and the U.S. Army confiscate pilfered U.S. military supplies of 10 trucks at Busan Kukje market.
- Kim Il Sung sends a letter to Stalin to pledge "the war will be fought until the last minute."
- The Soviet Union and North Korea celebrate the second anniversary of the mutual agreement on the economic and cultural cooperation and assistance.

March 18, Sunday (February 11, by lunar calendar, 丁巳日 Red Snake) Very Clear
267 Day of the War

War Situation
- ROK troops confront 1,500 Communist troops in the northwest of Hongcheon.
- The spokesman of the Eighth U.S. Army refutes what was broadcast in China regarding the use of poison gas in the war.

At Home
- Kim Hoon, Minister of Commerce and Industry leaves for Tokyo to participate in a Trade and Commerce Negotiation between Korea and Japan.
- The Stevedores Union of Busan port asks the U.S. Combat Operation Center to raise their wages.

March 19, Monday (February 12, by lunar calendar, 戊午日 Yellow Horse) Very Clear
268 Day of the War

War Situation
- The Armored Reconnaissance Unit of the U.S. Army engages in combat with a Communist platoon supported by field guns and mortar.
- The Communist troops are routed to north of the 38th parallel.

At Home
- An advance party of 112 Government offices departs for Seoul, but the reconstruction plan for the capital is withheld for the time being.
- Calling-up of about 200,000 reservists of the Second Peoples' Force is abandoned due to lack of the training facilities.
- The UN Forces distribute food to 60,000 citizens who stayed back in Seoul.

Overseas

- China admits taking 58,000 citizens of Seoul away forcibly.
  - It is reported that they chose to go to North Korea when Chinese troops retreated.

March 20, Tuesday (February 13, by lunar calendar, 己未日 Yellow Sheep) Clear and Cloudy
269 Day of the War

War Situation
- In the north of Seoul, a reconnaissance Unit of the ROK Army and two platoons of the Communist troops engage in combat.
- General Kale of the British Army Education Center visits the frontlines commenting that there would be little possibility of the Chinese troops again retaking the initiative.

At Home
- The Ministry of Finance makes an announcement to prohibit circulation of so-called "Inminkwon" (North Korean currency banknotes) and other Communist currencies.
- The National Defense Corps dissolves all of its training centers.
- 120 assemblymen of the National Assembly submit a bill to upgrade the status of Busan City.
- Lee Sung-joo, Director of South Gyeongsang Province asks the people to refrain from playing *gut*(shaman ritual)."

March 21, Wednesday (February 14, by lunar calendar, 庚申日 White Monkey) Clear and Cloudy
270 Day of the War

War Situation
- The ROK troops approach the eastern part of the 38th parallel.
- The 26th Military Unit of the Chinese 3rd Field Corps appears on Korean peninsula.

At Home
- Foreign Minister Lim Byung-jik sends a letter to Secretary Acheson regarding the issue of the UN Mediation Committee.
- Vice-Minister of Home Affairs makes an announcement about arresting an espionage ring of the North Korean security agency.

March 22, Thursday (February 15, by lunar calendar, 辛酉日 White Rooster) Very Clear
271 Day of the War

War Situation
- The Eighth U.S. Army begins an all-out offensive as of 8 a.m.

At Home
- The National Assembly organizes a special security mission team.
- The Government proclaims "the enforcement regulations on the law on grain security."

- Minister of Defense, Shin Sung-mo announces a statement on a partial lifting of the Emergency Martial Laws.

March 23, Friday (February 16, by lunar calendar, 壬戌日 Black Dog) Very Clear
272 Day of the War

War Situation
- The U.S. 187th Airborne Corps (3,000 according to Voice of America) launches an air-mobile operation in the Munsan area to block the retreat routes of the North Korean 1st Corps troops.

At Home
- President Syngman Rhee makes a special statement that 500,000 of the ROK Army Forces are able to protect their homeland even if the UN Forces would withdraw after advancing across the border.
- Minister of Finance, Baik Doo-jin delivers a strong message to encourage the tax officials to perform their professional obligations to thoroughly collect due national taxes.
- The Jeonnam Textile Company restores its power plant to full operating capacity.

An Airdrop Operations of Munsan to exterminate the enemy in the north of Seoul (1951. 3. 23)

March 24, Saturday (February 17, by lunar calendar, 癸亥日 Black Pig) Cloudy and Clear
273 Day of the War

War Situation

- A reconnaissance Unit of the ROK Army crosses the 38th parallel, and returns to its original post after a clash with the Communist troops.
- The Communist troops offer strong resistance in the northern sector of Cheongpyeong.

At Home

- President Syngman Rhee states that advancing to the Korea-Manchuria border should be continued, and no ceasefire would be possible until the last minute to achieve it.
- The plenary session of the National Assembly passes a bill related to "the special law on wartime taxation," and holds an interim special hearing on the so-called "poster incident."
- The investigation section of the National Police arrests a bogus military captain.

March 25, Sunday (February 18, by lunar calendar, 甲子日 Blue Rat) Rainy and Cloudy
274 Day of the War

War Situation

- Reconnaissance Units of the ROK Army continue to cross the border.

At Home

- The Board of Audit and Inspection states that thorough auditing and budget control would be done.
- Ulsan Refinery requests the Commerce Ministry to provide counterpart funding from the U.S. Economic Commission.
- Patriot Hong Eon (a Korean woman journalist in America who fought against the Japanese colonization) passes away.

March 26, Monday (February 19, by lunar calendar, 乙丑日 Blue Ox) Clear and Cloudy
275 Day of the War

War Situation

- The allied troops engage in combat against a battalion of the Communist troops in the north of Chuncheon.
- Commander of the 7th Fleet of the U.S. Navy, Admiral Arthur D. Struble is replaced by Admiral Harold M. Martin.

At Home

- President Syngman Rhee gives special instructions to Minister of Home Affairs Cho Byung-ok and Minister of Agriculture Yoon Young-seon to expedite and reinforce the forest management and development of farmland.

Overseas

- UNESCO is preparing for the post-war programs for the education and economic reconstruction of the Korean Peninsula with a dollar value of U.S$ 10 million.
- China urges its people to increase the production of agricultural and industrial products in order to achieve the earlier completion of the Korean War.

March 27, Tuesday (February 20, by lunar calendar, 丙寅日 Red Tiger) Cloudy and Rainy
276 Day of the War

War Situation
- The ROK 1st Corps occupies Anyang.
- The ROK troops engage in fierce combat with the Communist troops at a hill located in north of Yangyang, and finally take control of it.

At Home
- The plenary session of the National Assembly passes a resolution calling for the lifting of Martial Law.
- The Government proclaims a Presidential Decree No. 465 "estalishment of Institue for sound thought guidance for the people."
- The Ministry of Education decides to simplify of the school system into 6-3-3-4 effective from the new semester and take necessary administrative procedures.

March 28, Wednesday (February 21, by lunar calendar, 丁卯日 Red Rabbit) Rainy and Clear
277 Day of the War

War Situation
- About 90,000 Chinese troops assemble en masse in the north of Chuncheon.
- The mobile strike team of the UN Forces launches bombardment from warships toward Wonsan (38th day) and Seongjin(19th day).
- A unit of large-size vehicles of the Communist Forces move between Pyongyang and Sookcheon.

At Home
- Proclaims a presidential decree (No. 466 retroactive to January 1.) on "The revised law on civilian employees attached to the Army."
- The Ministry of Social Affairs completes the "five-year plan for reconstruction of war-damaged housing," and prepares to set up "the war-damaged housing reconstruction committee."

March 29, Thursday (February 22, by lunar calendar, 戊辰日 Yellow Dragon) Very Clear
278 Day of the War

War Situation

- The UN Forces approach the defense lines of the Communist troops.
- The Communist troops in the rear area of Uijeongbu begin an all-out retreat operation.

At Home
- The National Assembly passes a bill on "The Relief Laws for Policemen."
- The National Assembly discloses "the scandal'" on the National Defense Corps. Total embezzlement amount: Cash of 2.3 billion won and 52,000 bags of grain.
- Prime Minister Jang Myeon asks the people to lead a more austere and frugal life.
- The Military Police headquarters call for more attention to be paid to the so-called "bogus military police."

March 30, Friday (February 23, by lunar calendar, 己巳日 Yellow Snake) Very Clear
279 Day of the War

War Situation
- The ROK Army advances 12.8 km to the north.
- In the areas of Chuncheon and Gimhwa, 80,000 Communist troops assemble and prepare for their combat operations.
- Small but sporadic attacks are continuously launched by the Chinese troops.

At Home
- The plenary session of the National Assembly has a closed meeting where the "Geochang Incident" and the "Poster Incident" are discussed. The session also decides to set up the investigation committee to probe the Geochang Incident.
- The Joint Investigation team of ROK and U.S. Armies begins an intensive confiscation of the military goods and supplies at Kukje market.

March 31, Saturday (February 24, by lunar calendar, 庚午日 White Horse) Cloudy and Rainy
280 Day of the War

War Situation
- The ROK Army approaches 16 km north of the 38th parallel.
- The U.S. Tank Units penetrate the 38th parallel from the north of Uijeongbu and safely return to their original positions.

At Home
- The Government nominates the Joseon Coal Distribution Company and six other companies as state-run enterprises.
- The Government proclaims "the Special Accounts Law" to recover from war damages
- The Government finishes the special training course program for 123 administrators to reconstruct the recovered areas of the North Korea.
- The Ministry of Defense makes an announcement on "the Regulations on daily duty man

at the Ministry headquarters."

Overseas

- President of France, Vincent Auriol, visits the UN.

April 1, Sunday (February 25, by lunar calendar, 辛未日 White Sheep) Rainy and Cloudy
281 Day of the War

War Situation

- The 4ᵗʰ Field Army of Chinese Communist Forces is replaced by its 3ʳᵈ Army.

At Home

- Refugees return to Seoul.
- The Ministry of Telecommunication and Postal Services opens direct telephone services: Busan-Gyeongju, Busan-Masan, Busan-Cheonan and Yongsan-Uijeongbu.
- New postage stamps (5, 20, 50, and 100 Won) are issued.
- Commodity price index of Busan doubles from that of Jan. 1. Jumped 6.3-fold in comparison with the before-the-war index.

Overseas

- 180 Government officials of East Germany escape to West Germany in March.

April 2, Monday (February 26, by lunar calendar, 壬申日 Black Monkey) Cloudy
282 Day of the War

War Situation

- The ROK Army advances about 3.2 km to the north of the 38ᵗʰ parallel.
- The UN Forces re-cross the frontier from the western frontline.

At Home

- The National Assembly rejects the bill for the establishment of a Suppression Operations Corps.
- The National Assembly establishes its Government Inspection Team.
- The National Assembly decides to petition the UN, the U.S. President for opposition to "Peace negotiation on a ceasefire at 38ᵗʰ parallel and the establishment of a buffer zone."

April 3, Tuesday (February 27, by lunar calendar, 癸酉日 Black Rooster) Cloudy
283 Day of the War

War Situation

General Ridgway, Commander of Eighth U.S. Army(back) and General MacArthur are on the way to the frontlines (1951. 4. 3)

- The UN Forces launch a large-scale offensive against the Chinese Communist Army and cross the 38th parallel.
- The ROK Army crosses the Imjin River and combats several companies of the enemy troops.

At Home
- The National Assembly adopts a resolution opposing "the peace negotiations with China and the establishment of a demilitarized zone."
- Prime Minister Jang Myeon issues his statement that only the unification of the Korean peninsula could contribute to world peace.
- The Ministry of Transportation establishes its plan for the construction of 4,800 vessels.

April 4, Wednesday (February 28, by lunar calendar, 甲戌日 Blue Dog) Clear
284 Day of the War

War Situation
- The ROK Army occupies Ganseong.
- The ROK Army penetrates Kaesong.

At Home
- The development project for Jeju Island is launched as planned with a loan of 1.8 billion won.
- The Cabinet Notice on the lift of Emergency Martical Law (No. 12) and the declaration of Martial Law (No. 13) is proclaimed.

April 5, Thursday (February 29, by lunar calendar, 乙亥日 Blue Pig) Cloudy and Rainy
285 Day of the War

War Situation
- The UN Forces drive all enemy troops away from south of the 38th parallel.
- The UN Forces seize Yanggu and Inje.

At Home
- Presidential Decree No. 468 is proclaimed on "the Local Broadcasting System."
- Public notice on "the special laws related to Government-vested farm lands" (Law No. 185).
- Attack on the special investigation team for the Geochang Incident by an unidentified mob takes place and its mission fails.
- American Veterans Association awards a Medal of Honor to President Syngman Rhee.
- A ceremony takes place to celebrate the reconstruction of the Han River railroad bridge.

April 6, Friday (March 1, by lunar calendar, 丙子日 Red Rat) Rainy and Clear

War Situation

- The U.S. Army opens all-out assaults against the enemy troops in the hills located between Hangye and Inje.
- The U.S. Army advances to the north from the northwest of Yongdong.
- The 1st Infantry Division's Commander, Baek Seon-yeop is promoted to Major General and assumes the Commanding position of 1st ROK Corps. Brigadier General Kang Moon-bong takes his place.

At Home

- Minister of Defense, Shin Sung-mo makes a statement related to the Students Volunteer Soldiers Corps saying that the TI & E (Troop Information and Education) team would be disbanded except for full-time official soldiers.
- The Monetary Policy Committee decides to increase the interest rates of bank deposits and loans including the rediscount rate.

Overseas

- Syria solicits an investigation to the UN Security Council in relation to the bombing incident caused by Israel.
- The Prime Minister of Israel makes a statement that they do not want a war.

April 7, Saturday (March 2 by lunar calendar, 丁丑日 Red Ox) Cloudy and Clear
287 Day of the War

War Situation

- The 2nd Infantry Division of the ROK Army advances north in the eastern frontline.
- All-out retreat operation of the Chinese Army is completed in the mid-west zone.

At Home

- The Government informs the customs office that the export of scrap iron will be handled only by the Ministry of Transportation.
- Byun Young-tae is appointed as Minister of Foreign Affairs while Lee Myo-mook is assigned as Minister of the Korean Embassy in the U.K. and Jeon Kyu-hong as Minister of the Korean Embassy in France respectively.

April 8, Sunday (March 3, by lunar calendar, 戊寅日 Yellow Tiger) Clear
288 Day of the War

War Situation

- The Advance Force of U.N. Forces is halted in the Chuncheon area due to strong resistance by the Communist troops.
- The ROK Marine lands in the Ongjin peninsula and continues to advance toward the

Songnim-myeon area.
- BOT (Burst on target) by F80 fighters against the oil tank terminal located in Sukcheon.

At Home
- Defense Minister, Shin Sung-mo makes a public announcement on the lifting of Emergency Martial Law in provinces such as South Gyeongsang, North Gyeongsang, South Chungcheong, North Chungcheong (except for Chungju and two other areas), South Jeolla and North Jeolla. Instead the Security Status Martial Law was announced in its place.
- Joseon Transportation Corporation receives a Government-guaranteed loan in the amount of 7.4 billion won for the reconstruction of war damages.
- The population of Seoul reaches 320,000.

April 9, Monday (March 4, by lunar calendar, 乙卯日 Blue Rabbit) Very Clear
289 Day of the War

War Situation
- ROK Army advances into Ganseong.
- The Chinese Army destroys 11 sluice gates of the Hwacheon Reservoir and flees to the north after discharging the water.
- The enemy mobilizes its transportation task team on a large scale and assembles in Cheorwon, Gimhwa and Hwacheon.

At Home
- President Syngman Rhee states that plan for the Foreign Capital Induction and inflation control measures are prepared.
- The Korean American Association in Hawaii donates U.S$1, 800 to the President to help purchase artificial limbs for those injured in the war.

April 10, Tuesday (March 5, by lunar calendar, 庚辰日 White Dragon) Cloudy
290 Day of the War

War Situation
- The UN Forces continue to advance toward the north after seizing Gorangpo Bay.
- Massive bombing is carried out against the concentration zone of the enemy Forces in Cheorwon and Gimhwa.
- Fierce air combat takes place in Sinuiju.

At Home
- The Government decides to file a request with the UN for the compensation fund and interest.
- About 100,000 refugees swarm to the Han River like a great human tide.

- The Government dissolves the Korea Trade Corporation (a Government agency).

Overseas
- The 7th Fleet of the U.S. Navy conducts WASEX ("War at sea exercise") over four days along the Taiwan Strait.
- The World Confederation of Governments Conference discusses a ceasefire of the Korean War, etc.

April 11, Wednesday (March 6, by lunar calendar, 辛巳日 White Snake) Cloudy and Clear
291 Day of the War

War Situation
- UN reconnaissance unit enters Inje.
- U.S. 1st Corps and 9th Corps start their so-called "indomitable attack operation."
- The U.S. Air Force performs 113 air strikes in rainy weather. And the allied ground Forces kill 615 Communist soldiers capturing 30 prisoners.

At Home
- Lee Cheol-won, Director of the Public Information Office states that the dismissal of General MacArthur is astonishing news to the Korean people.
- The Ministry of Commerce prepares a draft bill on "the Government's management of the important materials and supplies."

Overseas
- UN Secretary-General Trygve Lie refuses to comment on the dismissal of General MacArthur.

April 12, Thursday (March 7, by lunar calendar, 壬午日 Black Horse) Very Clear
292 Day of the War

War Situation
- Strong resistance by the Communist troops continues in the southern area of the Hwacheon Reservoir.
- The UN Forces attack with flamethrowers to the warfare positions of the Chinese troops south of the Seolcheon River.
- China reinforces its combat forces by 180,000 soldiers and the total number of the Chinese Army reaches 690,000. (Meanwhile the UN Forces numbers about 500,000.)

At Home
- ROK President Syngman Rhee has an important meeting with Frank Pace, U.S. Secretary of the Army.
- Paik Nak-jun, Minister of Education, gives a briefing on the re-education of North Korean teachers who fled to South Korea.

- The Local Administration Bureau of the Ministry of Home Affairs submitted a bill on the revision of the "Local Tax Law."
- Yang Yu-chan is appointed as Ambassador to the U.S.

April 13, Friday (March 8, by lunar calendar, 癸未日 Black Sheep) Very Clear
293 Day of the War

War Situation
- The Communist Army begins to re-attack the entire frontline.

At Home
- ROK President Syngman Rhee leaves for Jinhae to celebrate the 406th anniversary of Admiral Lee Sunshin's birthday.
- The Government decides to export all of locally produced tungsten through the cooperation between the Ministry of Commerce and the Special Committee for the Industrial reconstruction.

Overseas
- Secretary of Defense George C. Marshall Jr. opposes the idea of the reinforcement of the U.S Marine Corps.
- John Foster Dulles, adviser to the Secretary of State leaves for Japan.
- French Prime Minister submits a bill to increase tax by 55 billion won.

April 14, Saturday (March 9, by lunar calendar, 甲申日 Blue Monkey) Cloudy
294 Day of the War

War Situation
- The UN Forces advance toward Cheorwon.
- The UN Forces frustrate the enemy's counter-offensive in Yeoncheon.
- The ROK Forces reach most of the Kansas lines.

At Home
- President Syngman Rhee meets U.S. Senator, Warren G. Magnuson to discuss the Fisheries Agreement.
- Cho Byung-ok, Minister of Home Affairs comments on the execution of "by-elections to elect National Assembly members.

Overseas
- It was reported that the Chinese troops might withdraw from Indo-China.
- United States Senator William F. Knowland says that the dismissal of General MacArthur might cause unnecessary discord in America.

April 15, Sunday (March 10, by lunar calendar, 乙酉日 Blue Rooster) Cloudy and Clear

War Situation

- The ROK Marine Corps lands at Jinnampo Bay with support from the commando Unit.
- The U.S Navy Fleets continue bombing against the ports such as Wonsan, Cheongjin and Seongjin port.
- The UN destroyer squadron bombards Jangsan located in the south of Jinnanmpo.

At Home

- The newly appointed Commander of the Eighth U.S. Army, Lt. General James A. Van Fleet arrives at Jinhae airport to meet President Syngman Rhee and American Ambassador John J. Mucho.
- The Gyeonggi Provincial Government establishes its provisional office at Suwon.
- A ring of robbers is arrested in one big raid in Yeonchon-gun.

Overseas

- UN Secretary-General Lie arrives in Athens, Greece.
- The Japanese Emperor visits General MacArthur and holds a discussion lasting about 45 minutes.

April 16, Monday (March 11, by lunar calendar, 丙戌日 Red Dog) Cloudy
296 Day of the War

War Situation

- A tank battalion of the UN Forces enter Yanggu, east end of Hwacheon Reservoir.
- The ROK Fleet shoots down a Communist fighter plane and brings down another fighter by anti-aircraft fire on the western coast.
- General Ridgway appoints General Doyle Overton Hickey as Chief of Staff.

At Home

- Byun Young-tae is appointed as Minister of Foreign Affairs.
- The National Assembly (the 58th main session) rejects a bill regarding the issuance of national bonds.
- The Bank of Korea decides to sell off the foreign exchange accounts allocated for export, which are overdue.
- The death sentence is pronounced on those who masterminded the People's Court in Goreyong.
- A fire breaks out at a synthetic rubber factory in Gwangju and three buildings are completely burnt down with losses amounting to 11 million won.
- The U.S. CIC issues a report on the spying activities of North Korean agents in South Korea.
- Korean patriot, Na In-hyup passes away.

April 17, Tuesday (March 12, by lunar calendar, 丁亥日 Red Pig) Clear
297 Day of the War

War Situation
- The ROK Army occupies Ganseong and advances north.
- The resistance of the Communist Forces in the Inje area is weak.
  The UN Air Force launches night firing against Pyongyang, Kumsung, Sinuiju and Anak.
- The first group of U.S. repatriated soldiers leaves Korea according to the Law on the rotational system for American soldiers.

At Home
- President Syngman Rhee expresses his thanks, on behalf of Korean people, to the UN member countries for their special aid for necessities and supplies.
- The National Assembly deals with a political issue through its special re-investigation committee: the so-called "poster incident" involving Defense Minister Shin Sung-mo.
- A Danish Telecom company cuts off the under-sea cables connecting Pohang-Bangeojin.

April 18, Wednesday (March 13, by lunar calendar, 戊子日 Yellow Rat) Cloudy
298 Day of the War

War Situation
- The UN Forces re-seize Hwancheon and Hwacheon Reservoir.
- The Tank Mobile Mission Team of the U.S. Forces gun-fires the ammunition transporters of the Communist Army in the north of Yeoncheon.
- The most advanced type of U.S. submarines start to operate in the seas off Korea.

At Home
- The plenary session of the National Assembly discusses measures to help the landowners with change of profession.
- The National Assembly makes a report and holds closed-door meetings to discuss the "Geochang Incident."
- The Government makes a public announcement on the laws related to "the establishment of combat police forces" in the southwestern area.
- The opening ceremony takes place for Waegwan Railroad Bridge of Nakdong River.
- The Government decides to adopt a recruitment and pre-qualification policy to employ the Government officials through the screening committee for Government officials.
- The first number of "the Newspaper on Politics (represented by Han Chang Wan)" is inaugurated.

April 19, Thursday (March 14, by lunar calendar, 己丑日 Yellow Ox) Cloudy
299 Day of the War

War Situation

- On the central frontline, the resistance of the Communist Army is very fierce toward the reconnaissance task unit of the UN Forces.

At Home

- The main session of the National Assembly is adjourned in 10 minutes due to the absence of most assemblymen.
- Kim Yun-geun, Commanding General of National Defense Corps makes a public statement on the recent incident of the Corps.

April 20, Friday (March 15, by lunar calendar, 庚寅日 White Tiger) Cloudy
300 Day of the War

War Situation

- The UN Forces approach in the range of artillery fire to Cheorwon.

At Home

- President Syngman Rhee gives instructions to all of the Provincial Governors that peat digging (mining) in paddy fields should not be allowed before sowing while the use of firewood was also not permitted.
- The Congress of American Industrial Organizations donates relief goods and supplies worth U.S$3,600 through the World Relief Council. After the donation ceremony, the distribution was carried out for needy workers on the streets.
- The railroad and telephone services between Seoul and Busan are re-opened.

Overseas

- The Soviet Union made comments on the possible construction of the atomic bomb-making facilities at Yili of Xinjiang, China.
- Robert L. Sikes, of the United States House of Representatives comments during his interview with a magazine that nerve gas bombs would be much more effective and powerful than atomic bombs.

April 21, Saturday (March 16, by lunar calendar, 辛卯日 White Rabbit) Clear and Cloudy
301 Day of the War

War Situation

- The U.S. 1st and 9th Corps start to attack the Wyoming Line.
- The UN Forces engage a fierce fight against the enemy troops in the south of Cheorwon.

At Home

- Provost Marshal, Choi Kyung-rok makes a statement on the results of the final examination of the National Defense Corps Incident.
- The bombing test was done in Yeongdo, Busan.

• The Ministry of Health announces the preventive measures against epidemics, and performed DDT air spraying (dusting) in 16 major cities in the country.

April 22, Sunday (March 17, by lunar calendar, 壬辰日 Black Dragon) Clear and Cloudy
302 Day of the War

War Situation
- A regiment of the Communist Army penetrates into the south and west of the Gimhwa zone.
- A regiment of the Communist Army attempts to cross the Imjin River from the Gorangpo area.

At Home
- The total loss of grain damaged after the Korean War amounts to 812,379 seok (one seok is equivalent to 180.39 liters) worth 10,244,342,200 won.

Overseas
- The Soviet Union awards "Motherhood Medals" to the 33,000 women who bore more than

U.S. Forces are firing with 155mm howitzer at the Battle of Imjin (1951. 4. 22)

10 children as a child-bearing incentive.

April 23, Monday (March 18, by lunar calendar, 癸巳日 Black Snake) Clear
303 Day of the War

War Situation
- The UN Forces advance to the point of 6.4 km toward the southern part of Cheorwon, but withdraw to the original position.
- The UN Corps of Engineers destroys one bridge on the Hantan River including its pontoon (bridge).
- The Commander of the U.S. Far East Air Forces states that the enemy's all-out air attack could not be prevented without bombing Manchuria.

At Home
- Lee Si-young, Vice President of South Korea returns to Busan after the trip to the Gyeongbuk area to observe and inspect the aftermath of the National Defense Corps incident. He deplores the mistreatment of the soldiers mobilized for the National Defense Corps.
- The Government decides the standard consumption rate of the National bonds: 3 % up in case of precious metals; and 20% up in case of high-class entertaining restaurants (Gisaeng houses).
- The Seoul City Government finishes the allocation of 3,600 tons' relief grain to each of the district offices.

April 24, Tuesday (March 19, by lunar calendar, 甲午日 Blue Horse) Very Clear
304 Day of the War

War Situation
- The Communist Forces initiate movements along the penetration points in the south of Gimhwa, but are successfully blocked by the reinforced UN Forces.
- The UN Forces pull out up to the 38th parallel and renounce most of the frontlines along the Imjin River.

At Home
- The Korea-Japan Trade Agreement comes into effect.
- The Martial Law Command (Div. of the Civilian Affairs) of Gyeongsang Provinces returns a part of the commandeered estates to the owners, starting from esates in Busan.

April 25, Wednesday (March 20, by lunar calendar, 乙未日 Blue Sheep) Clear and Cloudy
305 Day of the War

War Situation

- About 20,000 soldiers of the Communist Army penetrate into the south of Jawol-ri.
- The 1st Infantry Division of the ROK Army rescues 40 soldiers of Britain's 29th Gloucestershire Regiment.

At Home
- The National Assembly decides to augment the Forces of the ROK Army by 10 Divisions. The main session of the National Assembly unanimously agrees to ask the U.S. Government to help with the arming of the 10 ROK Army's Divisions.
- The Finance and Economic Committee of the National Assembly reduces the amount of interest incurred on the Government's compensation money.
- The Government orders Seoul citizens to evacuate. (For the third time since the outbreak of the war)

April 26, Thursday (March 21, by lunar calendar, 丙申日 Red Monkey) Clear and Cloudy
306 Day of the War

War Situation
- The UN Forces speed up the withdrawal from the central frontlines.
  -The UN Forces block the attack of the Communist Army at a point 27.3 km northeast of Seoul.
  -The UN Forces take counter-offensive from the northeast of Seoul and advance about 3.2 km.

At Home
- President Syngman Rhee awards the Order of Military Merit (the 2nd grade silver medal) to Commander of General Oliver P. Smith of the U.S. 1st Marine Division.
- The Ministry of Social Affairs estimates the total number of refugees to be 5,350,675 persons.
- An ex-professor of Kim Il Sung University who was arrested as a political espionage agent is sentenced to two years' imprisonment.

April 27, Friday (March 22, by lunar calendar, 丁酉日 Red Rabbit) Cloudy and Rainy
307 Day of the War

War Situation
- The UN Forces withdraw from the Chuncheon-Seoul national highway.

At Home
- The National Assembly examines the bill of "the law on the punishment of sniper criminals."
- Korean Ambassador to the United States, Yang Yoo-chan returns home to receive a letter of credence.
- The Task Force team for administrative construction withdrew from Seoul.

April 28, Saturday (March 23, by lunar calendar, 戊戌日 Yellow Dog) Rainy and Cloudy
308 Day of the War

War Situation
- The U.S. 1st Corps occupies the golden lines of northern Seoul.
- The ROK 1st Infantry Division initiates battle in Hwajeon-ri.

At Home
- The National Assembly starts to investigate the beating attack on a journalist.
- The Ministry of Education establishes "the provisional measures for war-time school education."
- Police Chief Kim Tae-seon gives emergency special instructions to the police to ensure "all policemen's selfless devotion and sacrifice to the country."

April 29, Sunday (March 24, by lunar calendar, 乙亥日 Yellow Pig) Cloudy and Clear
309 Day of the War

War Situation
- The UN Forces withdraw from the entire frontlines due to the augmented units of the Chinese Army.
- The ground troops of the UN Forces kill or injure 4,100 Communist soldiers and capture 80.

At Home
- The UN Special Commission for New Korea discusses matters related to food problems.
- Mayor of Seoul, Lee Gi-boong, announces that Seoul residents had withdrawn from their hometown with the remainder of 250,000 out of 450,000.
- The Federation of Korean Trade Unions decides to replace "May Day" with "day for hard-working and victory."

April 30, Monday (March 25 by lunar calendar, 庚子日 White Rat) Very Clear
310 Day of the War

War Situation
- Some elements of the UN Forces in the eastern zone of Inje begin to make retrograde movement by some 1 km due to attack by a Communist regiment.
- The 19th Field Army of the Chinese Forces prevail near the Ui-dong area, but retreat 12 km due to the strong counter-offensive by the UN Forces.

At Home
- The plenary session of the National Assembly is engaged in a heated controversy over the abolition of "the National Defense Corps" and "Homeland Defense Corps." The final decision is made on the abolition of them.

- The Ministry of Education decides to adopt the standard 1,000 Chinese characters to be taught in elementary schools.
- The Ministry of Social Affairs restricts the entry of refugees to South and North Gyeongsang Provinces.
- The National Classical Music Institute is established. The state-managed measures to promote the classical court music of royal families are passed by the National Assembly.

Overseas
- The Soviet Union Navy's specialists are said to have assisted with mine laying in Shantou Harbor.
- U.S. President Truman requests Congress to approve a military budget amounting to U.S$ 60,679,414,690.

May 1, Tuesday (March 26, by lunar calendar, 辛丑日 White Ox) Cloudy and Clear
311 Day of the War

War Situation

- The Eighth U.S. Army states that the front lines show a minor confrontation with the Communist troops.

At Home

- The plenary session of the National Assembly abolishes the pending bill related to "the special law on the farm lands."
- Huh Jeong, Minister of the Social Affairs has a press interview to speak about the issue on 400,000 refugees staying in the areas of Seoul and Incheon.
- In South Gyeongsang Province, the training program is finished for the administration personnel to serve in North Korea.

May 2, Wednesday (March 27, by lunar calendar, 壬寅日 Black Tiger) Very Clear
312 Day of the War

War Situation

- The UN Forces repel the Communist troops which attacked their beachhead.
- The Chinese troops move to the east from the north of Seoul.

At Home

- The plenary session of the National Assembly passes the bill to disorganize the Joint Investigation Headquarter."
- The Cabinet Meeting abolishes the market price index of the aid and relief goods which cause the consumer price hike.

May 3, Thursday (March 28, by lunar calendar, 癸卯日 Black Rabbit) Clear and Cloudy
313 Day of the War

War Situation

- The UN Forces engage a combat with unidentified Communist troops at the south east of Chuncheon.
- The UN Artillery Units and ground Forces repel an offensive by the Communist troops near Inje.

At Home

- President Syngman Rhee makes an address to the ROK soldiers saying that the final victory will be ours.

- Byun Young-tae, Minister of Foreign Affairs has a press interview to stress the importance of hard-line policy toward the Soviet Union.
- The Financial Supervisory Commission submits its proposal regarding "the regulations on interest and financing business."

Overseas
- United States representative, H.R. Gross requests UN member countries to block the export of armaments to China.
- The Republic of Korea appeals to the UN Economic and Social Council to stop acts of genocide done by the North Korea (or in collaboration with the Soviet Union and China).

May 4, Friday (March 29, by lunar calendar, 甲辰日 Blue Dragon) Cloudy
314 Day of the War

War Situation
- The UN and ROK Forces begin to take counter-offensives advancing northward Bongilcheon - Chuncheon-Inje- Sokcho.
- The friendly Forces repel the Communist troops from the northwest to the north.

At Home
- Wayne Geisinger, the special advisor to President Syngman Rhee states that the Chinese troops can be easily beaten if 500,000 Korean troops are properly armed and well equipped.
- Shin Sung-mo, Minister of Defense praises the Military Medical School for its contribution by giving awards.
- Daegu District Tribunal Court gives sentences to those charged with "Incident of National Defense Corps.": 3 years and 6 months for Col. Yoon Ik-hyun of the Headquarters, 4 months for Lt. Col. Kang Suk-han of the Headquarters, 6 months for Lt. Col. Park Chul of the 15th Training Camp Unit, and 3 years for Col. Lim Byung-eon of the 25th Training Camp Unit.

May 5, Saturday (March 30, by lunar calendar, 乙巳日 Blue Snake) Cloudy and Clear
315 Day of the War

War Situation
- A Reconnaissance Unit of the UN Forces enter Inje killing 255 of the Communist troops with 57 captured.
- General Ridgway, Commander of the UN Forces issues his affirmative position to take a strategic military initiative on the front lines of Korea.

At Home
- The Government organizes "the Committee for Economic Reconstruction" which consists

US tanks and soldiers racing to Uijeongbu City (1951. 5. 6).

of Prime Minister (in charge of chairman) and Ministers of Administration & Planning, Home Affairs, Agriculture, Industry, Social Affairs, Transportation, and Postal and Telecommunication (as committee members).
- The UN Council for Korean Unification and Reconstruction examines an overall status of Korean industry and economy, and return to Busan via Daegu.
- A rally by "the Chinese Residents' Anti-Communist Association in Korea" takes place at Dong-A theatre in Busan.

May 6, Sunday (April 1, by lunar calendar, 丙午日 Red Horse) Clear
316 Day of the War of the war

War Situation
- UN Air Forces locates a large number of the Communist transporters, 4,000 units in the major supply roads in the North Korea.

At Home
- Beginning 00:00 hours, Summer Time begins.
- The Government decides to reduce the national bonds issuance to the amount of 40 billion won.
- The Ministry of Foreign Affairs of North Korea appeals to the President of the UN General Assembly and Chairman of UN Security Council, accusing the biological warfare of the U.S. Army.

May 7, Monday (April 2, by lunar calendar, 丁未日 Red Sheep) Cloudy and Rainy

War Situation
- A reconnaissance of the UN Forces penetrates the 38th parallel near Inje.
- A reconnaissance of the UN Forces breaks into Chuncheon.
- The ROK Army advances 5km in the northwest of Euijeongbu.

At Home
- The Government nominates 4 Ministers: Lee Gi-boong as the Minister of Defense; Lee Sun-yong as Minster of Home Affairs; Cho Jin-man as Minister of Justice; and Lim Mun-hwan as Minister of Agriculture.
- The National Assembly reports on the Incident of National Defense Corps.
- The Central Committee for the Absorption of National bonds suggests to each of the Ministry concerned the measures on how to absorb and dispose the national bonds issued.

Overseas
- It is rumored that the secret agreement of military alliance is to be made between China and the Soviet Union. : China would send an additional troops(600,000) to Korean peninsula, and the Soviet Union is to newly organize 10 Divisions which consist of volunteer troops from friendly countries and are well equipped with Russian armaments.

May 8, Tuesday (April 3, by lunar calendar, 戊申日 Yellow Monkey) Cloudy and Rainy
318 Day of the War

War Situation
- The UN Forces advance 32 km to the north of Seoul via Uijeongbu roads approaching the 38th parallel.
- The ROK Army crosses Gokneung River in the northwest of Seoul advancing 27km toward the north of Seoul.
- The UN Air Force kills 300 of the Communist troops.

At Home
- The plenary session of the National Assembly argues over an alleged conspiracy of embezzlement of the National Defense Corps fund in amount of 100 million won which was misappropriated as political funds.
- Huh Jeong, Minister of Social Affairs comments on an imminent problem on "Relief and Aid for the war victims and refugees."

May 9, Wednesday (April 4, by lunar calendar, 己酉日 Yellow Rooster) Very Clear
319 Day of the War

War Situation

- The ROK Army enters Ganseong.
- The UN Air Force bombards Sineuiju airport, and engages an air battle, the largest ever recorded shooting down 38 enemy fighters.

At Home
- President Syngman Rhee visits the front lines including Gapyeong and Cheongpyeong.
- Lee Si-yeong, Vice-President submits his resignation after accusing the Incidents of the National Defense Corps and Geochang .
- Korea, Japan and Hong Kong conclude an agreement on "the Exchange of postal stamps and parcels."

May 10, Thursday (April 5, by lunar calendar, 庚戌日 White Dog) Cloudy and Rainy
320 Day of the War

War Situation
- The main Forces of the Communist troops continue to retreat to the north of Moonsan.
- The ROK Army destroys 6,000 of the Communist troops which were trying to envelop Seoul from its western section.

At Home
- President Syngman Rhee invites representatives of all political parties, and accepts the resignation of Vice-President, Lee Si-yeong.
- The Bank of Korea and the commercial banks release the funds to enable farmers to purchase fertilizer and agricultural tools and machinery.
- The Bank of Korea issues its first edition of monthly research bulletin. (Represented by the research department of the Bank of Korea)

May 11, Friday (April 6, by lunar calendar, 辛亥日 White Pig) Cloudy and Clear
321 Day of the War

War Situation
- The Communist troops in the middle of front lines advance southward near Gapyeong.
- Lt. General Frank W. Milburn, Commander of the U.S. 1st Corps delivers a letter of encouragement to praise a heroic battle of the ROK 1st Division.

At Home
- The National Assembly accepts the resignation of Vice-President, Lee Si-yeong with a voting, 115 vs. 1.
- President gives credentials to the newly appointed Ministers of Defense, Agriculture including a special envoy minister to the Korean Embassy in the U.K.
- President Syngman Rhee has a press interview that he has no intention to run for next presidential election.

The refugees are on the line to register at the concerned authorities to receive grain rations(1951. 5. 12)

May 12, Saturday (April 7, by lunar calendar, 壬子日 Black Rat) Clear
322 Day of the War

War Situation
- The Communist troops begin to make a move in the south east of Hwacheon.
- The Chinese troops secure a beachhead in the south of Soyang River.
- The Communist troop employs smoke cover from the east of Gimhwa up to the north of Inje.

At Home
- The law(No. 195) regarding "the Abolition of the law on the National Defense Corps is proclaimed"
- The abolition of the law(No.196) and the Emergency Order (No.9) regarding "the Homeland Defense Order in emergency" are proclaimed.
- The Ministry of Education decides to permit Korean students to go to Japan for further studies.

May 13, Sunday (April 8, by lunar calendar, 癸丑日 Black Ox) Cloudy and Clear
323 Day of the War

War Situation

- The Communist troops advance southward by a large scale to secure beachheads in the south of Soyang River.
- The ROK Army repels offensives of Communist troops near Inje for 8 times.

At Home

- The National Assembly has an argument over the issue of the U.S. nationality held by the newly-appointed Minister of Home Affairs.
- The American hospital ship called "Haven" invites 400 of Korean orphans on the occasion of "Mother's Day".

May 14, Monday (April 9, by lunar calendar, 甲寅日 Blue Tiger) Cloudy
324 Day of the War

War Situation

- The UN Forces advance toward the northwest of Inje along the northern part of Soyang River, and engage a fierce combat with 2 battalions of the Communist troops.
- The UN Air Force bombards an assembly spot of the Communist troops in the north of Chuncheon killing 175.

At Home

- The National Assembly discusses the matter of nationality of Lee Soon-yong, Minister of Home Affairs.
- The plenary session of the National Assembly passes a resolution on "the investigation on Geochang Incident."
- The plenary session of the National Assembly adopts a bill for the election of Vice-President of the Nation on May 16".

Overseas

- The Council of Europe (Conseil de l' Europe) decides to establish two offices of refugee resettlement and the jobless relief.
- The New Fascist League finishes its conference.

May 15, Tuesday (April 10, by lunar calendar, 乙卯日 Blue Rabbit) Rainy and Cloudy
325 Day of the War

War Situation

- The Communist troops substantially increase their forces in the Chuncheon and Inje areas.
- Lee Gi-boong, Minister of Defense has 5 hours' conference with three Supreme Commanders of the ROK Army on board LCI near Busan.

At Home

- President Syngman Rhee issues a statement on the resignation of Vice-President, Lee

Si-yeong and reshuffle within the Government.
- Kim Seong-soo is elected as a Vice-President. : three times' voting with 78 out of 151 seats. The second runner, Lee Gap-seong secures 73 votes.
- The Ministry of Industry announces that all the trade transactions be dealt with on "letter of credit (L/C) basis except for Japan.

May 16, Wednesday (April 11, by lunar calendar, 丙辰日 Red Dragon) Cloudy
326 Day of the War

War Situation
- The Communist troops break into the front lines of the ROK Army in the south of Inje.
- The Chinese troops begin its second spring offensive.
- The Communist troops commit strong elements of troops into a beachhead in the south of Bukhan River.

At Home
- Chung Yoon-jo is appointed as a special aide for Prime Minister in charge of public relations and publicity.
- The Government asks the National Assembly to withhold the by-election for the Assembly members.
- The opening ceremony for the National T.B. Sanatorium for the Disabled Veterans takes place.
- The Government proclaims the enforcement of "the regulations on payment of compensation to informers who report or disclose" the underground money benefiting enemies."

May 17, Thursday (April 12, by lunar calendar, 丁巳日 Red Snake) Cloudy and Clear
327 Day of the War

War Situation
- The Chinese troops are estimated to be about 95,000. They begin to attack the front lines in the west.

At Home
- President Syngman Rhee asserts that the constitution be revised for the direct election of president and that the bicameral system be adopted.
- The United States Economic Cooperation Administration (ECA) authorizes the Army to purchase the goods to be supplied to the Republic of Korea in amount of U.S$6,956,000.
- The Bank of Korea closes its balance sheet for the first period (12 June 1950 and 31 March 1951) on 17 May marking the net profit 170 million won.

May 18, Friday (April 13, by lunar calendar, 戊午日 Yellow Horse) Cloudy and Clear
328 Day of the War

War Situation
- The UN Forces finish the retreat operation toward the south from the front lines.
- The ROK troops in the southwest of Inje retreat to their strategic defense lines, and 10,000 of the Communist troops start to penetrate.
- The Communist troops break into Uijeongbu.

At Home
- Vice-President Kim Seong-soo gives his inaugural address at the National Assembly.
- In response to a motion made by Vice-Speaker of the National Assembly, the issue over the nationality related to Lee Soon-yong, Minister of Home Affairs has been resolved (disregarded).
- Some private importers and public institutions import a large quantity of luxury items which can be produced locally. It arouses criticism.

Overseas
- The UN General Assembly passes a bill to prohibit the export of strategic items to China and the North Korea.
- The Dutch Army authority announces that 170 of voluntary troops will be dispatched to the South Korea at the end of the year.

May 19, Saturday (April 14, by lunar calendar, 己未日 Yellow Sheep) Clear and Rainy
329 Day of the War

War Situation
- The Communist troops break Cheongpyeong - Gapyeong and Hangye - Chuncheon keeping to advance to the south.

At Home
- The plenary session of the National Assembly agrees to ask the Government to protect and assure the personal livelihood of ex-vice president, Lee Si-yeong.
- The "Shinjeong Hoe" and "Gonghwa Club" in the National Assembly agree to integrate into one group.
- The National Police of Korea and the U.S. Counter-Intelligence Center agree to the mutual limit of criminal investigation of both sides.

May 20, Sunday (April 15, by lunar calendar, 庚申日 White Monkey) Clear and Cloudy
330 Day of the War

War Situation
- The ROK troops in the East Sea area retreat to the south of the 38th parallel.

- The 3rd Division of the Communist troops breaches the defense lines between Hangye and Poongam.

At Home
- The Ministry of Defense establishes the committee to investigate various matter related to military services.
- The Government awards badges for the wounded soldiers to the disabled veterans for the first time.
- Mayor of Busan City gives stern warnings to landlords that excessive rental charges and forced evacuation of tenants would be severely punished.

May 21, Monday (April 16, by lunar calendar, 辛酉日 White Rooster) Rainy
331 Day of the War

War Situation
- On the central front lines, the Chinese troops commit 4 Units to the north of Poongam to counter-attack the U.S. 2nd Division nearby.
- The 4th offensive of the Communist troops is frustrated on the 6th day, and they begin to retreat from the beachhead in the south of Namhan River.

At Home
- The National Assembly passes a bill related to "the Emergent Measures for War-damages."
- The Government asks the U.S. authorities concerned to implement the mid-term payment out of the UN credit.
- Paik Nak-jun, Minister of Education, asks the military authority concerned to return the school spaces which have been used for the military operations.
- J. Donald Kingsley, Director of UNKRA(UN Korean Reconstruction Agency) states that the total loss and damage caused by the Korea War stands at U.S.$ 500-1,000 million and the number of civilian casualties is about 1 million.

May 22, Tuesday (April 17, by lunar calendar, 壬戌日 Black Dog) Rainy and Cloudy
332 Day of the War

War Situation
- The Chinese troops abandon their beachhead near Cheongpyeong and retreat to the north.
- The Communist troops show a stronger resistance at the point of 15km north of Seoul.

At Home
- The National Assembly proposes to release 40,000 of the POWs who are from the South Korea.
- The Government proclaims "the law for issuance of patriotic lottery", and "the law for

special financial account."
- The Association of Customs Clearance Agencies is established to ensure the more effective administration of Customs Clearance.
- The postal service begins for POWs.

Overseas
- China issues a written refutation to oppose the prohibition of export to China.

May 23, Wednesday (April 18, by lunar calendar, 癸亥日 Black Pig) Very Clear
333 Day of the War

War Situation
- The Communist troops begin to take all-out retreats from the front lines.
- The UN Forces counter-attack from the central front lines capturing Hangye.

At Home
- The two National Assembly negotiating groups called "Shinjeong Hoe" and "Gonghwa Club" agree to be integrated into one single group called "Gonghwa Minjeong Hoe(Republic and Democratic Political Group).
- Lee Gi-boong, Minister of Defense asks the people to show deep sympathy and compassion toward the wounded veterans.

May 24, Thursday (April 19, by lunar calendar, 甲子日 Blue Rat) Clear and Cloudy
334 Day of the War

War Situation
- The UN Forces begin to take all out offensives without notable resistance from the hostile troops.
- The Armored Reconnaissance Units of the UN Forces breach the 38th parallel on the central front lines.

At Home
- President Syngman Rhee negates the alleged withdrawal of the American troops from Korean peninsula commenting on the necessity of reinforcing the U.S. troops.
- President Syngman Rhee gives instructions to withhold the removal of temporary housing facilities for the refugees for the time being.
- Kim Hoon, Minister of Industry announces measures to prevent the Korean export items from flowing into China.
- President Truman submits his special message to the Congress in connection with the foreign aid fund in amount of U.S$ 8.5 billion.

May 25, Friday (April 20, by lunar calendar, 乙丑日 Blue Ox) Cloudy

335 Day of the War

War Situation
- The UN Forces breach the 38th parallel from the northwest of Chuncheon.
- The UN Forces engage a fierce battle with the Communist troops in the northeast of Hangye.
- An advance unit of the ROK Army advances 16 km north of Gorangpo.

At Home
- Kodier, special aid in charge of administration to the UN Secretary General visits Korea.
- The Economic Reconstruction Committee reviews a draft of the reconstruction planning submitted by the Division of Material Mobilization of the Economic Planning Office.
- The Office of the Public Information issue an announcement to prohibit the import and use of Japanese musical records and albums.
- Seoul-Busan Railroad newly operates No. 7 and No.8 trains.

May 26, Saturday (April 21, by lunar calendar, 丙寅日 Red Tiger) Rainy
336 Day of the War

War Situation
- The ROK Army occupies Yangyang.
- The U.S. Forces and French troops make a fast penetration into Hongcheon and Inje securing their strong bridgeheads north of the 38th parallel.

At Home
- President Syngman Rhee awards "Military Distinguished Service medals" to the U.S. troops.
- The Government issues a strong message to oppose the cease-fire of the war.
- A ring of 100 armored guerillas attacks Cheongju city.
- The Ministry of Defense appoints the new top staff. : Major Gen. Yoo Jae-heung as Deputy Chief of Staff, Brig. Gen. Yang Guk-jin as Assistant Chief of Staff for administration, and Brig. Gen. Lee Jun-sik as Assistant Chief of Staff for operation(G-3).

Overseas
- The Swedish representative of the UN 3 member mediation committee reveals that he received a message from the Soviet Union which expresses its intention to respond to a negotiation table for peaceful solution of the Korean War.

May 27, Sunday (April 22, by lunar calendar, 丁卯日 Red Rabbit) Cloudy and Clear
337 Day of the War

War Situation
- The U.S. 2nd Division occupies Inje and Hyeonri.

- The Communist troops surrender near Hwacheon.

At Home
- The Ministry of Industry makes an urgent decision to supply water and electricity to Gimpo plain.
- The Bureau of the Property Custody announces the punishment for illegal transaction and lending of the Government-vested properties.

May 28, Monday (April 23, by lunar calendar, 戊辰日 Yellow Dragon) Clear
338 Day of the War

War Situation
- The Communist troops flee from Hwacheon.
- An American mother whose son was dispatched to the Korean War as the first UN officer leaves England for Korea and meets with his wounded son, Second Lt. Martin on the medical ship at Busan port.

At Home
- Defense Minister, Lee Gi-boong, makes a statement that initiative response is desired in case of drafting re-call.
- Joseon Minju-dang (Korean Democratic Party) issues a statement to oppose the cease fire.

May 29, Tuesday (April 24, by lunar calendar, 己巳日 Yellow Snake) Clear
339 Day of the War

War Situation
- The ROK 1st Corps occupies Ganseong.
- The Communist troops begin to show the most stubborn resistance for a week at Moonsan, Gorangpo and the south west of Yeoncheon.

At Home
- The Ministry of Commerce and Industry transfers all of the administration services (procedures and formalities) to the Customs Office and the Bank of Korea.
- Kim Chong-won, Director-General of the Civil Affairs Bureau of the South Geongsang Martial Law Command announces the requisition of all civilians' jeeps.

May 30, Wednesday (April 25, by lunar calendar, 庚午日 White Horse) Rainy
340 Day of the War

War Situation
- The UN Air Force destroys the Communist troops' large depot of military supplies in the north east of Gimhwa.

At Home

- Shin Ik-hee, Speaker of the National Assembly makes a statement that the general election in North Korea is expected on the occasion of the 1st anniversary for May 30 Election Day.
- The Ministry of Agriculture decides the total quantity and purchase price of rice: 400,000 seok (a seok is equivalent 5.12 U.S. bushels) at 23,000 won per seok.

Overseas

- The United States Government and Hitachi of Japan commit the largest contract ever made with the contract value in amount of U.S.$ 5 million(1.8 billion won).

May 31, Thursday (April 26, by lunar calendar, 辛未日 White Sheep) Very Clear
341 Day of the War

War Situation

- The UN Forces encircle 2,000 of the Communist troops between the roads of Inje-Hyeonri.
- The newly-arrived cruiser, Los Angeles of the U.S. Navy begins the night bombardment toward the military facilities of the Communist troops in Ganseong and Goseong.

At Home

- The 11th provisional session of the National Assembly convenes.
- A conference is held by the members' representatives of The Association of Daehan (Korean) Finance Institutions, severely criticizing the self-righteous and bureaucratic management of the Association.

June 1, Friday (April 27, by lunar calendar, 壬申日 Black Monkey)Very Clear
342 Day of the War

War Situation
- The friendly troops repel the strong resistance from the Communist troops in the north west of Hwacheon.
- The Chinese Corps d'elite breaks into the front lines, and tries to reinforce the defense of the areas such as Cheorwon, Gimhwa and Pyeonggang.
- The UN Forces establish the bridgeheads in the west of Yeoncheon, in the north of Jeokseong and Imjin River.

At Home
- President Syngman Rhee announces to nationalize 42 enterprises including some of major industries and finance corporations.
- Assault on an assemblyman, Cho Gwang-seop, takes place.
- The Office of Foreign Capital Management makes a decision on how to deal with imported relief goods.

June 2, Saturday (April 28, by lunar calendar, 癸酉日 Black Rooster) Very Clear
343 Day of the War

War Situation
- The ROK Army occupies Goseong.
- The UN troops counter-attack the strong resistance in the central front lines advancing 3.2km.

At Home
- The National Assembly adopts "the Multiple Exchange Rate System".
- The Civil Affairs Department decides to levy customs duties on the imported relief goods.
- The newly-appointed Commander of the 5th U.S. Air Force visits President Syngman Rhee with the U.S. Ambassador John L. Mucho.

Overseas
- President Truman signs "the Act to prohibit foreign aid to the countries exporting the strategic items to the Communist bloc."

June 3, Sunday (April 29, by lunar calendar, 甲戌日 Blue Dog) Clear, Cloudy and Rainy
344 Day of the War

War Situation

- The U.S. 1st Corps start "pile hammering" operation.
- The ROK Capital Division starts to engage a combat to capture Hyangrobong hill.

At Home
- The National Assembly agrees to inquire into the true state of the incident of Cheongju assault and to hold the people involved liable for the results.
- The total number of the smugglings disclosed by Busan Customs Office in May turns out to be 106 cases in amount of 202,000,000 won.

June 4, Monday (April 30, by lunar calendar, 乙亥日 Blue Pig) Clear and Cloudy
345 Day of the War

War Situation
- The Communist troops in Inje give up their beachhead due to air strikes launched by the U.S. Air Force.
- The UN Forces take the hills located in the north east of Yeongpyeong.
- Major Gen. Yoo Jai-heung is appointed as Chief of Staff of the ROK Army.

At Home
- Baik Doo-jin, Minister of Finance makes a statement to adopt "the Multiple Exchange Rate System."
- Kim Tae-seon, the National Police Chief announces that all of the police stations located in south of Chuncheon come to their normal operation.

June 5, Tuesday (May 1, by lunar calendar, 丙子日 Red Rat) Cloudy and Clear
346 Day of the War

War Situation
- The Communist troops begin to advance from the north-west of Yanggu.

At Home
- The plenary session of the National Assembly adopts a resolution to oppose the cease-fire.
- The Governor of Gyeonggi Province demands the residents living in the north of Han River to evacuate.

June 6, Wednesday (May 2, by lunar calendar, 丁丑日 Red Ox) Very Clear
347 Day of the War

War Situation
- The Communist troops strongly resist from the north east and north of Yanggu area.
- The Communist troops begin to retreat from the western front lines but continue to engage a limited battle in the rear lines.

At Home
- The telephone service opens between Busan and Seoul.
- The railway line opening is completed between Cheongryangri and Chuncheon.

Overseas
- The United States Government demands the Soviet Union to punish two Russian soldiers who killed an American soldier.

June 7, Thursday (May 3, by lunar calendar, 戊寅日 Yellow Tiger) Clear and Cloudy
348 Day of the War

War Situation
- The UN fleets bombard the port of Wonsan.
- The U.S. Air Force launches heavy bombing on the railway system near Sariwon-Haeju.

At Home
- President Syngman Rhee states that the Government would deal with the export of iron scraps exclusively.
- The National Assembly agrees with the officials concerned of the Ministry of Defense and the Ministry of Home Affairs on how to deal with the punishment in connection with so-called "Cheongju Incident".
- Kim Seok-gwan, Minister of Transportation states that recovery of railway system for normal operation is done in 90%.

June 8, Friday (May 4, by lunar calendar, 己卯日 Yellow Rabbit) Very Clear
349 Day of the War

War Situation
- The ROK 7th Division begins to engage a battle in Gunryang-hyun.
- The Communist troops weaken their delaying operation in the mid-eastern front lines and begin to retreat.

At Home
- President Syngman Rhee issues a firm statement to oppose the cease fire at 38th parallel.
- President Syngman Rhee, Defense Minister and the ROK Navy Chief of Staff visit the refugee camps at Geoje Island.
- The Eighth U.S. Army demands the withdrawal and retreat to the residents living in the north of Han River except for Seoul citizens.

June 9, Saturday (May 5, by lunar calendar, 庚辰日 White Dragon) Very Clear
350 Day of the War

War Situation

The U.S. 7th Infantry Division is engaged in a battle to advance to Wyoming lines on the north of Jeokgeun Mountain. (1951. 6. 9)

- The U.S. 9th Corps occupies the left half of the Wyoming Line.
- The Communist troops abandon the Iron Triangle (Cheorwon, Gimhwa and Pyeonggang) and begin to retreat to Geumseong.

At Home
- President Syngman Rhee has a press interview to speak about opposing the cease fire at the 38th parallel.
- The National Assembly has a heated argument over the disbandment of "The Patriotic League for Nation-saving Mobilization".
- The Office of Public Information (The Special Committee for Propaganda Counter- measures) makes decision on ritual formalities related to "the Day of National Crisis."
- Prime Minister Jang Myeon visits the western front lines in Seoul, Daejeon and Daegu.

Overseas
- The United States Secretary of State gives the 6th witness saying that President Truman ordered him to examine and collect various information and how to aid the Taiwan Government.

June 10, Sunday (May 6, by lunar calendar, 辛巳日 White Snake) Clear and Cloudy
351 Day of the War

War Situation

- Van Fleet, Commander of the Eighth U.S. Army announces the occupation of Cheorwon and Gimhwa.
- The ROK Army counter-attacks the Communist troops and regains Ganseong.
- The strong resistance by the hostile troops continues in the areas of Yanggu and Hwacheon.

At Home

- The telephone lines open between Seoul and Suwon.
- The Provost Martial of the Eighth U.S. Army arrests a ring of theft including 5 American soldiers and one Korean 1st Lieutenant for the military goods and supplies, and announces that they would be brought to the military court for punishment.

June 11, Monday (May 7, by lunar calendar, 壬午日 Black Horse) Cloudy and Clear
352 Day of the War

War Situation

- The U.S. 9th Corps occupies the right half of the Wyoming Line.
- The resistance by the Communist troops weakens in the areas of the northern zones of Hwacheon and Yanggu.

At Home

- Proclamation No.15 is announced by the Cabinet on "the indefinite postponement of the by-election for the National Assembly members."
- Prime Minister Jang Myeon discusses with John B. Coulter, Commander of the Eighth U.S. Army on the return of the Korean farmers to their farm lands in the north of Han River.
- Byun Young-tae, Minister of Foreign Affairs asserts in the National Assembly that the rumored cease-fire at the 38th parallel is groundless.

June 12, Tuesday (May 8, by lunar calendar, 癸未日 Black Sheep) Cloudy and Clear
353 Day of the War

War Situation

- The UN troops move from Cheorwon and support the friendly Forces in Gimhwa advancing 3km after repelling the residual elements of the Communist troops.
- The UN Forces in Gimhwa zone counter-attack the Communist elements which are in retreat toward Geumgsung.

At Home

- Prime Minister Jang Myeon has a press interview on the increase of foreign exchange rate and the rumored cease-fire.
  : Impossible to return to Seoul and the rumor of cease-fire at the 38th parallel is absolutely

groundless expressing a hope of advancing to the border in the north. The official exchange rate between Korean won and U.S. dollar is unchangeable.

June 13, Wednesday (May 9, by lunar calendar, 甲申日 Blue Monkey) Very Clear
354 Day of the War

War Situation
- The UN troops begin to launch reconnoitering operations in the area of Imjin River.
- Commander of the Eighth U.S. Army, Gen. Van Fleet states about the over-all status of the front lines.
  - : The UN Forces have sufficient military power. The enemy has lost a capability to conquer Seoul. There is, however, a possibility that the Communist troops might have established their beachheads beyond the north of Imjin River.

At Home
- President Syngman Rhee enters Seoul to look around the status of recovery asserting that the Government would return to Seoul immediately after the general conditions permit and expresses his satisfaction on the morale of the soldiers on the front lines. The return to Seoul would be done when food and other preparations are readily available.

Overseas
- The strategic conference between North Korea, China and the Soviet Union takes place between June 13 and 14, and they come to agreement on the cease fire at the 38th parallel.

June 14, Thursday (May 10, by lunar calendar 乙酉日 Blue Rooster) Cloudy
355 Day of the War

War Situation
- The ROK Army repels the 2nd offensive of the Communist troops in the north of Ganseong.
- The Air Force bombs the airports in Suncheon and Sariwon areas.

At Home
- President Syngman Rhee visits the U.S. hospital ship called "Haven"(which deals with obstinate diseases.)
- The evacuation order to the people living in the north of Han River is lifted.

June 15, Friday (May 11, by lunar calendar, 丙戌日 Yellow Dog) Clear
356 Day of the War

War Situation
- The ROK Army counter-attacks the Communist troops in the north of Ganseong for three days repelling them under cover of the UN fleets.

- The Communist troops in the forest zone near Gimhwa and Hangye attack the UN troops in advancing operation.

At Home
- The Military authority lifts the evacuation order to the farmers living in the north of Han River.
- The railroad services start to operate up to Chuncheon, Dongdoocheon and Moonsan.

June 16, Saturday (May 12, by lunar calendar, 丁亥日 Red Pig) Cloudy and Clear
357 Day of the War

War Situation
- The advancing Forces of the ROK Army are frustrated by a strong resistance from the Communist troops in the south of Geumseong.
- The UN Forces engage a number of sporadic combats with the enemy troops in the north west of Yeoncheon area.

At Home
- The Ministry of Transportation announces the completion of repairing the railway systen below the south of the 38th parallel.
- The railroad services start to operate up to Moonsan, Dongdoocheon and Chuncheon.

Overseas
- The Central Committee of the Chinese Communist Party gives instructions and asks for necessary cooperation in connection with sending the delegation of entertainment and support to North Korea.

June 17, Sunday (May 13, by lunar calendar, 戊子日 Yellow Rat) Very Clear
358 Day of the War

War Situation
- The Communist Forces show a desperate resistance to protect Geumseong.
- The U.S. 10th Corps occupies the Kansas Lines.

At Home
- The Chairman of the Foreign Affairs Committee of the National Assembly severely refutes so called "the newly- proposed plan" for cease-fire.
- In Daegu, a big rally to invoke the opposition for the cease fire takes place.
- Chung Ill-kwon, Chief of Staff of the ROK Joint Army-Navy-Air Forces, announces a plan to send the military officers to the U.S. military schools.

June 18, Monday (May 14, by lunar calendar, 己丑日 Yellow Ox) Clear
359 Day of the War

War Situation

- The friendly Ground and Air Forces jointly repel the Communist troops which penetrate into the west of Ganseong.
- The UN troops cross the 38th parallel from Gorangpo area.

At Home

- The number of patients contaminated by epidemics sharply increases.
- The consumer price index of Busan is 6.5 times higher than that of pre-war period and 21.5 times higher than that of the year 1947.

June 19, Tuesday (May 15, by lunar calendar, 庚寅日 White Tiger) Cloudy and Rainy
360 Day of the War

War Situation

- The UN troops fight their way despite heavy shell-firing done by the Communist troops and make the deepest penetration ever launched in the year.
- The Communist troops stop to retreat at the new outposts in Gimhwa and in the north of Cheorwon.

At Home

- Brig. Gen. Kwon Joon, ex-Commander of the 87th Infantry Division of the National Government of China (Taiwan)'s Army interviews with POW on the front lines. He said that 60 % of the Chinese troops used to serve for the National Government of China (Taiwan)'s Army and they are still willing to fight for Generalissimo Chiang Kai Shek.

June 20, Wednesday (May 16, by lunar calendar, 辛卯日 White Rabbit) Clear and Cloudy
361 Day of the War

War Situation

- The resistance by the Communist troops weakens in the north of Wontong.

At Home

- The UN Forces Command replaces MPC(Military Payment Certificate) with the new certificates which put the black market into a great disarray and the old MPC's price shows a big drop.
- The Central Committee of Jomin-dang(Korean Democratic Party) decides to make a plan on the administration execution policy and procedures in the occupied North Korea area.

June 21, Thursday (May 17, by lunar calendar, 壬辰日 Black Dragon) Rainy
362 Day of the War

War Situation

- The friendly Forces gain an advantageous position after a battle in the south of Goseong.

- The Communist troops continue to make movements in the northeast of Hwacheon and near Mt. Baekam.
- The UN Tank Units enter Kaesong.

At Home

- The Special Task Mission Team arrests a Communist guerilla who secretly breaks into the building of the National Assembly.

June 22, Friday (May 18, by lunar calendar, 癸巳日 Black Snake) Clear and Cloudy
363 Day of the War

War Situation

- The 2nd offensive attempted by the Communist troops is blocked in the north of Inje.
- A Medical Support Unit of Norway arrives in Korea.

At Home

- Kim Hoon, Minister of Commerce and Industry says that the thermal power plants located in Dangin-ri and Susaek are under repair for normal operation.
- The rumor that the strategic materials to be used for electricity are lost is groundless.
- Prime Minister Jang Myeon sends a letter requesting Shin Ik-hee, Speaker of the National Assembly to request the witness hearing by the 11 assemblymen in connection with the Incident of National Defense Corps.

Overseas

- 16 countries engaged in the Korea agree not to issue any joint statement on the occasion of war break-out day (25 June).
- Italy agrees to join the UN member countries of the Western Europe on the prohibition of export to North Korea and China.

June 23, Saturday (May 19, by lunar calendar, 甲午日 Blue Horse) Clear and Cloudy
364 Day of the War

War Situation

- The Communist troops show much stronger resistance on all of the front lines.
- The UN Air Force launches the first bombing on Supoong Dam in the northern part of North Korea.

At Home

- Son Won-il, the ROK Naval Chief of Staff, states that intensive crackdown will be carried out on smuggling vessels.
- Lee Soon-yong, Minister of Home Affairs says that refugees' returning to Seoul is too early and solicits their patience until further notice.

June 24, Sunday (May 20, by lunar calendar, 乙未日 Blue Sheep) Cloudy and Clear
365 Day of the War

War Situation
- Fierce battles take place on all front lines, the Communist troops appearing on the western zone.
- The UNC troops retreat after a half day's fierce battle on the hills near Pyeonggang.

At Home
- President Syngman Rhee nominates Major General Lee Jong-chan as Chief of Staff of the ROK Army and Commander of Martial Law.
- UNKURC announces the commencement of reconstruction project for Korea.

June 25, Monday (May 21, by lunar calendar, 丙申日 Red Monkey) Cloudy and Clear
366 Day of the War

War Situation
- The Communist troops launch fierce reconnoitering operations of mini-scale on all front lines.
- The Reconnaissance Units meet little confrontation on the western front lines.

At Home
- The events for War Memorial Day (the first year) take place in various places.
- The anti-Communist rally to remind the people of Korean War is held at Choongmuro Plaza in Busan.

June 26, Tuesday (May 22, by lunar calendar, 丁酉日 Red Rooster) Clear
367 Day of the War

War Situation
- The Reconnaissance Units of the troops are engaged in battles in the area of Ganseong.
- The UN Forces retreat from the hills in the northeast of Gimhwa but regain them.

At Home
- President Syngman Rhee meets with General Matthew B. Ridgway, Supreme Commander of the UN Forces.
- The Government convenes an urgent Cabinet Meeting to discuss the cease fire proposal by the U.S.S.R.

June 27, Wednesday (May 23, by lunar calendar, 戊戌日 Yellow Dog) Clear and Cloudy
368 Day of the War

War Situation
- The Reconnaissance Units of the UN Forces confront with strong resistance from the

Communist troops in the areas of Inje.

At Home
- The Ministry of Home Affairs states that necessary aid and relief are prepared for about 200,000 North Korean refugees who are expected to evacuate to the south due to the advancing of the UN Forces to the north.
- The Director of the Public Information Office gives warnings about the groundless rumor related to the cease fire.

June 28, Thursday (May 24, by lunar calendar, 己亥日 Yellow Pig) Clear
369 Day of the War

War Situation
- The friendly troops repel the Communist troops in the southwest of Ganseong.
- Small scale of battles takes place in Yanggu.

At Home
- Minkukdang (Democratic National Party) issues a statement to oppose the negotiation for the Armistice agreement.
- Radio Pyongyang reports that the cease fire would be accepted on the condition of recovering the 38th parallel to the original state before the war.

June 29, Friday (May 25, by lunar calendar, 庚子日 White Rat) Clear
370 Day of the War

War Situation
- All of the front lines come to a state of lull.
- The Command of the UN Forces proposes the cease- fire to the Communist troops.

At Home
- The plenary session of the National Assembly unanimously passes a resolution to oppose the cease-fire at the 38th parallel.

June 30, Saturday (May 26, by lunar calendar, 辛丑日 White Ox) Very Clear
371 Day of the War

War Situation
- The Reconnaissance Units of the friendly troops engage many battles in Ganseong area.
- The UN Forces retreat from the hills in the northeast of Gimhwa but regain them.

At Home
- President Syngman Rhee issues a statement to oppose the cease-fire negotiation.

Overseas
- The UN Forces issues a memorandum. : The authorities concerned is closely examining

the proposal made by Malik, and the retreat of any troops from the 38th parallel is an act of profiting the enemy.
- A UK Government high-level official says that the UN troop is building the bridgeheads for permanent use on the 38th parallel.

July 1, Sunday (May 27, by lunar calendar, 壬寅日 Black Tiger) Cloudy
372 Day of the War

War Situation
- The fleets of the UN Navy and the UN Air Force jointly launch shelling on Mongeum-po area on the western coast.

At Home
- The nationwide rally for "the national unification and no ceasefire at the 38th parallel" takes place in Busan.
- The Bank of Korea(BOK) begins the exchange service for the bank notes issued by BOK and the North Korean Bank.
- The Ministry of Education establishes an intergrated school which can accommodate children remaining in Seoul.

Overseas
- The U.S. National Peace Convention sponsored by the State of Georgia issues a declaration of basic principles including the cease- fire issue on the Korean peninsula.
- Yang Yu-chan, Korean Ambassador to the U.S. delivers to the U.S. State Department the Korean Government's message which includes 5 major principles for the cease-fire issue.

July 2, Monday (May 28, by lunar calendar, 癸卯日 Black Rabbit) Clear and Rainy
373 Day of the War

War Situation
- The UN Forces engage 3 hour battle with a platoon of the Communist troops in the northeast of Gimhwa and repel them.
- The Police Force of the South Jeolla Province launches, with support by jet fighters, a mop-up operation in a hangout of the Communist guerilla in Mt. Baeka killing 77.

At Home
- President Syngman Rhee convenes an urgent Cabinet Meeting at his temporary residence, and discusses how to deal with and respond to the cease-fire proposal by the Communist side.
- The National Assembly passes a recommendation to the Government requesting to send a delegation to the UN in order to oppose the cease-fire at the 38th parallel.

July 3, Tuesday (May 29, by lunar calendar, 甲辰日 Blue Dragon) Rainy, Windy and Clear
374 Day of the War

War Situation
- The UN Forces occupies several important hills of the Iron Triangle after a fierce battle.

At Home
- President Syngman Rhee has a press interview saying that the Korean people do want and need a peace, but they don't accept any kind of cease-fire at the 38th parallel.
- President Syngman Rhee sends a telegram to President Truman to express the opposition of cease-fire at the 38th parallel.

July 4, Wednesday (June 1, by lunar calendar, 乙巳日 Blue Snake) Cloudy and Windy
375 Day of the War

War Situation
- A small scale of battle takes place in the northeast of Inje.
- The Communist troops respond to the proposal for the cease-fire meeting suggesting the preliminary meeting to be held on July 8 at Kaesong.

At Home
- President Syngman Rhee sends the congratulatory messages to President of the U.S. and President of the Philippines on the occasion of their Independence Day.
- The U.S. Ambassador to the South Korea, Mucho expresses his worries about the exclusion of the Korean interests in "the Treaty of Peace" between U.S. and Japan.

July 5, Thursday (June 2, by lunar calendar, 丙午日 Red Horse) Cloudy and Rainy
376 Day of the War

War Situation
- The maneuvering Force of the UN troops begins to retreat from the northern section of the Iron Triangle (1.2 km from the south of Pyeonggang) on the central front lines.
- Gen. Ridgway, Supreme Commander of the UN Forces agrees on the cease-fire meeting to be held on the 8th of July demanding the protection of 3 liaison officers and 2 interpreters.

At Home
- The National Assembly exchanges a series of heated interpellation over the issue of cease-fire.
- Shin Ik-hee, the Speaker of the National Assembly gives a lecture on the current situation and says that the people should not be misled by the rumor on cease-fire.

July 6, Friday (June 3, by lunar calendar, 丁未日 Red Sheep) Cloudy and Clear
377 Day of the War

War Situation

- The port of Wonsan is continually under bombardment of the UN warships (up to the 141st day)
- George Stratemyer, Commander of the Far East Air Forces order the stop of bombing operation within the 8 km of Kaesong and on the passage of the Communist delegation after 4 p.m. of the July 4 when the Communist delegation is expected to arrive for the cease-fire talk.

At Home
- The student soldiers of the ROK 3887 Unit donates U.S.$ 210,000 to the ROK Army's Bureau of Information and Education for the purpose of scholarship fund for the student in the rear areas.
- The Radio Communication Station of the ROK Army is established in Seoul.

July 7, Saturday (June 4, by lunar calendar, 戊申日 Yellow Monkey) Cloudy
378 Day of the War

War Situation
- On the front lines, minor confrontations take place sporadically.
- The UN warship and carrier-based planes severely bombard the port of Wonsan.

At Home
- The first class of the Armor School and the third class of the Officer Candidate School have a joint graduation ceremony at the ROK Army Infantry School in Donghae.
- Shin Sung-mo, the newly- appointed Korean Representative to Japan leaves for Tokyo to take his new office.

Overseas
- Ales Kiro, Greek representative to the United Nations report to the UN that the strength of the Greek troops engaged in the Korean War would be doubled from one battalion to 2 battalions.

July 8, Sunday (June 5, by lunar calendar, 己酉日 Yellow Rooster) Rainy, Windy and Rainy
379 Day of the War

War Situation
- The preliminary meeting for the armistice agreement is finished.
  : the meeting takes place at Naebong-jang with the presence of the Chief of UN liaison officers, Colonel of the U.S. Air Force, Andrew J. Kinney, Colonel of the U.S. Marine, James Murray, Lt. Col. Lee Soo-young of the ROK Army together with the delegation of the Communist side such as Col. Chang Chun-san of the North Korean Army, Chai Cheng-won, the Chinese liaison officer and Kim Il-pa from the North Korean delegation.
- The Truce delegation agrees to have a main session on the 10th at Kaesong.

At Home

- Governor of the New Jersey State, Dewy, visits President Syngman Rhee.

July 9, Monday (June 6, by lunar calendar, 庚戌日 White Dog) Rainy, Windy and Rainy
380 Day of the War

War Situation

- The UN Forces drive away the stubborn resistance of the Communist troops in the south of Geumseong, advancing 4,828 m.
- Governor of the State of New Jersey, Dewy, visits the front lines and air-inspects the outposts of the Communist troops.

At Home

- The Government Legislation Office examines the draft law of Industrial Bank which includes integration of commercial bank.
- The South Gyeongsang Province decides to drive a big scale rice-saving campaign.

July 10, Tuesday (June 7, by lunar calendar, 辛亥日 White Pig) Rainy, Windy and Cloudy
381 Day of the War

War Situation

- Minor crashes are often noted on the front lines.
- The main conditions for the Truce agreement proposed by Nam II, Chief of the North Korean delegation: 1) All foreign troops should withdraw. 2) The 10 km of the demilitarized zone should be made. 3) Exchange of POWs.

At Home

- Lee Chol-won, the Director of the Office of Public Information emphasizes the unification of the Korean peninsula by free election in North Korea in his comment on the rumored coalition Government between the two Koreas.
- In Masan, a rally is held by the Association of the Patriotic organizations to oppose the truce moves.
- In Busan, many anti-truce demonstrations take place.

Overseas

- A Chinese daily newspaper called "Ta Kung Pao (Daegongbo in Korean, 大公報)" in Hong Kong reports on the news related to the Korean truce: the Communist delegation demands the withdrawal of the UN Forces to the south of the 38th parallel and the setting-up of the demilitarized zone.

July 11, Wednesday (June 8, by lunar calendar, 壬子日 Black Rat) Cloudy, Windy and Rainy
382 Day of the War

War Situation
- The UN Air Force attacks an airport and 4 facilities in Pyongyang in the night.
- The agreement is made in regard to the detailed procedures of the truce meetings.

At Home
- The Cheif Commanders of the ROK Army, Navy and Air Force and Maj. Gen. Baik Seon-youp have a conference at Munsan.
- The Seoul City and the association of all town and district offices hold a united rally to oppose the truce moves and to advocate the national unification.
- The Daehan (Korean) Youth League takes to the street to oppose the truce moves.

July 12, Thursday (June 9, by lunar calendar, 癸丑日 Black Ox) Rainy and Cloudy
383 Day of the War

War Situation
- The UN Air Force fighter-bombers launch the repeated bombings against Soonan, Hwnagju, Sinanju, Sinmak and Pyongyang including the airports.

At Home
- The National Assembly passes a bill related to "the law on jurisdiction of military court."
- Gukmin Hoe (the National Association) and 5 other associations hold street march advocating the completion of national unification.

July 13, Friday (June 10, by lunar calendar, 甲寅日 Blue tiger) Rainy
384 Day of the War

War Situation
- The UN Forces repulse the fierce resistance of the enemy in the southeast of Geumseong.
- The UN Air Force fighter-bombers launch the repeated night-bombings against Soonan, Hwnagju, Sinanju and Sinmak including the airports.

At Home
- Seoul-Busan railroad service begins to operate once a day.

July 14, Saturday (June 11, by lunar calendar, 乙卯日 Blue Rabbit) Rainy
385 Day of the War

War Situation
- The UN Forces repel the counter-offensive of the enemy troops in Yuseong and Yanggu.
- The U.S. Marine fleets destroy the command posts of the 4 Communist regiments.

At Home
- In Busan, a big nationwide rally takes place adopting a resolution to oppose the truce agreement.

- UNKRA(UN Korean Reconstruction Agency) issues a statement on its plan of investment in amount of U.S.$ 250,000,000 for the reconstruction of Korea.

July 15, Sunday (June 12, by lunar calendar, 丙辰日 Red Dragon) Rainy and Cloudy
386 Day of the War

War Situation
- The UN fleets launch high-powered bombings toward 4 ports in the east coast.
- The Communist delegations for the truce negotiation basically agree on the 3 principles proposed by the UN delegation, such as neutralization of 3.1km radius of Kaesong and the unlimited use of access roads.

At Home
- It is reported that a representative of the U.S. military delegation sent a message to the Korean Government that indicates that the demonstrations by the Korean people would be harmful to the on-going armistice negotiations.

July 16, Monday (June 13, by lunar calendar, 丁巳日 Red Snake) Rainy and Cloudy
387 Day of the War

War Situation
- The fighter-bombers of the U.S. 5th Air Squadron launch the concentrated bombings against the supply access roads of the Communist troops.
- The Communist delegation for the truce negotiation demands to secure the neutralization of the conference place as agreed upon.

At Home
- The National Assembly has a secret hearing from the prime minister about the Government's policy and attitude toward the Peace Treaty with Japan.
- The Radio Pyongyang airs a statement to urge the withdrawal of all foreign troops from the Korean peninsula.

July 17, Tuesday (June 14, by lunar calendar, 戊午日 Yellow Horse) Cloudy and Clear
388 Day of the War

War Situation
- The UN fleets continue to bombard the port of Wonsan.
- The 5th truce negotiation takes place at Kaesong.

At Home
- Many rallies to oppose the truce negotiation are held throughout the country.
- The North Korean refugees in Geoje Island have a mass rally to oppose the armistice.

Overseas

ROK Sergeant eats lunch at abandoned house in Munsan (1951. 7. 17)

- The Iran Government informs to the UN that they would prohibit the export of strategic items to China.
- The Supreme Assembly of the Philippines determines to oppose the Peace Treaty with

Japan concluded by the Committee of the Peace Treaty.

July 18, Wednesday (June 15, by lunar calendar, 己未日 Yellow Sheep) Clear
389 Day of the War

War Situation
- The UN fleets with the support of the Air Force bombard the shore batteries of Wonsan port.
- The delegations for Truce negotiation agree upon the two main points on meeting proceedings.

At Home
- The Government determines to pay the farmers for the purchase of crops in cash on the spot.
- Baik Doo-jin, the Minister of Finance and Lim Mun-hwang, the Minister of Agriculture answered at the Assembly that the Government is ready to provide the farmers with cash payment.
- In relation to the truce negotiations, the Japanese Press Corps visits Korea for the first time since Korea was liberated.

July 19, Thursday (June 16, by lunar calendar, 庚申日 White Monkey) Rainy, Windy and Rainy
390 Day of the War

War Situation
- The U.S. Air Force launches 470 sorties despite the bad weather, bombing the main logistic depots of the Communist troops including bridges.
- The main arguing point of the 7th Truce negotiation table is reported to be the withdrawal of every country's troops.

At Home
- The National Assembly adopts a recommendation to the Government requesting to send a diplomatic delegation to the U.S. and pursue diplomatically the revision of article 4(concerning the reverted properties) of the draft Peace Treaty with Japan.
- Minkuk-dang (the Peoples' Party) issues a statement to demand the revision of the article 4 (related to the issue of reverted properties) of the draft Peace Treaty with Japan.

July 20, Friday (June 17, by lunar calendar, 辛酉日 White Rooster) Rainy, Windy and Rainy
391 Day of the War

War Situation
- The reconnaissance planes of the UN Forces engage long hours' gun firing with the Communist troops in Yanggu, Inje and Ganseong.

- B29 squadron raider-bombs the railway facilities of Gowon and logistics center of Hamheung.

At Home
- The Ministry of Defense and the Ministry of Home Affairs jointly begin the repair works of the national roads throughout the South and North Gyeongsang Provinces.
- The Headquarters of the Defense Ministry and all the branch offices move to the Sujeong Elementary School in Busan as a new integrated office building.

Overseas
- The 10 countries of the UN dispatching troops in the Korean war support the statement issued by Dean Acheson, Secretary of State on the previous day refusing to discuss the withdrawal of foreign troops from Korea on the Truce negotiation table.
- The United States and the United Kingdom send the invitation to 49 countries including the U.S.S.R to the signing ceremony of the Peace Treaty with Japan.

July 21, Saturday (June 18, by lunar calendar, 壬戌日 Black Dog) Rainy, Windy and Cloudy
392 Day of the War

War Situation
- All of the front lines show no particular confrontation.
- The 8th meeting for the truce negotiation takes place at Kaesong.

At Home
- Lee Cheol-won, the Director of the Office of Public Information strongly supports the statement of Dean Acheson, Secretary of State advocating the continued presence of the UN Forces until the Chinese troops are withdrawn and the invaders are driven out.

July 22, Sunday (June 19, by lunar calendar, 癸亥日 Black Pig) Rainy, Windy and Cloudy
393 Day of the War

War Situation
- On the eastern front lines, the attack by the reconnaissance unit of the Communist troops is repelled.
- B29 squadron drops more than 2,500 tons' bombs destroying Hwangju and Sariwon airport.

July 23, Monday (June 20, by lunar calendar, 甲子日 Blue Rat) Cloudy, Windy and Clear
394 Day of the War

War Situation
- The UN Forces occupies a hill of target in the south of Geumseong.
- The UN Air Force launches the bombing in the night targeting Hwangju and the airport of

Yeongyoo including Anju and supply depot of the Communist troops in Jaeryeong.

At Home

- The National Assembly issues a statement to support the statement of Dean Acheson, the U.S. Secretary of State regarding the withdrawal of the foreign troops from Korea and to advocate the unification of Korean peninsula under the sovereignty of the Republic of Korea.

July 24, Tuesday (June 21, by lunar calendar, 乙丑日 Blue Ox) Clear
395 Day of the War

War Situation

- A fierce battle takes place in the southwest of Kaesong.
- The UN Forces repels the 8 time attacks by the reconnaissance Units of the Communist troops in the mid-east front lines.

At Home

- Lee Gi-boong, the Minister of Defense and Byun Young-tae, the Minister of Foreign Affairs arrive in Seoul to have consultation before the resumption of negotiations.
- The Pyongyang Broadcasting asserts that the issue of the U.S. troops' withdrawal be included on the agenda for the Truce agreement.

July 25, Wednesday (June 22, by lunar calendar, 丙寅日 Red Tiger) Clear
396 Day of the War

War Situation

- The advance unit of the UN troops occupies their target position north of Gorang-po.
- The British light cruiser and the U.S. destroyer launch the bombarding on the port of Wonsan.
- The 9th session for the truce negotiation takes place.

At Home

- The Police Chief of South Gyeongsang Province issues a statement about the strict application and control of "the registration system for the accommodation facilities such as hotel and inn" as well as much more intensive control of food pricing.
- The Korean Disabled Veterans Association files a petition concerning the Government's positive support for relief and aid.

Overseas

- The Philippines Committee on Peace Treaty decides to reject the proposed draft of Peace Treaty with Japan.
- The Indonesian Government announces that they would ask the U.S.A to deal with the matter of reparation.

July 26, Thursday (June 23, by lunar calendar, 丁卯日 Red Rabbit) Clear
397 Day of the War

War Situation

- The UN Air Force launches bombing on Gangdong, Suncheon, Pyongyang and Wonsan including the enemy's 8 bases of antiaircraft artillery.
- The 10th meeting for the truce agreement takes place at Kaesong and comes to agreement on 5 major items as stated below. :
  1) Adoption of agenda and schedule.
  2) Under the condition of non-hostile activities, the demilitarized zone would be set up.
  3) Detailed procedures and to ensure the cease-fire including the establishment of the surveillance and supervisory control agency by defining its function, rights and authority.
  4) All matters relevant to the exchange of POWs.
  5) Withdrawal of the foreign troops and peaceful solutions of the Korean peninsula together with follow-up recommendations to be made to each Government concerned.

At Home

- Pyongyang Broadcasting reports on the necessity of the foreign troops' withdrawal.

July 27, Friday (June 24, by lunar calendar, 戊辰日 Yellow Dragon) Clear, Windy and Clear
398 Day of the War

War Situation

- Fierce battles take place at the northeast of Yanggu and Inje.
- The UN Air Force launches bombing against the motor vehicles unit of the enemy troops on numerous positions including the military depots of Youngmi-dong and Yangduck.
- The spokesman of the UN Forces, Brig. Gen. Nichols says that the exchange of POWs includes 75 civilians.

At Home

- The plenary session of the National Assembly has heated argument over the issue of conscription system in presence of the Vice-Minister of Defense.
- The Government and UNKRA have consultation on how to execute and proceed with the reconstruction programs.
- The UN Korean Unification and Reconstruction Committee consents to the UNKRA's plan.

July 28, Saturday (June 25, by lunar calendar, 己巳日 Yellow Snake) Clear, Windy and Clear
399 Day of the War

War Situation

- Heavy battles are exchanged at the northeast of Yanggu.
- No progress is made at the 12th meeting for the Truce agreement.

At Home

- The National Assembly has an interpellation with the Government on the issues of the military affairs administration and the security measures in the rear regions.
- The demonstrators in Seoul take to the street to oppose the truce agreement.
- The Central Court-martial Jurisdiction begins the trials in relation with "the Incident of Geochang Massacre of the Civilians."

July 29, Sunday (June 26, by lunar calendar, 庚午日 White Horse) Clear, Cloudy and Clear
400 Day of the War

War Situation

- The squadron of UN Air Force launches the nocturnal air-attack on Pyongyang and Wonsan including the enemy's motor vehicle unit operating on the access road.

At Home

- Major general Baik Seon-youp of the UN delegation for the Truce negotiation visits Lee Gi-boong, the Minister of Defense in Seoul.
- The Law No. 210 is proclaimed concerning "the jurisdiction of the martial court."

July 30, Monday (June 27, by lunar calendar, 辛未日 White Sheep) Cloudy, Clear and Cloudy
401 Day of the War

War Situation

- The 14th meeting for the Armistice agreement is held at Kaesong.
- The both representatives of the Armistice negotiation parties continue to hold on their own positions related to the establishment of demilitarized zones.

At Home

- Kim Dong-seong of the National Assembly and some other lawmakers suggest to the Government that refugees camps be established in Kanghwa Island.
- The National Alliance of the Patriotic Associations holds a mass rally in Busan demanding the revision of the draft Peace Treaty with Japan.

Overseas

- The first meeting of the UN Special Committee takes place to discuss the issue of the missing POWs.
- The UN Economic and Social Council holds the 13th meeting at Geneva.

July 31, Tuesday (June 28, by lunar calendar, 壬申日 Black Monkey) Clear
402 Day of the War

War Situation

- The UN Air Force bombs Pyongyang.

- The Civilian Affairs and Information Bureau of the UN Forces announces its official opinion on the matter of demarcation line (de-militarized zone -DMZ) emphasizing on the importance of setting -up of the DMZ on what the front lines currently stand at.

At Home
- The Cabinet Meeting decides to establish a refugees' camp directly operated by the Government in Ganghwa Island for the refugees in the region of the Imjin River.
- 1.2 million refugees assemble in Gyeonggi Province.
- Robert T. Oliver, special advisor to President Syngman Rhee suggests to the Korean Government to keep silent with regard to the armistice negotiation.

August 1, Wednesday (June 29, by lunar calendar, 癸酉日 Black Rooster) Cloudy and Clear
403 Day of the War

War Situation
- The negotiation for the Armistice agreement shows no progress, with both parties sticking to their own basic positions.
- Vice Admiral Joy C. Turner, representative of the UN troops for the Armistice negotiation asserts that fair and realistic demarcation lines be established. He refutes the proposed idea of setting DMZ on the 38th parallel line by quoting the Hague Convention regarding a military ceasefire.

At Home
- The Minister of Defense Lee Gi-boong, denies a rumor that Baik Seon-youp, representative of the Korean delegation for the Armistice Conference would withdraw from his assigned post at Kaesong.
- Donald J. Kingsley, the Director of UNKRA says that all reconstruction programs of UNKRA would be carried out intensively if an Armistice agreement is successfully concluded.

Overseas

A ROK soldier guards the bridge at Imjin River (1951. 8. 3)

- *The Shanghai Daily News* reports that China continues to send its medical doctors and nurses to North Korea.
- The U.S. Government establishes the Defense Supply Management Agency.

August 2, Thursday (June 30, by lunar calendar, 甲戌日 Blue Dog) Clear
404 Day of the War

War Situation
- The UN Forces begin to advance to the south of Geumseong from the mid-eastern frontlines.
- B-26 light-duty squadron bombs the depot of ammunition equipment in Pyongyang.

At Home
- The Monetary Policy Committee makes a decision to release KRW 2 billion as a limited lending to assist the financial structures of the local Governments in the country.
- In Busan, a rally of the families of the kidnapped by the Communists takes place to plea for the rescue of the patriotic kidnapped people.

August 3, Friday (July 1, by lunar calendar, 乙亥日 Blue Pig) Cloudy and Clear
405 Day of the War

War Situation
- The UN Forces advance 1km from the southeast of Geumseong.
- The UN delegation for the Truce agreement says that the present defense lines will never be surrendered.

At Home
- The National Assembly decides to re-examine the Incident of the National Defense Corps.
- The Constitution Committee is established. The members from the Assembly are So Seon-gyu, Chung Heon-ju, Nam Song-hak, Kim Bong-jo, Lee Do-young while the members from the Justice of Supreme Court are Kim Byung-ro, Kim Chan-young, Baik Han-seong, Kim Du-il and Kim Woo-shik.

August 4, Saturday (July 2, by lunar calendar, 丙子日 Red Rat) Clear, Cloudy, Windy and Clear
406 Day of the War

War Situation
- The UN Forces repel the counter-attack by the Communist troops to the south of Geumseong.

At Home
- The Korean Anti-tuberculosis Institute is established.
- The UN relief goods arrive in Busan(blankets, soap, rubber, clothes, salt, etc.)

- The United States announces plans to purchase the materials and equipment for Korea in Japan.
- The Chilean Government decides to prohibit the export of strategic items to the Communist countries.

August 5, Sunday (July 3, by lunar calendar, 丁丑日 Red Ox) Rainy, Windy and Clear
407 Day of the War

War Situation
- The resistance by the Communist troops continues in the southeast of Geumseong.

At Home
- Commander of the Military Conscription Affairs, Col. Kim Jong-won, admits that the firing order was given in order to interupt investigation of the special inspection team of the National Assembly.
- The first commencement ceremony of the ROK Air Force Academy takes place at Jinhae in the presence of President Syngman Rhee.

August 6, Monday (July 4 by lunar calendar 戊寅日 Yellow Tiger) Clear
408 Day of the War

War Situation
- The UN Forces completely repel an attack by two companies of Chinese troops southeast of Geumseong.
- The Communist troops broadcast a message asking for the reopening of the Armistice negotiation with an apology comment in relation to the violation of the neutral zone.

At Home
- Lee Gi-boong, the Minister of Defense states at a press conference that the method of conscription for the soldiers would be reformed.
- A big rally to oppose the Armistice agreement takes place.

August 7, Tuesday (July 5, by lunar calendar, 乙卯日 Blue Rabbit) Cloudy, Windy and Clear
409 Day of the War

War Situation
- The UN Forces repel a counter-offensive by the Communist troops west of Cheorwon.

At Home
- A certain number of dongs (* Dong is the smallest administrative unit) ask for certificates of national bonds purchase when they called up on the conscription roll call.
- The Director of the Office of Public Information announces that severe punishment would

be imposed upon the import of Japanese publications into the country.

August 8, Wednesday (July 6, by lunar calendar, 庚辰日 White Dragon) Cloudy and Clear
410 Day of the War

War Situation
- The UN Forces continue their resistance at the west of Geumseong.
- Minor confrontations are noted northwest of Yeoncheon and west of Gorang-po.

At Home
- Yang Yoo-chan, Korean Ambassador to the United States exchanges views with President Truman.

August 9, Thursday (July 7, by lunar calendar, 辛巳日 White Snake) Cloudy and Clear
411 Day of the War

War Situation
- The UN Navy forces attacks Yeonan and Haejoo and bombard the port of Wonsan.
- The Communist Party at the Armistice Conference responds to the message of Gen. Ridgway, and commits to securing neutrality hoping for the re-opening of the Armistice Conference.

At Home
- The Legislation Committee of the National Assembly sets up a plan to reform the structure of the Government's organization.
- Lee Gi-boong, the Minister of Defense talks with Baik Seon-youp, representative at the Armistice Conference

August 10, Friday (July 8, by lunar calendar, 壬午日 Black Horse) Clear
412 Day of the War

War Situation
- The ROK Navy's escort ship Aprok launches repeated bombarding against the Communist troops' facilities near Yeonan.
- The Communist side at the Armistice Conference refuses to discuss any kind of alternative other than the 38th parallel to define the demarcation (demilitarized) line.

At Home
- Australian Minister of the Foreign Affairs Richard G. Casey highly praises the patriotic spirit of the Korean people before his departure from Korea.
- The 8th Discharge Ceremony of the Honorary Disabled-soldiers takes place at the ROK Army No. 839 Unit in the presence of President Syngman Rhee.

Overseas

- The U.S. Government accepts the request for the rights of compensation claims requested by the French Government regarding the Peace Treaty with Japan.

August 11, Saturday (July 9, by lunar calendar, 癸未日 Black Sheep) Clear
413 Day of the War

War Situation
- The UN troops repulse an assault by the Communist troops to the northwest of Yanggu despite the unfavorable weather.
- The Australian troops and the ROK Navy launch attacks on the enemy in the lower part of the Han River.

At Home
- The Ministry of Social Affairs issues an announcement on "the guidelines on the war-time national movements or campaigns."
- Huh Jeong, Minister of Social Affairs, makes a statement on a plan to accommodate the North Korean refugees who assemble in the west coast areas.
- The Commander of the Eighth U.S. Army sends a message asking the refugees to refrain from going back to their hometowns in the North.

August 12, Sunday (July 10, by lunar calendar, 甲申日 Blue Monkey) Clear
414 Day of the War

War Situation
- Small-scale clashes occur at the mid-east frontlines.

At Home
- The Government begins to import the necessary goods for daily life by using the foreign currency reserve.

Overseas
- Soviet Ministry of Foreign Affairs accepts an invitation to the Armistice Conference with Japan via its Embassy in Washington.

August 13, Monday (July 11, by lunar calendar, 乙酉日 Blue Rooster) Clear
415 Day of the War

War Situation
- The UN Air Force squadron bombs an assembly area of the enemy in the northwest of Pyongyang and the west of Daedong River.
- The ROK Air Force attacks the enemy's military quarters and artillery posts.

At Home
- The Emergency Martial Law is lifted in the three counties such as Choongju, Jecheon and

Bombardment is launched at close assaults carried out on the enemy position of 773 highlands which was called "Bloody Ridge" at Bukbang-myeon Yanggu. (1951. 8. 13)

Danyang, instead, the Security Status Martial Law is proclaimed.

August 14, Tuesday (July 12, by lunar calendar, 丙戌日 Yellow Dog) Clear
416 Day of the War

War Situation

- The Allied troops repel an attack by the Communist troops south of Geumseong.
- The ROK Air Force launches bombing raids on the outpost of anti-aircraft artillery in the north of Soonan and an armory of Pyongyang.

At Home

- Shin Ik-hee. Speaker of the National Assembly issues a statement on the occasion of Liberation Day saying, " Let us try our best to fight against communism together with our allies."
- The Government imports necessary goods with its foreign exchange reserve.

August 15, Wednesday (July 13, by lunar calendar, 丁亥日 Red Pig) Clear and Cloudy

War Situation
- The Allied Forces repel an attack by the Communist troops at Ganseong on the eastern frontlines.

At Home
- The Liberation Day ceremony takes place in the hall of the National Assembly in the presence of President Syngman Rhee.
- Kim Dae-woon is arrested on charges of being involved in the Incident of the National Defense Corps.
- On the occasion of Liberation Day, a mass rally organized by Seoul citizens takes place at the Seoul City Hall.

Overseas
- Zhou En-lai, Chinese Minister of Foreign Affairs publishes a statement regarding the proposed Peace Treaty between the United States and Japan and its conference held in San Francisco.
- The U.S. Government issues the full text of the Peace Treaty with Japan.

August 16, Thursday (July 14, by lunar calendar, 戊子日 Yellow Rat) Cloudy and Clear
418 Day of the War

War Situation
- The U.S. State Department announces that the number of American casualties for the past week has reached 20, which is the lowest number since the war broke out.
- At the 26th meeting at Kaesong for the negotiation of the Armistice agreement, the Communist side agrees to establish a joint special committee to seek solutions for the issue of demarcation lines.

At Home
- The Legislation and Judicial Committee of the National Assembly passes the bill on the revision of the National Government Organization Act, with partial amendment.
- The court trial begins for Kim Byung-sik and seven other persons on charges of being involved in the Incident of Ganghwado Massacre (allegedly conducted by the militiamen and police Forces. About 200 unarmed civilians were killed.)

August 17, Friday (July 15, by lunar calendar, 己丑日 Yellow Ox) Clear
419 Day of the War

War Situation
- The UN Air Force launches 24 hours of serial bombings, destroying the transportation grid of the Communist troops.

- The ROK Air Force launches nighttime bombings on the supply access roads and main military targets in Sinanju, Pyongyang, Gangdong, Deokcheon and Seongcheon.

At Home
- President Syngman Rhee visits Jeju Island.
- The Government submits the detailed lists of the equipment and materials to be mobilized for the reconstruction programs of UNKRA.
- The Government assigns a new military attaché to the Embassy in Washington.

August 18, Saturday (July 16, by lunar calendar, 庚寅日 White Tiger) Clear, Cloudy and Rainy
420 Day of the War

War Situation
- The Allied Forces retreat due to pressure exerted by the Communist troops from the north and northwest of Yanggu.
- The Communist troops are repelled in the north and northeast of Cheorwon.

At Home
- The Democratic National Party issues a statement regarding the pressing issues including the revision of the constitution.
- The Korean Chamber of Commerce submits a recommendation to the Government in relation to food distribution.

Overseas
- Professor Thomas Banner of Illinois University is appointed as the first superintendent of the UNESCO Korea Reconstruction Commission.
- Japan appoints its plenipotentiaries for the U.S.-Japan Peace Treaty Conference and Premier Yoshida is appointed as their head.

August 19, Sunday (July 17, by lunar calendar, 辛卯日 White Rabbit) Cloudy, Windy, Clear and Cloudy

421 Day of the War

War Situation
- Fierce battles occur in the areas of Ganseong on the east coast including the eastern part of Geumseong and the middle area of Cheorwon.
- Spokesman of the UN delegation for the Truce agreement gives a briefing on the truth of "the Firing Incident" within the neutral zone of Kaesong" by the UN troops.

At Home
- The prohibition of crossing the Han River troubles most of the refugees assembling near the river.
- Seoul Mayor, Kim Tae-seon re-issues a warning that it is too early for Seoul citizens to

return to the capital city.

August 20, Monday (July 18, by lunar calendar, 壬辰日 Black Dragon) Cloudy, Windy and Rainy
422 Day of the War

War Situation
- The U.S. Air Force launches bombing attacks on Sinanju, Youngmidong, and the railroad switchyards of Maengjoong-dong.
- The 4th Joint Special Committee for the Truce meeting takes place at Kaesong.

At Home
- UNKRA is ready to execute various basic projects in the amount of US$ 250 million.
- Commander of the United Nations Civil Assistance Corps Korea (UNCACK), Col. Coyle, says that one of UNCACK's primary missions is, first of all, to help the war refugees suffering starvation.

August 21, Tuesday (July 19, by lunar calendar, 癸巳日 Black Snake) Cloudy, Windy and Cloudy
423 Day of the War

War Situation
- A fierce battle occurs at Ganseong.

At Home
- The Eighth U.S. Army demands again that the refugees should not proceed to the North.

August 22, Wednesday (July 20, by lunar calendar, 甲午日 Blue Horse) Cloudy, Windy and Cloudy
424 Day of the War

War Situation
- The ROK Army repels the Communist troops on a hill located west of Ganseong.
- The 6th Joint Special Committee for the Truce meeting takes place at Kaesong.

At Home
- The National Assembly puts the two bills on an agenda to deal with "the Government Organization Law" and "the Law on the Establishment of the Ministry of Reconstruction.
- The Ministry of Industry decides to add some import items such as medical and chemical products to its import plan.

August 23, Thursday (July 21, by lunar calendar, 乙未日 Blue Sheep) Cloudy, Windy and Cloudy
425 Day of the War

War Situation
- The ROK Capital Division occupies Hill 924.
- Offensive and defensive battles continue southwest of Ganseong.

At Home
- The Martial Law Command establishes its Division of Civil Affairs.
- UNKRA begins to execute its own projects.

August 24, Friday (July 22, by lunar calendar, 丙申日 Red Monkey) Cloudy, Windy and Clear
426 Day of the War

War Situation
- The UN Air Force destroys about 400 vehicles of the enemy on the roads of North Korea.
- The commander of the Communist troops officially informs that the negotiation for the Armistice Agreement and the joint committee meeting will be stopped immediately.

At Home
- The National Assembly has different voices on "the Government Organization Law."
- The Government proclaims "the Law on the Government-vested Properties.

August 25, Saturday (July 23, by lunar calendar, 丁酉日 Red Rooster) Clear
427 Day of the War

War Situation
- The UN Forces re-take the target hills of Gimhwa and Geumseong.
- Hand-to-hand battles occur northwest of Ganseong.
- Commander of the Eighth U.S. Army, General Van Fleet sends a message praising the brave spirit of the ROK soldiers.

At Home
- Minister of Social Affairs, Huh Jeong says that 25,000 tons of rice for relief is being distributed to every province of the country.
- The Ministry of Defense establishes the 4th Bureau which deals with overall conscription affairs.
- The evacuation begins for refugees in Yeonpyeong Island to be relocated to Jindo Island.

Overseas
- Brigadier General William E. Christ is nominated as Commander of the United Nations Civil Assistance Corps Korea (UNCACK).
- The U.S. State Department announces that the Indian Government will not participate in the Armistice Conference.

August 26, Sunday (July 24, by lunar calendar, 戊戌日 Yellow Dog) Clear, Cloudy and Clear
428 Day of the War

War Situation
- B-29 squadron launches bombing on the railway facilities of Gunwoori and the airport of

Pyeongri.

- The effective pacification activities by the South Jeolla Provincial Police help to convert the loyalty of 175 guerillas as of August 25.

At Home
- The Government authorities concerned review appropriate policy for the export of tungsten.
- The Government discusses the overall management matters in relation with UNKRA's economic policy and programs.

August 27, Monday (July 25, by lunar calendar, 己亥日 Yellow Pig) Clear
429 Day of the War

War Situation
- The ROK 11th Division occupies Hill 884.
- The South Jeolla Provincial Police launches a mop-up operation at Sangchi, killing 100 guerillas.

At Home
- The National Assembly passes the Government's proposal regarding the additional annual budget and raises the meal price for the soldiers.
- The Public Prosecutors Office summons lawmakers to investigate the Incident of the National Defense Corps: Suh Min-ho, Park Seung-ha, Nam Song-hak and Kim Jong-hee.

August 28, Tuesday (July 26, by lunar calendar, 庚子日 White Rat) Cloudy, Windy and Cloudy
430 Day of the War

War Situation
- A battle occurs north of Ganseong, and the counter-offensive of the Communist troops is repelled under the cover of the Navy's firing on the western zone.

At Home
- Commander of the Eighth U.S. Army, Gen. Van Fleet visits Mayor of Seoul City expressing his interest in the coming-back- home of Seoul citizens.
- The ROK Navy establishes its military police.

Overseas
- The Burmese Government officially refuses to endorse the draft U.S.-Japan Peace Treaty.
- The Secretary-general of the Arab League announces that the League's member countries will participate in the Armistice Conference with Japan.

August 29, Wednesday (July 27, by lunar calendar, 辛丑日 White Ox) Cloudy and Clear
431 Day of the War

Military priest gives mass on the battlefield for soldiers (1951. 8. 28)

War Situation
- The Allied Forces repel the Communist troops in the west and east of Ganseong and occupy two strategic hills.
- UN Forces Command issues a statement explaining the notice of Gen. Ridgway to the Communist Army.

At Home
- Director of the Office of Public Information issues a warning against sub-standard cartoons.
- Assemblymen Kim Yong-hwa with joint signatures of 58 other members sumbits a proposal regarding the moving of the Capital to Daejeon.

August 30, Thursday (July 28, by lunar calendar, 壬寅日 Black Tiger) Cloudy and Clear
432 Day of the War

War Situation
- The UN air squadron continues day-long bombing on the Communist troops assembled in the Heavy Artillery Unit and Ganseong area.
- The 1st Fighter Wing of the ROK Air Force launches bombing north of Haejoo.

At Home
- President Syngman Rhee sends his message to the National Assembly soliciting serious consideration on the system of "the Minister of State for Political Affairs."
- Before the conclusion of the Peace Treaty with Japan, a dispute arises over the issue of territorial sovereignty of Dokdo.
- The U.S. Forces accept a proposal made by the Seoul Bureau of the Civilian Affairs of the Martial Law to allow the daily necessities to be brought to Seoul.

August 31, Friday (July 29, by lunar calendar, 癸卯日 Black Rabbit) Cloudy, Windy and Clear
433 Day of the War

War Situation
- The UN Forces repel fierce resistance by the Communist troops on the north of Yanggu and occupy a strategic hill.
- The Allied troops destroy the guerillas in the Sancheong area.

At Home
- The police chief of South Gyeongsang Province announces the annihilation of the guerillas in the Sancheong area.
- The Military Affairs Command begins to carry out the registration for the Second Peoples' Force.

Overseas
- The Association of Korean Businessmen in Japan establishes the Korean Reconstruction Committee.
- The Ministry of Foreign Affairs of Japan expresses its opinion that Jukdo (=Dokdo) Island belongs to the territory of Japan.

September 1, Saturday (August 1, by lunar calendar, 甲辰日 Blue Dragon) Windy and Clear
434 Day of the War

War Situation
- The Allied Troops partially retreat from the north and northwest of Yanggu but recapture it by advancing.
- The ROK Air Force launches bombing of the Sinwon area of Hwanghae Province.

At Home
- Minister of Finance Baek Doo-jin announces that the national bonds issued before liberation day would be paid out by the Japanese Government.
- Henry Kissinger, professor of Harvard University visits Korea in order to examine various opinions of Korean society regarding the United States policy toward to the Korean Peninsula.

Overseas
- The ANZUS Treaty (Australia, New Zealand and United States Security Treaty) is signed in San Francisco.
- The United States begins to launch a nationwide campaign to save Korean war victims and refugees by marking the month of September as the "Month of Medical Assistance for Korea."

September 2, Sunday (August 2, by lunar calendar, 乙巳日 Blue Snake) Clear, and Cloudy Clear
435 Day of the War

War Situation
- The UN Forces engage in heavy battles in the mid-frontlines and mid-eastern frontlines occupying eight strategic hills.
- The UN fleets launch devastating bombing of the assembly zones of the Communist troops in East Sea coast.

At Home
- President Syngman Rhee issues a stern warning to the Japanese fishing vessels which violate the MacArthur Line.
- The law on the "Korean Mint Corporation" is proclaimed and takes effect.

September 3, Monday (August 3, by lunar calendar, 丙午日 Red Horse) Clear, Cloudy and Rainy
436 Day of the War

War Situation

- The 1st Regiment of the ROK Marine Corps occupies Punchbowl (in the bowl-shaped Haean-myeon valley).
- Fierce battles occur in the mountains of the mid-east frontlines, where the UN Forces occupy strategic positions.

At Home
- President Syngman Rhee issues a statement about his policy on Japan opposing the rearmament of Japan.
- The Ministry of Foreign Affairs refutes the Japanese claim about their territorial rights of Dokdo Island.
- The Korean Disabled Veterans' Association issues its positive counter-measures on so-called "bogus members of the Association."

September 4, Tuesday (August 4, by lunar calendar, 丁未日 Red Sheep) Cloudy, Rainy and Clear 437 Day of the War

War Situation
- The ROK 5th Division engages in a battle on Hill 1121 near Gachilbong beginning September 4 and continuing through October 14.

U.S. Marines aircraft are coming back to their aircraft carrier after bombing North Korean Army's outpost (1951. 9. 4)

- The head representative of the UN Forces responds to the Communist representative without accepting a claim made by the Communist Party dated September 3.

At Home
- The Government begins to investigate matters related to the missing or lost books of cultural heritages or values in every library of the country.
- Prosthesis makers (for artificial arms and legs) arrive from the United States.

September 5, Wednesday (August 5, by lunar calendar, 戊申日 Yellow Monkey) Cloudy and Clear
438 Day of the War

War Situation
- The U.S. 2nd Division fiercely engages in 18 days' battle and finally occupies "the Ridge of Blood" to the north of Yanggu.
- The Commander of the U.S. 2nd Logistic Support Command (or Quartermaster Depot) awards an honorary medal to the Commander of Busan Port Operation Command.

At Home
- The Cabinet Meeting decides to strictly crackdown on smuggling.
- The National Assembly brings up on the agenda the draft law proposed by the Government regarding "the Law on Property Tax."
- Ninety prisoners flee from the Geoje POW Camp by boat escaping to the mainland.

Overseas
- Japan and the Philippines begin preliminary negotiations on compensation matters related to war damages.

September 6, Thursday (August 6, by lunar calendar, 己酉日 Yellow Rooster) Clear, Cloudy and Clear
439 Day of the War

War Situation
- The allied troops occupy three strategic hills northeast of Yanggu.
- Commander of the UN Forces, General Ridgway, responds to the Communist Party regarding the Armistice Conference, proposing a meeting between the liaison officers from both parties in order to choose a new meeting venue.

At Home
- President Syngman Rhee issues a statement criticizing Korea's reliance on Japan for the import of war supplies.
- The Bank of Korea asks the holders of the national bonds issued by Japan before the liberation date for due registration.

September 7, Friday (August 7, by lunar calendar, 庚戌日 White Dog) Cloudy, Rainy and Cloudy

440 Day of the War

War Situation
- The UN Forces continue to launch partial attacks on the eastern frontlines.
- B-29 squadron launches bombing on a switchyard of Jeongju and a steel bridge of Sinanju.

At Home
- The National Assembly passes a bill regarding "the sending of the delegation to deal with the Clearance of the UN Compensation Fund."
- The Foreign Affairs Committee of the National Assembly demands early release of the prisoners who were forced to become the soldiers of the North Korean Army.

Overseas
- The UN Economic and Social Council passes a resolution to adopt the "Long-term Land Reform Planning" proposed by the United States.
- The Indonesian Government holds the Cabinet Meeting and agrees to sign the Peace Treaty with Japan.

September 8, Saturday (August 8, by lunar calendar, 辛亥日 White Pig) Rainy
441 Day of the War

War Situation
- The Communist troops attack the bridgehead of the allied troops to the east of Gimhwa.
- B-29 squadron launches bombing of Sunan Airport.

At Home
- President Syngman Rhee gives secret orders to every Minister concerned to seek solutions on "how to spread out and accommodate the refugees" presently living in the mass refugee camps into the other farming villages.
- The joint memorial service for fallen soldiers takes place at the Relief Hospital for the wounded soldiers in Masan.

September 9, Sunday (August 9, by lunar calendar, 壬子日 Black Rat) Rainy, Cloudy and Clear
442 Day of the War

War Situation
- The UN Forces and the Communist troops engage in battles in the north of Geumseong and Yanggu.
- The UN troops and their Tank Units retake their strategic positions on the west of Yeoncheon.

At Home
- The Civilian Affairs Command of the Martial law announces strict crackdown on the illegal

cross-border people.

- Ex-vice commander of the Eight U.S Army, General Coulter leaves Suyeong Airport for Japan.

September 10, Monday (August 10, by lunar calendar, 癸丑日 Black Ox) Cloudy
443 Day of the War

War Situation
- The U.S. 5th Air Force reports that huge numbers of Communist troops' vehicle units are moving in the night from the Korea-Manchuria border to the west and the mid-frontlines.

At Home
- The Military Court opens its trial indicting Col Kim Jong-won and other officers.
- The landowners of North Jeolla Province set up "the Landowners' Association for National Security" and plan to invest their land capital in domestic enterprises.
- The total sales of the relief and assistance goods amount to KRW 17.4 billion.

September 11, Tuesday (August 11, by lunar calendar, 甲寅日 Blue Tiger) Clear
444 Day of the War

War Situation
- Day-long battles take place on the north of Inje.
- The UN Forces admit the accidental misfiring by the UN aircraft in the Kaesong area.

ROK officers leave to study in the United States (1951. 9. 12)

- General Ridgway of the UN Forces proposes the abolition of the neutral zones to the Joint Chief of Staffs.

At Home
- The Military Affairs Command of the South Gyeongsang Province orders its Military Police to strictly crackdown on the draft dodgers of the Second Peoples' Force.
- The National Students Defense Corps proposes to launch a campaign for the reconstruction of school classrooms.

Overseas
- Zhu De, Chinese General announces at the 1st Political Strategic Meeting that China would establish its Navy Force and would strengthen the its ability for the coastal defense.
- The Executive Committee of UNICEF (United Nations International Children's Emergency Fund) decides to contribute clothes worth US$ 450,000.

September 12, Wednesday (August 12, by lunar calendar, 乙卯日 Yellow Rooster) Cloudy
445 Day of the War

War Situation
- The allied Forces repel a battalion of the Communist troops to the west of Ganseong occupying a target hill.
- The enemy units attack the minesweepers of the UN Forces operating near the Galma peninsula north of Wonsan. The safeguard destroyer and carrier-borne aircraft destroy the main outposts of the enemy's battery

At Home
- President Syngman Rhee donates soap to the soldiers on the frontlines through his secretary.

September 13, Thursday (August 13, by lunar calendar, 丙辰日 Red Dragon) Cloudy and Clear
446 Day of the War

War Situation
- The UN Forces launch an attack on the Communist troops north and northeast of Yanggu. The enemy, however, shows strong resistance.
- The UN Air Force locates the Communist Tank Units at Yeoncheon area, bombing them with napalm.

At Home
- The Police Chief of the South Gyeongsang Province instructs to rigidly control the shirkers of the intellectual class evading military service.
- The investigation team of North Gyeongsang Province leaves for the drought-stricken areas.

Overseas
- The U.S. Air Force announces formation of a new unit of guided-armament company equipped with unmanned fighter bombers as of October 1.
- A broadcasting station in West Germany reports that the Soviet Union has demanded that its satellite countries to support the supply of military equipment and materials to North Korea.

September 14, Friday (August 14, by lunar calendar, 丁巳日 Red Snake) Cloudy and Rainy
447 Day of the War

War Situation
- Fierce battles take place on the frontlines in the areas of Geumseong and Idong.
- The Turkish and Ethiopian troops repel the attack of the Communist troops on the east frontlines.

At Home
- President Syngman Rhee visits the mid-frontlines, and meets with General Van Fleet, Commander of the Eighth U.S. Army.
- Seoul Mayor Kim Tae-seon says that the City Government would obtain hard coal (anthracite) of Hwasoon Mines to help the Seoul citizens with their winterizing.

September 15, Saturday (August 15, by lunar calendar, 戊午日 Yellow Horse) Cloudy
448 Day of the War

War Situation
- Heavy battles continue on the ridges of the northern part of Yanggu.
- A joint operation of the military and police Forces repulses the guerilla Unit that attacked and occupied the police station of Samga at Hapcheon.

At Home
- The Ministry of Communication and Postal Services issues commemorative stamps in appreciation of the UN troops' participation in the Korean War and their sacrifice rendered to help the Korean people.
- Minister of Social Affairs, Huh Jeong issues a statement on the war refugees and victims numbering 8 million.

September 16, Sunday (August 16, by lunar calendar, 己未日 Yellow Sheep) Clear
449 Day of the War

War Situation
- Hand-to-hand battles occur in the Yanggu area.
- The ROK Air Force extends Gangneung Airport.

At Home
- South Jeolla Province plans to establish the Gwangju University in Gwangju.
- According to the South Jeolla Province's revised plan related to the high school system, the total number of public high schools is 31, while the private high school reaches nine.
- The founder of a religious body Tae eul-gyo (sect), Lee Do-sool is arrested on charges of abduction, fraud and stirring public order and sentiment.

September 17, Monday (August 17, by lunar calendar, 庚申日 White Monkey) Cloudy
450 Day of the War

War Situation
- In the valley of the Soyang River in the basin of the northeast Inje River, the UN troops advance 12.8 km, occupying the main positions of the target hills.
- General Ridgway proposes reopening of the Armistice Conference.

At Home
- The Government decides to strengthen the anti-Communist movements.
- The Headquarters of the UN Forces warn the North Korean civilians to evacuate.

September 18, Tuesday (August 18, by lunar calendar, 辛酉日 White Rooster) Cloudy and Clear
451 Day of the War

War Situation
- The UN troops initiate long-hour offensive against the Communist troops, occupying the main hills of " Heartbreak Ridge" to the north of Yanggu.
- The Headquarters of the UN Forces reconfirms its position on the reopening of the Armistice Conference.

At Home
- The Cabinet Meeting refuses the draft bill to establish "the Minister of State for Political Affairs" and "The Central Economic Committee." The Assembly-submitted bill on the revision of the Governmental Organization Law" is reviewed, and the Cabinet Meeting decides to return it to the Assembly with notes stating the Government's different opinions.
- The Ministry of Agriculture and Forestry decides to give a priority right to the landowners to purchase the stocks of the Government-vested enterprises.

Overseas
- The United States Department of Agriculture issues an announcement on the relaxation of export limitations of cotton.
- West Germany Chancellor Konrad Adenauer stresses that the rearmament of West Germany is one of the best ways to ensure world peace.

September 19, Wednesday (August 19, by lunar calendar, 壬戌日 Black Dog) Clear
452 Day of the War

War Situation
- The UN troops retreat by a narrow range from the north and the northwest of Yanggu.
- The Communist Party requests a liaison officers' meeting at Panmunjom on September 20 (at 06:00 a.m).

At Home
- Minister of Transportation, Kim Seok-kwan announces that 100 Korean ships brought to Japan at the end of the Japanese colonial period would be returned to the Korean Government upon endorsement by the UN Forces.
- Minister of Foreign Affairs Byun Young-tae emphasizes the necessity of Korea-Japan Talks.

September 20, Thursday (August 20, by lunar calendar, 癸亥日 Black Pig) Clear
453 Day of the War

War Situation
- The 1st Division of the U.S. Marine Corps occupies Hill 812.
- Commander of the Communist troops delivers a memorandum through the liaison officers of both parties. An immediate meeting for the Armistice Conference is suggested at

The first reconnaissance helicopter of the U.S. Marines(1951. 9. 20)

Kaesong without any preconditions about the re-opening of the Conference.

At Home
- President Syngman Rhee issues an important statement regarding the re-opening of the Armistice Conference under the below-mentioned conditions.
  1) The Chinese troops should be withdrawn;
  2) Disarmament of the North Korean troops;
  3) Free elections in North Korea under the supervision of the United Nations;
  4) Setting up a deadline for the Truce Agreement;
- The Ministry of Social Affairs prepares for the measures to provide necessary assistance to the injured and disabled war veterans.
- Minister of Social Affairs, Huh Jeong says that unscrupulous landlords exploiting the refugee tenants would be strictly punished.

September 21, Friday (August 21, by lunar calendar, 甲子日 Blue Rat) Clear, Cloudy and Clear
454 Day of the War

War Situation
- The allied troops advance 32km from the north of Yeoncheon.
- Two battalions of North Korean troops show strong resistance on the two positions of the eastern frontlines.

At Home
- The Cabinet Meeting prepares a statement explaining the reasons for opposing the proposed new system on "the Minister of State for Political Affairs" and" The Central Economic Committee."
- Director of the Office of Public Information stresses the importance of anti-air raid drills as well as the spiritual armament of the people.
- An agreement between the Republic of Korea and the World Health Organization is concluded and takes effect.

September 22, Saturday (August 22, by lunar calendar, 乙丑日 Blue Ox) Clear
455 Day of the War

War Situation
- An offensive by the Communist troops is repelled in the mountainous areas northeast of Yanggu.
- The UN troops initiate an offensive toward the highest hill of "Heartbreak Ridge" northeast of Yanggu.

At Home
- The Cabinet Meeting passes a bill regarding "the Law of Korea Industrial Bank (to be

called "the Korean Development Bank").
- "The National Culture Co." is established (represented by Lee Eun Sang).

September 23, Sunday (August 23, by lunar calendar, 丙寅日 Red Tiger) Clear and Rainy
456 Day of the War

War Situation
- The U.S. Infantry Division occupies the main hill of Heartbreak Ridge," repelling an offensive by Communist troops.
- Commanding General Ridgway responds to the Communist Party for the Armistice Conference agreeing on the re-opening of the meeting.

At Home
- The Korea Chamber of Commerce and Industry (KCCI) recommends a draft bill to the authorities concerned regarding the revision of "the Special Law on Tax."
- The Japanese immigration control law is placed on the agenda of the Japanese parliament, causing controversies and arguments in Korea because the law allows the forceful deportation of the Korean residents living in Japan.

Overseas
- The Hong Kong police authorities limits the activities of political exiles (defectors) and third party pressure groups.

Prime Minister Jang Myeon (middle) and his cabinet members(1951. 9. 23)

September 24, Monday (August 24, by lunar calendar, 丁卯日 Red Rabbit) Cloudy
457 Day of the War

War Situation

- The ROK Navy destroyer, "Aprok," bombs the bridgeheads of the North Korean troops near Gojeo, Geumnamri on the east coast, but is attacked by shelling from the North Korean Unit.

At Home

- The Ministry of Finance issues a notification on the special exchange of the Joseon Bank-issued notes.
- The self-reporting period is announced for the straggler soldiers.
  - During the period October 1-15, those who voluntarily report to the authorities would be treated with generosity for whatever reason they might have been motivated.

September 25, Tuesday (August 25, by lunar calendar, 戊辰日 Yellow Tiger) Clear and Cloudy
458 Day of the War

War Situation

- The battles in the mountains continue on the eastern frontlines.
- The U.S. Navy battleship New Jersey launches heavy firings on the beachheads of the Communist troops in the south of Goseong.

At Home

- The National Assembly finishes 15 days' recess for the purpose of a field survey on the local situations and reopens its regular session.
- The Cabinet Meeting decides the conscription age at 25 years for the soldiers to be drafted for the Second Peoples' Force.

September 26, Wednesday (August 26, by lunar calendar, 己巳日 Yellow Snake) Cloudy and Clear
459 Day of the War

War Situation

- The 7th Infantry Division occupies Mt. Baiseok.
- The battles continue in the northeast of Geumseong.

At Home

- Minister of Defense Lee Gi-boong is interviewed about the establishment of the No. 1 Bureau for Audit and Inspection. Its main responsibility is to oversee any wrongdoing or misconduct of the military servicemen and its civilian employees.
- The Director of the Office of Public Information stresses the role of journalists in wartime, giving warnings to some corrupt newspapermen.

September 27, Thursday (August 27, by lunar calendar, 更午日 White Horse) Clear
460 Day of the War

War Situation
- The Communist troops continue occupying the hills on "Heartbreak Ridge" north of Yanggu, launching artillery attacks on the UN troops.
- The UN Navy Squadron launches bombardments on the outposts of the Communist troops' artillery and mortar fire units on "Heartbreak Ridge."

At Home
- President Syngman Rhee asks the people to use brown rice and to improve their eating habits.
- The Monetary Policy Committee decides to re-establish the system of the national bonds deposit.
- The Director of the Office of Public Information gives a warning on the excessive issue of ID cards for the media.

Overseas
- A joint session of both Houses of the United States Congress agrees on the total amount of foreign aid being U$ 7,483,400,000.
- The Soviet Union and East Germany sign an economic cooperation agreement in Moscow.

September 28, Friday (August 28, by lunar calendar, 辛未日 White Sheep) Clear, Cloudy and Clear
461 Day of the War

War Situation
- Sporadic battles occur in the mountainous areas of northeastern Yanggu.
- An offensive by the Communist troops is repelled northwest of Cheorwon.

At Home
- The Cabinet Meeting proclaims No.21 notification on" the matter related to the conscription for soldiers." Beginning the 1st of October, the call-up for the Second Peoples' Force is for those aged between 19 and 25.
- The Central News Agency of North Korea continues to criticize the incident of a "violation" by the UN troops penetrating into the neutral zone of Kaesong.

September 29, Saturday (August 29, by lunar calendar, 壬申日 Black Monkey) Rainy, Cloudy and Clear
462 Day of the War

War Situation
- The Communist troops continue to augment their military force resisting north of Yanggu.
- Battles continue in the southeast of Geumseong.

- The UN troops engage in a battle to try to occupy the three hills of the western part of Cheorwon and are successful in taking two of them.

At Home
- The conscription rate for soldiers stands at 26 %, and the commander of the Military Service Affairs demands a second call-up for the evaders who should abide by due registration for the conscription order. An additional warning is given to those who do not respond to the re-call would be severely punished.

September 30, Sunday (August 30, by lunar calendar, 癸酉日 Black Rooster) Clear
463 Day of the War

War Situation
- The ROK Army troops engage in hand-to-hand battle on the western frontlines of "Heartbreak Ridge" northwest of Yanggu occupying the top of the mountain.
- A heavy battle to occupy the target hills takes place southwest of Cheorwon. The UN infantry Division launches a sudden attack and retakes No.3 hilltop with the support of flame throwers.

At Home
- The Government proposes a bill for the Law on the Temporary Land Income Tax so that income tax incurred from land would be paid in kind.
- The Monetary Policy Committee decides the purchase price for the grains harvested in the autumn.

- Korean Ambassador to the United States, Yang Yoo-chan reports to the Foreign Ministry on the United States' notification regarding the compensation fund for Korea.

An injured soldier is looking at the bullet hole of his helmet

October 1, Monday (September 1, by lunar calendar, 甲戌日 Yellow Dog) Clear and Windy
464 Day of the War

War Situation
- The 8th Infantry Division occupies Mt. Baikseok.
- Battles occur five times in the north of Gorangpo.

At Home
- The plenary session of the National Assembly discusses the management system for the sake of the prisoners of Geoje POWs Camp.
- The Government allows the establishment of an agency by the Japanese shipping companies in Korea.
- The South Gyeongsang Provincial Police begin to maneuver the operation to induce self-reporting and submission of the Communist guerillas.

October 2, Tuesday (September 2, by lunar calendar, 乙亥日 Yellow Pig) Clear
465 Day of the War

War Situation
- The UN troops launch heavy firing by barrage against the Communist troops on the hillsides northwest of Gorangpo.
- B-29 squadrons bomb the Suncheon railway bridge.

At Home
- The National Assembly passes emergency legislation to provide aid for the bereaved families of fallen soldiers and policemen including disabled war soldiers.
- The National Assembly issues a status report on the Korean laborers employed by the UN troops.
- The Government submits a bill related to "the revised law on the disposal of the Government-vested properties."

Overseas
- Beijing Broadcasting Station reports that some Japanese prisoners are noted on the western frontlines of Korea.

October 3, Wednesday (September 3, by lunar calendar, 丙子日 White Rat) Cloudy and Windy
466 Day of the War

War Situation
- The U.S. 1st and 9th Corps launch the Commando Operation.

- The U.S. battleship *USS New Jersey* launches artillery attacks on the Communist troops south of Goseong.
- Commander of the Communist troops responds to the message dated Sept. 27 sent by General Ridgway and refuses the suggested reopening of the Armistice Conference by changing the meeting place to Songhyeon-ri.

At Home

- The ceremony to celebrate the National Foundation Day takes place at the National Assembly.
- Minister of Defense, Lee Gi-boong issues a statement on the change of methods to take out materials from the Gyeonggi Province and Incheon area.
- The ceremony for the foundation of Mint Corporation is held.

October 4, Thursday (September 4, by lunar calendar, 丁丑日 Red Ox) Clear
467 Day of the War

War Situation

- The Communist troops keep on firing from the bridgeheads of "Heartbreak Ridge" north of Yanggu.
- The British Commonwealth Royal Army repulses the resistance of the Communist troops on the west of Yeoncheon, taking a target hill.

At Home

- The Martial Law Commander issues a proclamation on the prohibition of illegal possession of arms.
- The economic circle tries to seek reasonable and effective solutions on how to operate the UN compensation fund for Korea.

October 5, Friday (September 5, by lunar calendar, 戊寅日 Yellow Tiger) Clear
468 Day of the War

War Situation

- The UN troops advance 4.8-6.4km on the western frontlines to control advantageous positions after engaging in a four-day offensive battle.
- The U.S. 3rd Infantry Division breaks into the defending lines of the Chinese troops north of Cheorwon.

At Home

- The Ministry of Education sets up appropriate measures to educate school-aged refugees.
- The Office of Public Information issues guidelines to prohibit the selling of literary works by writers who went to North Korea, including their literary activities.
- Korean Airlines obtains permission from the UN Forces Command to fly non-regular

services between Japan and Korea (Busan and Tokyo).

October 6, Saturday (September 6, by lunar calendar, 己卯日 Yellow Rabbit) Clear and Cloudy
469 Day of the War

War Situation
- The U.S. and French Forces launch a heavy and sudden attack on the top hills of the Heartbreak Ridge" mainly with flame throwers and gun and bayonet fighting.
- The U.S. 1ˢᵗ Calvary Division and the Greek Infantry Unit repulse a strong counter-offensive by Chinese troops north of Yeoncheon.

At Home
- The Government proclaims the enforcement regulations on "the Temporary Tax Income Law."
- It is reported by an informed source that Kim Il Sung has fallen ill.

October 7, Sunday (September 7, by lunar calendar, 庚辰日 White Dragon) Cloudy
470 Day of the War

War Situation
- The allied troops occupy a hill north of Yanggu.

At Home
- The Provincial Police of South Gyeongsang Province moves its headquarters of the emergency alert command to Jinju.
- The Korean Mission in Japan announces the schedule and agenda for Korea-Japan Talks.

October 8, Monday (September 8, by lunar calendar, 辛巳日 White Snake) Cloudy and Clear
471 Day of the War

War Situation
- The ROK Army repels the North Korean troops from the hills northwest of the valley in Inje.

At Home
- Twenty six lawmakers are referred to the Disciplinary Committee of the National Assembly due to absence without due notice or reason.
- Minister of Foreign Affairs issues a statement to oppose the proposal made by the Communist party that the meeting place for the Armistice Conference should be stretched out to the neutral zone.

Overseas
- Meeting of the UN Special Committee for Forced Labor takes place in Geneva.
- The United States urges Korea and Japan to conclude the mutual agreement for trade and fishing matters.

October 9, Tuesday (September 9, by lunar calendar, 壬午日 Black Horse) Clear
472 Day of the War

War Situation
- The 38th Regiment of the U.S. 2nd Infantry Division engages in a fierce hand-to-hand battle with the Chinese troops on No.1 Hill of "Kim Il Sung Ridge" northwest of Yanggu.

At Home
- The Cabinet Meeting selects the Government's delegation headed by Prime Minister, Jang Myeon to represent Korea at the 6th UN General Assembly.
- The Korean Residents in Japan Human Rights Association begin to promote their human rights movements in line with Korea-Japan Talks.

October 10, Wednesday (September 10, by lunar calendar, 癸未日 Black Sheep) Clear
473 Day of the War

War Situation
- The allied troops occupy the two hills north of Yanggu.
- The liaison officers of the UN Forces meet with their counterparts of the Communist Forces. They survey Sacheongyo Bridge and its vicinity located on the south of Panmunjom to

U.S. Marines fire 4.5 inch rocket to the Chinese troops in Yanggu, Gangwon Province (1951. 10)

choose a new meeting venue for the Armistice Conference.

At Home

- As a provisional measure for the recovered areas north of the 38th parallel, the Government decides to establish an office of site-operation.
- Minister of Defense, Lee Gi-boong, issues a statement on the matters such as remuneration, etc. related to the Korean laborers employed by the U.S. Forces.

October 11, Thursday (September 11, by lunar calendar, 甲申日 Blue Monkey) Clear
474 Day of the War

War Situation

- The U.S. 1st Cavalry Division repulses the strong resistance by the Communist troops north of Yeoncheon.

At Home

- The Defense and Educational Committees of the National Assembly prepares a special measure to withhold the conscription of 10,198 students.
- The Ministry of Social Affairs and the Office of Public Information decide to organize "a night for entertaining the bereaved families of the fallen soldiers and policemen" by touring

Working-level staff officers from the both sides for the Armistice negotiation are looking at the map to decide on Military Demarcation Lines (1951. 10. 11)

the major cities throughout the country.

Overseas

- The Ministry of Foreign Affairs of the Philippines Government issues a diplomatic white paper regarding "the US - the Philippines Security and Defense Agreement" and "the Peace Treaty between the USA and Japan."

October 12, Friday (September 12, by lunar calendar, 乙酉日 Blue Rooster) Clear and Windy
475 Day of the War

War Situation

- The UN troops repel the resistance by the Communist troops northwest of Yanggu, capturing the five main hills.

At Home

- The Government selects the delegation to represent the Government at the UN General Assembly.
- Minister of Finance announces the implementation of the system of the limits of monthly currency issuance.

October 13, Saturday (September 13, by lunar calendar, 丙戌日 Red Dog) Cloudy and Windy
476 Day of the War

War Situation

- The UN troops repel the Communist troops on the six hills located northwest of Yanggu.
- The Korean representative for the Armistice Conference, Maj. Gen. Lee Hyeong -geun, says that Korean people want the unification of Korea and do not want to continue with the Armistice Conference any longer.

At Home

- The National Assembly agrees upon the Government's proposal that the highest honor of medal would be awarded to Franklin D. Roosevelt, Winston Churchill and Chang Kai-shek, respectively.
- The National Assembly gives its consent to the agreement between the Republic of Korea and the World Health Organization.

October 14, Sunday (September 14, by lunar calendar, 丁亥日 Red Pig) Cloudy and Windy
477 Day of the War

War Situation

- 36 U.S. Saber-jet fighters and 30 MIGs engage in dog fights in the skies above Sinanjoo.
- The 4th meeting with the liaison officers takes place for the Armistice Conference.

At Home

- A joint meeting by the responsible officials in charge is held. They are from the Department of the Civilian Affairs of the U.S. Army, the Ministry of Industry, the Planning Office of the Government, the Ministry of Communication and Postal Services, the Ministry of Transportation and other officials of the Government's agencies involved.
- A nationwide rally is successfully held by The Korean -Japanese Human Rights Association, passing five different resolutions including a permission of residence right to be given to the Korean residents in Japan.

Overseas
- The Central Committee of the Chinese Communist Party is to deliver the strategies of the Chinese troops to the Chinese representative, Lt. Gen. Teng Hua for the Armistice Conference.
- The Japanese liner Kongomaru carrying UN troops is stranded at the port of Sasebo on the way to Busan.

October 15, Monday (September 15, by lunar calendar, 戊子日 Yellow Rat) Cloudy, Windy and Clear
478 Day of the War

War Situation
- The U.S. 38th Regiment advances along the Bukhan River and occupies the top position of "Heartbreak Ridge."
- The ROK Army and the U.S. troops advance 5.5km from the northwest of Yanggu, occupying four strategic hills.
- The 5th meeting of the liaison officers for the Armistice Conference shows no progress.

At Home
- The Ministry of Industry issues import licenses to the laver manufacturers which have earned US$ 10,000 in 1950 by exporting laver. The items to be imported are: working shoes, sports shoes, pencils, etc.

October 16, Tuesday (September 16, by lunar calendar 己丑日 Yellow Ox) Clear
479 Day of the War

War Situation
- Commander of the UN Forces, General Ridgway, says that the present frontlines are considered to be "demarcation lines (or Truce lines)."

At Home
- The Cabinet Meeting passes the two bills related to the revision of the Constitution in connection with the "Direct election of the President" and "the Bicameral System."
- The total amount of national taxes collected for the first half of the year is KRW 76.7 billion while the Seoul Tax Office collects only 28 % of the target amount.

October 17, Wednesday (September 17, by lunar calendar, 庚寅日 White Tiger) Clear
480 Day of the War

War Situation

- The UN troops start to advance to Geumseong and occupied about 40 strategic hills for five days.
- The U.S. 1st Cavalry Division attacks the bridgeheads of the Communist troops northwest of Yeoncheon.

At Home

- The Cabinet Meeting passes a resolution on the revision of the Constitution in connection with "Direct election of President" and" the Bicameral System."
- About 500 Communist guerillas attack Okcheon causing 141 casualties, 17 wounded, and 68 kidnapped including damages to seven Government buildings, etc.

October 18, Thursday (September 18, by lunar calendar, 辛卯日 White Rabbit) Clear
481 Day of the War

War Situation

- The UN troops repel a fierce offensive by the Communist troops northeast of Ganseong.
- The U.S. 15th Armored Regiment occupies a hill northwest of Yeoncheon.

At Home

- The Minister of Social Affairs, Huh Jeong announces that the bereaved families of patriotic martyrs would be paid as a part of their living expenses: KWR 100,000 per household for the total of 100 households.
- The Minister of Agriculture and Forestry, Lim Moon-hwan advises the people to promote eating of brown rice as a means to improve their eating habits during the wartime.
- It is reported that Kim Kyu-sik has passed away in prison of the North Korea.

October 19, Friday (September 19, by lunar calendar, 壬辰日 Black Dragon) Clear and Cloudy
482 Day of the War

War Situation

- The ROK Capital Division completely secures the positions of the Nam River and advances to the south of Goseong.
- The 9th meeting of the liaison officers is held, and the Communist party accepts the establishment of a neutral zone near Moonsan and Kaesong.

At Home

- The plenary session of the National Assembly passes a bill on "the Law related to the improvement of wartime living conditions."
- On the occasion of the third year since the establishment of diplomatic and trade relations

between the USSR and the North Korea, Kim Il Sung sends a thank-you message to Stalin.

Overseas
- The delegation to represent Korea at the Korea-Japan Talks arrives at Haneda Airport.
- President Truman signs the resolution to formally end the war against Germany.

October 20, Saturday (September 20, by lunar calendar, 癸巳日 Black Snake) Cloudy and Windy
483 Day of the War

War Situation
- The UN troops regain the two hill positions southeast of Geumseong which were lost during the previous night.

At Home
- The National Assembly begins to discuss matters related to "the local election" and " the incident of riots in the POW camps."
- The Korean Residents Association in Japan holds a nationwide rally accepting a resolution for the Korea-Japan Talks.
- Chief of Staff of the ROK Army, Lee Jong-chan, issues an announcement for the establishment of "the Command of the Mt. Jiri Combat Operation."

October 21, Sunday (September 21, by lunar calendar, 甲午日 Blue Horse) Cloudy and Windy
484 Day of the War

War Situation
- The 6th Infantry Division occupies Mt. Gyoam.
- The UN troops occupy an important hill southwest of Geumseong.

At Home
- UN relief goods are imported, comprising 1,736 boxes of medicines, 46 boxes rubber materials, and others.
- The suicide attempt by a wounded officer is caused by his anger and dissatisfaction over his life, and becomes a social issue.

October 22, Monday (September 22, by lunar calendar, 乙未日 Blue Sheep) Cloudy
485 Day of the War

War Situation
- The allied Forces launch bombing focused on an assembly of Communist troops north of Geumseong.
- The UN Tank Units re-penetrate into Geumseong.

At Home

- The Vice-Minister of Home Affairs says that the present force of the national police is hard to maintain security of the nation, and is unable to perform necessary operations for mopping-up of guerillas.
- The Commander of the British Commonwealth Royal Army in Korea says that the lesson learned from the Korean War is a painful reminder of the Communists' invasion.
- The Minister of Social Affairs issues instructions to all governors of the local provinces, asking them to set up necessary measures to deal with the refugees.

Overseas
- The United Nations Commission of Korea (UNKOK) submits the recommendation in its 6th report to continue necessary support and assistance to enable Korea to achieve its unification and independence.
- The United Nations Commission for Unification and Rehabilitation for Korea (UNCURK) submits a report on the current situation of Korea.

October 23, Tuesday (September 23, by lunar calendar, 丙申日 Red Monkey) Cloudy, Windy and Clear
486 Day of the War

War Situation
- The allied troops attack a reconnaissance unit of the Communist troops northwest of Yanggu.
- A UN reconnaissance unit attacks a hill located west of Yeoncheon.

At Home
- The Ministry of Home Affairs submits a report on the overall security situation of the nation including the operation plans to mop up the guerillas.
- The United Nations Korean Reconstruction Agency (UNKRA) donates the new editions of "The Annual Report of the United Nations" to the United Nations Association, Republic of Korea, including other books.

October 24, Wednesday (September 24, by lunar calendar, 丁酉日 Red Rooster) Cloudy, Windy and Clear
487 Day of the War

War Situation
- The UN troops advance 457m from the west of Geumseong.
- The UN Tank Unit advance to the southwest of Geumseong, destroying the defense walls in construction of the Communist troops.
- Major General Lee Hyung-geun is appointed as a new representative in the Ceasefire negotiation.

At Home

- On the occasion of commemorating the UN Day, President Syngman Rhee appeals to the people of the free world emphasizing the important missions of the UN -organized projects which should be implemented as soon as possible as scheduled.
- The Government re-organizes the delegation to strengthen the representation for the Korea-Japan Talks.
- Yang Yoo-chan, Head of Korean representatives for the Korea-Japan Talks meets with General Ridgway.

October 25, Thursday (September 25, by lunar calendar, 戊戌日 Yellow Dog) Clear and Windy
488 Day of the War

War Situation
- The 27th main session of the Armistice Conference is held.
  - Nam Il, Chief representative of the Communist Party proposes that all matters related to the negotiation should be handled by the Joint Subcommittee," while the joint committee of liaison officers handles other matters related to administration, guarantee of security and investigation of incidents. The UN's representative, the vice Admiral C. Turner Joy accepts the proposal.

At Home
- Media reporters from South Korea and North Korea meet and exchange conversation.
- The ROK Navy hold the 2nd Honorary Discharge Ceremony of the wounded soldiers.

October 26, Friday (September 26, by lunar calendar, 己亥日 Yellow Pig) Clear
489 Day of the War

War Situation
- The UN troops advance 914m from the southeast of Geumseong, and its infantry element destroys a cluster of pillboxes (touchka) of the Communist troops.
- The 8th Joint Subcommittee is held for the Armistice Conference:
  1) The Communist Party suggests a new proposal on the demarcation lines.
  2) Based on the axis of the current 160km battle lines near Jineung-dong(16km north of Munsan), both sides should withdraw 24km. On those conditions, the Communist side demands from the UN delegation that the UN troops withdraw from the Ongjin Peninsula.

At Home
- The National Assembly passes a bill related to the law to prohibit the raising of contributions (donation money).
- The supplementary call-up for the Second Peoples' Force is implemented.

Overseas

- President Truman signs the final draft bill related to "the Law on Prohibition of Military and Economic Aid." By the enactment of this law, the USA Government cannot provide any military or economic assistance to those countries which export certain strategic or military items to the Soviet Union and Soviet bloc countries.

October 27, Saturday (September 27, by lunar calendar, 庚子日 White Rat) Clear, Cloudy and Clear
490 Day of the War

War Situation
- The UN troops occupy a strategic hill southeast of Geumseong.

At Home
- President Syngman Rhee issues his opinions on the 2nd presidential election and the formation of a new political party.
- The Ministry of Social Affairs explains about a plan for the schedule of the people's return to their   houses.

October 28, Sunday (September 28, by lunar calendar, 辛丑日 White Ox) Clear and Windy.
491st Day of the War

War Situation
- The ROK 8th Infantry Division engages in a 23-day operation, and finally occupies the strategic Hill 1090.
- A meeting is held between the UN liaison officers and their counterparts of the Communist Side. They agree to establish a new joint agency in charge of safety and security concerned with the Armistice negotiation.

At Home
- The Ministry of Defense announces the abolition of "the detailed notices on the postponement of conscription for the Secondary People's Force.
- The Wonju Police Station arrests a political spy from North Korea.

October 29, Monday (September 29, by lunar calendar, 壬寅日 Black Tiger) Clear
492 Day of the War

War Situation
- Three consecutive offensives by the Communist troops are attempted from the east and the southeast of Geumseong.
- The UN troops occupy two strategic hills northwest of Yeoncheon.

At Home
- All banks start to deal with the deposit accounts system for children.
- The Banking Cooperative begins to provide banking loans for the purchase of cattle for

farming.

- The Korean Association of the Disabled Veterans files an application with the Ministry of Industry regarding the Comprehensive Technical School for the disabled or wounded veterans.

October 30, Tuesday (October 1, by lunar calendar, 癸卯日 Black Rabbit) Clear
493 Day of the War

War Situation

- The UN troops attack the Communist troops on the hill of the eastern frontlines, destroying 40 firing positions in the pits of earth and woodwork.
- The 12th session of the Joint Subcommittee is held for the Armistice Conference.

At Home

- Syngman Rhee issues a statement on the abolishment of postponement for the conscription of the military service.
- The Central Vocational Guidance Agency of the Disabled Veterans establishes the Special Relief Center for Teachers Training and issues an announcement for recruitment.

Overseas

- The U.S.-Japan Pacific Market Conference takes place in Tokyo.
- The United States Atomic Energy Commission (AEC) carries out America's third atomic bomb test.

October 31, Wednesday (October 2, by lunar calendar, 甲辰日 Blue Dragon) Clear
494 Day of the War

War Situation

- The UN troops repel an attack by 200 Communist troops southeast of Geumseong.

At Home

- The Director of Military Affairs, Ministry of Defense, issues a statement on the abolishment of postponement for the conscription of the Second Peoples' Force as well as the regular conscription system.
- The Office of Public Information announces that the collection of all empty cartridges used by the U.S. Army would be done by the Korean Association of Theological School Construction.

At the end of 1951, the number of UN troops was sufficient and it was possible for the shift of the military mission. U.S. soldiers are being on board to go back to their hometown.

One week before the Thanksgiving Day, A U.S. Sergeant First Class takes out and holds the turkey from the food supplies that arrived at Busan Port.

The soldiers of U.S. Marines are eating turkey flown by a helicopter.

November 1, Thursday (October 3, by lunar calendar, 乙巳日 Blue Snake) Cloudy and Clear
495 Day of the War

War Situation
- The UN troops repel an offensive of the Communist tropps toward the bridgeheads held by the UN forces southwest of Geumseong.
- The 14th session of the Joint Subcommittee is held.
- Regarding the demarcation lines, most of the agenda items are agreed upon except for defining the zone of "Heartbreak Ridge" which is linked to the Gimhwa, Idong, and the east coast lines.

At Home
- The Ministry of Social Affairs establishes an assistance and relief plan to support the bereaved families of the fallen military servicemen and policemen as well as the families of the military and the police in active service.
- The Jeju Police Station arrests Cho Mong-ku who allegedly masterminded the 4.3 Incident.

Overseas
- The three battalions of the British Commonwealth Royal Army stationed in Hong Kong leaves for Korea.
- The U.S. Atomic Energy Commission carries out its fourth nuclear bomb test near Las Vegas.

November 2, Friday (October 4, by lunar calendar, 丙午日 Red Horse) Clear
496 Day of the War

War Situation
- The UN troops retreat from the outpost lines west of Yeoncheon due to an attack by the Communist troops.
- The UN troops repel the two consecutive reconnaissance actions of the Communist troops southeast of Geumseong.

At Home
- The Ministry of Transportation strongly protests to the Japanese Government over the unnecessarily rigid control of entry into Japanese ports by Korean ocean-going vessels.
- The National Police discloses an incident about the illegal detention cells and violations such as confinement and assault.
- North Korea dismisses Huh Ga-I, the first secretary of the Joseon (Korean) Labor Party.

November 3, Saturday (October 5, by lunar calendar, 丁未日 Red Sheep) Clear
497 Day of the War

War Situation
- The UN troops repel three offensives by the Communist troops southeast of Geumseong.
- The USS New Jersey bombs Wonsan and Heungnam.

At Home
- The police arrest the captain and crew of a ship who were going to stow themselves away into Japan.
- Seoul City holds a large departure ceremony for the youngmen joining the Army.
- The UN troops issue a communique regarding the negotiation for the Armistice.

November 4, Sunday (October 6, by lunar calendar, 戊申日 Yellow Monkey) Cloudy and Clear
498 Day of the War

War Situation
- The UN troops continue repelling the Communists' attacks until midnight.
- The 17th Joint Subcommittee meeting for the Armistice negotiation is held. The Communist party refuses the proposal made by the UN delegation in connection with the demilitarization of Kaesong.

At Home
- Representatives of the Korean Government, the UN Forces and SCAP (Supreme Commander of the Allied Powers) hold a secret meeting on the reconstruction plans for the Korean economy.

November 5, Monday (October 7, by lunar calendar, 己酉日 Yellow Rooster) Rainy
499 Day of the War

War Situation
- The UN troops recapture two hilltops northwest of Yeoncheon.
- The two parties of the Armistice negotiation reach a deadlock over the issue of the delineation of the demarcation lines.

At Home
- The National Assembly passes a resolution opposing the idea of conceding the Yeonbaek and Ongjin areas to North Korea.
- The Government establishes a Special Investigation Committee in order to prevent the illegal transactions of relief aid goods on the black market.
- An attack by Communist guerillas on passenger carriages on a railroad causes 24 casualties.

November 6, Tuesday (October 8, by lunar calendar, 庚戌日 White Dog) Rainy
500 Day of the War

War Situation

- The UN troops advance 1.8-2.7 km northwest of Ganseong.
- The UN troops retreat from the two hilltops northwest of Yeoncheon due to pressure by the Chinese troops.

At Home

- The Ministry of Telecommunication and Postal Services raises the telegram and telephone rates by an average of 22%.
  - The population of Incheon City increases to 300,000.
- The Association of Seoul City's Dong offices holds a city-wide rally to demand that Kaesong be retained as part of the territory of the South during the Armistice negotiation.

Overseas

- The Korean delegation to represent the 6th UN General Assembly leaves for Paris.
- The fourth meeting is held of the shipping affairs subcommittee for the preliminary Korea-Japan Talks.

November 7, Wednesday (October 9, by lunar calendar, 辛亥日 White Pig) Rainy and Cloudy
501 Day of the War

War Situation

- The UN Infantry Unit repels the offensive by the Chinese troops on the hilltops near the Imjin River west of Yeoncheon.
- The 20th Joint Subcommittee meeting is held for the Armistice negotiation.
- Both parties for the Armistice negotiation engage in a bitter tug-of-war (November 7-16) over the issue, regarding:
  1) an immediate decision to define the demarcation lines;
  2) defining the demarcation lines at the time of signing the Agreement.

At Home

- The Government concludes a financial agreement with the Command of the UN Forces and Japan in connection with the transfer of accounts.
- The North Korean Broadcasting reports that Park Dong-jo, the vice-minister of North Korea dies during execution of important duties.

November 8, Thursday (October 10, by lunar calendar, 壬子日 black Rat) Rainy and Clear
502 Day of the War

War Situation

- The UN Troops launch a sudden attack on the outposts of the Communist troops north of Inje.

- The UN troops retake a hilltop northwest of Yeoncheon.

At Home
- The Korean Women's Youth Corps holds a ceremony in the Busan Cultural Theatre to erect and present bronze statutes honoring three U.S. Generals, MacArthur, Ridgway, and Van Fleet.
- The Mission of the ROK in Japan begins a survey on the status of Korean residents visiting and living in Japan.

November 9, Friday (October 11, by lunar calendar, 癸丑日 Black Ox) Clear and Cloudy
503 Day of the War

War Situation
- All along the frontline, small-scale reconnaissance activities are seen.
- The 22nd Joint Subcommittee meeting for the Armistice negotiation reaches a deadlock over the issue on the delineation of the demarcation lines.

At Home
- The Ministry of Finance finishes its survey on the quantity of crops harvested in accordance with the Temporary Land Income Tax Law.

November 10, Saturday (October 12, by lunar calendar, 甲寅日 Blue Tiger) Clear
504 Day of the War

War Situation
- The UN troops repel six separate attacks by the Communist troops southwest of Geumseong.

At Home
- Following joint operations by the three Provincial Police Stations (North Jeolla, South Chungcheong and North Chungcheong Provinces), successful mopping-up is completed against the Communist guerillas.
- The Politburo of the Central Committee of the Labor Party of North Korea (Joseon Rodong Dang) adopts a resolution to strengthen the relief projects for the war victims and refugees.

Overseas
- The United Nations Security Council discusses the issue of Kashmir, and adopts a resolution. The terms of conditions proposed by Dr. Frank Graham are set forth in the Resolution clarifying the demilitarization of Kashmir. (9 ayes, 0 nays, 2 withdraws)

November 11, Sunday (October 13, by lunar calendar, 乙卯日 Blue Rabbit) Cloudy
505 Day of the War

War Situation

- The UN troops repulse an offensive of five battalions of Communist troops on the eastern frontlines.
- The 24th Joint subcommittee meeting for the Armistice talks is held, but no progress is made.

At Home
- The Central Urban Planning Council reviews the plan for reconstruction of the five major cities.
- The Daehan (Korean) War-bereaved Families Association is founded as a non-profit corporation.

November 12, Monday (October 14, by lunar calendar, 丙辰日 Red Dragon) Rainy and Clear
506 Day of the War

War Situation
- The UN troops repel the two reconnaissance units of the Communist troops northwest of the eastern basin.
- The UN troops occupy two strategic hilltops southwest of Geumseong.
- The 25th Joint Subcommittee meeting for the Armistice talks is held without any particular results.

At Home
- The plenary session of the National Assembly discusses the bill of "the Labor Standard Law" and decides to re-examine it.
- Minister of Defense Lee Gi-boong, issues a statement on "the homecoming of the soldiers" and the counter-measures to resolve related issues.
- The passenger service of Jeolla railway between Yeosu and Suncheon reopens. The service had been suspended due to the transportation of military personnel.

November 13, Tuesday (October 15, by lunar calendar, 丁巳日 Red Snake) Clear
507 Day of the War

War Situation
- The UN troops repel numerous attacks by 5 Communist troops south of Goseong.
- An Infantry Unit of the UN troops occupies two strategic hilltops southwest of Geumseong.
- The 26th Joint subcommittee meeting for the Armistice talks is held.

At Home
- The Minister of Defense Lee Gi-boong announces the augmentation of the ROK military Forces.
- Representatives from the Korean Government, the UN Forces Command, the UN Office of Civilian Affairs and UNKRA (The United Nations Korea Reconstruction Agency) meet for a

discussion of Korean economic problems.
- The Korea-Japan Talks encounter some difficulties due to the issue of the Korean residents in Japan.

November 14, Wednesday (October 16, by lunar calendar, 戊午日 Yellow Horse) Clear and Cloudy
508 Day of the War

War Situation
- UN troops repel attacks by the Communist troops south of Geumseong.

At Home
- The Ministry of Transportation reports on the incident of attacking the trains by the Communist guerillas:
  - Eighty armed guerillas attacked the Youngdong Railway Station on the Gyeongbu-line setting fire to its building.
- The Board of Inspection and Audit decides "the guidelines on the Inspection and Audit."

November 15, Thursday (October 17, by lunar calendar, 己未日 Yellow Sheep) Cloudy and Clear
509 Day of the War

War Situation
- The UN troops retreat from the north of Yanggu due to fierce attacks by the enemy troops but re-occupy their positions.
- The UN troops repel the night attacks by the Chinese troops west of Cheorwon.

At Home
- The Monetary Policy Committee endorses the lending allocations: KRW1.2 billion for the welfare housing construction and KRW1.46 billion for the supply of tap-water.
- Vice-ministers and high-ranking officials from every Government ministry visit the wounded and disabled soldiers.

Overseas
- The 7th Shipping Business Subcommittee for the Korea-Japan Talks is held.

November 16, Friday (October 18, by lunar calendar, 庚申日 White Monkey) Rainy and Clear
510 Day of the War

War Situation
- The UN troops occupy a strategic hill west of Cheorwon.
- The U.S. Far East Air Force destroys the railway systems in the center of the North Korea.
- The 29th Joint Subcommittee session for the Armistice Conference is held.
- Long hours' discussion and debate are exchanged to decide the timing of defining the

military demarcation lines but no tangible results emerge.

At Home

- The inspection team of the Board of Inspection and Audit leaves for Japan to inspect all organizations representing the Government in Tokyo.

November 17, Saturday (October 19, by lunar calendar, 辛酉日 White Rooster) Clear, Cloudy and Clear

511 Day of the War

War Situation

- The ROK 6th Infantry Division occupies Hill 949.
- The UN troops occupy a strategic hill west of Cheorwon.
- The 30th Joint Subcommittee for the Armistice Conference is held.

At Home

- Martial Law Commander Lee Jong-chan issues a proclamation to prohibit the wearing of military uniforms by civilians.
- The Police Station of the North Gyeongsang Province launches a winter operation to mop up the guerillas.

Korean women make flour with grinding wheat by using a treadmill and sifting (1951. 11. 18)

• The ferry, No. 3 Haenam, sinks in the sea off Jindo Island with the loss of 60 passengers.

November 18, Sunday (October 20, by lunar calendar, 壬戌日 Black Dog) Rainy and Clear
512 Day of the War

War Situation
• The UN troops advance 1.8km from the mid-frontlines occupying three strategic hills on the east of the Bukhan River.
• The 1st Infantry Division of the British Commonwealth Royal Army re-takes a strategic hill west of Yeoncheon.

At Home
• The Vice-Minister of Defense visits the recuperation center for the disabled veterans at Dongnae.
• The Ministry of Transportation presents the results of the investigation related to the Incident of the Ferry, No 3. *Haenam* that was wrecked in the sea off Jindo Island of South Jeolla Province.
• The police of South Jeolla Province resume operations to mop up the Communist guerillas.

November 19, Monday (October 21, by lunar calendar, 癸亥日 Black Pig) Clear, Cloudy and Clear
513 Day of the War

War Situation
• The elements belonging to the ROK 6th Infantry Division and 8th Infantry Division repel the attack twice by the reconnaissance units of the Communist troops southeast of Geumseong.
• The UN troops repulse a battalion of the Chinese troops west of Yeoncheon.
• The 32nd Joint Sub-Committee session is held for the Armistice Conference.
  - The Communist side commits to respond to the proposal made by the UN troops before November 21.

At Home
• The Prime Minister Jang Myeon meets with Secretary of State Acheson and discusses the problems of Korea and the U.S.-Korea alliance.
• The Liberal Party is founded, and Syngman Rhee is elected as its chairman.

November 20, Tuesday (October 22, by lunar calendar, 甲子日 Blue Rat) Clear
514 Day of the War

War Situation
• Hand-to-hand battles occur south of Goseong.
• The ROK troops break through the defense lines of the Communist troops southeast of

Geumseong and advance 6.4km.

At Home

- The National Assembly passes two proposals concerning "the strengthening of the relief and assistance projects for the disabled veterans" and "the recommendations to the Government on the restoration of the Seoul and Busan railway line."
- The Ministry of Defense begins registration of the reservist officers in preparation for future military training of students.
- The Korean Women's Party is founded (and is represented by Lim Yeong-shin).

November 21, Wednesday (October 23, by lunar calendar, 乙丑日 Blue Ox) Clear
515 Day of the War

War Situation

- The Communist troops attempt to attack the bridgehead of the ROK troops southeast of Geumseong but fail.
- The UN troops repel a sudden offensive by the Communist troops west of Yeoncheon.
- The 33th Joint Subcommittee session is held for the Armistice Conference.

At Home

- The Prime Minister, Jang Myeon reports to President Syngman Rhee on what was discussed with the US Secretary of State Acheson.
- The ROK Army sends its orders for mopping-up operation in the southwest area of the country.

Overseas

- A nationwide campaign rally to oppose the Forced deportation of Korean residents in Japan" takes place in spite of the warnings given by the chairman of Hukuoka Prefecture and Police.

November 22, Thursday (October 24, by lunar calendar, 丙寅日 Red Tiger) Clear, Cloudy and Windy
516 Day of the War

War Situation

- The UN troops repel the reconnaissance assault by the Communist troops southeast of Geumseong and east of the Bukhan River.
- The 34th Joint Subcommittee meeting of the Armistice Conference takes place.
- Both parties for the Armistice Conference announce that the demarcation lines fixed and agreed upon by the negotiating parties would be effective and operational from November 23.

At Home

- Acting Prime Minister Huh Jeong submits an official letter to the National Assembly to oppose using Daejeon City as a temporary capital.
- The Minister of Social Affairs Huh Jeong has a press interview, talking about the assistance to the bereaved families of fallen war-heroes and the distribution of relief goods to them.
- Chief of Staff of the U.S. Air Force, General Hoyt Vandenberg says that the US Air Force will not hesitate to bomb the main military basis of the Chinese troops in Manchuria if the negotiation for the Armistice agreement comes to a rupture.

November 23, Friday (October 25, by lunar calendar, 丁卯日 Red Rabbit) Rainy, Clear, Cloudy and Clear
517 Day of the War

War Situation
- The staff officers of the both parties for the negotiation of the Armistice agreement begin to define and fix "the present lines of ground contact."

At Home
- The National Assembly passes "the proposal on the revised plan of railroad fare for the soldiers of the UN troops and ROK Army."
- About five hundred refugees die over the past five months in the refugee camp of Jeonju of North Jeolla Province.

November 24, Saturday (October 26, by lunar calendar, 戊辰日 Yellow Dragon) Clear and Windy.
518 Day of the War

War Situation
- The UN troops lose the two outposts southwest of Geumseong, but re-capture them.
- In order to secure more favorable positions for the demarcation lines, fierce hand-to-hand battles occur west of Yeonchoen.

At Home
- Acting Prime Minister, Huh Jeong issues an announcement on the status of the total damages inflicted by the War.
  - The total property losses amount to KRW 7.65 trillion, while the number of totally burnt buildings is 514,900.
- The Minister of Foreign Affairs, Byun Yeong-tae issues a statement on the Korea-Japan Talks.

Overseas
- The 11th meeting of the Korea Japan Shipping Business Subcommittee is held.

November 25, Sunday (October 27, by lunar calendar, 己巳日 Yellow Snake) Rainy

519 Day of the War

War Situation
- The UN troops occupy a strategic hill west of Yeoncheon after a 24-hour battle.
- The meeting by the staff officers for the Armistice Conference reaches agreement on 75% of the present lines of ground contact,

At Home
- The Cabinet Meeting decides to permit the sellers of seafood to the UN troops to dispose of the foreign exchange owned by them. It is one of the ways to remove the embargo on seafood exports.
- The ROK Army holds the 13th Honorary Discharge Ceremony for Disabled Veterans at the parade ground of the ROK Army Unit No. 839

November 26, Monday (October 28, by lunar calendar, 庚午日 White Horse) Clear and Windy
520 Day of the War

War Situation
- The UN troops continue to secure the strategic hills (called "Little Gibraltar") west of Yeoncheon.
- Through the staff officers for the Armistice Conference, the final agreement is made on present lines of ground contact by both sides for 232km of the frontline.

At Home
- President Syngman Rhee expresses his opinion through a press interview on the time-limited ceasefire line.

November 27, Tuesday (October 29, by lunar calendar, 辛未日 White Sheep) Cloudy, Windy and Clear
521 Day of the War

War Situation
- The ROK 6th Infantry Division fights against the Chinese troops southeast of Geumseong, and recapture the strategic hilltops along the upper stream of the Bukhan River.
- Temporary demilitarized lines are agreed upon. Both parties begin to discuss Item No.3, the ceasefire and detailed issues related.

At Home
- The Government organizes the Temporary Public Hygiene Inspection Team as a part of its agencies so as to conduct better control of entertainment business houses.
- A Ceremony for the Day of the Disabled Veterans takes place at Dong-A Theatre in Busan.
- A meeting of the presidents of all universities decides how to postpone the conscription of the students.

Staff officers from the both sides for the Armistice agreement are signing the map of demarcation line (1951. 11. 27)

November 28, Wednesday (October 30, by lunar calendar, 壬申日 Black Monkey) Clear
522 Day of the War

War Situation
• The UN troops repel an assault by the Communist troops northwest of Yanggu.

At Home
• Acting Prime Minister Huh Jeong announces that a proposal for the revised draft of the Constitution would be submitted to the National Assembly within a few days.
• Acting Prime Minister Huh Jeong visits a refugees' camp which was burnt.

November 29, Thursday (November 1, by lunar calendar, 癸酉日 Black Rooster) Clear
523 Day of the War

War Situation
• The UN troops retake the outposts northwest of Yanggu.
• The UN Artillery Unit launches bombarding from the western frontlines on the target positions of the enemy troops.

• The 30th main session of the Armistice Conference is held.

At Home
• The Cabinet Meeting issues a statement on the negotiation for the Armistice agreement posing three questions to the UN:
1) Should the United Nations maintain its position to keep the peace in Korea on the condition that the Chinese troops do not remain on Korean territory ?
2) Is the United Nations trying to take necessary measures to ensure security and safety for the people of North Korea?
3) Is the United Nations willing to impose the necessary timeframe for the Korean unification to be achieved by satisfying its inherent purposes?
• The Government passes a resolution for the revised plan of the Constitution.

November 30, Friday (November 2, by lunar calendar, 甲戌日 Blue Dog) Clear and Cloudy
524 Day of the War

War Situation
• The reconnaissance unit of the Communist troops attacks the bridgehead of the UN troops on the southwest of Geumseong, but is repelled.
• The 31st meeting for the Armistice Conference is held.

At Home
• The Government issues an official announcement on the revised Constitution in relation to the "direct election of national president and vice-president" and the establishment of the bicameral system of the National Assembly.
• As of December 1, the Minister of Defense, Lee Gi-boong proclaims emergency martial law in the areas where the Communist guerillas make frequent appearances.
• The Emergency Operational Mission of the South Jeolla Provincial Police proclaims a curfew in limited areas.

Overseas
• The Political Committee of the United Nations ratifies the proposal for an unofficial conference of the Four Nations' Disarmament Special Committee of the United Nations jointly made by the three countries including Andrey Vyshinsky, representative of the USSR, and Pakistan.
• The meeting for Subcommittee of the Korea-Japan Talks is held in order to deal with various matters on "nationality." The Committee discusses the practical matters related to deportation and other nationality problems.

The soldiers of U.S. Marines 1st Division are riding a heavy cargo helicopter

A U.S. tank is firing to the enemy position near Chuncheon (1951. 12)

December 1, Saturday (November 3, by lunar calendar, 乙亥日 Blue Pig) Clear
525 Day of the War

War Situation
- The UN troops repulse the counter-offensive by the Communist troops south of Geumseong.
- The 32nd main session for the Armistice Conference is held.
  - The UN party offers the four proposals including no more Forces to be reinforced during the ceasefire period.

At Home
- The National Assembly adopts a resolution to oppose any ceasefire whose purposes are contradictory to the UN Charter.
- Presidential decree No. 577 for "the order for students' military training" is proclaimed.
- Martial Law Commander, Maj. Gen. Lee Jong-chan, issues a proclamation of Emergency Martial Law in the areas of the North Chungcheong Province, and the Jeolla Provinces including parts of Gyeongsang Provinces.
  - Except for Busan and Daegu, the whole of South Korea is subject to the Emergency Martial Law. The National Police establishes its Command of Frontlines at Namwon and begins its joint operation with the military mission to mop up the Communist guerillas.

Overseas
- The U.S. State Department states that there are about 18,000 guerillas in the southern areas of South Korea.

December 2, Sunday (November 4, by lunar calendar, 丙子日 Red Rat) Clear and Windy
526 Day of the War

War Situation
- The U.S. Marine Corps together with a special unit of British Commonwealth Royal Army launches a landing on the east coast near Dancheon, and destroys the communication and transportation facilities of the Communist troops.
- The UN troops retreat from the southwest of Pyeonggang due to the attack by the Communist troops, but re-take its original positions.

At Home
- The Korean Relief Society for the Bereaved Families of the Veterans has a joint meeting with the representative of the surviving families and many officials concerned with relief missions and services.

- Lee Jong-chan, Commander of the Martial Law issues a statement regarding the mop-up operation to annihilate the Communist guerillas under the Martial Law.

December 3, Monday (November 5, by lunar calendar, 丁丑日 Red Ox) Clear
527 Day of the War

War Situation
- The UN troops repel the reconnaissance assaults by the Communist troops on the eastern frontlines.
- The ROK Air Force begins to attack the guerilla positions on Mt. Jiri.

At Home
- The Ministry of Social Affairs pays living expenses to the bereaved families of the patriotic forefathers.
- Commissioner General of the National Police Agency, Kim Tae-seon inspects the situation of the Jeolla Provinces, and discloses the results of the guerillas' defection for the past many days.

December 4, Tuesday (November 6, by lunar calendar, 戊寅日 Yellow Tiger) Clear and Rainy
528 Day of the War

War Situation
- The UN troops repel the reconnaissance Units of the Communist troops on the northwest of the eastern front lines and southwest of Geumseong.
- The 35th main session for the Armistice Conference is held.
- The Joint Subcommittee conferences are held.

At Home
- Commissioner General of the National Police Agency, Kim Tae-seon has a press interview briefing on the overall situation of the battles in the local areas.
- The ROK Army begins to launch the operation to mop up the Communist guerillas.

December 5, Wednesday (November 7, by lunar calendar, 己卯日 Yellow Rabbit) Clear
529 Day of the War

War Situation
- The UN troops repel the reconnaissance Units of the Communist troops on the eastern frontlines.
- A meeting for the Armistice Conference is held.
  The Communist party delivers a written answer to the liaison officer of the UN troops in connection with the response to the questions raised by the UN delegation dated December 4.

At Home

- President Syngman Rhee broadcasts his message asking the people to more positively help with mopping-up of the guerillas in Mt. Jiri. A special statement on the occasion of launching mopping-up operation to annihilate the Communist guerillas.
- Commander of the Eighth U.S. Army, General Van Fleet, inspects the field operation of guerilla mop-up operations.

December 6, Thursday (November 8, by lunar calendar, 庚辰日 White Dragon) Clear and Windy
530 Day of the War

War Situation

- The UN troops repulse the attacks by the reconnaissance unit of the Communist troops in the areas of Mundeungri of Yanggu.

At Home

- The Ministry of Social Affairs establishes the appropriate counter-measures against the moving of the refugees who would be coming down to the south of the military demarcation lines to be temporarily fixed.

December 7, Friday (November 9, by lunar calendar, 辛巳日 White Snake) Clear, Windy and Rainy
531 Day of the War

War Situation

- No particular confrontation is noted all through the 233.3km of battle lines.
- The staff officers of the UN troops and the Communist Army finish the field works to define the demilitarized zone.

At Home

- The Minister of Home Affairs, Lee Soon-yong issues an announement on "the Regulations on the National Police Academy."
- "The International Friendship Football Matches" is held at the playground of the ROK Infantry Academy at Dongnae.

Overseas

- Mao Zedong sends a message related to the exchange of POWs to be dealt with by the Armistice Conference. He adds that the United States has no basic rights to ask China to seek the missing soldiers of the U.S. troops.

December 8, Saturday (November 10, by lunar calendar, 壬午日 Black Horse) Clear and Windy
532 Day of the War

War Situation

- Few confrontations, in general, are noted on the battle lines.
- The UN troops repel the night attack by the Communist troops south of Pyeonggang and southwest of Geumseong.

At Home
- The Civil Affairs Bureau of South Gyoengsang Province announces the self-reporting period for the dodgers of conscription (December 8-12).
- Most of the farmers in North Gyeongsang Province suffer from the implementation of "the Land Income Tax."
- Seoul Railroad Police Chief Lee In-gang , the chief criminal of the incident of stealing copper wire is sentenced to 6 years imprisonment.
- In Busan many rallies are held by the students to oppose the Armistice.

December 9, Sunday (November 11, by lunar calendar, 癸未日 Black Sheep) Clear and Windy.
533 Day of the War

War Situation
- The UN Infantry elements recapture the three outposts which were lost on December 7.
- The UN troops repel the attacks by the two battalions of the Communist troops in the Pyeonggang area.

At Home
- Three lawmakers of the U.S. House of Representatives, including MacClass, visit the front lines.
- Through the Voice of America, The Prime Minister Jang Myeon delivers a brief report on his activities during the period of his participation as the representative of the Republic of Korea to the United Nations.
- One million students deliver their letter of resolution to the Speaker of the National Assembly to oppose the Armistice agreement.

Overseas
- The Four Nations' Disarmament Special Committee of the United Nations prepares a report to present to the UN Political Committee.
- A delegation of East Germany which is to participate in the general session of UN Political Committee to review and assess the various matters related to the general election in Germany arrives at Paris.

December 10, Monday (November 12, by lunar calendar, 甲申日 Blue Monkey) Clear and Cloudy
534 Day of the War

War Situation
- The Joint Subcommittee meeting of the Armistice Conference is held. The UN delegate

proposes the establishment of a subcommittee to discuss and finalize the matters related to the exchange of POWs.

- The staff officers of both parties for the Armistice Conference sign an agreement to finalize the temporary border lines for the demilitarized zone.

At Home

- Both parties to the Armistice Conference sign the agreement to finalize the temporary border lines for the demilitarized zone.
- An Australian soldier is indicted and charged with the murder of a Korean soldier.

December 11, Tuesday (November 13, by lunar calendar, 乙酉日 Blue Rooster) Clear
535 Day of the War

War Situation

- A U.S. Air Force F-86 fighter plane shoots down two MIGs and destroys another two.

At Home

- The Minister Extraordinary and Plenipotentiary Kim Yong-sik, assigned to the Korean Mission in Japan, has a press interview in which he explains the tasks and operation of the Mission.

December 12, Wednesday (November 14, by lunar calendar, 丙戌日 Red Dog) Clear
536 Day of the War

War Situation

- The UN troops attack the bridgehead of the Communist troops west of Yeoncheon.
- The UN Air Force Squadron continues to bomb the bridgeheads on the frontlines and supply routes of the enemy troops.

At Home

- The Defense Command of Jeju Island reports on the results of mopping up the Communist guerillas.
- A mass rally for the anti-ceasefire campaign is held in Seoul.

December 13, Thursday (November 15, by lunar calendar, 丁亥日 Red Pig) Clear
537 Day of the War

War Situation

- The reconnaissance units of the UN troops engage twice in battles in western frontlines.
- The Joint Subcommittee for the Armistice Conference does not come to any conclusion due to the different opinions on the matters related to "the Neutral Nations Supervision" and "the exchange of POWs."

At Home

- The National People's Party (called "Minkuk -Dang") issues a statement on opposing the exchange of POWs who come from South Korea.
- The Anti-Communist POWs in Geoje Island POW camp delivers a letter of appeal to the National Assembly and ask for setting themselves free.

December 14, Friday (November 16, by lunar calendar, 戊子日 Yellow Rat) Clear, Snowy, Clear and Windy
538 Day of the War

War Situation
- The U.S. 25th Infantry Division sends its reconnaissance unit to attack the bridgehead of the Communist troops southwest of Pyeonggang.
- A reconnaissance unit of the UN troops engages in a five-hour battle with the Communist troops northwest of Gorangpo.

At Home
- The Planning Board asks the Korea Civil Affairs Agency of the United Nations for aid in the amount of US$ 500 million.
- The Korean Veterans Association is inaugurated.
- The Korean representative to the United Nations affirms Korea's opposition to an Armistice agreement.

December 15, Saturday (November 17, by lunar calendar, 己丑日 Yellow Ox) Clear
539 Day of the War

War Situation
- Reconnaissance activities are sporadically noted on the entire frontline.
- The sessions for the Armistice Joint Subcommittee including the POWs Exchange Subcommittee are held.

At Home
- The Government unifies the allocation of grain for the refugees including its transportation to be managed by the Ministry of Agriculture and Forestry.
- The Ministry of Defense establishes a plan for the students' military training targeting all high schools and universities throughout the nation.

December 16, Sunday (November 18, by lunar calendar, 庚寅日 White Tiger) Clear
540 Day of the War

War Situation
- The UN troops repulse the attacks of the Communist reconnaissance unit north of the eastern frontline.

- The UN troops launch a sudden attack on an outpost of the Communist troops south of Panmunjom, and withdraw after a battle.

At Home
- The Government announces that 40,000 POWs express their pledge of allegiance to the country.

Overseas
- An adviser to the U.S. Secretary of State, Dulles, leaves for Tokyo after touring the frontlines of Korea.

December 17, Monday (November 19, by lunar calendar, 辛卯日 White Rabbit) Clear
541 Day of the War

War Situation
- The Turkish troops in south of Pyeonggang repel the attack of the Communist troops on the outpost.
- The sub-committee for POWs Exchange takes place: The Communist party request the UN Representatives to agree upon the complete release of POWs in arrest.

At Home
- A mass rally takes place at Daegu to oppose the Armistice agreement.
- Pyongyang Broadcasting Service reports that the Communist troops occupy the two Islands on the west coast, namely, Sukdo and Yukdo, which were occupied by the ROK Army.

December 18, Tuesday (November 20, by lunar calendar, 壬辰日 Black Dragon) Cloudy and Clear
542 Day of the War

War Situation
- The UN troops repulse an enemy unit northwest of Cheorwon.
- Brigadier General Nicols issues a statement on the release of POWs who come from South Korea.
- The POWS Exchange Subcommittee for the Armistice Conference is held. The Communist party agreed to submit the list of POWs and both parties are supposed to exchange their list of POWs at 3 p.m.

At Home
- President Syngman Rhee issues a statement on Major General Dean who is reported to be alive.
- In Dangjin, eighty persons die due to a maritime accident.

December 19, Wednesday (November 21, by lunar calendar, 癸巳日 Black Snake) Cloudy and Clear
543 Day of the War

War Situation
- Battles occur between the Reconnaissance Units of both sides' troops in Gimhwa and Geumseong.
- Northwest of Cheorwon, a battalion unit of the Communist troops launches a fire-attack.

At Home
- The 11th Temporary session of the National Assembly opens.
- A mass rally is held at Deoksu Palace to oppose the Armistice and release the people kidnapped by North Korea.
- A mass rally by the Seoul citizens is held at Deoksu Palace.

December 20, Thursday (November 22, by lunar calendar, 甲午日 Blue Horse) Clear
544 Day of the War

War Situation
- The UN troops retreat from the upper part of Bukhan River due to an attack by the Communist troops.
- The Joint Subcommittee for the Supervision of the Armistice is held. For the efficiency of the proceeding of the conference, all the detailed principles are entrusted to the assistant chief of staff officers from both parties.

At Home
- Chief of Staff of the ROK Army, General Lee Jong-chan issues a statement on the final court sentences related to the Geochang Incident.
- The Ministry of Education distributes the wartime study books for the students.

Overseas
- The 24th Shipping Business Subcommittee of the Korea-Japan Talks is held. Both parties exchange a list of the ships which are to be returned to the other party's country. The parties agree to adjourn until January 8.

December 21, Friday (November 23, by lunar calendar, 乙未日 Blue Sheep) Clear and Rainy
545 Day of the War

War Situation
- The U.S. 7th Infantry Division finishes the construction of the roads for tanks on the roads accessible to "Heartbreak Ridge" in 50 days.
- The Communist troops south of Pyeonggang and west of Geumseong try to attack the outpost of the UN troops but are repelled.

At Home

- A mass rally takes place in the North Chungcheong Province to oppose the ceasefire without unification.
- The UN Forces Command and UNKRA sign to agree to the Korean reconstruction plan.

December 22, Saturday (November 24, by lunar calendar, 丙申日 Red Monkey) Rainy
546 Day of the War

War Situation
- An attack by the Communist troops is repelled in the Yeoncheon area.
- The POWs Exchange Joint Subcommittee for the Armistice agreement is held. The UN party demands an immediate exchange of the list of the wounded and sick prisoners.

At Home
- The National Assembly transfers to the Government the petition for releasing the kidnapped South Korean patriots, and also asks the Government to take special measures at the armistice conference for early solution of it.
- According to the Military Affairs (conscription) Command of South Gyongsang Province, the "report to call" rate to the conscription for the Secondary Peoples' Force is considerably poor in Busan and other major cities.

December 23, Sunday (November 25, by lunar calendar, 丁酉日 Red Rooster) Clear
547 Day of the War

War Situation
- The UN troops repel the Communist Unit west of Ganseong.
- The UN troops repel the attacks by the Communist reconnaissance Unit southwest of Geumseong.

At Home
- The Minister of Defense, Lee Gi-boong urges the early release of the POWs who are engaged in the war as the volunteers and pledge to commit their loyalty to the home country.
- The Australian Minister of Army, Francis arrives in Korea to visit the Australian Army Units.

December 24, Monday (November 26, by lunar calendar, 戊戌日 Yellow Dog) Clear
548 Day of the War

War Situation
- B29 Air Squadron bombs Taecheon Airport and bridges of Sinanju occupied by the Communist troops.
- The representative of the Communist troops refuses the proposal made by the International Red Cross to visit POW camps in control of the Communist Army.

At Home
- The Police Chief of Seoul Police Department has a press conference on the overall situation of security in Seoul.
- The ROK Army officers including Brig. General Kim Chang-gyu and 9 officers leave for the United States at the invitation of the U.S. Air Force College.

Overseas
- Beijing Broadcasting Station reports that the security of POWs is a much more imminent concern rather than a field survey of the POW camps.
- Prague Broadcasting Station reports that a decision has been made to send hospital trains to assist the North Korean troops.

December 25, Tuesday (November 27, by lunar calendar, 己亥日 Yellow Pig) Rainy
549 Day of the War

War Situation
- The 7th Infantry Division engages in the battle of "Christmas Hill" from December 25 to 28.
- An attack by the Communist troops is repelled northwest of Gorangpo.

December 26, Wednesday (November 28, by lunar calendar, 庚子日 White Rat) Snowy and Clear
550 Day of the War

War Situation
- A series of battles continue to secure the western outposts of Mundeungri.
- The Units of the UN troops engage in a three-hour battle near Panmunjom.

At Home
- The National Assembly has a special session to hear the status reports on the implementation of "the Temporary Land Income Law."
- The National Assembly is submitted with a bill on "the Revised Land Reform Law" which stipulates the additional postponement of three years for "the repayment for the distributed lands compensation."

December 27, Thursday (November 29, by lunar calendar, 辛丑日 White Ox) Clear and Cloudy
551 Day of the War

War Situation
- Battles occur in the hills west of Mundeungri.
- Light confrontations are noted on the central and western frontlines.
- The ROK Air Force launches an attack mission toward Wonsan.

At Home
- The association of the families whose family members were taken away forcibly by the

Communist North demand that their hijacked family members should be included in the list of POWs exchange members.
- A South Korean team is dispatched to take part in the World Table Tennis Championships.

December 28, Friday (December 1, by lunar calendar, 壬寅日 Black Tiger) Clear
552 Day of the War

War Situation
- The UN troops recapture the outpost positions west of Mundeungri.
- A total of 3,609 guerillas are killed during the mop-up operation in Mt. Jiri. The casualty rate of the ROK Army is 50 dead and 52 wounded.

At Home
- The National Assembly, The Ministry of Agriculture and Forestry and the National Federation of Fisheries Cooperatives agree to the basic policy for the implementation of land improvement projects: 80% of financial subsidy by the Government's treasure and the balance (20%) to be borne by the farmers.
- Lawmaker Chung Soon-jo of the Democratic People's Party submits a bill for a new revised constitution based on a combination of the bicameral system and the parliamentary cabinet system.

Overseas
- Beijing Broadcasting Station blames the UN delegation saying that they are totally responsible for the delay of the Armistice agreement.

December 29, Saturday (December 2, by lunar calendar, 癸卯日 Black Rabbit) Clear and Cloudy
553 Day of the War

War Situation
- Battles are continuously waging west of Gorangpo.
- 3,060 Communist guerillas are killed during the Mt. Jiri mop-up operation.

At Home
- The number of patients suffering from tuberculosis is on the rapid increase. The Government begins inoculation against TB for the first time in Korea.
- The Jangsoo Police Station of the North Jeolla Province initiates meetings with a band of the Communist guerillas to induce them to defect.

December 30, Sunday (December 3, by lunar calendar, 甲辰日 Blue Dragon) Cloudy and Rainy
554 Day of the War

War Situation
- The winter temperature on the frontlines is 20 degrees C below zero.

- The UN troops repel the two companies of Communist troops west of Gorangpo after nine hours of fierce battles.

At Home
- Pyongyang Broadcast Stations reports that the Communist troops occupy the two islands near Haeju Bay called Daesuap and Sosuap.

December 31, Monday (December 4, by lunar calendar, 乙巳日 Blue Snake) Cloudy and Clear
555 Day of the War

War Situation
- Hand-to-hand battles takes place west of Gorangpo.
- The UN Representative of the Joint Armistice Supervision Committee for the Armistice agreement, Lerner criticizes the Communist side for seeking to augment their Air Force power.

At Home
- Due to the Government's extreme "belt-tightening financial policy," the industries concerned severely suffer from the financial sources.
- The price index at the end of the year stands at 3,368.5 (1947=100)
- The total amount of currency in circulation is KRW 577 billion.

"The United States is not thinking of a truce until all UN POWs are released, and is opposed to a truce that may threaten the safety of Korea."

- Dean Acheson, United States Secretary of State

1952

The Year of Black Dragon, *Dangi* 4285

January 1, Tuesday (December 5, by lunar calendar, 丙午日 Red Horse) Clear and Windy
556 Day of the War

War Situation
- The POWs Exchange Subcommittee comes to an agreement to release the detained civilians.
- The Communist Forces agree, in principle, on the proposition of the UN Forces regarding the problem of detained civilians and pledge to provide information on about 50,000 UN POWs omitted from the list.

At Home
- The price index has risen 13 times higher than that of the before-war index.
- The Government applies to join the United Nations.

Overseas
- John F. Dulles, an adviser to the Secretary of State, comments in a radio interview, "I think, there will be no real peace in Korea that can solve even all the political problems."

A group of squad members of the 23rd Regiment of the U.S. 2nd Division proceed to inspect the Mt. Geumgang area (Jan. 1, 1952)

January 2, Wednesday (December 6, by lunar calendar, 丁未日 Red Sheep) Clear, Cloudy, Clear and Windy

557 Day of the War

War Situation

- The U.S. State Department announces that the toll of casualties of the U.S. military in the Korean War has amounted to 103,739.
- The POWs Exchange Subcommittee meeting takes place. The delegation of the UN Forces presents six conditions for POWs exchange and agrees, in principle, with the Communist delegation, on all the processes for the POWs exchange.

Overseas

- The U.S representative of the UN Forces, Coen, asserts in the UN Political Committee, "The UN Forces' participation in the Korean War is an exemplary realization of collective actions and the UN has to take a new resolute step in case the ceasefire of the Korean War fails."
- The Chinese Communist Forces and the North Korean Army reject the proposals of the UN Forces about the repatriation issue of POWs.

January 3, Thursday (December 7, by lunar calendar, 戊申日 Yellow Monkey) Clear and Windy

558 Day of the War

War Situation

- The UN Forces retreat from their outpost position in the west of Mundeungri due to aggressive pressure by a company of the Chinese Communist Army.
- The UN Forces jet-fighter squadron bombs the railroad facilities in Shinanju, Pyongyang, and other areas.

At Home

- Huh Jeong, The Minister of Social Affairs, issues an advance notification on a registration program of the war victims.

January 4, Friday (December 8, by lunar calendar, 己酉日 Yellow Rooster) Clear

559 Day of the War

War Situation

- The UN Forces fleet launches continuous bombardment on Wonsan in the East Sea.
- The police combat unit under the control of the National Police Headquarters announces the wartime accomplishments of the year, including 7,880 battles, 52,571 enemy killed, 8,536 arrested, and 43,937 defectors.

At Home

- Five ice manufacturing plants are planned to be built in South Korea, aiming to produce

180 tons of ice a day

- Kim Suk-gwan, the Minister of Transportation, announces that 92 percent of railway facilities are restored.
- Due to the delay of notification of the POW list by the headquarters of the ROK Army, the public opposition grows.

Overseas

- Coen, the U.S. representative to the UN, warns that the Soviet Union's new dangerous attempt to shift the Korean War Armistice talks to the UN Security Council will cause the talks to break down.
- Archbishop Francis Spellman is invited by General Van Fleet, Commander of the Eighth U.S. Army to commemorate Christmas in Korea and leave for Haneda Airport in Tokyo.

January 5, Saturday (December 9, by lunar calendar, 庚戌日 White Dog) Clear and Windy
560 Day of the War

War Situation

- A hard battle continues to secure an outpost position west of Gorangpo.
- A U.S. Sabre jet comes across 40 MIG-15 jet fighters over the Sinanju area.

At Home

- The ceasefire talks discuss the issue of releasing the abducted civilians.
- The 839 Unit of ROK holds the 15th honorable discharge ceremony for disabled soldiers.

Overseas

- North Korea applies again for admission to the UN.

January 6, Sunday (December 10, by lunar calendar, 辛亥日 White Pig) Rainy, Cloudy and Clear
561 Day of the War

War Situation

- Clashes continue all day long west of Gorangpo and the Communist Army maintains strong resistance.
- The Supervision Subcommittee of the Armistice requests to submit a new plan for a military airfield problem.

At Home

- The opening and naming ceremony of Sangmudae (a military school for the infantry) is held in Gwangju attended by President Syngman Rhee and General Van Fleet, Commander of the Eighth U.S. Army, and other honor guests

January 7, Monday (December 11, by lunar calendar, 壬子日 Black Rat) Clear, Cloudy and Windy
562 Day of the War

U.S POWs in North Korean POW camp (1952. 1. 7)

War Situation
- The U.S. heavy cruiser, *U.S.S Rochester*, bombards the Communist Forces' positions for nine hours nearby Ganseong.
- B-29 fighter-bomber squadron bombs Cheongcheon River Railway Bridge.

At Home
- The Ministry of Commerce & Industry reports that exports for the year 1951 amounts to 15,560,960 dollars and the imports 26,106,498 dollars.
- The Seoul City Government makes a plan to organize a grain association to control the escalating rice price.

January 8, Tuesday (December 12, by lunar calendar, 癸丑日 Black Ox) Clear and Windy
563 Day of the War

War Situation
- The First Infantry Division of ROK Army engages in a hard battle with four battalions of the Chinese Communist Forces, which have counterattacked from the flank of Sasiri Hill west of Gorangpo and kills 1,000 enemy combatants.
- The UN Forces make a counter-proposal for the exchange of POWs. The UN Forces submit a new six article proposal which is an amendment of the proposal submitted on January 2.

At Home
- South Gyeongsang Province Civil Affairs Department of the Korea Martial Law Command

carries out the draft of regular workers at the request of the Eighth U.S. Army.

January 9, Wednesday (December 13, by lunar calendar, 甲寅日 Blue Tiger) Clear and Windy
564 Day of the War

War Situation
- A platoon of the Communist Forces makes a surprise nighttime attack on the outpost position of the UN Forces west of Mundeungri.
- An Armored Unit of the UN Forces raids the positions of the Communist Forces west of Yeoncheon.
- The Mustang fighter squadron of the UN Forces supports with napalm bombs in a guerrilla mopping up operation in the Mt. Jiri district.

At Home
- The amount of grain receipts according to the Land Income Tax Law sums up to 881,276 seok(one seok= rice 144kg) which comprises 85% of the target collection amount (1,032,747 seok).
- Single line of the wireless telegraph (dots and dashes in Morse code) is restored between Busan and Hong Kong.

Overseas
- The Chinese Communist Government submits the amendment of Article 3 on the agenda of the Armistice talks.
- *Radio Beijing* supports the Russian representative's plan of January 3 which tried to shift the Korean War Armistice talks to the United Nations Security Council.

January 10, Thursday (December 14, by lunar calendar, 乙卯日 Blue Rabbit) Cloudy and Rainy
565 Day of the War

War Situation
- A Dutch cruiser supported by the U.S. Navy carry out concentrated bombarding Seongjin on the east coast.
- A B-29 fighter-bomber squadron bombs a railway bridge on the west side of Seongcheon.

At Home
- President Syngman Rhee visits the flagship, Wisconsin of the U.S. Seventh Fleet, and bestows the Order of Military Merit [Taegeuk] on its Commander, The Vice Admiral Harold M. Martin.

January 11, Friday (December 15, by lunar calendar, 丙辰日 Red Dragon) Clear and Windy
566 Day of the War

War Situation

- The Reconnoitering Unit of the UN Forces engages in hand-to-hand combat in the Communist position southwest of Pyonggang.
- The UN Fleet bombs the military facilities of the Communist Forces in Wonsan, Hamhung and Seongjin.

At Home
- The Government spokesperson announces that the Government has presented a petition in opposition to the indiscriminate and unconditional exchange of 5,500 North Korean POWs confined in Geoje POW camp

Overseas
- The UN General Assembly passes a bill for installing a Disarmament Commission consisted of 12 nations proposed jointly by the U.S.A, the UK and France (The result: 42 yays, 5 nays, 7 abstentions)
- The UN General Assembly rejects the bill of Russia which requested to discard the Mutual Security Act of the U.S. (approbation 42 vs. opposition 5)

January 12, Saturday (December 16, by lunar calendar, 丁巳日 Red Snake) Clear and Windy
567 Day of the War

War Situation
- The combat situation is limited to reconnoitering activities all along the front.
- A troop of the UN Forces attacks the high ground position of the Communist Forces west of Cheorwon.

At Home
- The Ministry of Education launches a plan to restore the school buildings. 573 elementary school classrooms built according to the first year plan for 1952.
- Forty-nine Government officials are selected to be dispatched overseas.
- The Army Chief of Staff, Major general Lee Jong-chan, is promoted to Lieutenant General. The Navy Chief of Staff, Rear Admiral Son Won-il, is promoted to Vice Admiral. The Field Battle Commander, Major General Paik Sun-yup is promoted to Lieutenant General.

January 13, Sunday (December 17, by lunar calendar, 戊午日 Yellow Horse) Clear, Cloudy and Snowy
568 Day of the War

War Situation
- The UN Forces loses an advance position nearby Panmunjom
- The U.S. battleship, *U.S.S Wisconsin*, bombs the battery site of the Communist Forces nearby Ganseong.
- 325 Communist guerrillas who have tried to escape are killed or captured on the west

position nearby Mt. Jiri.

At Home
- Gambling fever spreads in rural communities.
- The aid goods for Koreans from the U.S. Economic Cooperation Administration arrived (Contents: 1,247 bags of clothes, 1,300 tons of grain, 1,448 bags of raw cotton, 877 bags of cloth)

January 14, Monday (December 18, by lunar calendar, 己未日 Yellow Sheep) Snowy, Clear and Windy

569 Day of the War

War Situation
- The First Infantry Division of the ROK Army engages in combat for about four hours to recapture the outpost position on Sasi-ri nearby Gorangpo. (Captured by the enemy on December 28)
- The UN Air Forces fly 575 sorties in spite of extremely heavy snow and storms.

At Home
- The regular cargo line service between Korea and America is established.
- The Ministry of Health announces that 360 bottles of DaiAsol, a kind of Hansen's disease medicine, arrive through the UN Civil affairs department and are allotted to every Provincial Authorities.
- The North Korea Authorities rejects the entry of the representative of the International Red Cross into North Korea.

Overseas
- Mao Zedong issues a directive, "Don't reveal our weakness in case enemy aircraft raid our border during the Armistice talks."

January 15, Tuesday (December 19, by lunar calendar, 庚申日 White Monkey) Clear
570 Day of the War

War Situation
- All the ground combats remain in a lull.
- The combat in the west of Gorangpo has continued for the past 19 days
- The UN Fleet bombards the naval base of the Communist Forces in Wonsan, Heungnam and Seongjin.

At Home
- The Liberal Party resolves to oppose to a bill for constitutional amendment proposed by the Government.
- Each political faction engages in a heated competition for the Chairman of the National

Assembly Standing Subcommittees.

January 16, Wednesday (December 20, by lunar calendar, 辛酉日 White Rooster) Clear
571 Day of the War

War Situation
- The ROK Army supported by the artillery and tank units in the northwest of Yeoncheon returns after a battle with Chinese Forces.
- An F-86 jet fighter squadron damages two MIG-15 fighters.
- The U.S. Department of State announces that the number of the U.S victims amounts to 104,383 persons.

At Home
- President Syngman Rhee asks the UN Forces Commander General Ridgway to resolve the loans of the UN Forces.
- The National Assembly plenary session passes a bill to release the POW.

Overseas
- The French Army drives out four battalions of the Ho Chi Minh Army which have tried to recapture Hoa Binh.
- The Russian Government announces that off limits areas for foreigners proclaimed in 1948 will be enlarged in number to 22 more cities.

January 17, Thursday (December 21, by lunar calendar, 壬戌日 Black Dog) Clear and Windy
572 Day of the War

War Situation
- The UN light bomber squadron attacks the vehicle unit of the Communist Forces on the main supply route at night.
- The UN Forces Commander General Ridgway visits the frontline and has an important conference with the UN representative Mr. Joy, and other UN Armistice representatives.

At Home
- President Syngman Rhee makes a special statement that all Koreans have been eager for the constitutional amendment.
- The Advisory Committee to the UN Korean Recovery Committee approves U.S.$250,000,000 dollars as a Korean Recovery Fund.

January 18, Friday (December 22, by lunar calendar, 癸亥日 Black Pig) Clear
573 Day of the War

War Situation
- A Thunder jet fighter squadron destroys 3 locomotives and 9 freight cars of the Communist

Forces and damages a locomotive and 12 freight cars in Sinanju.

At Home

- President Syngman Rhee makes an official declaration to set up a Peace Line, the so-called Syngman Rhee Adjacent Sea Line.
- The regular session of the National Assembly rejects the second bill for constitutional amendment (the Government bill of a direct presidential election system) (19 in favor, 143 against, 1 abstention)

Overseas

- The French Army fiercely attacks the Vietnamese Communist Forces in Nam Dinh located 112.6 km southeast of Hanoi.

January 19, Saturday (December 23, by lunar calendar, 甲子日 Blue Rat) Clear
574 Day of the War

War Situation

- Six B-29 fighter bombers bomb the Daedong River railroad bridge.
- Squadron leader major Kim Du-man establishes a record of 100 sorties.

At Home

- The Ministry of Agriculture and Forestry decides upon a policy to give priority to landowners when selling Government-vested rice-polishing mills.

January 20, Sunday (December 24, by lunar calendar, 乙丑日 Blue Ox) Clear
575 Day of the War

War Situation

- 80 Sabre jet fighters conduct an air battle with 60 MIG fighters of the Communist Forces over Sinanju.
- 183 Communist guerrillas are mopped up at 7 spots on Mt. Jiri.
- The UN Forces representative of the POW Exchange Subcommittee declares a partial amendment of the POW exchange program.

At Home

- The inauguration ceremony of the Korea Military Academy (four-year course) is attended by President Syngman Rhee and General Ridgway, UN Forces Commander.

January 21, Monday (December 25, by lunar calendar, 丙寅日 Red Tiger) Clear and Cloudy
576 Day of the War

War Situation

- The representative of the Communist Forces criticizes severely the UN side insisting that the UN Forces are going to hand over POWs of the Communist Forces to South Korea and

Taiwan Nationalist Government.

At Home
- The Ministry of Agriculture and Forestry decides that Government vested rice-polishing mills are open to landowners for their occupational changes

Overseas
- The representative of the Taiwan Nationalist Forces denies the insistence of their Yunnan invasion.

January 22, Tuesday (December26, by lunar calendar, 丁卯日 Red Rabbit) Clear
577 Day of the War

War Situation
- The UN Forces reconnoitering unit clashes with a platoon of the Communist Forces northwest of Gorangpo.
- The UN Air Force bombs the harbors and supply bases of the Communist Forces.

At Home
- Twelve chairpersons of the National Assembly standing committees are elected (Liberal party: 8; Minu Party: 2; Min-guk Party; and nonpartisan 1)

January 23, Wednesday (December 27, by lunar calendar, 戊辰日 Yellow Dragon) Clear
578 Day of the War

War Situation
- The UN Tank Units fiercely attack a *tochka* position southeast of Geumseong.
- The UN Tank Units and Infantry troops clash with Communist Forces on the Hill in the west of Cheorwon for six hours.

Overseas
- The representatives of the Chinese Communist Forces, Zhu De and Zhou Enlai grant an audience to the representative of the North Korean Forces
- General Eisenhower advocates the Integration of Europe.

January 24, Thursday (December 28, by lunar calendar, 己巳日 Yellow Snake) Cloudy and Clear
579 Day of the War

War Situation
- The ROK Navy takes over four torpedo boats from the U.S. Forces.
- Staff officers hold a meeting. The representative of the Communist Forces hands over a map to his counterpart in which POW camps in North Korea are indicated and agrees to specify the positions of the POW camps.

At Home

- The Minister of Social Affairs, Choi Chang-sun, holds a press conference announcing a plan to set up technical schools for disabled veterans.
- The Minister of Commerce and Industry announces that the factories are restored up to 50% of before-war state.

January 25, Friday (December 29, by lunar calendar, 庚午日 White Horse) Clear and Windy
580 Day of the War

War Situation
- The UN Forces recapture a Hill west of Yeoncheon and then return.
- The Armistice Supervisory Sub-Commission is held. The representative of the UN Forces proposes three plans to advance in the supervisory problems of the Armistice.

At Home
- The number of newly registered trading companies reaches 283.
- The National Taxation Bureau undertakes to impose corporate tax on 250 medium and small firms.
- The Bank of Korea pays the excess of the limited trade account to Japan in conformity with the Korea-Japan trade agreement.

January 26, Saturday (December 30, by lunar calendar, 辛未日 White Sheep) Clear
581 Day of the War

War Situation
- The UN Forces search party engages the enemy northeast of Panmunjom for two hours.
- The POWs Exchange Subcommittee is held. The Communist Forces hand over to the UN side the list of 68 detained foreigners.

At Home
- Renewal of the Korea-Japan trade agreement is discussed.
- The Ministry of Foreign Affairs announces a counter statement to Japan's criticism of Korea's proclamation of sovereignty over adjacent seas.

Overseas
- Three nations, including the U.S.A, UK and France, submit a resolution to hold the UN Special General Assembly for the Korean problem.
- The six nation meeting for establishing the Allied Command Europe is held in Paris.

January 27, Sunday (January 1, by lunar calendar, 壬申日 Black Monkey) Clear and Rainy
582 Day of the War

War Situation
- The UN Forces launch a surprise attack on a position of the Chinese Communist Forces

southeast of Geumseong.

- The POWs Exchange Subcommittee is held. The representative of the Chinese Communist Forces agrees that the staff officer conference is entrusted with right of determining the details of the Armistice clauses mutually agreed.

At Home

- Notices blaming the rejection of the constitutional amendment are posted.

January 28, Monday (January 2, by lunar calendar, 癸酉日 Black Rooster) Rainy
583 Day of the War

War Situation

- The POWs Exchange Subcommittee meeting is held. The UN Forces proposes a draft of 14 conditions about POWs exchange which are to be included in the Armistice agreement.

At Home

- President Syngman Rhee delivers an address in the welcoming ceremony of Seoul citizens held in the Capitol Plaza, saying "I hope our Government can return to Seoul within one or two months."

January 29, Tuesday (January 3, by lunar calendar, 甲戌日 Blue Dog) Cloudy and Clear
584 Day of the War

War Situation

- The UN Forces repulse the attack of the Communist Forces in the north of Goseong County on the eastern front.
- The POWs Exchange Subcommittee is held.
  The Communist Forces reject the UN Force's POWs exchange draft agreement of January 28, but only agree to exchange the injured prisoners first in case the Armistice agreement comes into effect.

At Home

- A member of the U.S. Congress comments on America's consideration of using nuclear weapons against North Korea.

Overseas

- The Armistice Conference discusses the practical procedures of the Armistice including a ceasefire and truce.

January 30, Wednesday (January 4, by lunar calendar, 乙亥日 Blue Pig) Cloudy and Clear
585 Day of the War

War Situation

The Communist Forces attack a position of the UN Forces northwest of Gorangpo.

The ROK Air Force acquires an additional F-51 jet fighter.

At Home

- President Syngman Rhee arrives in Jinhae.
- The acting Prime Minister, Huh Jeong mentions that the Syngman Rhee Line (the so-called Peace Line) has legal justification.

January 31, Thursday (January 5, by lunar calendar, 丙子日 Red Rat) Cloudy, Clear and Windy
586 Day of the War

War Situation

- The UN Forces repulse the Communist Force's assault on the outpost position in the upper region of the Bukhan River.
- The U.S. Fifth Air Force confirms the Communist Forces' use of anti-aircraft guns equipped with the radio locator.

At Home

- The total number of refugees reaches 7,274,712 and 3,510,000 persons of them are accommodated in 868 refugee camps in the whole country.
- Financial institutions implement a new saving system called the Anonymous Time Deposit.

February 1, Friday (January 6, by lunar calendar, 丁丑日 Red Ox) Clear
587 Day of the War

War Situation
- A B-29 bomber squadron launches a nighttime bombing of Seongcheon Bridge.
- The staff officers meeting for the supervising Armistice.
  The UN Forces nominate Switzerland, Sweden and Norway as member states of the Neutral Nations Supervisory Commission at Panmunjom.

At Home
- The founding ceremony of the Korean Veterans Association is held in the auditorium of the Military Manpower Administration.

February 2, Saturday (January 7, by lunar calendar, 戊寅日 Yellow Tiger) Cloudy and Windy
588 Day of the War

War Situation
- Eighteen F-86 jet fighters of the UN Air Forces engage in an air battle with 55 MIG Jet fighters of the Communist Forces in the sky over Sinuiju.
- Forty-nine Communist guerrillas are killed in the southwest regeion.

At Home
- The Chief Justice of the Supreme Court informs the National Assembly of the fact that 14 suits of May 30 election law violation are formally accepted.

Overseas
- The Korean issue is submitted to the Joint Political, Economic, and Social Committee of the UN General Assembly.

February 3, Sunday (January 8, by lunar calendar, 己卯日 Yellow Rabbit) Clear, Cloudy and Windy
589 Day of the War

War Situation
- A Mustang fighter unit of the UN Forces bombs a supply depot and a Communist Force unit in Jinhae.
- The chief delegate of the Communist Forces, Nam Il, agrees to have a parallel discussion on agenda No. 5 .

At Home
- The Minister of National Defense, Lee Gi-boong, announces a way of mail exchanges with POWs.

- An opening ceremony of the restored railroad bridge of the Bukhan River is held.

February 4, Monday (January 9, by lunar calendar, 庚辰日 White Dragon) Clear and Windy
590 Day of the War

War Situation
- The UN Forces retreat from a position in the northwest of Yeoncheon due to fierce attacks of the Communist Forces.
- The POWs Exchange Subcommittee is held.
  The following four articles are in principle agreed after discussing the propositions suggested by the Communist Forces on February 3.
  (1) Injured prisoners are to be exchanged first
  (2) Panmunjom is designated as an exchanging place
  (3) References for the dead during the detained period are to be exchanged
  (4) The repatriation of the refugees of the both sides is to be assisted.

February 5, Tuesday (January 10, by lunar calendar, 辛巳日 White Snake) Clear
591 Day of the War

War Situation
- A squadron of B-29 bombers bomb Sinanju Railroad Bridge.
- The staff officers meeting for supervising the Armistice is held.

At Home
- The Assembly by-election is held in eight districts.

February 6, Wednesday (January 11, by lunar calendar, 壬午日 Black Horse) Cloudy, Windy and Rainy
592 Day of the War

War Situation
- A mixed unit of the UN Forces attacks the Communist Forces position in the southeast of Pyeonggang.
- Both the UN and the Communist Forces agree in the Armistice meeting, that the Joint Subcommittee composed of Red Cross members of both parties visit POW camps to assist the repatriation of the prisoners.

At Home
- President Syngman Rhee blames the rejection of the Government's bill for constitutional amendment.
- The Minister of National Defense, Lee Gi-boong, explains the promulgation of the Martial Law and its class change.

Overseas
- The Chinese Armistice representative of Korean War submits the principle recommendation on the fifth agenda.

February 7, Thursday (January 12, by lunar calendar, 癸未日 Black Sheep) Cloudy and Clear
593 Day of the War

War Situation
- A surprise attack troop of the UN Forces operates a penetration assault on the Communist position in the south of Panmunjom.
- The staff officers meeting for the POW problems is held.
  The UN Forces withdraw their exchange proposal to exchange detained Communist prisoners in the UN Forces with non-military people of Korean nationality detained in the Communist Forces on condition that the UN party gives more Communist prisoners in number than the Korean detainees.

At Home
- The Ministry of Social Affairs sets up 30 houses for the war victims in Yeongdo, Busan.
- Martial Law is declared in Gimje, Gurye and Damyang-gun in Jeollabuk/nam-do province.

February 8, Friday (January 13, by lunar calendar, 甲申日 Blue Monkey) Cloudy and Windy
594 Day of the War

War Situation
- Minor battles in the northeast of the Eastern Front and in the west of Mundeungni Valley.

At Home
- The victims of starvation are on sharp increase in the six counties of North Gyeongsang Province. due to a severe drought
- Monuments for the fallen soldiers are built nationwide, and in Seoul War Comrade Memorial Tower is] built.

Overseas
- The Mutual Security Headquarters of the U.S. announces that Taiwan receives U.S.$415,000 and the Philippines U.S.$75,000 as financial aid.
- Queen Elizabeth II's accession to the throne in the United Kingdom.

February 9, Saturday (January 14, by lunar calendar, 乙酉日 Blue Rooster) Cloudy, Clear and Windy
595 Day of the War

War Situation
- A reconnoitering attack of the Communist Forces is repulsed by the UN Forces in the

northeast of Gimhwa.

- The staff officers meeting on the POWs problems agrees to establish a Joint Red Cross team.

At Home

- As the price of rice soars, the Government releases its holding rice to sell in the 10 places in Busan.

February 10, Sunday (January 15, by lunar calendar, 丙戌日 Red Dog) Cloudy, Windy and Rainy
596 Day of the War

War Situation

- Ground combats show calm situation.
- The UN Forces have a battle with the Communist Forces in the north of Gorangpo.
- In the staff officers meeting on the problem of monitoring the Armistice, the UN Forces proposed to establish eight monitoring entrances on both sides.
- In the staff officers meeting on the problem of POWs, the proposition of the UN Forces consisting of 11 articles is discussed article by article.

At Home

- The Director of Public Information Office makes a statement that the Republic of Korea is not able to accept the UN's compromise for the joint control on the Han River estuary.
- The Ministry of Agriculture and Forestry announces the release of the Government holding rice unlimitedly to settle the rice price.

February 11, Monday (January 16, by lunar calendar, 丁亥日 Red Pig) Clear, Cloudy and Windy
597 Day of the War

War Situation

- The Seventh Division of the ROK Army secures the Christmas Hill with a fierce fighting.

At Home

- The tax collection situation of the Busan District Tax Service at the end of January reaches 88% of the collection rate, 91% of the storage in kind.

Overseas

- The military committee of the North Atlantic Treaty Organization (NATO) is held in Lisbon.

February 12, Tuesday (January 17, by lunar calendar, 戊子日 Yellow Rat) Rainy, Windy and Clear
598 Day of the War

War Situation

- The UN Forces repulse a reconnoitering attack of the Communist Forces to a position in the Mundeungri Valley at night and killed 96 Communist soldiers.

- 40 Communist guerillas are killed and 1 captured.
- The war result of the combat police forces are as follows:
  2,752 enemy combatants are shot dead, 1,150 captured and 90 defected since the beginning of mop-up operation in the southwest region of Korea.

At Home
- The Parliamentary inspection team points out a problem that the nation-wide conference of the inspection section chiefs of police bureau is held just before the by-election.

February 13, Wednesday (January 18, by lunar calendar, 己丑日 Yellow Ox) Clear, Cloudy and Windy
599 Day of the War

War Situation
- The three attacks by the Communist Forces on the UN positions are all repulsed on the eastern front.
- The staff officers meeting for monitoring the Armistice is held. The UN Forces proposed to decide the number of the entrances to be seven.
- The staff officers meeting for the POW issue is held. Both representatives agree to finish the POW exchange within two months after the signing of the Armistice agreement.

At Home
- The Ministry of Education conducts an investigation of the number of legal aged children for the elementary school and takes measure to expand the range of the legal age for the elementary school.

February 14, Thursday (January 19, by lunar calendar, 庚寅日 White Tiger) Rainy
600 Day of the War

War Situation
- 1,000 Communist soldiers fail to break through the position of the UN Forces in the Mundeung Valley.
- The staff officers meeting for the POW issue is held. The Communist Forces submit a new program.

At Home
- The regular session of the National Assembly is resumed after 20 days' recess for the parliamentary inspection on the administration.

Overseas
- The second anniversary celebrating the Sino-Soviet Treaty of Friendship and Alliance is held at all social levels of Beijing.
- The United States announces that the United Nations Korean Reconstruction Agency is financed 10 million dollars.

February 15, Friday (January 20, by lunar calendar, 辛卯日 White Rabbit) Rainy and Cloudy
601 Day of the War

War Situation
- The UN Artillery Unit heavily bombards the Communist Forces position in the north of Mundeungri.
- A company strength of the Communist Forces attacks a position of the UN Forces in the upper region of the Bukhan River.

At Home
- The Government expresses its intention to permit the imports of foreign grains to alleviate the hardness of the food situation.
- The UN relief supplies arrive, including about 3,000 bags of raw cotton, about 4,000 bags of clothes, and 170 boxes of automobile components.

February 16, Saturday (January 21, by lunar calendar, 壬辰日 Black Dragon) Rainy, Cloudy and Clear
602 Day of the War

War Situation
- Seven units of the UN Forces heavily attack a position of the Communist Forces on the western front.
- The UN Forces reject Russia to join the Neutral Nations Armistice Supervisory Commission.

At Home
- The Members of the National Assembly argue badly with the Cabinet Members about the happening of posting notices insisting recall of the member of the Assembly and a special committee is constituted in the Assembly.
- BRIDGE OF FREEDOM opens for returning of POWs.

February 17, Sunday (January 22, by lunar calendar, 癸巳日 Black Snake) Cloudy and Windy
603 Day of the War

War Situation
- A Reconnoitering attack of the Communist Forces is repulsed from a position of the UN Forces in the northeast of Panmunjom.
- Eighty Communist guerrillas are killed and 21 captured in the northeast district.

Overseas
- The British Government announces that it is to carry out the first nuclear test of its own in Australia within this year.

February 18, Monday (January 23, by lunar calendar, 甲午日 Blue Horse) Clear, Cloudy, Clear and Windy

604 Day of the War

War Situation

- The UN Forces fiercely fight against the Chinese Communist Forces in the east of Geumseong.
- A riot of the leftists happens in the POW camp in Geoje Island.

At Home

- The National Assembly resolves to investigate the protesting demonstration against rejection of the constitutional amendment bill.

  An impeaching demonstration to the rejection of the Government's constitutional amendment bill is held in front of the Assembly.

February 19, Tuesday (January 24, by lunar calendar, 乙未日 Blue Sheep) Clear
605 Day of the War

War Situation

- The outpost troops of the UN Forces retreat due to the strong pressures of a company strength of the Chinese Communist Forces in the upper region of the Bukhan River.

At Home

- The National Assembly resolves to submit a questionnaire to President Syngman Rhee about the demonstration incident for recalling the members of the Assembly.
- An investigation shows that the number of the poor and needy people is 420,000 in Seoul.
- The president of the Korean Agricultural Science Institute, Woo Jang-choon, has devoted himself to studying thremmatology.

February 20, Wednesday (January 25, by lunar calendar, 丙申日 Red Monkey) Clear
606 Day of the War

War Situation

- The UN Forces engage the Chinese Communist Forces in the west of Cheorwon.
- A battalion of the Chinese Forces attempts to land on Yangdo Island near the port of Seongjin.

At Home

- President Syngman Rhee makes a statement requesting the National Assembly to listen to the opinions of the people about the rejection of the constitutional amendment bill and also asking the Assembly members to act sincerely in accordance with public opinion about the presidential election.

  The Taiwan Government delivers a draft of the overall peace treaty to the representative of Japan

- The 9th board meeting of the North Atlantic Treaty Organization is held in Lisbon.

February 21, Thursday (January 26, by lunar calendar, 丁酉日 Red Rooster) Clear and Windy
607 Day of the War

War Situation
- The ROK Marine Corps stationed on Yangdo Island near the port of Seongjin repulse a battalion of the Communist Forces trying to land.
- An American destroyer and a New Zealand cruiser sink 15 of 20 transport ships of the Communist Forces which have tried to land at Yangdo Island.

At Home
- The Ministry of Social Affairs allocates 500,000 pieces of clothes and other relief goods to each province in commemoration of the March 1st Independence Movement.
- The U.S. Ambassador to Korea, John J. Mucho, has a discussion with the UN Committee for Unification and Rehabilitation of Korea to weaken President Syngman Rhee's campaign against the Korean War Armistice.

Overseas
- On the second day of the Lisbon conference, the foreign ministers of 14 nations hold a meeting.
  A secret session hears a report on the Soviet Union and its recent international policy.

February 22, Friday (January 27, by lunar calendar, 戊戌日 Yellow Dog) Clear, Cloudy, Clear and Rainy
608 Day of the War

War Situation
- In the staff officers meeting for monitoring the Armistice, the Communist Forces insist to have 30,000 troops for replacement troops and five entrances for surveillance.
- In the staff officers meeting for the POW issue, the UN Forces submit a new codified plan for POW exchange including all the principles previouslly agreed on the 13th of this month.

At Home
- *Radio Pyongyang* broadcasts that the North Korean Foreign Minister, Park Heon-yeong, insists that the U.S. Forces systematically have sprayed large amounts of bacteria along the frontlines and rear areas by plane.

February 23, Saturday (January 28, by lunar calendar, 己亥日 Yellow Pig) Clear and Windy
609 Day of the War

War Situation
- A reconnoitering attack of the Communist Forces is repulsed from the southeast of Yeoncheon.

- Thirteen Communist guerrillas are killed and one captured in three locations in the southeast area.
- In the staff officers meeting for monitoring the Armistice.
  The Communist Forces agree on the suggestion of the UN Forces including both parties' approval of 35,000 soldiers for replacement during the Armistice.

At Home
- Foreign newspapers report the facts about the Geoje Island POW camp riot incident.

February 24, Sunday (January 29, by lunar calendar, 庚子日 White Rat) Cloudy and Clear
610 Day of the War

War Situation
- A search party of the UN Forces engages a platoon of the Communist Forces in Yeoncheon.

Overseas
- In the compensation subcommittee of the Korea-Japan Talks, Korea explains the proposition about the right to demand compensation.

February 25, Monday (February 1, by lunar calendar, 辛丑日 White Ox) Rainy, Snowy, Rainy and Windy
611 Day of the War

War Situation
- A platoon of the UN Forces engages two platoons of the Chinese Communist Forces in the west of the Mundeungri Valley.
- The U.S. Mustang fighter unit attacks a supply base of the Communist Forces near Ganseong and Geumseong.

At Home
- A fishing boat imported by the aid of the U.S. Economic Cooperation Administration is actually found unusable.

February 26, Tuesday (February 2, by lunar calendar, 壬寅日 Black Tiger) Rainy, Cloudy and Clear
612 Day of the War

War Situation
- In the staff officers meeting for monitoring the Armistice, the Communist Forces reject the proposition of the UN Forces, which has included an article to rule out the Soviet Union from the Armistice commission.

At Home

The children perform for the U.S. soldiers of the warship U.S.S Wisconsin which has been anchored in Busan harbor.

- The Ex-Minister of Defense, Shin Sung-mo is accused under suspicion of the Geochang incident and sent to the civil court instead of the military court.

February 27, Wednesday (February 3, by lunar calendar, 癸卯日 Black Rabbit) Clear, Cloudy and Windy
613 Day of the War

War Situation
- A Reconnoitering Unit of the UN Forces conducts a search on the Hills nearby Geumseong and Gimhwa, engaging the Chinese Communist Forces.
- The Communist Forces fire propaganda bombs on the west front to the UN Forces position.

At Home
- The arguments for a direct presidential election are escalating between the President and the National Assembly.

Overseas
- The Joint Chiefs of Staff delivers the final decision of the United States against the compulsory repatriation of POWs to the UN Forces Commander, Matthew Ridgway

February 28, Thursday (February 4, by lunar calendar, 甲辰日 Blue Dragon) Clear and Rainy

War Situation

- The UN Air Forces heavily attack the supply railroad of the Communist Forces.
- Twenty-eight Communist guerrillas are killed and 11 captured at two spots in Yeongnam and eight spots in the northwest area.

At Home

- The price of rice soars to KRW56,000.

February 29, Friday (February 5, by lunar calendar, 乙巳日 Blue Snake) Clear and Rainy
615 Day of the War

War Situation

- The UN Forces tank unit advances to the positions of the Communist Forces in the north and the east of Geumseong and wages battle for three hours.
- The controversy over the Armistice talks continues.

At Home

- The amendment bill of the Local Government Act is submitted to the National Assembly.

March 1, Saturday (February 6, by lunar calendar, 丙午日 Red Horse) Clear, Cloudy and Clear
616 Day of the War

War Situation

- The UN Forces repulse company strength Chinese Communist Forces west of Cheorwon in the central frontline.
- In the POWs Exchange Subcommittee, the representative of the Communist Forces rejects the UN Forces' request for the immediate exchange of the injured POWs of both sides.

At Home

- The 33rd anniversary of the March 1st Independence Movement is celebrated in Chungmuro Square in Busan attended by President Syngman Rhee and Speaker of the National Assembly, Shin Ik-hee, announcing a "National Declaration."
- The Miners Union of the Korean Confederation of Trade Unions declares strikes

Overseas

- Some Chinese activists create a small riot in Hong Kong.

March 2, Sunday (February 7, by lunar calendar, 丁未日 Red Sheep) Clear, Cloudy, Windy and Clear
617 Day of the War

War Situation

- As the Armistice talks face an emergency, there are skirmishes on all the frontlines
- The UN Forces engage the reinforced Chinese Communist Forces in the east frontline.
- In both the staff officers meeting for monitoring the Armistice and the POWs Exchange Subcommittee, the representative of the UN Forces blames the Communist Forces' violation of the agreement on designating neutral countries and exchanging the references of POWs.

At Home

- The 5th graduation of the Naval Academy is held on Jinhae campus.

Overseas

- The United States Government considers extending the scope of the collective security clause of the North Atlantic Treaty Organization to West Germany.

March 3, Monday (February 8, by lunar calendar, 戊申日 Yellow Monkey) Clear, Windy and Cloudy
618 Day of the War

War Situation

- The Communist Forces fire propaganda leaflet shells totaling 251 to date.

- In the POWs Exchange Subcommittee, the representative of the UN Forces, Major General R. E. Libby, announces that the meeting has made no progress and that the Communist Forces claim that the riot of the Geoje camp happened due to the unfair treatment of the POWs.

At Home
- President Syngman Rhee clarifies that the goal of Korean War is the reunification of Korea, criticizing the Armistice talks as a kind of intolerable insult toward Koreans.

March 4, Tuesday (February 9, by lunar calendar, 己酉日 Yellow Rooster) Clear and Rainy
619 Day of the War

War Situation
- 28 Sabre jet fighters engage in an air battle with 50 MIG fighters over the Yalu River.

At Home
- The capital city Seoul will be completely recovered by May
- A send-off ceremony of 148 heroic souls from Gangwon and Chungbuk Province who have been enshrined in the Beomeosa Temple in Dongnae is held at the platform of the Busan station attended by the Prime Minister, Huh Jeong and the Minister of Defense, Lee Gi-boong.

Overseas
- The UN Forces Commander, Ridgway, removes a ban of taking aerial photos in Japan at the request of Associated Press.

March 5, Wednesday (February 10, by lunar calendar, 庚戌日 White Dog) Clear, Windy and Cloudy
620 Day of the War

War Situation
- The UN search party of the mid-east front battle with the Communist Forces for 90 minutes northeast of Geumseong.
- 26 Sabre jet fighters of the U.S. Forces engage in an air battle with 70 MIG jet fighters of the Communist Forces over the national boundaries between Korea and Manchuria.

At Home
- The Minister of Defense, Lee Gi-boong, removes the Emergency Martial in the South Gyeongsang and North Gyeongsang Provinces at 06:00 on February 3.
- The Central Committee for Urban Planning passes the restoring plan of Seoul.

March 6, Thursday (February 11, by lunar calendar, 辛亥日 White Pig) Clear, Rainy and Cloudy
621 Day of the War

War Situation

- A search party of the UN Forces kills 49 soldiers and wounds 40 soldiers of the Communist Forces in the eastern frontline.
- The UN Forces the Mundeung-ri Valley recapture the hill position.

At Home
- The Minister of National Defense, Lee Gi-boong, declares lifting the Martial Law in Yeongnam Province.

March 7, Friday (February 12, by lunar calendar, 壬子日 Black Rat) Rainy and Windy
622 Day of the War

War Situation
- The mop-up operation of the Communist guerrillas develops into a heated state on Mt. Jiri. As a result 57 guerrillas are killed and 24 guerrillas captured.

At Home
- The President Syngman Rhee has an interview with foreign reporters about the Armistice issues.

March 8, Saturday (February 13, by lunar calendar, 癸丑日 Black Ox) Rainy and Cloudy
623 Day of the War

War Situation
- B-26 fighter-bombers and the Marine Air Squadron bomb the main transportation facilities of the Communist Forces in North Korea.
- The Eighth U.S. Army Commander, General Van Fleet, gives a warning about the possibility of the 900,000 Communist soldiers' assembling.
- 23 Communist guerrillas are killed in the mountains of southern Gwangju.

At Home
- The Minister of Agriculture and Forestry, Ham Inseop, submits his resignation, taking the responsibility for the soaring rice price.

March 9, Sunday (February 14, by lunar calendar, 甲寅日 Blue Tiger) Cloudy, Clear, Windy and Rainy
624 Day of the War

War Situation
- UN aircraft attack the supply routes of the Communist Forces and destroy more than 50 strategic locations of the railroads.
- The police Force of the Mt. Jiri district clashes with the enemy, and as a result, 43 guerrillas are killed, two captured, and two defected.

At Home

- The Ministry of Foreign Affairs obtains a map that a Japanese oceanographer has recorded Dokdo islets as Korean territory.

Overseas
- The 3rd Deputy Chief of Staff of the U.S. Army and 10 staff officers arrive in Taipei to inspect the National Chinese Army of Taiwan.

March 10, Monday (February 15, by lunar calendar, 乙卯日 Blue Rabbit) Rainy, Clear, Windy and Cloudy

625 Day of the War

War Situation
- The UN Forces recapture the outpost position in the northeast of Panmunjom.
- 100 fighter bombers of the UN Forces drop 500,000 tons of bombs on a supply line of the Communist Forces near Suncheon.
- The mop-up operation of guerrillas has conducted heavy attacks for five days on Mt. Jiri.

At Home
- The Korean Ambassador to the United States and the chief delegate of the Korea-Japan Talks, Yang Yu-chan announces a statement about the nationality of the Korean residents in Japan and shipping issues.

March 11, Tuesday (February 16, by lunar calendar, 丙辰日 Red Dragon) Clear and Windy

626 Day of the War

War Situation
- Communist guerrillas are completely mopped up in the area of the Mt. Jiri.
- In the staff officers meeting for monitoring the Armistice, a joint team for translation examines English, Chinese and Korean translations of the 72 Armistice principles already agreed.

At Home
- The National Assembly makes a decision to investigate the real state of the POWs who have been incarcerated in POW camps.
- A member of the National Assembly, Chun Jin-han, calls for a general strike and to make a report to the International Labor Organization about the labor dispute in Joseon Textile Co.

March 12, Wednesday (February 17, by lunar calendar, 丁巳日 Red Snake) Clear, Windy and Cloudy

627 Day of the War

War Situation
- The Communist Forces in the eastern frontline attack under the support of artillery and

mortars at night.

- Seven B-29 fighter bombers from the Okinawa base attack the Communist Forces' airport in Pyongyang with 70 tons of bombs.

At Home

- The Director of Public Information Office announces that the Government recommends the use of *Hangeul*, the Korean alphabet.
- The Ministry of Social Affairs allocates 26,930 tons of relief grains for March to each province Government according to the resolution of the National Relief Committee.
- The UN Forces stationed in the school campuses are to withdraw before the Government's returning to Seoul.

Overseas

- The Chinese People's Committee for world peace and against the United States' aggression (Chairperson: Lee De Chian, vice-chairperson: Liao Cheng Zhi, Cheon Chi Wen) hold an enlarged meeting and organize an investigation team of bacteriological warfare.
- The U.S. Mutual Security Agency announces a new aid quota for Taiwan and the Philippines.

March 13, Thursday (February 18, by lunar calendar, 戊午日 Yellow Horse) Cloudy and Rainy
628 Day of the War

War Situation

- The Fifth Squadron of the U.S. Air Force heavily attacks ground targets of the Communist Forces.
- A riot breaks out at the Geoje POW camp.
  The stone-throwing riot is suppressed immediately and 12 POWs of the Communist Forces are killed and 26 are wounded, and an officer of the U.S. Army and a Korean are wounded.

At Home

- Evidence is discovered, which will help resolve ship problem in the Korea-Japan talks.
- The rice price exceeds the average domestic price index and it is 40% higher than the international price.

March 14, Friday (February 19, by lunar calendar, 己未日 Yellow Sheep) Clear and Windy
629 Day of the War

War Situation

- The UN Air Forces destroy 18 Communist ground positions and antiaircraft positions with 400 sorties.

- The U.S. Department of Defense announces the military achievements since the beginning of the Korean War:

  The number of casualties in combat areas is 1,153,965 persons, while the number of casualties in non-combat areas is 328,494 persons and the number of POWs is 132,231 soldiers.

Overseas
- The U.S. Secretary of State, Dean Acheson, requests the International Red Cross to investigate infectious diseases to counter the bacteriological warfare of North Korea.

March 15, Saturday (February 20, by lunar calendar, 庚申日 White Monkey) Clear, Cloudy and Windy

630 Day of the War

War Situation
- The UN tank Forces advance on the eastern front.
- The Police Force Unit of Southwest District achieves brilliant war results, killing 59 enemy combatants, capturing six and getting six more to defect to South Korea.
- In the staff officers meeting for monitoring the Armistice, the UN Forces suggest an overall compromise proposal including five articles for the Armistice.

At Home
- The refugee registration is implemented all over the country with 10,464,491 refugees registered.
- In the announcement of a riot out-breaking in the Geoje POW camp, the director of the camp, Francis Dodd, explains that the riot happened accidentally in a heated atmosphere.

March 16, Sunday (February 21, by lunar calendar, 辛酉日 White Rooster) Clear
631 Day of the War

War Situation
- Nine B-29 fighter bombers drop 50,000 tons of bombs on the airport of the Communist Forces near Sariwon.
- The Eighth U.S. Army Commander, General Van Fleet states that the cause of the riot is the UN Forces' hospitable treatment of the prisoners.

At Home
- The Ministry of Social Affairs announces that the total number of refugees is 7,451,629 persons (as of the end of February)

March 17, Monday (February 22, by lunar calendar, 壬戌日 Black Dog) Clear
632 Day of the War

War Situation

- The warship *U.S.S Wisconsin* heavily attacks the positions of the Communist Forces.
- The carrier-base aircraft and the U.S. Marine Corps fighters attack 141 spots on the railroads.

At Home

- The Ministry of Agriculture and Forestry allocate about 500,000 seok(1seok is equivalent to 180 liters) of rice to each provincial Government.
- The Seoul City Government is prudently considering the problem of removing non-licensed private markets before returning of the Central Government.

March 18, Tuesday (February 23, by lunar calendar, 癸亥日 Black Pig) Clear, Cloudy and Rainy
633 Day of the War

War Situation

- The ROK Army has a battle with two squads of the Communist Forces in the west of Cheorwon.
- The UN Forces artillery unit in the western frontline repulses Chinese Communist Forces six time attacks.

At Home

- President Syngman Rhee states that the presidential candidacy for the next election will be open to anybody.
- The National Assembly plenary session resumes.

Overseas

- The trade talks for amendment between the United Kingdom and Japan is held in the United Nations Command.

March 19, Wednesday (February 24, by lunar calendar, 甲子日 Blue Rat) Rainy, Cloudy, Clear and Windy
634 Day of the War

War Situation

- The Eighth U.S. Army Commander Van Fleet, predicts that there will be no offensive in spring season by the Communist Forces.
- The problem of entrance of monitoring the Armistice is agreed.
  The compromise proposal about the entrances submitted by the UN Forces:
  (South Korea: Busan, Gangneung, Gunsan, Incheon [Including Seoul airport]
  North Korea: Hamheung [including Heungnam], Jinnampo [including Pyongyang airport], Sinuiju, Cheongjin, Manpojin).

At Home
- The National Assembly passes a bill to cancel the Gwangmu press law and rejects the bill of the newspaper and periodical publication law.

March 20, Thursday (February 25, by lunar calendar, 乙丑日 Blue Ox) Clear
635 Day of the War

War Situation
- Due to a heavy snow only reconnoitering skirmishes happen.
- The UN naval vessels bomb and the naval facilities of the Communist Forces in succession.
- In the staff officers meeting for monitoring the Armistice, the UN Forces submit an amendment plan for the entrances. (South Korea: Busan, Gangneung, Gunsan, Incheon [including Seoul airport] North Korea: Sinuiju, Heungnam, Sinanju [including Pyongyang airport], Cheongjin, Manpojin). The Communist Forces agreed on this revised plan.

At Home
- Swindlers alluring people with emigration appear.

March 21, Friday (February 26, by lunar calendar, 丙寅日 Red Tiger) Clear
636 Day of the War

War Situation
- The UN Forces withdraw from the western frontline due to the hard offensive of the Communist Forces.
- The staff officers meeting for monitoring the Armistice is held.

At Home
- The Ministry of Agriculture and Forestry decides to release 50,000,000,000 won for farming funds.
- The highest rice price reaches 75,000 won by a large-size du in the Busan market.

Overseas
- The U.S. Secretary of Defense, Robert A. Lovett, reports on the Indochina War in the Foreign Affairs Committee, announcing that a party of the Chinese Communist Forces crossed the border and joined the Ho Chi Minh Forces.

March 22, Saturday (February 27, by lunar calendar, 丁卯日 Red Rabbit) Cloudy, Windy and Rainy
637 Day of the War

War Situation
- The F-51 Mustang fighters of the Korean Air Force heavily bomb the Communist railroad.
- In the staff officers meeting for monitoring the Armistice, the Communist Forces submits

The helium gas balloon for indicating the Armistice talks (March 22, 1952)

an amendment to limit the activities of the Neutral Nations' Supervisory Commission for Armistice at the five entrances in the rear area of North Korea.

At Home
- The Ministry of Commerce and Industry announces financing of 15,100,000,000 won as operating fund for the factories in operation.

March 23, Sunday (February 28, by lunar calendar, 戊辰日 Yellow Dragon) Clear and Windy
638 Day of the War

War Situation
- Small arms combat happen in the northwest basin in the eastern front.
- The U.S. 5th Air Force has full engagements in the skies over North Korea.
- An F-51 propeller fighter squadron destroys nine assembly areas of the Communist Forces in northeastern Pyongyang.

At Home
- The Ministry of Finance decides on 50,000,000,000 won of farming funding which is

a curtailed amount from the originally requested budget 119,000,000,000 won by the Ministry of Agriculture and Forestry

March 24, Monday (February 29, by lunar calendar, 己巳日 Yellow Snake) Clear and Windy
639 Day of the War

War Situation
- The UN Navy bombards a town which is occupied by the Communist Forces on the west coast.
- The Eighth U.S. Army Commander, General Van Fleet, points out the Communist Forces' insincerity toward the Armistice talks.
- In the staff officers meeting for exchanging POWs, confidential talks are suggested to resolve the deadlock.

At Home
- The Korea-Japan Talks encounter a crisis due to Japanese insistence on their property rights in Korea.
- The Government makes a decision to punish the military uniformed civilians.

Overseas
- The Korea-Japan Talks on the property rights issue is held.
- The Japanese representative insists they still keep the right of the property possessed by the Japanese in Korea during the Japanese colonial era.

March 25, Tuesday (February 30, by lunar calendar, 庚午日 White Horse) Clear and Windy
640 Day of the War

War Situation
- The UN Artillery Unit finds 400 soldiers of the Communist Forces and heavily attacks them in the western Gorangpo.
- UN Thunder jet fighters destroy three tanks of the Communist Forces in Geumcheon.
- In the staff officers meeting for monitoring the Armistice, the UN Forces accept the map of five entry points in North Korea which are suggested by the Communist Forces.

At Home
- The Government requests Japan to return the ashes kept by the Japanese Government, of those who have passed away after a compulsory manpower draft of Japan.
- The graduation ceremony of the elementary school for refugees is held at Bumingwan in Busan.

March 26, Wednesday (March 1, by lunar calendar, 辛未日 White Sheep) Clear and Cloudy
641 Day of the War

War Situation

- The UN Forces launch three onslaughts on Gureung Hill which has been occupied by the Communist Forces in the western Mundeungri valley.
- The UN bomber squadron destroys the railroad network of the Communist Forces between Jeongju and Sinanju.

At Home

- The Ministry of Commerce and Industry resolves to fund the second recovery project of Hwacheon Hydro power Plant and Yeongwol Thermal power plant.
- The value of the U.S. dollar in the black market increases suddenly at the exchange rate of 25,100 won to one dollar and at the exchange rate of 10,200 won to an Army note (APC).

Overseas

- The Chinese Communist Forces command rallies to welcome the investigation team on bacteriological warfare which has visited North Korea.
- The Japanese Government states that they have asked the United States to rent 60 small warships for protecting their coasts.

March 27, Thursday (March 2, by lunar calendar, 壬申日 Black Monkey) Cloudy and Clear
642 Day of the War

War Situation

- Reconnoitering skirmishes occur on the east and west frontlines.
- In the staff officers meeting for monitoring the Armistice, the Korean translation for the United Nations Command in the Armistice agreement document is discussed.

At Home

- The 37th National Assembly plenary session passes the special account bill for the Farmland Reform Projects.
- The civilian aircraft of the South Korean airline, Unnamho, departs on a maiden flight to Taipei, carrying a Korean cultural goodwill mission to China.
- A counterfeit dollar bill, the first in Korea, is seen in a bank window of the Bank of Korea.

March 28, Friday (March 3, by lunar calendar, 癸酉日 Black Rooster) Clear
643 Day of the War

War Situation

- The UN Navy continuously attacks the east and west coasts of North Korea.
- B-26 fighter bombers attack the road and railroad traffic in North Korea.
  The Communist Forces suggest transferring the issue of Russia's participation in the Neutral Nations' Supervisory Commission for the Armistice to a High-Level Meeting.
  The Communist Forces suggest replacing the title of Korea in the English document to

Joseon.

At Home
- President Syngman Rhee asks the Eighth U.S. Army Commander, General Van Fleet, to release South Korean POWs who are accommodated in the Geoje POW camp.
- A businessman is criticized for applying to buy a luxury velvet loom.

Overseas
- The Vice-Minister of the UN Secretariat, Cordier, states in Tokyo that the UN representative of the Armistice talks is fully representing South Korean people.

March 29, Saturday (March 4, by lunar calendar, 甲戌日 Blue Dog) Clear
644 Day of the War

War Situation
- A small reconnoitering attack of the Communist Forces occurs.
- Twenty-seven Communist guerrillas are killed at Nogodan in South Jeolla Province capturing seven rifles.

At Home
- Present price index is soaring seventy times compared to the year 1947 index.

March 30, Sunday (March 5, by lunar calendar, 乙亥日 Blue Pig) Clear, Cloudy, Rainy and Windy
645 Day of the War

War Situation
- Two platoons of the Communist Forces attack a position of the UN Forces in the northern Ganseong in the eastern frontline.
- In the staff officers meeting for monitoring the Armistice, the Communist Forces reject the UN's request to rule out Russia from the Neutral Nations Supervisory Commission.

At Home
- The Korea-U.S. tungsten agreement is concluded.
- The press corps accredited to the National Assembly submit a petition pointing out undemocratic elements of the Publication Law.

March 31, Monday (March 6, by lunar calendar, 丙子日 Red Rat) Rainy
646 Day of the War

War Situation
- The UN Forces repulse a reconnoitering attack of the Communist Forces on the outpost position of the UN Forces in the northern Ganseong on the eastern front.
- A search party of the UN Forces has a battle with the Chinese Communist Forces in the West Hill of Yeoncheon.

At Home

- The Financial Bureau of the Ministry of Finance establishes a foreign currency reporting system at immigration to strengthen foreign exchange management (to take effect on April 1).
- The prohibition of selling boiled rice is to be in effect on April 1.

Overseas

- The Policy Planning Bureau of the U.S. State Department submits a "memorandum on the Chinese POWs."

The Chinese culture and art group visit the Chinese Embassy in Pyongyang with the author, Ba Jin (right of the flag holders) as its leader.

April 1, Tuesday (March 7, by lunar calendar, 丁丑日 Red Ox) Rainy, Cloudy, Windy and Clear
647 Day of the War

War Situation
- The UN Forces repulse two battalions of the Chinese Communist Forces in western Munsan and southern Panmunjom at night.
- The joint subcommittee agrees to consider the issue of monitoring the Armistice.

At Home
- President Syngman Rhee states that he wants the Chinese Nationalist Forces to attack mainland China.
- The supporters of the constitutional amendment to a cabinet system agreed to launch a signature campaign.

April 2, Wednesday (March 8, by lunar calendar, 戊寅日 Yellow Tiger) Clear
648 Day of the War

War Situation
- The UN Forces repulse a company of the Chinese Communist Forces in southern Panmunjom at dawn.
- The UN Air Forces attack a position of the Communist Forces in southern and western Panmunjom.

At Home
- The imported grains purchased, for the first time, with the Government's holding dollars arrive at Busan Harbor, including 9,000 tons of barley produced in America.
- The Korea-U.S. joint committee reviews the reimbursement methods of the distributed farmland.

Overseas
- The Vietnamese Armed Forces under the command of the French Forces gradually meet strong resistance in the course of mop-up operation against three battalions of the Vietminh Communist Forces assembling at the Song Coi delta 80.4 km to the southeast of Hanoi.

April 3, Thursday (March 9, by lunar calendar, 己卯日 Yellow Rabbit) Clear
649 Day of the War

War Situation
- F-86 Sabre jet fighters engage in an air battle twice in the skies over North Korea.

- The UN fighter bombers attack the Communist Forces supply line and railroad.

At Home
- The Minister of National Defense, Sin Tae-yeong, announces that registered ID pocketbooks are delivered to veterans and the Second Peoples' Force.
- The repeal act of the Special Treatment of Treacherous Activities Law is officially proclaimed.
- The Monetary Policy Committee decides to issue a new 500-won note from the Bank of Korea.

April 4, Friday (March 10, by lunar calendar, 庚辰日 White Dragon) Clear
650 Day of the War

War Situation
- UN jet fighters continuously attack all around the fronts with napalm bombs.

At Home
- Prime Minister Jang Myeon, makes a report to the National Assembly about the situation in the UN General Assembly for processing Korean issues.
- The repeal Act of the Newspaper Law is officially proclaimed. The Newspaper Law is enacted by the Korean Empire.

April 5, Saturday (March 11, by lunar calendar, 辛巳日 White Snake) Clear
651 Day of the War

War Situation
- The UN Air Force continuously attacks Haeju and Jinnampo.
- The organizing ceremony of the Second Corps is held and attended by President Syngman Rhee.

At Home
- The constitutional amendment bill to the parliamentary governent system is disclosed.
- The Ministry of Social Affairs announces free distribution of 300,000 seok of rice to the refugees and destitute persons.

Overseas
- The UN Forces announces the capacity of the newest U.S. nuclear weapons carrier , B-60 which is fitted with the newest 8-engines and has super medium width, flying 965.6 km per hour.

April 6, Sunday (March 12, by lunar calendar, 壬午日 Black Horse) Clear and Cloudy
652 Day of the War

War Situation

The ROK Army Soldiers relieving stress from the fierce battles to recapture the hill with a consolation performance. (1952. 4. 2)

- The UN Forces recapture the retreated outpost position in the western Cheorwon .
- A liaison officer of the Communist Forces protests that the UN Air Force attacked their supply vehicle of the Armistice representative of the Communist Forces running toward the Kaesong neutral zone.

At Home
- The Labor Bureau of the Ministry of Social Affairs proceeds a negotiation with the Eighth U.S. Army to increase the wages of dock workers.

April 7, Monday (March 13, by lunar calendar, 癸未日 Black Sheep) Rainy and Cloudy
653 Day of the War

War Situation
- The UN Forces engage the Communist Forces at eastern Panmunjom.
- B-29 fighter bombers bomb the Jeongju railroad bridge.

At Home

- Political circles fall into confrontations due to the issue of constitutional amendment to a direct presidential election system.
- The Minister of National Defense, Sin Tae-yeong announces the cancelation of Martial Law in some regions before holding the local elections.

Overseas
- The Chairman of the U.S. Joint Chiefs of Staff, Omar Nelson Bradley, states that he hopes for a peaceful settlement of the Korean War, adding that the Communist Forces' request to invite Russia to the Neutral Nations' Supervisory Commission for Armistice is meaningless.

April 8, Tuesday (March 14, by lunar calendar, 甲申日 Blue Monkey) Clear and Cloudy
654 Day of the War

War Situation
- A scouting unit of the UN Forces engages the Chinese Communist Forces in northern Cheorwon.
- The Joint Supervisory Subcommittee is deadlocked continuously.

At Home
- The National Assembly passes a motion to give a Government guaranteed loan of 7.4 billion won to Joseon Transportation Co. Ltd. as a fund for company operation and facility repairs.

April 9, Wednesday (March 15, by lunar calendar, 乙酉日 Blue Rooster) Clear
655 Day of the War

War Situation
- The UN fighter bombers attack railroad facilities of the Communist Forces between Jeongju and Suncheon.
- The Commander of the U.K. Far East Ground Forces, General Charles Keightley, states an optimistic view to accomplish peace within 6 months after a meeting with the UN chief delegate.

At Home
- The Ministry of Agriculture and Forestry conducts research on the actual situation of the filature industry to stabilize the price of thread.

April 10, Thursday (March 16, by lunar calendar, 丙戌日 Red Dog) Clear and Windy
656 Day of the War

War Situation
- The UN fighter bombers attack supply lines of the Communist Forces throughout North Korea.

- A Mustang unit of the ROK Air Force bombs the Gyeomipo supply center.

At Home
- The Constitutional Amendment Promotion Committee to the parliamentary government system is organized.
- The Financial Union establishes the savings in kind system as a way of increasing national savings.

Overseas
- President Truman requests the Congress to approve 1,457,100,000 dollars as a national defense budget, explaining that most of it is additional expenses for the Korean War.

April 11, Friday (March 17, by lunar calendar, 丁亥日 Red Pig) Cloudy and Windy
657 Day of the War

War Situation
- F-86 Sabre jet fighters bomb a supply train in southern Sinuiju.
- The 5th U.S. Air Force fighters attack the Communist Forces position in northern Geumseong.

At Home
- The Government is considering the possibility of appointing an acting Prime Minister.
- Three Ministers including Ministry of Social Affairs, Ministry of Home Affairs and Ministry of Agriculture and Forestry announce the steps for refugee farmers to return home.

April 12, Saturday (March 18, by lunar calendar, 戊子日 Yellow Rat) Rainy, Windy and Cloudy
658 Day of the War

War Situation
- The UN Forces recapture the outpost in the western Mundeungri Valley at dawn after a short evacuation.

At Home
- The Special Account Law for the Farmland Reform Projects (Law No. 241) is published.
- Some burglaries are reported at the U.S. Army PX in Incheon.

Overseas
- Looking forward to the Armistice of the Korean War to be accomplished on May 1, the relevant UN authorities push ahead with a plan to hold the UN Special General Assembly

April 13, Sunday (March 19, by lunar calendar, 己丑日 Yellow Ox) Rainy, Windy and Cloudy
659 Day of the War

War Situation
- The UN carrier-based aircraft unit attacks the supply centers and Cheongjin industrial

facilities in North Korea.

At Home
- The Seoul City Government completes a city master plan
- The special envoy, Mayer, and his entourage dispatched by President Truman arrive at the Suyeong Airport.

April 14, Monday (March 20, by lunar calendar, 庚寅日 White Tiger) Cloudy, Windy and Clear
660 Day of the War

War Situation
- The UN Forces recapture an outpost in the eastern Bukhan River area after a temporary evacuation due to the strong attacks of the Communist Forces.
- A search party of the Communist Forces is repulsed three times in western Munsan.
- The Armistice Supervisory joint subcommittee holds a talk for 15 seconds and is then deadlocked.

At Home
- The Ministry of Social Affairs establishes a policy to support the refugees who are not able to settle down at home.
- The Provost Marshal, Sim Eon-bong, hold a press conference about the problem of phony soldiers and military draft evaders.

April 15, Tuesday (March 21, by lunar calendar, 辛卯日 White Rabbit) Clear and Windy
661 Day of the War

War Situation
- The UN Forces evacuate an outpost in the western frontline.
- The UN Navy fleet moves out for an operation in the Korean waters and the 17th Task Forces attack the railroads in the triangle zone of Hamheung, Wonsan and Yangdok.

At Home
- The Korea-U.S. conference is held in the Cabinet Conference room of the Capitol building.
- A memorial hall is built in Mangyeongdae in commemoration of the 40th birthday of Kim Il Sung.

April 16, Wednesday (March 22, by lunar calendar, 壬辰日 Black Dragon) Clear, Cloudy, Windy and Clear
662 Day of the War

War Situation
- The UN Forces in the eastern frontline repulse the Communist Forces in the northern basin and in southwestern Geumseong.
- The Armistice Supervisory joint subcommittee has a talk for 23 seconds and is then

deadlocked.

At Home
- The second day of the Korea-U.S. conference;
  The Korean party presents a proposition about the military and economic aids and the repayment of the UN Forces loans and then the discussion procedure is decided.

April 17, Thursday (March 23, by lunar calendar, 癸巳日 Black Snake) Cloudy, Rainy, Windy and Cloudy
663 Day of the War

War Situation
- The UN Forces in western Munsan repulse four times the reconnoitering attacks of the Communist Forces.
- The Communist Forces urge the UN Forces to resume the talks for the POW exchange problem which has been in recess.

At Home
- A total of 7,922 POWs in the Geoje POW camp present a petition against the compulsory repatriation to the Speaker of the National Assembly, Shin Ik-hee.
- The political powers against the constitutional amendment to the parliamentary cabinet system organize a preparatory meeting for the joint struggle committee of national political groups against the constitutional amendment.

Overseas
- The atomic weapon testing center announces that a flying saucer was witnessed in the sky over the northern Nellis Air Force Base near Las Vegas.

April 18, Friday (March 24, by lunar calendar, 甲午日 Blue Horse) Clear, Cloudy and Clear
664 Day of the War

War Situation
- The confidential staff officers meeting for exchanging POWs agrees to resume its meeting on April 19.

At Home
- The National Assembly plenary session passes a bill of the Government budget.
- The National Assembly decides to send the petition of the POWs in the Geoje POW Camp objecting to the compulsory repatriation, to the Panmunjom Armistice Talks through the Ministry of National Defense.

Overseas
- The Chief delegates' informal talks of the two countries is held to resolve the stagnation of the Korea-Japan Talks.

April 19, Saturday (March 25, by lunar calendar, 乙未日 Blue Sheep) Rainy
665 Day of the War

War Situation

- A search party of the UN Forces engages the Chinese Forces with grenades in northern Cheorwon.
- The Armistice Supervisory Joint Subcommittee decides to transfer the issue of monitoring of armistice again to the staff officers meeting.

At Home

- The third day of the Korea-U.S. conference resumes.
- The National Assembly plenary session decides to take fundamental measures against famine.
- The Director of the Public Information Office, Lee Cheol-won, announces the Government position on the constitutional amendment of the parliamentary government system.

April 20, Sunday (March 26, by lunar calendar, 丙申日 Red Monkey) Rainy and Clear
666 Day of the War

War Situation

- A search party of the UN Forces engages the Communist Forces in Cheorwon.
- The staff officers meeting for exchanging POWs continues confidential talks.

At Home

- The promotion committee of the parliamentary government system announces the reasons to enforce the constitutional amendment.
- The Minister of Justice, Seo Sang-hwan, announces a statement against the parliamentary government system.
- *Radio Pyongyang* announces that Kim Il Sung accepted the offer of Stalin to donate 50,000 tons of wheat flour.

April 21, Monday (March 27, by lunar calendar, 丁酉日 Red Rooster) Clear
667 Day of the War

War Situation

- A search party of the UN Forces attacks a position of the Communist Forces northeast of Geumseong.

At Home

- The National Assembly establishes a plan to dispatch a surveillance team to create a free atmosphere of local parliament elections.
- The judge in the Suwon Branch of Seoul District Court, Gwon Sun-yeong, requested to confirm if the Special Action Decree Article 9 on the criminal punishment under

emergency is unconstitutional.

April 22, Tuesday (March 28, by lunar calendar, 戊戌日 Yellow Dog) Cloudy and Clear
668 Day of the War

War Situation
- A Cavalry Regiment of the Chinese Communist Forces appears.
- The staff officers meeting for monitoring the Armistice discusses the problem of the airport and the neutral nation.
  The representative of the Communist Forces insists that in case the designation problem of the neutral nations is not agreed, each party can freely designate the neutral nations after announcing the common acceptance principle.

At Home
- The U.S. Provost Marshal of Seoul district requests to refrain from submitting a counterfeit application form of carrying in daily necessities.

April 23, Wednesday (March 29, by lunar calendar, 己亥日 Yellow Pig) Cloudy and Windy
669 Day of the War

War Situation
- The UN Air Forces launch a nighttime attack on the supply unit of the Communist Forces in the area between Pyongyang and Sariwon.

At Home
- The leader of the UN Korean Reconstruction Agency, Kingsley, arrives at Suyeong airport.
- The Minister of Health and Welfare, Choi Jae-yu, states that lepers will be isolated in Sorok Island.
- About 2,000 civilian detainees are moved to a refugee camp in Busan from the Geoje POW Camp and this movement started on April 21.

Overseas
- The UN Command and the U.S. Far East Command announce that at the same time of effectuation of the U.S. peace treaty with Japan, the UN Command and the U.S. Far East Command will be renamed respectively.
- The optimism for a Korean Armistice has declined in Washington.

April 24, Thursday (April 1, by lunar calendar, 庚子日 White Rat) Cloudy and Rainy
670 Day of the War

War Situation
- Hand to hand combat with grenades develops in southwestern Pyeonggang.
- The UN Navy bombards the supply storages and artillery units of the Communist Forces

in Cheongjin.
- Around 100 Communist guerrillas launch a surprise attack and set fire to a post office and district office in Hadong-eup in South Gyeongsang Province.

At Home
- The National Assembly ratifies the agreement between Korea and the World Health Organization for the Korean health promotion (Treaty No. 10, proclaimed on November 27, 1951).
- The U.S. Ambassador to Korea, John J. Mucho, sends a report on the current opinions to replace Prime Minister Jang Myeon and trends of the political power groups related to the constitutional amendment.

April 25, Friday (April 2, by lunar calendar, 辛丑日 White Ox) Rainy and Clear
671 Day of the War

War Situation
- A search party of the Communist Forces is repulsed in southern Geumseong.
- Communist guerrillas appear in the first and second election precinct of Hadong County, disturbing local election.

At Home
- The Foreign Minister, Byeon Yeong-tae, expresses his regret over the Japanese unilateral interruption of the Korea-Japan talks.
- The local election under the Local Government Act is implemented in electoral precincts in 1,397 cities and 4,263 eup and myeon all over the country.

April 26, Saturday (April 3, by lunar calendar, 壬寅日 Black Tiger) Cloudy and Clear
672 Day of the War

War Situation
- The UN artillery unit repulses the nighttime attack of the Communist Forces in southeastern Gimhwa.
- The UN fighter bombers attack railroads of the Communist Forces.
- UN bombers bomb railroad of Communist Army in Seoncheon district.

At Home
- The graduation of the Seoul University is held granting the first doctorates after the national independence. (Doctorate Degree of Literature: 2 students, Doctorate Degree of Medicine: 1 student, Doctorate Degree of Engineering: 3 students)

Overseas
- The UN Command in Japan notifies the Japanese Government of the abolition of the MacArthur Line.

Graduation of Seoul University during the war (1952. 4. 26)

April 27, Sunday (April 4, by lunar calendar, 癸卯日 Black Rabbit) Cloudy
673 Day of the War

War Situation
- The UN Forces repulse an attack of the Communist Forces in the area between Gimhwa and Geumseong.
- B-29 fighter bombers bomb a railroad bridge in Jeongju.
- F-86 Sabre jet fighters shoot down three MIG jet fighters of the Communist Forces.

At Home
- The Ministry of Agriculture and Forestry explains the situation to import foreign rice.

April 28, Monday (April 5, by lunar calendar, 甲辰日 Blue Dragon) Rainy and Windy
674 Day of the War

War Situation
- A search party of the UN Forces attacks an outpost position of the Communist Forces in southeastern Gimhwa.
- On the request of Nam Il, representative of the Communist Forces, the plenary session of the Armistice talks is indefinitely postponed.

At Home
- Fifty boxes of aid packages arrive, which have been collected by American elementary and junior-high school students in an aid campaign for Korean students.

Overseas

- The U.S. delegation to the UN notifies the UN Security Council of replacement of the UN Commander.
- President Truman appoints the UN Commander, Gen. Matthew Ridgway, as the Commander of the North Atlantic Treaty Organization Forces and Gen. Mark Wayne Clark as the UN Commander.

April 29, Tuesday (April 6, by lunar calendar, 乙巳日 Blue Snake) Rainy, Cloudy and Clear
675 Day of the War

War Situation

- The UN Air Force bombers destroy 46 enemy spots on the main roads of the east coast at night.
- The Armistice talks are completely adjourned for the first time since five months ago.

At Home

- The Government imported 60,000 tons of foreign grains with the Government's holding fund of 7,000,000 dollars.
- The rice price soars to 90,000 won per one du.(1 du is equivalent to 1.8 liter)

Overseas

- The UN Commander, Mark Wayne Clark, announces his stance to maintain General Ridgeway's policies.

April 30, Wednesday (April 7, by lunar calendar, 丙午日 Red Horse) Clear and Windy
676 Day of the War

War Situation

- The UN Forces in the eastern frontline repulse many search attacks of the Communist Forces in mountainous area in Seosan.
- Artillery exchanges occur between the UN Forces and the Communist Forces on the western frontline.

At Home

- The Minister of National Defense, Sin Tae-yeong, gives an order of hunting prohibition to all officers and soldiers on the front.
- The Nakdong River bridge repair work is completed and reopened at a cost of 249,670,000 won.

Overseas

- The Executive Yuan of the Taiwan Nationalist Government approves the Peace Treaty between the Republic of China and Japan.

May 1, Thursday (April 8, by lunar calendar, 丁未日 Red Sheep) Clear
677 Day of the War

War Situation
- Reconnaissance clashes occur in all the frontline areas.
- Artillery battles between the two sides fiercely rage on the western front.
- The Communist Forces notify the UN Forces of their intention to resume the regular session of the Armistice talks.

At Home
- The Ministry of National Defense begins to hand out soldier's bounty to the families of fallen soldiers.
- The political circles face a complicated situation due to the constitutional amendment to the parliamentary government system and the legislative bill about political movements.
- The Korea-Japan trade agreement has been renewed for another year.
- The U.S. electricity delegation converses with the Korean side and makes a decision to restore the Hwacheon thermoelectric power plant.
- The Chairman of the Korean Federation of Labor Unions Chun Jin-han, makes an address for May Day and requests the National Assembly to legislate the Labor Law.

Overseas
- 250 of the second Korean Military Officer Corps arrives at American military schools and relative institutions.

May 2, Friday (April 9, by lunar calendar, 戊申日 Yellow Monkey) Clear, Cloudy, Windy and Rainy
678 Day of the War

War Situation
- The UN Air Forces heavily attack transportation routes of North Korea.
- The 45th regular session of the Armistice talks is resumed.
- A Japanese journalist starts reporting on the Armistice conference for the first time.

At Home
- The Foreign Minister, Byeon Yeong-tae, asks the Japanese Government to follow the MacArthur Line.
- The police arrested persons related to the case of the nation saving fighters alliance.

May 3, Saturday (April 10, by lunar calendar, 己酉日 Yellow Rooster) Rainy and Windy
679 Day of the War

War Situation

- The U.S. Far East Air Force announces the damages caused since the outbreak of war.

  The loss of Air Force planes of the Communist Forces: 564 planes (uncertainty: 122)

  The loss of Far East Air Force planes: 657
- The U.S. Air Forces limit the number of flight of the entire Air Forces except in Korea.
- Brigadier General Nichols announces that the conference agreement has not been reached.

At Home

- The Government decides to dispatch a search team for the remains of the draftees in Japan.
- The political circles crash with the issue of the constitutional amendment and ratifying the prime minister.
- The ROK Navy holds a naming ceremony for four naval vessels donated by the United States.

Overseas

- The U.S. Army Chief of Staff, Collins, states about the situation of the deployment of the U.S. Force as follows: residual mainland: 1 corps, Korea: 6 divisions, Japan: 2 divisions, Europe: 5 divisions.

May 4, Sunday (April 11, by lunar calendar, 庚戌日 White Dog) Rainy and Windy
680 Day of the War

War Situation

- The UN Forces capture a position in northwest Yeoncheon after a fierce battle.
- The UN Air Forces shoot down five MIG jet fighters of the Communist Forces in an air battle over around Yalu River.
- Ten guerrillas are killed and two captured in the cleanup operation of Communist guerrillas on Mt. Jiri.

At Home

- Foreign Minister Byeon Yeong-tae announces plans to defend the Korean proclamation on the ocean sovereignty declared by President Syngman Rhee.
- The Government opens a letter of credit to import rice produced in Thailand.

Overseas

- The U.S. Department of Defense expresses its position about the POWs of the Communist Forces:

  The fact that 75% of the POWs of the Communist Forces rejected the compulsory repatriation contradicts the claim by the Communist Forces that they are volunteer soldiers.

May 5, Monday (April 12, by lunar calendar, 辛亥日 White Pig) Cloudy, Windy and Clear
681 Day of the War

War Situation
- The UN Forces repulse an attack of the Communist Forces in northwestern Yeoncheon, northern Gimhwa and southern Goseong.
- Fighter bombers and carrier-base aircrafts attack the traffic routes of the Communist Forces at night.
- The Eighth U.S. Army Commander, General Van Fleet, states that the matter of Armistice and war depends on the decision of the Communist Forces.

At Home
- The rice price in Seoul is soaring again.
- The U.S. State Department makes an analysis of the political struggles between the National Assembly and President Syngman Rhee.

May 6, Tuesday (April 13, by lunar calendar, 壬子日 Black Rat) Cloudy, Clear and Windy
682 Day of the War

War Situation
- The UN Air Forces launch combined attacks on the main railroad supply routes of the Communist Forces for five to six days.
- The 49th regular conference is held for 15 minutes.
- The representative of the Communist Forces, Nam Il, calls for a recess after reading a prepared statement.

At Home
- The 50th National Assembly plenary session ratifies Chang Taek-sang as the Prime Minister, with the votes of 95 ayes and 81 noes.
- The Constitutional Council dismisses the Seoul High Court's requisition to decide the constitutionality of the Treatment of State-Reverted Property Act.

May 7, Wednesday (April 14, by lunar calendar, 癸丑日 Black Ox) Cloudy, Rainy and Cloudy
683 Day of the War

War Situation
- A riot occurs in the Geoje POW camp and the director of the camp, Brig. Gen. Francis T. Dodd, is abducted in the middle of the conference with the POWs, at about 14:15 hours and the accompanying Lieutenant Colonel Raible escapes.
- The UN Forces Commander, General Ridgway, announces a statement on the Armistice.

At Home
- The Government concludes the Korea - U.S. tungsten agreement.

340

- The Minister of Social Affairs, Choi Chang-sun, and the Parliamentary inspection team states that farmers of the entire country barely manage to stay alive with herb-roots and tree-barks due to a serious food shortage.

Overseas
- The UN Forces Commander, General Wesley Clark arrives in Tokyo and states that he will exert himself to fulfill the duty of the UN Forces and to finalize an Armistice of the Korean War.

May 8, Thursday (April 15, by lunar calendar, 甲寅日 Blue Tiger) Cloudy, Windy and Clear
684 Day of the War

War Situation
- The UN tank Forces destroy two battalions of the Communist Force and 90 tochka positions in the area between Geumseong and Gimhwa.
- The UN representative, Joey, announces that the Armistice talks make no progress and got no better and the Communist Forces request repatriation of all 132,000 POWs.

At Home
- The Prime Minister, Chang Taek-sang, gives an order to enforce official discipline as his first official step since taking office, the first step of which is to ban Government officials from entering tea rooms and luxurious restaurants and 191 cases of violation are exposed in the first day surveillance.

May 9, Friday (April 16, by lunar calendar, 乙卯日 Blue Rabbit) Cloudy and Rainy
685 Day of the War

War Situation
- The Communist Forces implement searches and attacks in all of the frontline.
- A fierce seesaw battle is carried out for seven days in the northern Yeoncheon.
- The Eighth U.S. Army Commander, General Van Fleet, rushes to Geoje.
- The former UN Forces Commander, Ridgway, orders Van Fleet, to rescue Brigadier General, Dodd and to use armed force if necessary.

At Home
- UN Forces Commander, General Clark and the former UN Forces Commander, General Ridgway pays a courtesy call on President Syngman Rhee in the temporary president residence in Busan.
- The Government releases 200,000 seok of rice as an emergency food measure.
- The Second Peoples' Force soldiers are drafted in South Gyeongsang Province.

Overseas
- The UN Forces Commander, Clark and the former UN Forces Commander, Ridgway

return to Tokyo after a 38-hour inspection tour of Korea.

May 10, Saturday (April 17, by lunar calendar, 丙辰日 Red Dragon) Rainy and Cloudy
686 Day of the War

War Situation
- The UN ground Forces recapture several spots on the western frontline.
- The POWs of the Communist Forces release Brig. Gen. Dodd, the commander of a POW camp.

At Home
- The first election of provincial assembly members is held.
- Incheon port workers begin a slowdown to raise their wages.
- The General Administration of Civil Aviation of China (CAAC) launches a new airliner for the Taipei-Tokyo-Seoul flight.

Overseas
- A senior official in Washington states that the U.S. Government considers requesting Russia to facilitate the Armistice agreement of the Korean War.

May 11, Sunday (April 18, by lunar calendar, 丁巳日 Red Snake) Cloudy and Clear
687 Day of the War

War Situation
- The UN Forces repulse search activities of the Communist Forces in all the frontline.
- The U.S. medium bombers attacked the main railroad network of North Korea at night.
- The Brigadier General, Dodd arrives at the Eighth U.S. Army Command in Seoul.

At Home
- The Prime Minster, Chang Taek-sang, delivers to the chiefs of each organization the urgent instruction to enforce official discipline such as not allowing Government officials to enter high-class restaurants.

May 12, Monday (April 19, by lunar calendar, 戊午日 Yellow Horse) Clear and Cloudy
688 Day of the War

War Situation
- The UN Forces repulse the Communist Forces after grenade battles in the northwest Yeoncheon and in the northeast Panmunjom.
- The UN Forces Commander, Clark announces a statement in Tokyo, including the contents of the agreement between the new chief of the Geoje POW camp, Major General Coalson and war prisoners for releasing the Brigadier General, Dodd;
  (1) To treat POWs in accordance with international law and to try to avoid bloodshed in the

Geoje camp,

(2) To stop screening war prisoners and rearming.

(3) To permit the representative of war prisoners to make an organization

At Home

- The Government projects a compromise proposal of the constitutional amendment for the direct presidential election system and the parliamentary government system.
- The Special Disciplinary Committee for Government officials decide on ways to suspend or expel the officials who use tea houses and high-class restaurants.

Overseas

- The Japanese Government deports 410 Korean-Japanese from Sasebo to Busan. (Two of the three are ex-convicts)
- The U.S. Joint Chiefs of Staff council requests the Far East Command to report on the Dodd case.

May 13, Tuesday (April 20, by lunar calendar, 己未日 Yellow Sheep) Clear
689 Day of the War

War Situation

- The UN Forces repulse search parties of the Communist Forces in western Mundeung-ri valley, the eastern frontline and the western frontline from the mid-night through the dawn of May 14.
- The U.S. First Marine Division defeats night reconnaissance parties on the western frontline.
- The 56th main talks argue about the issues of POWs continuously for 35 minutes.

At Home

- The Government forecast a bumper crop of wheat and barley this year and announces it will make a thorough survey of the expected yields.
- The Seoul city Government decided to repair the historical remains in Seoul such as Junghwajeon, Bosingak Pavilion ravaged by the Korean War.

May 14, Wednesday (April 21, by lunar calendar, 庚申日 White Monkey) Clear
690 Day of the War

War Situation

- The new Commander of Geoje POW camp, Brigadier General Boatner, takes his office.
- In the 57th main conference the representative of the UN Forces, Joy, condemns that the Communist Forces have not carefully examined the final compromise plan of the UN Forces, only repeating their own propaganda with a lot of differences between both parties.

- The representative of the Communist Forces, Nam II, only repeats his criticism on the POW treatment by the UN Forces for 30 minutes.

At Home
- The Government announces the Constitutional Amendment Proposal (The Notice of the State Council, Article No. 36)

  The Government notifies the constitutional amendment proposal of the direct presidential election system and the bicameral parliament. As a result, two constitutional amendment proposals are announced including the parliamentary government system.

Overseas
- The UN Forces Commander, Clark summons former Commander of Geoje POWs camp, Dodd and the new Commander, Coalson to Tokyo to collect actual information about releasing Dodd.

May 15, Thursday (April 22, by lunar calendar, 辛酉日 White Rooster) Clear
691 Day of the War

War Situation
- The U.S. Marine Corps repulse a search party of the Communist Forces in the western Gorangpo.
- The 58th main conference of the Armistice talks get bogged down on the POW issue without any result for 48 minutes.
- The representative of the Communist Forces, Nam II, fiercely accuses in the meeting that the UN Forces have been experimenting with gas warfare, bacteriological warfare and atomic bombs.

At Home
- The Korea National Red Cross begins to provide the communications service and family news for the soldiers' family.
- The Government authorities begins to arrest the evaders of draft registration in South Gyeongsang Province.

Overseas
- The UN Forces Commander, Clark, announces that the case of the Geoje POWs was planned to disturb the exchange of POWs.

May 16, Friday (April 23, by lunar calendar, 壬戌日 Black Dog) Clear
692 Day of the War

War Situation
- Light reconnoitering skirmishes continues all along the frontline.
- F-51 mustang fighters of the ROK Air Forces destroy 55 assembling positions of the

Communist Forces together with the U.S. Navy planes.

• The representative of the Communist Forces, Nam Il, rejects the Free Repatriation Plan of POWs in a 28-minute speech.

At Home

• The National Assembly announces that more than 17,000 POWs of the North Korean Army submitted a petition against the repatriation to the National Assembly three weeks previously and pledged to combat communism.

May 17, Saturday (April 24, by lunar calendar, 癸亥日 Black Pig) Clear and Cloudy
693 Day of the War

War Situation

• The UN tank Forces destroy 70 bunkers and arms dumps in the middle-western frontline.

• The protest by POWs in the Geoje camp continues. The UN guard strengthens security Forces and constructs defense works around the camp.

At Home

• The political circles argue about the constitutional amendment plan submitted by the Government.

• The first joint wedding ceremony of the disabled veterans (six couples) is held in the Donga Theater in Busan.

Overseas

• The UN Forces Commander, Clark, states that the 187th Airborne Infantry Regiment is to be dispatched to the Geoje camp for strengthening security force and illegal acts by POWs will not be tolerated any more.

May 18, Sunday (April 25, by lunar calendar, 甲子日 Blue Rat) Clear and Cloudy
694 Day of the War

War Situation

• The Philippine troops rush a position of the Chinese Communist Forces and kills 40 soldiers of the Communist Forces in hand-to-hand fight in western Cheorwon.

• The Communist Forces bombards heavily in the eastern and western frontline and 4,000 shots are fired all the frontline.

• About 14,000 POWs of the Communist Forces in South Korean POW camps pledge to combat against communism, singing the Korean National anthem.

• 430 prisoners out of 700 to 800 women POWs in the Geoje camp hope to return after the Armistice agreement.

At Home

• The Korean Residents Association in Japan rebuts the distorted propaganda of the

Japanese Government.
- Eighty draft evaders are arrested in Busan.

May 19, Monday (April 26, by lunar calendar, 乙丑日 Blue Ox) Rainy and Cloudy
695 Day of the War

War Situation
- The Philippine troops fiercely attack the Communist Forces positions in Cheorwon.
- The 3rd U.S. Air Force Rescue Crew rescues a helicopter pilot who has crashed in the camp of the Communist Forces.
- In the 62nd main conference of the Armistice talks, the Communist Forces only continue to blame the UN Forces.

At Home
- The Liberal Party and the Korean Youth Organization hold a joint protest meeting against unpatriotic members of the National Assembly in the Chungmuro Square in Busan.

Overseas
- *Beijing Radio* announces that the regional peace conference proposed by China is attended by the social organizations from the U.S.A, Canada, India, Australia, and other seven countries and fully empathized by all parties.
- Russia shuts down the railroad between Berlin and Munich.

May 20, Tuesday (April 27, by lunar calendar, 丙寅日 Red Tiger) Clear
696 Day of the War

War Situation
- POWs of the Communist Forces caused a riot to reject the medical treatments in the POW camp in Geoje Island. A POW is killed and 85 POWs were wounded and a guard is wounded.

At Home
- The Cabinet Meeting decides to organize the wartime system of the Busan city and to stop furnishing deluxe cars for ministerial ranking officials, providing jeeps instead.
- The members of the National Assembly organize a meeting called *Shilla Hoe* consist of 48 members as an amity circle of anti-Gukmindang line in the rally promotion group of the constitutional amendment.

The members of the National Assembly including the Samwoojangpa faction and Minwoohoepa faction, who had supported the bill of approval of the prime minister nominee, Chang Taek-sang, postponed forming a parliamentary negotiation body. Instead, they organized Shilla Hoe.

May 21, Wednesday (April 28, by lunar calendar, 丁卯日 Red Rabbit) Clear
697 Day of the War

War Situation
- The UN Tank Forces attack the targets of the Communist Forces located in northwest Gimhwa and southern Pyeonggang.
- B-29 fighter bombers attack Sinheung-dong railroad bridge at night.

At Home
- Some minor officials are arrested under the suspicion of complicity in the corruption of rationed rice.
- Neglectful measures of the Central Relief Committee and the Federation of the financial association cause huge damages to the relief grains imported from foreign countries.

May 22, Thursday (April 29, by lunar calendar, 戊辰日 Yellow Dragon) Cloudy, Windy and Rainy
698 Day of the War

War Situation
- The Communist Forces attack outpost of the UN Forces on the western frontline in Yeoncheon.
- The Eighth U.S. Army Commander, General Van Fleet, carries out an inspection of the Geoje POW Camp.

At Home
- The Prime Minster, Chang Taek-sang, announces plans to shut down 80% of high-class Korean-style restaurants and expresses the abolition of luxury vehicles for Cabinet Ministers.
- General Van Fleet allows 40 jeeps to be rented in place of luxury official vehicles.

Overseas
- *Beijing Radio* claims that the case of the Busan POW Camp is a part of a homicide plan of the United States.
- The U.S. Senate passes the amendment bill of the Immigration and naturalization Law.

May 23, Friday (April 30, by lunar calendar, 己巳日 Yellow Snake) Clear
699 Day of the War

War Situation
- The UN Air Forces planes heavily bomb munition industrial complexes in Jinnampo and Pyongyang.
- The Commander of the Geoje POW camp, Boatner reorganizes the Camp headquarters.

At Home
- The Cabinet council makes a resolution to promote public welfare stability during the war.

- The Seoul District Prosecutor's Office propels to establish a special investigation agency for enforcing official discipline and preventing illegal acts.

Overseas
- The U.S. Army Command demotes the former Commander of the Geoje POW camp, Brigadier General Dodd and Coalson to ranks of Colonel.

May 24, Saturday (May 1, by lunar calendar, 庚午日 White Horse) Clear
700 Day of the War

War Situation
- Ground combats are generally calm.
- F-84 Jet fighters and F-51 mustang fighters of the Korean Air Forces attack the railroad between Gwaksan and Sinanju.
- Twenty companies of the British Armed Forces and the Canadian armies move from Seoul to Geoje to guard it.

At Home
- The Government declares Martial Law in South Gyeongsang, South Jeolla and North Jeolla provinces.
- The Korea-U.S. Economic Cooperation Agreement (Meyer Agreement) is signed.
- The Minister of National Defense, Sin Tae-yeong, announces re-declaration of emergency Martial Law in some parts of Korea.

May 25, Sunday (May 2, by lunar calendar, 辛未日 White Sheep) Clear
701 Day of the War

War Situation
- The UN Forces repulse the Communist Forces in the western Bukhan River.
- The UN tank unit attacks in succession a position of the Communist Forces in the triangle zone on the central front.
- The UN Forces repulse two companies of the Communist Forces which have tried to attack outposts of the UN Forces in northwest Yeoncheon.

At Home
- The ROK Army Chief of Staff, Lee Jong-chan, rejects the dispatch of Martial Law Army to Busan.
- The Minister of National Defense Sin Tae-young holds a press conference related to the Martial Law in Busan;
  The proclamation of Martial Law in Busan district was to defend supply bases and to prevent Communist guerrillas' plots in connection with the case of Seo Min-ho, member of the National Assembly, and to carry out military actions freely.

348

Overseas
- The spokesman of the Chinese Communist Forces and North Korean Forces state that the U.S. Forces oppressed POWs of the Communist Forces.

May 26, Monday (May 3, by lunar calendar, 壬申日 Black Monkey) Cloudy and Clear
702 Day of the War

War Situation
- The UN Forces repulse the Communist Forces which have attacked outposts in western Yeoncheon.
- The armed forces from six countries including Korea, the U.S.A, the UK, Greece, Canada, and Netherlands, guard the Geoje POW camp.
- The chief delegate of the UN Forces, Harrison hold a press conference;
  (1) The proposal of April 28 is final, in which the UN Forces have tried to protect the dignity of human rights for war prisoners.
  (2) The riot of war prisoner camp has been committed by the instruction of the Communist Forces
  (3) The UN Forces will stand by until the time a new situation appears if the Communist Forces do not change their position.

At Home
- A political upheaval is caused by the Government's enforcement of the constitutional amendment. The military police takes a commuter bus boarded by 45 members of the National Assembly to some place for reasons of inspection refusal in front of South Gyeongsang provincial Government building and arrests ten members of the National Assembly.
- The U.S. Joint Chiefs of Staff order a strategy for the Armistice talks to be implemented by the UN Forces Commander, General Clark

May 27, Tuesday (May 4, by lunar calendar, 癸酉日 Black Rooster) Rainy and Clear
703 Day of the War

War Situation
- The UN Forces repulse the attacks of the Communist Forces in western Cheorwon.
- A reconnoitering skirmish happens on the east of the conference hall in Panmunjom.
- The 67th main conference resumes but argues about the war prisoner issues for 34 minutes and declares a recess.

At Home
- The Public Information Office announces the case under investigation that several members of the National Assembly received political funds from the International Communist Union

A citizen rally for cleanup of the National Assembly and reforming Government (May 28, 1952)

for a clandestine operation.
- President Syngman Rhee converses with General Van Fleet concerning the declaration of Martial Law in Busan.
- The National Assembly discusses the case of taking the National Assembly bus to the police.

May 28, Wednesday (May 5, by lunar calendar, 甲戌日 Blue Dog) Clear
704 Day of the War

War Situation
- The UN Forces engage in the three positions of the Communist Forces in the western Gorangpo on the western frontline.
- B-29 fighter bombers attack the Huichon railroad bridge.
- The representative, Harrison, blames the Communist Forces for taking advantage of the Armistice talks as a venue to promote their propaganda.

At Home
- The National Assembly passes a resolution to lift the Marital Law in Busan with 96 ayes vs 3 noes.
- The UN Korean committee has a talk with President Syngman Rhee, advising to release arrested members of the National Assembly.

May 29, Thursday (May 6, by lunar calendar, 乙亥日 Blue Pig) Clear and Cloudy

350

705 Day of the War

War Situation
- The UN Forces repulse the Chinese Communist Forces which attacked in northwestern Yeoncheon.
- A riot happened in the Yeongcheon POW camp.
- The representative, Harrison, states that the UN Forces' measure for screening the war prisoners is the fairest one.

At Home
- President Syngman Rhee receives a resolution of dissolving the National Assembly which has been made by the representatives of six provincial parliaments, and blames the interference of foreign countries and the National Assembly.
- The National Assembly questions the Government about the case of sufferings of National Assembly members and the replacement of the security police chief.

Overseas
- The Acting Secretary of State, Bruce, provides the measures of pressing Syngman Rhee Government to the U.S. Ambassador to Korea.
- The Secretary of State, Acheson, and the France Foreign Minister, Schuman, completed a three-day meeting to disuss overall global issues.

May 30, Friday (May 7, by lunar calendar, 丙子日 Red Rat) Clear
706 Day of the War

War Situation
- The UN Forces in the eastern front repulse the attack of the Communist Forces which started from the night of May 29.
- The 70th main conference of the Armistice talks;
The representative of the Communist Forces, Nam Il blames the riots at the Yeongcheon and Geoje-do POWs camps at night on May 29 and insists immediate stop of the massacre by the UN Forces.

At Home
- The National Assembly passes a motion(82 to 0) to release the arrested member of the National Assembly on suspicion of receiving funding by the International Communist Group.
- The UN Korea Committee makes a strong statement for the Korean Government to lift the Martial Law in Busan.

May 31, Saturday (May 8, by lunar calendar, 丁丑日 Red Ox) Clear
707 Day of the War

War Situation
- The UN Tank Forces, Artillery Units. Construction battalion and each troop destroy positions of the Communist Forces through closely cooperating operations in the Bukhan River area.
- The 71st main conference of the Armistice talk argue about the POW issues for 35 minutes.

At Home
- The Government establishes a plan to privately import fertilizers.
- The Minister of Agriculture and Forestry, Ham In-seop, emphasizes that overall food controls are not possible.
- The rice price is 110,000 won per 10 *doe (1 doe is equivalent to 1.8 liter)*

Overseas
- Mao Zedong sends telegraphs to Stalin about the reasons of stagnation of the Armistice talks of the Korean War and the possible countermeasures.
- The first section Commander of the Chinese Communist Forces, Deonghwa, is assigned to North Korea, performing his duty as the deputy Commander of the Chinese Communist Forces as well as a political commissar.

June 1, Sunday (May 9, by lunar calendar, 戊寅日 Yellow Tiger) Cloudy and Clear
708 Day of the War

War Situation
- All of the frontlines are in a lull.
- The UN Forces repulse the attacks of the Communist Forces in a position in the eastern Bukhan River.
- A bomber squadron of the UN Forces bombs the Hui Cheon railroad bridge.

At Home
- The National Assembly discusses the process of the constitutional amendment.
- President Syngman Rhee agrees to have a meeting with the delegation of the National Assembly to discuss the issue of lifting Martial Law.
- The Ministry of Agriculture and Forestry comes under criticism from the public regarding the fertilizer import plan through a private trade company.
- The dock workers in Busan suffer considerable losses due to the revision of the contract between Busan Port Logistics and U.S. Armed Forces.
- The total amount of Korea's foreign exchange reserves reaches U.S.$ 18,334,000, £7,400 and HK$849.

Overseas
- The Chinese People's Liberation Army starts the Culture and Education Movement with the goal to improve the 80% illiteracy rate of the whole Army up to the level of graduating elementary school more than 80% of the Army.
- The United States conducts a nuclear test at the Nevada Test Site (NTS) attended by as many as 1,000 persons involved.

June 2, Monday (May 10, by lunar calendar, 己卯日 Yellow Rabbit) Clear and Cloudy
709 Day of the War

War Situation
- A reconnaissance party of the UN Forces engages the Communist Forces in the Mundeungri Valley, and Heartbreak Ridge.
- A company of the U.S. Army Forces incinerates the flags of North Korea in the Geoje POW Camp.

At Home
- The Social Affairs Division of Busan City announces that the total number of war orphans and famine children is 285. (Boy: 203, Girl: 82)

- E. Allan Lightner, the U.S. chargé d'affaires to Korea, reports about the general tendencies of Korean politics.

June 3, Tuesday (May 11, by lunar calendar, 庚辰日 White Dragon) Cloudy, Windy and Clear
710 Day of the War

War Situation
- A reconnaissance party of the Communist Forces attacks a position of the UN Forces in eastern Cheorwon.
- A search party of the Chinese Communist Forces attacks an outpost of the UN Forces in northwestern Yeoncheon, but fails.

At Home
- *Shilla Hoe* decides to promote the selected amendment bill to the Constitution.
- The pro-Government members of the National Assembly refuse to attend the National Assembly, so the National Assembly is suspended.

June 4, Wednesday (May 12, by lunar calendar, 辛巳日 White Snake) Rainy, Windy and Clear
711 Day of the War

War Situation
- The UN Tank unit attacks a position of the Chinese Communist Forces in southern Pyeonggang.
- A bomber squadron of the UN Forces bombs the main transportation network of the Communist Forces of North Korea.
- The 85th, 96th, and 60th U.S. Infantry Units dash into the 85th camp in the Geoje POW camp with tank support and incinerate the North Korean flags and Communist banners.

At Home
- President Syngman Rhee gives strict instructions to the Minister of Home Affairs and the Chief Martial Law Commander not to arrest the members of the National Assembly if they are unrelated to the case of the Communist conspiracy.

Overseas
- General Clark, the UN Forces Commander, returns to Tokyo after an inspection of the Korean fronts.
- Robert A. Lovett, the U.S. Secretary of Defense, issues instructions on the measures to resolve the Korean political crisis to General Clark, the UN Forces Commander.

June 5, Thursday (May 13, by lunar calendar, 壬午日 Black Horse) Clear and Rainy
712 Day of the War

War Situation

- A reconnaissance party of the UN Forces engages in the western Bukhan River.
- Boatner, the Commander of the POW camp, announces instructions to stop feeding POWs in three buildings in the Geoje POW Camp in accordance with the Geneva Convention

At Home
- President Syngman Rhee sends a letter to U.S. President Truman evaluating the Korean political situation.
- The National Assembly passes a motion to investigate the members of the National Assembly who were related to the case of the Communist conspiracy in the disciplinary committee;

  The Assembly plenary session is held by 95 members of the National Assembly and decides to investigate the members of the National Assembly who were related to the case of the Communist conspiracy in the disciplinary committee.
- A strong typhoon hits the entire country, and the amount of damage reaches 1 billion won.

June 6, Friday (May 14, by lunar calendar, 癸未日 Black Sheep) Rainy, Windy and Clear
713 Day of the War

War Situation
- The U.S. 2nd Division engages the battle of Bulmo Hill.(6.6-8.1)
- The U.S. 45th Division launches the counter operation and occupies 11 forward combat bases.

At Home
- The National Assembly annuls the interpellation related to lifting Martial Law in Busan due to the absence of the Cabinet Members.
- The Minister of Home Affairs, Lee Beom-seok, holds a press conference with foreign press on the issues such as arresting the members of the National Assembly.

Overseas
- Nam II, the chief representative of communist side requests withdrawal of the detention plan of POWs of the U.S. Army Forces in the representative meeting of both parties in the Armistice Conference.

June 7, Saturday (May 15, by lunar calendar, 甲申日 Blue Monkey) Rainy, Clear, Cloudy and Windy
714 Day of the War

War Situation
- The UN Forces capture the main hills in western Cheorwon.
- The UN Forces representative, Harrison, calls a three-day recess in spite of the rejection of the Communist Forces party.

At Home

- The Ministry of Agriculture and Forestry orders local administrative agencies to distribute fertilizers on time for farming even on credit.

June 8, Sunday (May 16, by lunar calendar, 乙酉日 Blue Rooster) Clear
715 Day of the War

War Situation
- The UN Forces engage in battle with the Communist Forces in western Cheorwon.
- The U.S. marine aircraft shoots down a Yak fighter of the Communist Forces in an air battle over Haeju.
- B-29 bombers attack the railroad bridge between Jeongju and Namsi and the Seoncheon railroad bridge.
- The UN Forces reject the second suggestion of the Communist Forces to resume the Armistice Conference.

At Home
- President Syngman Rhee expresses his position on the present political situation, emphasizing the direct presidential election system.
- A Government official insists that Lee Gangguk has planned to overthrow the Korean Government visiting North Korea and Japan.

June 9, Monday (May 17, by lunar calendar, 丙戌日 Red Dog) Cloudy, Windy and Clear
716 Day of the War

War Situation
- The UN Forces repulse an attack of the Communist Forces in western Cheorwon.
- The U.S. Army Forces stationed in Geoje have a drill for dispersing of the POWs.
- The liaison officer of the Communist Forces requests resumption of the Armistice Conference in the liaison officers meeting of both sides, but the UN Forces reject it.

At Home
- Ten members of the National Assembly including Jeong Sunjo, submit a resolution to guarantee the functioning of the National Assembly.
- The authorities of the UN Forces in Korea delivers a letter requesting release of the members of the National Assembly and to lift Martial Law.

Overseas
- The chief of the UN Korean Reconstruction Agency, Kingsley, announces that he has sent to Korea 1,500 tons of paper goods and 7,500,000 copies of textbooks for Korean students.

June 10, Tuesday (May 18, by lunar calendar, 丁亥日 Red Pig) Cloudy, Windy, Rainy and Clear

717 Day of the War

War Situation
- The UN Forces repulse an attack of the Chinese Communist Forces on a Hill in western Cheorwon.
- The dispersed accommodation of POWs in Geoje is conducted;
  War prisoners resist the plan of the dispersed accommodation.
  As many as 6,000 prisoners accommodated in CAMP 76 are dispersed into 12 new camps accommodating 500 prisoners each. In the course of this dispersion a riot happens and a soldier of the U.S. Army is killed, 13 soldiers are wounded, 30 POWs of the Communist Forces are killed and 136 POWs are wounded.

At Home
- The Cabinet Meeting passes the bill of the direct presidential election.
- The representative members of various social levels in South Jeolla Province gather in Busan requesting dissolution of the National Assembly.
- The Bureau of Public Information of the Eighth U.S. Army Command announces the importing of aid grains.

June 11, Wednesday (May 19, by lunar calendar, 戊子日 Yellow Rat) Rainy and Clear
718 Day of the War

War Situation
- The Chinese Communist Forces attacks the strategically important position of the UN Forces under the covering of the artillery and trench mortar in the western Cheorwon.
- A body of the anti-Communist POW is found in the Camp77 in Geoje.
- The 79th main conference of the Armistice Conference is held;
  The representative of the Communist Forces, Nam Il, complains about the UN Forces' way of treatment of POWs.

At Home
- The Assembly plenary session passes a resolution to guarantee the functioning of the National Assembly. A resolution to safeguard the Constitution is passed.
- *Shilla Hoe* agrees with Samujang-pa(the Liberal Party's Hapdong-pa) about adopting the selected amendment bill to the Constitution in case of the constitutional amendment.

Overseas
- President Truman sends a letter to the U.S. Secretary of Defense, Robert A. Lovett, suggesting that the representatives of five neutral nations are to inspect the Geoje POW camp.

June 12, Thursday (May 20, by lunar calendar, 己丑日 Yellow Ox) Clear

719 Day of the War

War Situation

- The UN Forces repulse an attack of the Communist Forces in the basin of the northern frontline.
- As many as 500 anticommunism POWs are rescued in the course of re-accommodating movement of the 95th CAMP.
- The 80th main conference of the Armistice Conference is held;
  The representative, Harrison, states that there are no more concessions of the UN Forces and urges the Communist Forces to accept the final suggestion of April 28.

At Home

- The National Assembly passes an urgent motion to request the President to attend the Assembly.
  The argument of presidential term is continued following the previous day's debate and a motion to close the debate is suggested but failed to be put to a vote due to several members' default.
- Shilla Hoe(led by Chang Taek-sang) completes a draft of the selected amendment bill to the Constitution.

June 13, Friday (May 21, by lunar calendar, 庚寅日 Yellow Tiger) Cloudy
720 Day of the War

War Situation

- The UN tank Forces attack a position of the Communist Forces in southern Pyonggang.
- The ground troops of the UN Forces (the 45th U.S. Division) seize two hills under the cover of the Air Forces in the western Cheorwon.

At Home

- The National Assembly passes a motion to close the debate on the presidential term.
  A motion of termination on July 23 is moved but fails to be put to a vote due to three *Shilla Hoe* members' exit just before the voting.
- *Shilla Hoe* makes an appeal that the National Assembly and the Government have to try to autonomically resolve the critical situation in a spirit of cooperation.
- As many as 600 local lawmakers visit the National Assembly to protest and wage a wordy battle with the Speaker of the National Assembly.

Overseas

- The British Air Force announces that the pilots trained as core members of the Air Force will be dispatched to Korea.

June 14, Saturday (May 22, by lunar calendar, 辛卯日 White Rabbit) Rainy, Cloudy and Clear

Refugees and conscriptees lined up to take the transport ship (LST) (1952. 6.13)

721 Day of the War

War Situation
- The UN Forces engage in sporadic combat in northeastern Geumseong and northeastern Gimhwa.
- The U.S. Far East Air Force confirms that MIG fighters of the Communist Forces took part in night combat.

At Home
- President Syngman Rhee sends a letter to the National Assembly to promote the constitutional amendment to the direct presidential election system emphasizing that the present political situation has passed the moment which can be controlled by the negotiation of the Administration and the Assembly. It must be resolved by the National Assembly and the people. The President is insisting to pass such bills as the direct presidential election system and the bicameral system in respect for the people's opinion.
- The headquarters of the Liberal Party announce a critical statement against Shilla Hoe.
- Local assembly men continue to protest in front of the National Assembly Building.
  They hold a rally in front of the National Assembly Building and demand the dissolution of the National Assembly.

Overseas
- President Truman attends a launching ceremony of the world's first operational nuclear-powered submarine in Groton.
- The U.S. Ambassador to Korea, Mucho, reports on the countermeasures to resolve the Korean political situation to the U.S. Department of State.

June 15, Sunday (May 23, by lunar calendar, 壬辰日 Black Dragon) Cloudy and Windy
722 Day of the War

War Situation
- A battalion of the Chinese Communist Forces counterattacks on a hill in western Cheorwon under the cover of artillery and mortars.
- The 83rd main conference of the Armistice Conference is held;
  The Communist Forces expresses an opinion to reject Neutral Nations' participation in screening of POWs.

At Home
- A compromise of the selected amendment bill to the Constitution proposed by *Shilla Hoe* receives 104 favorable signatures.
- The Liberal Party's Hapdong-pa announces that the selected amendment bill to the Constitution must be passed in order to resolve the present political crisis and explains that they will carry out political struggles through the Assembly activities from June 16.

June 16, Monday (May 24, by lunar calendar, 癸巳日 Black Snake) Clear and Windy
723 Day of the War

War Situation
- An artillery duel occurs in the Iron Triangle, resulting in more than 1,000 Communist soldiers killed in five days.
- A unit belonging to the 45th U.S. Division repulses a battalion's counterattack of the Chinese Communist Forces in the Iron Triangle.
- An explosion accident occurs in an ammunition dump of the UN Forces in Busan.

At Home
- The National Assembly rejects a resolution to disseminate the National Assembly's position to protect the Constitution.
- The political circles show delicate movements regarding the selected amendment bill to the Constitution.
- Local Government authorities face serious fiscal crises due to the enactment of an amended bill of room rent tax.

Overseas
- The Swedish Government strongly complains that a Russian fighter has shot down a rescue aircraft of Sweden.

June 17, Tuesday (May 25, by lunar calendar, 甲午日 Blue Horse) Clear and Cloudy
724 Day of the War

War Situation
- The Chinese Communist Forces stop the continuous night attacks on a hill in western Cheorwon for seven days.
- A squadron of B-26 fighter bombers launches nighttime attacks on the positions and a supply base of the Communist Forces in Pyongyang, Suncheon, and Yangdok.
- The 85th main conference of the Armistice Conference is held;
  The representative of the UN Forces protests against the intense and defiant propaganda of the Communist Forces and walks out after unilateral declaration of a three-day recess.

At Home
- The National Farmer Representative Meeting decides to criticize the Profit Tax Law from land and decides to request the dissolution of the National Assembly and the implementation of a general election in the Busan meeting.

Overseas
- The British Prime Minister, Winston Churchill, holds a talk with the Prime Minister of Australia, Menzies;
  They intensively discuss the Far East and Southeast Asian Policy and the issue of pushing

The barracks which are thrown into turmoil by riots in the Geoje POW camp (June 17, 1952)

forward with the joint military action plan.

June 18, Wednesday (May 26 by lunar calendar, 乙未日 Blue Sheep) Cloudy, Clear and Cloudy
725 Day of the War

War Situation

- The UN Forces in the northwest of Gimhwa repulse an attack of the Communist Forces on an outpost.
- The Chinese Communist Forces attack TWO positions of the UN Forces in southeastern Geumseong.

- The representative of the UN Forces of the Armistice Conference, Harrison, sends an official memorandum requesting to clearly specify the exact positions of 4 Communist POW camps.

At Home
- Political factions, *Shilla Hoe* and Samujang-pa in the National Assembly try to persuade the members of the National Assembly to pass the selected amendment bill to the Constitution.
- The National Assembly elects Shin Ik-hee as Speaker, Jo Bong-am and Kim Dong-sung as Vice-Speakers of the Special National Assembly Session.
- The U.S. Ambassador to Korea, Mucho, reports on the countermeasures to deal with the Korean political situation.

June 19, Thursday (May 27 by lunar calendar, 丙申日 Red Monkey) Rainy and Cloudy
726 Day of the War

War Situation
- The Chinese Communist Forces launch six tanks and 750 troops in a new attack on the UN Forces positions in southeastern Geumseong.
- A Mustang fighter unit of the 5th U.S. Air Force attacks the Jeunggang area of the Communist Forces in northern Geumseong.

At Home
- Seven members of the National Assembly and seven civilians are indicted on suspicion of violating the National Security Law in the military court held behind closed doors in the Busan district court, but the members of the UN Korea Committee and only some other foreigners can witness the trial.
- The Office of Public Information announces the case is related to the International Communist Party.
- The Korean Democratic Public Opinion Association conducts a poll about the constitutional amendment and the presidential election.

Overseas
- The U.S. Senate and House of Representatives pass a final draft approving that the U.S. Marine Corps be reinforced from 212,000 soldiers to 400,000 soldiers.

June 20, Friday (May 28, by lunar calendar, 丁酉日 Red Rooster) Cloudy, Windy and Clear
727 Day of the War

War Situation
- The UN Forces successfully defend their position in southeastern Geumseong
- Fighter bombers of the UN Forces making a sortie for covering operation attack field

artillery positions and the Communist Forces in Gimhwa, Cheorwon, Geumseong.
- A battalion of the UK Black Watch regiment arrives in Busan Harbor.

At Home
- Gukmindang Party members including Yi Si-yeong, Kim Seong-su, Cho Byung-ok, and others hold a Cultural Comrades meeting, but they fail in making a declaration of anti-dictatorship, protection of the Constitution and national salvation, as terrorists abruptly attack the meeting. (the so-called Case of the International Club in Busan).
- Hapdong-pa a faction of the Liberal Party announces the number of the members of the National Assembly in favor of the selected amendment bill to the Constitution reaches 115.

June 21, Saturday (May 29, by lunar calendar, 戊戌日 Yellow Dog) Cloudy and Windy
728 Day of the War

War Situation
- A regiment of the Communist Forces attacks the UN Forces' position under the cover of artillery in western Cheorwon.
- The UN Forces repulse the attacks of the Communist Forces on the UN Forces' position and kill 300 soldiers of the Communist Forces in western Cheorwon.
- A squadron of B-29 fighter bombers bombs the supply bases and the Communist Forces' bases at the rear of the main resistance line on the western and middle frontline.

At Home
- The National Assembly is aggravating confrontation between the political factions due to the introduction of the selected amendment bill to the Constitution.
- The Government Policy Committee discusses a bill for the security measure of a minimum living standard of civil servants.

Overseas
- Mao Zedong blames the U.S. authority's permission for five countries including Indonesia, to inspect the Geoje POW camp.

June 22, Sunday (Leap Month May 1 by lunar calendar, 己亥日 Yellow Pig) Cloudy, Windy and Rainy
729 Day of the War

War Situation
- The UN Forces repulse the attacks of the Communist Forces in eastern Geumseong.
- The UN Forces launch a surprise attack on the six Horseshoe Hills occupied by the Chinese Communist Forces in northeastern Cheorwon.
- The UN Forces Command announces the release of 27,000 civilian detainees from South Korea.

At Home

- Seoul City urges the Government to solve pending problems before its return to Seoul.
- The UN Forces Command announces the release of civilian detainees.

June 23, Monday (Leap Month May 2 by lunar calendar, 庚子日 White Rat) Rainy, Windy and Cloudy
730 Day of the War

War Situation
- Activities of both South and North search parties are carried out briskly all over the frontlines.
- Combat resumes around the Shanghai Hill in the northwestern Cheorwon.
- The UN Navy vessels covering the allied ground forces heavily attack the Communist Forces' positions in the eastern and western coasts.

At Home
- The National Assembly passes a resolution that the presidential term is to be extended in case the bill of the presidential term is not passed or the presidential election is not implemented.
- The National Assembly passes an urgent motion including such contents that the present president is to conduct his duty until the time next president is elected in case the presidential election is not to be implemented.

Overseas
- The British Minister of Defense, Alexander, discusses with the leading members of the U.S. Army Forces about the solution of the Korean War and the deadlocked Armistice

The National Assembly voting on a presidential term extension bill (1952. 6. 23).

Conference.

June 24, Tuesday (Leap Month May 3 by lunar calendar, 辛丑日 White Ox) Cloudy, Windy and Clear
731 Day of the War

War Situation

- The UN fighter bombers bomb four power plants, except for the Supung Power Plant following the previous day's bombing.
- The UN fighter bombers heavily bomb the troops and heavy gun positions of the Communist Forces all over the frontline.
- The U.S. Far East Navy announces that as much as 70% of the inner part and 90% of the outer part of the Supung Power Plant were destroyed by the bombing of June 23.

At Home

- As many as 400 Communist guerrillas attack the trains and set fire to nine passenger and freight cars and kill 45 passengers and injured three in the area between Honam Line intersection and Sinheung-ri.

June 25, Wednesday (Leap Month May 4 by lunar calendar, 壬寅日 Black Tiger) Cloudy and Rainy
732 Day of the War

War Situation

- B-29 fighter bombers attack the Gyeomipo steel factory.
- The 90th main conference of the Armistice Conference is held;
  The UN Forces criticize the fact that the Communist Forces have rejected the free repatriation of POWs, pointing out that Russia accepted the free repatriation of German POWs in World War II.

At Home

- A sniper attack on President Syngman Rhee happens in the Korean War Memorial ceremonies.
- *Shilla Hoe* announces a statement to rebut the news contents announcing the voluntary dissolution of the National Assembly.

June 26, Thursday (Leap Month May 5 by lunar calendar, 癸卯日 Black Rabbit) Cloudy and Rainy
733 Day of the War

War Situation

- The UN Infantry troops and Tank Forces attack the Communist Forces' positions in western Pyeonggang.
- The UN Forces recapture a Hill of the Communist Forces through five hours combat on the western frontline.

At Home

- The Public Information Office releases the second report of the full account of the attempted assassination of the President.

  The sniper is identified as Ryu Si-tae (62) an ex-member of Korean Heroic group, instructed by Kim Si-yeon how to use a pistol and also accompanied by him. Kim is an ex-member of the National Assembly belonging to the Democratic Nationalist Party.
- The cities and counties representatives of the Public Self-Determination Group go on a hunger strike in front of the National Assembly, requesting the voluntary dissolution of the National Assembly.

June 27, Friday (Leap Month May 6 by lunar calendar, 甲辰日 Blue Dragon) Clear and Cloudy
734 Day of the War

War Situation

- The UN Forces occupy the Shanghai Hill of the Chinese Communist Forces under the cover of the artillery and the Air Forces through eight-hour combat in western Cheorwon.
- The Eighth U.S. Army Command finishes reexamining 47,000 POWs in Geoje camp.
- The 92nd main conference of the Armistice Conference is held;

  The representative of the Communist Forces, Nam Il, indirectly mentions that the UN Forces bombed the power plants of North Korea blaming the UN Forces. The chief delegate of the UN Forces, Harrison, walks out after declaring a recess.

At Home

- The Prime Minister, Chang Taek-sang, gives an official order to prepare the countermeasures for the released volunteer POWs from South Korea.
- As many as 62 members of the non-National Assembly faction of the Liberal Party submit a dissolution bill of the National Assembly.

June 28, Saturday (Leap Month May 7 by lunar calendar, 乙巳日 Blue Snake) Cloudy and Rainy
735 Day of the War

War Situation

- The UN Forces repulse three attacks of the Chinese Communist Forces on Shanghai Hill in western Cheorwon.
- The Communist Forces attack two outposts of the UN Forces in the mid-west frontline in the heavy rain.
- The representative of the UN Forces in the Armistice Conference, Harrison, sends a letter to the representative of the Communist Forces, Nam Il, through a liaison officer.

At Home

- A special investigation team of the case of sniping at the President is organized.

- The criminal investigation bureau arrests the suspects involved in the case of sniping at the President.

June 29, Sunday (Leap Month May 8 by lunar calendar, 丙午日 Red Horse) Cloudy, Windy and Rainy
736 Day of the War

War Situation
- The UN Forces repulse the attacks of the Communist Forces on the two outposts in the western frontline.
- As many as 1,700 civilian detainees out of 27,000 civilian detainees in the POW camps of the UN Forces are firstly released.
- The 5th Air Force Commander Macas announces that 13 hydro-electric power plants in North Korea are completely destroyed.

At Home
- The transplantation of rice seedlings is delayed because of the drought in the middle and southern part.

June 30, Monday (Leap Month May 9 by lunar calendar, 丁未日 Red Sheep) Cloudy, Windy and Rainy
737 Day of the War

War Situation
- A battalion of the Communist Forces attacks the UN Forces' position near Heartbreak Ridge
- The UN Forces repulse the attacks of the Communist Forces on the Hill in western Cheorwon.

At Home
- The Public Self-Determination Group sieges the National Assembly building confining 80 members of the National Assembly.
- President Syngman Rhee declares that he has an intention to dissolve the National Assembly in case the selected amendment bill to the Constitution is rejected in his congratulatory address in the closing ceremony.
- The chief of the Public Security Bureau, Yun Wu-gyeong, warns again that wall posters without legal permission will be heavily punished.
- The U.S. Ambassador to Korea, Mucho, reports to the U.S. Department of State on the situations relevant to the civil demonstration against the National Assembly

Overseas
- The UK Government announces the white paper on the case of the Geoje POW camp and the Armistice issues of Korea.

July 1, Tuesday (Leap Month May 10, by lunar calendar, 戊申日 Yellow Monkey) Cloudy, Windy and Rainy

738 Day of the War

War Situation

- The UN Force repulses a battalion of the Communist Forces attacking a position of the UN Forces near Heartbreak Ridge.
- In the 93rd main conference of the Armistice Conference, Harrison, the chief representative of the UN Forces, presents the result of the Armistice Conference and explains the measures needed to resolve the deadlock. The UN Forces suggest deleting the names of the POWs from the list who did not want to be repatriated.

At Home

- The Ministry of Social Affairs implements the first Juvenile Vagrants Protection Period for a month of July all over the country.

July 2, Wednesday (Leap Month May 11, by lunar calendar, 己酉日) Rainy and Cloudy

739 Day of the War

War Situation

- A troop of the UN Forces attacks the Communist Forces' position in the northeastern Gorangpo.
- The Communist Forces request a recess of the main conference for 24 hours through the liaison officer of the Armistice Conference.
- The UN Forces agree on the suggestion of the Communist Forces.

At Home

- At the request of the National Assembly, the Korean Government fully mobilizes all of the intelligence agencies and broadcasting organizations to make the members of the National Assembly attend at the National Assembly.
- An official of the Commerce and Industry Ministry announces that a patrol boat of the Japanese Maritime Police inspected a Korean trade ship.

Overseas

- The UN Security Council states that the representative of the Chinese Nationalist Party (Taiwan), states that an epidemic occurred in China because the Chinese Government had failed in the experiment of bacteriological warfare.

July 3, Thursday (Leap Month May 12, by lunar calendar, 庚戌日 White Dog) Clear, Cloudy and Rainy

740 Day of the War

War Situation

- A troop of the UN Forces attacks a position of the Communist Forces in the eastern Panmunjom.
- A carrier-borne aircraft squadron of the U.S. Navy 77th Task Force bombs three power plants in Buryeong and Hochon in North Korea.
- The UN Forces authorities announce that they will displace as many as 35,000 POWs of the Chinese Communist Forces, the North Korean Communist Forces and detained civilians of North Korea into four new camps on four islands, namely, Jejudo, Geojedo, Yongchodo and Bongamdo.
- In the 94th main conference of the Armistice Conference, the Communist Forces accepted the proposal of the UN Forces related to POWs of July 1.

At Home

- In the First Plenary Session of the 13th Special National Assembly, 119 members of the National Assembly attend the opening ceremony and elect the Temporary Speaker, Jo Bong-am, and the Chairman of Plenary Committee, Ji Cheong-cheon.
- Ten members of the National Assembly accused of the International Communist Party's Fund attend on bail to deliberate the bill of the constitutional amendment. 146 members of the National Assembly attend at 5 p.m.
- Serious problems of excessive profits occur in the distribution process of the urgently imported food and fertilizer.

July 4, Friday (Leap Month May 13, by lunar calendar, 辛亥日 White Pig) Cloudy
741 Day of the War

War Situation

- The UN Forces' position in eastern Cheorwon repulses two attacks of the Chinese Communist Forces.
- The UN Forces' authorities start to displace the POWs of the Chinese Communist Forces on Geojedo.
- The information section of the Ministry of National Defense announces the total military achievements of cleanup operation on the rear Communist guerillas in June. (457 guerrillas are killed, 48 captured, 16 defected / 228 various rifles, 21 grenades and a radio are acquired.)
- The 95th main conference of the Armistice Conference is held behind closed doors.

At Home

- The National Assembly resumes the subcommittee of the nine political faction's representatives and continuously creates conflicts with the issue of the head of the

370

Government. An agreement was reached by the concession of the Democratic Nationalist Party and independent members of the National Assembly.

- The second plenary session of the 13th special National Assembly passes the direct presidential election system, the parliamentary government system and the bicameral parliament of the Upper House and the Lower House with ayes of 163 votes out of 166 present members.
- The National Assembly resumes the whole member of committee at 7 p.m., holds the Assembly plenary session at 8 p.m. and introduces the constitutional amendment bill.

Overseas
- Clark, the UN Forces Commander, delivers the Fourth-of-July oration.
- The U.S. Senate conference decides on the military budget of the 1953 fiscal year. ($46,600,000,000)

July 5, Saturday (Leap Month May 14, by lunar calendar, 壬子日 Black Rat) Cloudy, Clear and Cloudy

742 Day of the War

War Situation
- Sporadic skirmishes occur in all of the frontline.
- The battleship, *U.S.S Iowa*, and three aircraft carriers of the 7th U.S. Task Fleet heavily bomb Wonsan harbor for seven hours.
- The official spokesman of the UN Forces, Brig. Gen. Nichols, states that there is nothing special to announce, but the conference proceeds in a businesslike manner.

At Home
- President Syngman Rhee announces a special statement on the adoption of the constitutional amendment at the National Assembly, and emphasizes that the atmosphere of freedom in the presidential election will be guaranteed.
- The 23rd honorable discharge ceremony is held in the 839th Army camp of the ROK Army.
- The South Gyeongsang Provincial Assembly constitutes a special grain investigation team and inspects the grain controlling office.

Overseas
- The British Foreign Ministry announces that the U.S., the U.K. and France agreed on the final response to the Soviet mainly on the issue of the unified Germany.

July 6, Sunday (Leap Month May 15, by lunar calendar, 癸丑日 Black Ox) Clear
743 Day of the War

War Situation
- The UN Air Force announces the overall result of the artillery fire for the North Korean

power plants;
It has destroyed 13 power plants in North Korea over 18 months and has sallied 1,373 sorties per year.
- The Turkish Forces and the Thai Forces arrive in Busan.
- The UN Forces' spokesmen, Brig. Gen. Nicols states that if the both parties continue to discuss, there is a possibility to find a constructive solution.

At Home
- The cities and counties representatives of the Public Self-Determination Group send a plea to the President to dissolve the National Assembly.
- The South Jeolla Province Martial Law Command orders suspension of the train operation between Namwon and Irie for a while.

July 7, Monday (Leap Month May 16, by lunar calendar, 甲寅日 Blue Tiger) Cloudy and Windy
744 Day of the War

War Situation
- The Capitol Division engages in a battle for the summit of Capitol Hill.
- A company of the Communist Forces attacks the UN Forces' position under the cover of fourteen T34-type tanks made in the Soviet Union in southeastern Geumseong.
- The UN Forces' troops attack three outposts of the Communist Forces with flame throwers in the eastern Panmunjom.

At Home
- The Third Plenary Session of the 13th Special National Assembly calls recess on July 8 deciding to elect the Speaker and Vice-Speaker on July 10.
- The Government promulgates the selected constitution (the 1st amended constitution) decided by parliamentary approval.
- The Minister of Social Affairs, Choe Chang-sun announces that the release of civilian detainees will be completed by August 20.

Overseas
- The Policy Planning Committee of the Republican Party criticizes President Truman's policy of the U.S. Armed Forces withdrawal from South Korea, insisting that it has caused the Korean War.
- General Douglas MacArthur delivers the keynote address in the Republican National Convention.

July 8, Tuesday (Leap Month May 17, by lunar calendar, 乙卯日 Blue Rabbit) Rainy
745 Day of the War

War Situation

- The UN Forces repulse a counterattack of the Communist Forces on the UN Forces' position in southeastern Geumseong.
- The Communist Forces blame the UN Forces for killing two POWs and wounding eight POWs in the Geojedo camp the previous week.

At Home
- The Government transfers the Presidential and Vice-presidential election bill to the National Assembly.
- The Ministry of Health arrests 11 drug addicts in a raid on a drug den in Busan.
- Rumors continue that illegal gold transfers to foreign countries are prevalent in the market.

Overseas
- President Truman signs a bill for renting 18 frigate vessels and 50 amphibious transport ships to Japan.
- The International Peace Conference in East Berlin claims that a new Peace Treaty with Japan be signed, the Korean War be ended and foreign Forces be immediately withdrawn from Korea.

July 9, Wednesday (Leap Month May 18, by lunar calendar, 丙辰日 Red Dragon) Cloudy and Rainy
746 Day of the War

War Situation
- A unit of the UN Forces attacks the Communist Forces' position and engages them all day long in southern Goseong.
- An attack unit of the UN Forces retreats from a position of the western Bukhan River because of the counterattack of two companies by the Chinese Communist Forces.
- The U.S. Department of Defense announces that the total number of Korean War victims reaches 112,128 with 552 victims increased last year.
- The 6th secret main conference of the Armistice Conference is held for 26 minutes.

At Home
- President Syngman Rhee inspects the civilian POW camp in Yeongcheon accompanied by the Eighth U.S. Army Commander, General Van Fleet.
- The Cabinet Meeting passes the bill of the election of the president and vice president and the members of the National Assembly.
- The Prime Minister, Chang Taek-sang, announces that the Government's basic principle of the grain importing process is to import grains on commercial bases and free dispositions.
- The U.S. Ambassador to Korea, Mucho, makes a report about the meeting between President Syngman Rhee and Shin Ik-hee after passing the selected amendment bill to the Constitution.

July 10, Thursday (Leap Month May 19, by lunar calendar, 丁巳日 Red Snake) Rainy and Cloudy
747 Day of the War

War Situation

- The 5th Division of the ROK Armed Forces engages in the 351 Hill. (July 10 to 11)
- An attack unit of the UN Forces attacks the Communist Forces' position in the southern Pyeonggang.
- An attack unit of the UN Forces recaptures 3 Hills in the northwestern Cheorwon.
- The UN Forces Commander, Clark, entrusts the Eighth U.S. Army Commander, General Van Fleet, with full power for establishing the supply administration official Agreement in charge of the rear area of the Eighth U.S. Army.
- The 7th secret main conference of the Armistice Conference is held for 40 minutes.
- The spokesman of the UN Forces states that the possibility of the Armistice completion has been increased more than a year ago.

At Home

- The 4th Plenary Session of the National Assembly implements the vote to elect the speaker and vice speaker of the National Assembly. The speaker of the National Assembly: Shin Ik-hee. The vice-speakers of the National Assembly: Jo Bongam, Yun Chi-young
- The 13 criminals of the case of the President assassination attempt including Kyu Si-tae and Kim Si-yeon are sent to the Martial Law Enforcement Headquarters of the Yeongnam district.
- Some problems occur because the Ministry of Social Affairs has pushed the immigration policy without a thorough research.
- The Martial Law Enforcement Headquarters refutes the rumor of lifting the Martial Law.

Overseas

- The Ambassador of Indonesia to the U.S visits the U.S. Department of Defense and notifies that the Indonesia Government rejects the request of the U.S. to join the 5 Neutral Nations Commission for investigating the Geoje POW camp.
- The first parliamentary session of Western Germany passes the Treaty of Peace with NATO and the treaty of the allied command of Europe.

July 11, Friday (Leap Month May 20, by lunar calendar, 戊午日 Yellow Horse) Rainy
748 Day of the War

War Situation

- The UN Air Forces heavily bomb the Military industrial facilities and supply dumps with the largest artillery fire in Pyongyang, Hwangju and Sariwon since the beginning of the war.
- The 8th secret main conference of the Armistice Conference is held for 26 minutes getting no better result after formal proceedings

374

At Home

- The Cabinet Meeting decides to cancel the status of the Korea Mint Corporation as a Government corporation.
- The Minister of Communication, Cho Joo-young, states that International Telegraph and Telephone charges can be paid in Korean won.
- Choe Jae-ho is dispatched as the chief Korean delegate of the 13th Universal Postal Union Conference

Overseas

- The Singapore Legislature Council states to permit the Japanese entry.
- The head of the U.S. Naval Operations, Fechteler, leaves Washington, D.C. to visit the Far East area.

July 12, Saturday (Leap Month May 21, by lunar calendar, 己未日 Yellow Sheep) Cloudy and Rainy 749 Day of the War

War Situation

- A unit of the UN Forces engages 2 companies of the North Korean Forces to recapture main positions in the southern Goseong.
- The U.S. Far East Air Forces announces the military accomplishment of the Air Forces since the beginning of the Korean War;
  Damages of the Communist Forces: 1,245 airplanes are shot down including unconfirmed and damaged planes and as many as 980 MIG Jet fighters. 5,257 vehicles, 8,367 railroad cars, and 1,257 tanks are destroyed.
- Damages of the UN Forces: Total 719 airplanes comprising 266 jet fighters of the U.S. Air Forces, 322 various type air planes, 64 friendly forces aircrafts, 67 Marine Corps aircrafts.

At Home

- The 6th National Assembly plenary session introduces the bill of the President and Vice President election and begins the deliberation.
- The Cabinet Meeting decides the landowner's indemnity for the farmland reform
- The Ministry of Agriculture and Forestry comes into conflict with private firms in the course of processing the grains and fertilizers with the fund of tungsten exports.
- *Radio Pyongyang* blames that indiscriminate bombing of the UN airplanes destroyed many private buildings and killed 6,000 civilians.

Overseas

- The Chinese delegation attends the 7th International Film Festival held in Karlovy city, Czechoslovakia, submitting a documentary film "Resistance to America, Assistance to korea" and others.

July 13, Sunday (Leap Month May 22, by lunar calendar, 庚申日 White Monkey) Cloudy and Clear
750 Day of the War

War Situation
- A bomber squadron of the UN attacks the northern position in Goseong.
- The Chief of Staff in the U.S. Army, Collins inspects the eastern frontline with the UN Forces Commander, Clark, and the Eighth U.S. Army Commander Van Fleet.

At Home
- Restoration works of railroad bridges in Han River and Bukhan River are completed.
- The Financial Services Union announces to release ten billion won as the business operation funds.

July 14, Monday (Leap Month May 23, by lunar calendar, 辛酉日 White Rooster) Rainy
751 Day of the War

War Situation
- A unit of the UN Forces recaptures the northern Hill in Goseong again.
- The Chief of Staff in the U.S. Army, Collins, states that if the UN Forces is able to bombard Manchuria if necessary, but the UN Forces will discuss this problem with other nations concerned.
- The Chief of Staff in the U.S. Army, Collins, states that the enforcement of artillery fires will never affect the Armistice Conference in a press conference.
- The Communist Forces request 2 day recess of the secret main conference through liaison officers and the UN Forces agree on it.

At Home
- The 7th National Assembly plenary session continues to examine the bill for the President and Vice President election and completes the first reading.
- Public institutions and social organizations constitute the promotion committee for Government's returning to Seoul.
- The Ministry of Social Affairs announces the Analyses of Working Condition of the Nation.

Overseas
- President Truman signs the bill of approving $2,390,000,000 as the military construction costs.
- A news source of Washington reports that the large-scale offensive operations of the UN Air Force on Pyongyang and the Supung power plants will continue all the more.

July 15, Tuesday (Leap Month May 24, by lunar calendar, 壬戌日 Black Dog) Rainy
752 Day of the War

War Situation

- The Communist Forces attacks the UN Forces' position in the southeastern Geumseong.
- An infantry troop of the UN Forces attacks the Communist Forces' position under the cover of the tank Forces in the Cheorwon.
- A bomber squadron of the 5th U.S. Air Forces bombs a cement factory and an engine locomotive repair plant near Pyongyang. A squadron of B-29 bombers bombs the Hamheung switchyard.

At Home
- The 8th National Assembly plenary session passes the bill of the President and Vice President Election.
- The rally of the Seoul Special City Patriotic Organization booms Syngman Rhee for the second President.
- The Korean Farmers Federation proposes the plan of food measures such as postponing a collection of wheat and barley to the Government.

July 16, Wednesday (Leap Month May 25, by lunar calendar, 癸亥日 Black Pig) Rainy
753 Day of the War

War Situation
- The Communist Forces request 2 days recess of the secret main conference of the Armistice Conference again and the UN Forces agree on it.
- A liaison officer of the UN Forces hands over the disapproval note on the Communist Forces' criticism that the bombardment of July 1 destroyed the POW camp in Pyongyang.

At Home
- The National Assembly agrees on the case of the traffic enterprise special accounts in the National Treasury Liabilities Bearing Act.
- The Minister of National Defense, Sin Tae-yeong, announces the statement that the Government is to impose the Martial Law to clean up the disturbing Communist guerrillas in Muju-gun, North Jeolla Province.
- The Vice-Minister of Communication states that the wire telephone work was launched between Seoul and Busan in a press conference.

Overseas
- Sandifer reported Han Gil-soo's proposal to the U.S. Department of State, including such contents as: after removing Syngman Rhee, the Korean Peace Mission should be dispatched to Korea and the Soviet Union.
- ADN Communication of Eastern Germany reports a false propaganda that the Eighth U.S. Army Commander, Van Fleet, admitted a implementation of bacteriological warfare by himself.

July 17, Thursday (Leap Month May 26, by lunar calendar, 甲子日 Blue Rat) Rainy
754 Day of the War

War Situation

- Attacking Forces of the UN Forces attack the Communist Forces' Hill in the northeastern Cheorwon.
- The head of the U.S. Naval Operations, Fechteler, arrives in Seoul accompanied by the U.S. Far East Navy Commander, Briscoe.
- In the liaison officers meeting of the Armistice Conference ; the Communist Forces hand over the map specifying the locations of POW camps and informing that they are to build newly 6 POW camps after closing 3 POW camps.

At Home

- The Prime Minister, Chang Taek-sang, states that he is planning to reform the Government organizations in a press conference.
- The Prime Minister, Chang Taek-sang, announces the organization of the drought damage relief countermeasure committee with the Prime Minister as chairman.
- The 42nd Line train locomotive between Oryu-dong and Yeongdeungpo derails to be overturned with bursting of an inner firebox causing 13 passengers dead, 159 passengers wounded.

July 18, Friday (Leap Month May 27, by lunar calendar, 乙丑日 Blue Ox) Rainy and Clear
755 Day of the War

War Situation

- The head of the U.S. Naval Operations, Fechteler, joins the Flagship of the First Fleet, Iowa, and inspects the operation in Wonsan area.
- The UN Air Forces keeps activities to a minimum due to a bad weather.
- The 11th main conference of the Armistice Conference resumes after 4 days recess.

At Home

- President Syngman Rhee states that he is irrelevant to the out-of the Assembly faction of the Liberal Party.
- The naming ceremony of the freight vessel, Busan, purchased from Sweden is held.
- 35 persons besides the Chief of South Gyeongsang Provincial Police Office, Park Pyeong-bae are awarded the National Defense Medals.

Overseas

- The U.S. Ambassador to Indonesia states that the U.S. Government welcome the mediation for the Armistice of the Korean War by the prime minister, Nehru.

July 19, Saturday (Leap Month May 28, by lunar calendar, 丙寅日 Red Tiger) Rainy

The U.S. Engineering Battalion building a floating bridge on Hangang River.(1952. 7. 15)

756 Day of the War

War Situation

- The UN Force recaptures the other side of the Bulmo Hill in spite of a violent resistance of the Communist Forces.
- A ship plane squadron of the 77th U.S. Task fleet bombs the first and 3rd hydroelectric power plants in Changjin.
- The 25th U.S. Division Commander, Swift, leaves his office and Brig. Gen William is appointed as his replacement.

At Home

- The Government announces to implement the President and Vice President election on August 5.
- The Ministry of Foreign Affairs announces to dispatch Im Byeong-jik, Gu Yong-suk, Hwang Seong-su as the Korean representatives of the 18th General Assembly of the International Red Cross conference.
- The opening ceremony of the Han River Railroad Bridge is held attended by President Syngman Rhee and the Eighth U.S. Army Commander, General Van Fleet.

Overseas

- Magson, the member of the United States Senate, insists on the formation of a Pacific Alliance to protect manpower resources and material resources of the Pacific area from

invasions of the Communist enemies in the doctrine committee of the Democratic Party.
- The Royal Canadian Air Force launches a joint defense exercises with the U.S. Air Force in Quebec.

July 20, Sunday (Leap Month May 29, by lunar calendar, 丁卯日 Red Rabbit) Rainy, Cloudy and Clear
757 Day of the War

War Situation
- The Communist Forces retain control of the summit of Bulmo Hill and the steep slope in the northwestern area.
- The 13th secret main conference of the Armistice Conference is held for 12 minutes, making no progress.

At Home
- The Government establishes the 3rd plan of importing rice to ease the food situation.

July 21, Monday (Leap Month May 30, by lunar calendar, 戊辰日 Yellow Dragon) Rainy and Clear
758 Day of the War

War Situation
- A reconnaissance party of the UN Forces probes the roads between Geumseong Gimhwa and kills 50 soldiers of the Communist Forces.
- In the liaison officers meeting after the Armistice Conference, the Communist Forces requests an explanation for the 101 POWs of the Chinese Communist Forces omitted from the list of the POWs.
- The Chief delegate of the UN Forces, Harrison, announces the reshuffle of the spokesman of the UN Forces, Brig. Gen Nichols and appoints Ltc. Joseph Borchert as his replacement.

At Home
- The 11th National Assembly Plenary Session passes the bill of the Culture Protection Law.
- The National Assembly constitutes a special investigation team for the case of free disposition of imported fertilizers with the fund from tungsten exports.
- The accused in the case of assasination attempt of the President is charged with attempted murder and offending Peace and Order as of July 21.
- The Minister of Transport, Kim Seok-kwan, expresses an opposition to increase wages of harbor workers in a press conference.

July 22, Tuesday (June 1, by lunar calendar, 己巳日 Yellow Snake) Clear
759 Day of the War

War Situation

- A reconnaissance party of the UN Forces attacks a company of the Communist Force near Jeonghyeong Hill in western Cheorwon.
- The 15th secret main conference of the Armistice Conference is held just for 5 minutes.
- The spokesperson of the UN Forces, Brig. Gen. Nicholas, transferring as the Chief of Information of the U.S. Far East Air Force announces his leaving statement before the departure from Munsan.

At Home
- The special investigation team of the National Assembly for the malversation case of the fund from tungsten exports launches its investigation in to the Government departments including the Ministry of Agriculture and Forestry.
- Communist guerrillas attack the Yeongdong Station and the Mulgeum Station on the Gyeongbu line.
- The South Gyeongsang Province Recruiting Command arrests illegal dealer of the Second People's Force soldier's ID pocketbook.

Overseas
- The head of the U.S. Naval Operations, Admiral Fechteler, arrives in Hong Kong and states in a press conference that the defense preparation of Taiwan is better than expected.

July 23, Wednesday (June 2, by lunar calendar, 庚午日 White Horse) Clear
760 Day of the War

War Situation
- A clash on Bulmo Hill calms down and the Chinese Communist Forces still occupy the Sanjeong hill top.
- The Army Chief of Staff, Lieutenant General Lee Jong-chan is replaced by the First Corps Commander, Lieutenant General Paik Sun-yup.
- The 16th secret main meeting of the Armistice Conference ends within seven minutes.

At Home
- The 12th National Assembly plenary session passes an approval bill of the Government guaranteed loan, 65.3 billion won, for the Federation of the Korea Irrigation Association.
- The special investigation team of the National Assembly for the malversation case of the fund of tungsten exports launches to investigate the private enterprises.
- The Ministry of Social Affairs displays a street enlightenment squad for appealing to use domestic products and remove luxury goods.

Overseas
- The Japanese Government requests resumption of the Korea-Japan Conference.
- The 18th International Red Cross Conference is held in Toronto, Canada, attended by the delegates of China and North Korea.

- The six countries' Ministers of Foreign Affairs that joined the Schuman Plan hold a meeting.

July 24, Thursday (June 3, by lunar calendar, 辛未日 White Sheep) Clear
761 Day of the War

War Situation
- The artillery fire of the Communist Forces falls to the lowest level for the current month.
- A company of the Communist Forces probes an outpost of the UN Forces in western Munsan.
- The 17th secret main conference of the Armistice Conference is held and lasts 26 minutes.

At Home
- The National Election Management Committee officially receives the registration document of President candidacy of Dr. Syngman Rhee and Vice President candidacy of Lee Beom-seok and decides to get Dr. Rhee's accepting document for the candidacy.
- The UN Forces Command notifies the Korean Government of the restoration plan for the electric power facilities.

Overseas
- The head of the U.S. Naval Operations, Admiral Fechteler, inspecting the Far East area states that the U.S. Government has already deployed a bomber aircraft in Manila that can carry atomic bombs.
- The U.S. State Department spokesperson accuses the Communists of directing the anti-American movement in Iran.

July 25, Friday (June 4, by lunar calendar, 壬申日 Black Monkey) Clear
762 Day of the War

War Situation
- The Eighth U.S. Army Commander announces that the Second U.S. Division is engaged in a fierce battle on Bulmo Hill in northwestern Cheorwon.
- In the 18th secret main conference of the Armistice Conference, the Communist Forces requests a staff officers meeting to discuss the detailed rules and terms for the Armistice agreement draft and resumes the open session.
- Both the representatives of the UN Forces and the Communist Forces agree to close the secret discussion for exchanging POWs.
- The frontline command of the UN Forces announces that the 18th secret Conference accomplished nothing.

  In the secret conference, the Communist Forces insist on the compulsory repatriation of 116,000 Communist Forces' POWs including 20,000 Chinese POWs against the UN Forces' suggestion to repatriate 83,000 POWs who want to return home.

At Home

- The 13th National Assembly Plenary Session decides to investigate the docker wage disputes in the Culture and Social Committee.
- The Department of Justice of Martial Law Command in Yeongnam area decides to transfer the case of assassination attempt of the President to civil court.
- The Chief of Police Office in South Gyeongsang Province, Pak Pyeong-bae, states that the civil servants entering the tea rooms and lexurious restaurants are mostly known to be tax officials and teachers.

Overseas

- The policy planning committee of the U.S. Steel Labor Union in the Congress of Industrial Organizations officially decides to halt its strike.
- Puerto Rico obtains its autonomy authorized by the U.S. congress and renames itself as the Federation of Puerto Rico.

July 26, Saturday (June 5, by lunar calendar, 癸酉日 Black Rooster) Clear, Cloudy and Clear
763 Day of the War

War Situation

- Sporadic combats continue on the western frontlines.
- Activities of the UN Air Forces are hampered by low clouds and rain in North Korea.
- The 118th open main meeting of the Armistice Conference resumes.
- The representative of the UN Forces, Harrison, agrees to hold the staff officers meeting to review the draft of the Armistice agreement and then notifies a week recess of the main conference and walks out.

At Home

- The 4th superintendent meeting of the National Police Agency is held in the assembly hall of South Gyeongsang Province.
- The delegate of the 18th International Red Cross conference is dispatched. (Chief delegate: Im Byeong-jik)
- The Commander of the Seoul-Gyeonggi branch of the UN Korean Civil Affairs department announces permission for Seoul citizens to return to the capital city.
- The Emergency Martial Law is lifted throughout South Korea.

July 27, Sunday (June 6, by lunar calendar, 甲戌日 Blue Dog) Rainy
764 Day of the War

War Situation

- Small-scale reconnaissance activities of the Communist Forces take place on the western and middle frontlines.

- A U.S. officer and a North Korean detainee are wounded in the Bongamdo POW camp.
- The representative of the Communist Forces in the Armistice Conference, Nam Il, notifies the previous position of the Communist Forces through a liaison officer again, sending the complaining letter against the unilateral recess of the UN Forces.

At Home
- President Syngman Rhee accepts the nomination for the next presidential candidate in deference to the opinion of the people.
- The Central Election Management Committee decides that the national electorate is estimated to be 8.31 million persons.
- The recruiting district command in South Gyeongsang Province implements the commandeering of first-line workers at the request of the Eighth U.S. Army.
- The Cheongpyeong hydroelectric power plant maximizes the capacity of generating electric power in the rainy season.

Overseas
- In the Helsinki Olympics, Kim Seong-jip from Korea wins the third place and Choe Yun-chil, 4th place in the marathon; meanwhile Zatopek from Czechoslovakia wins first place.

July 28, Monday (June 7, by lunar calendar, 乙亥日 Blue Pig) Clear, Cloudy and Clear
765 Day of the War

War Situation
- The Communist Forces carry out a reconnoitering skirmish in the western Munsan, northwestern Yeoncheon and southeastern Geumseong.
- A search and attack unit of the Air Forces attacks the UN Forces' position in the southeastern Bulmo Hill.

At Home
- The National Assembly operates the crippled interpellation for the case of the fund from tungsten exports.
- Prime Minister Chang Taek-sang orders the guarantee of a free election atmosphere and prohibits the election campaign by civil servants.
- Im Young-sin, Lee Gap-seong, and Jeon Jin-han announce their presidential candidacy.
- One month extension of jurisdiction in court-martial is declared by the presidential decree after lifting of the Emergency Martial Law.

July 29, Tuesday (June 8, by lunar calendar, 丙子日 Red Rat) Rainy, Stormy and Clear
766 Day of the War

War Situation
- The UN Forces repulse a search and attack unit of the Communist Forces in three

locations between Panmunjom and Yeoncheon.
- President Syngman Rhee commends the U.S. 8226th Corps for their operation and maintenance of the Korean communication equipment.
- The Commander of the UN Forces, General Clark announces that Major General Sue Smith takes office as the Vice Chief of Staff of the UN Forces.

At Home
- Jang Myeon declares his intention not to run for the presidential election.
- The general court-martial for the violation case of the National Security Law withdraws the prosecution of seven members of the National Assembly and releases them on account of the prosecution suspension.
- The textile industry is revitalized after the foreign capital supervisory agency releases 10 billion won's worth of cotton yarn.
- The Far East Trade Conference is held in Washington examining the bill of establishing a new body for preventing the export of strategic goods to the Soviet-bloc States.

July 30, Wednesday (June 9, by lunar calendar, 丁丑日 Red Ox) Clear
767 Day of the War

War Situation
- A fighter bomber squadron of the UN Forces continuously attacks the main military bases of the Communist Forces on the frontlines.
- The Eighth U.S. Army Commander, General Van Fleet, states that the Armistice is directly related to the allies' military pressures on the Communist Forces and it is difficult to be instantly completed.

At Home
- President Syngman Rhee, in a exclusive interview with AP reporter insists that the UN Forces set a time limit for the Armistice Conference and emphasizes that if the Communist Forces do not accept it, a full-scale war must resume.
- The Ministry of Foreign Affairs strongly complains to the Japanese Government that the Japanese police boat illegally arrested Korean fishing vessels in the open waters near Tsusima Island on June 23.
- 500 civilian detainees from North Korea are released in three phases and the welcoming ceremony is held in front of the Busanjin Station.

July 31, Thursday (June 10, by lunar calendar, 戊寅日 Yellow Tiger) Rainy and Stormy
768 Day of the War

War Situation
- The Communist Forces attack the UN Forces' position in the northwestern Yeoncheon.

- The staff officers meeting of the Armistice Conference gets no better.

At Home

- Prime Minister Chang Taek-sang emphasizes the need to form a joint defense organization of free nations in the Asia-Pacific region.
- The Minister of Social Affairs, Choe Chang-sun, announces the end of the port strike and commits to improving the standard of living of the harbor workers.
- The General Court-Martial in Youngnam district holds a verdict hearing for the violation case of the National Security Law and sentences the three defendants to life imprisonment.
- The electric power delegation of the UN Forces Command postpones the joint meeting with Korean parties concerned as the Japanese Electric Power engineers are refused permission to enter the country.

Overseas

- The 10th Korean compulsory repatriation ship departs from Sasebo harbor in Japan including 228 stowaways.
- The U.S. Central Intelligence Agency reports on the progress of the election campaign in South Korea for President and Vice President and the chemical fertilizer deficiency of North Korea.
- The International Red Cross Conference in Toronto revises the 1925 Geneva Conventions and informs the Governments of all member nations.

A field artillery attack on an enemy's position on Bulmo Hill in Cheorwon.(July 30, 1952)

August 1, Friday (June 11, by lunar calendar, 己卯日 Yellow Rabbit) Clear
769 Day of the War

War Situation
- An infantry unit of the UN Forces seizes the summit of Bulmo Hill in western Cheorwon through eight hours of heavy conflict.
- In the staff officers' meeting of the Armistice Conference, the UN Forces agree on the modification of the wording for six articles in the draft of the Armistice agreement of the Communist Forces.

At Home
- The Cabinet Meeting passes the implementing outlines of the production responsibility system in the original form of the Ministry of Commerce and Industry.
- The Methodist minister, Lee Myeong-je escaping from North Korea, testifies that the North's Communists were actually defeated in the Korean War and the North Korean people are revolting against the Kim Il Sung regime.

August 2, Saturday (June 12, by lunar calendar, 庚辰日 White Dragon) Clear
770 Day of the War

War Situation
- Artillery Units and Aviation Corps of the UN Forces continue to lethally bomb positions of the Chinese Communist Forces in the northern Bulmo Hill.
- The UN Forces Command announces the establishment of the Korean Rear Area Command;
  Major General, Thomas W. Herren is appointed as the first Commander and the command is established in Daegu. It places under its command the U.S. Rear Base Command of the Eighth U.S. Army and the UN POW Camp Command and controls the civil relief works.
- In the staff officers' meeting in the Armistice Conference, both the representatives try to achieve a complete agreement on the terms of the Armistice agreement.

At Home
- President Syngman Rhee announces that he will not designate any vice-presidential candidate as his partner.

Overseas
- The 18th International Red Cross Conference in Toronto decides to request a fair investigation of the accusation by the Communist Forces that the UN Forces are implementing bacteriological warfare in Korea.

- The Far East Trade Conference in Washington agrees to restrict Japan's trade with the countries within the Soviet orbit by joining Japan into the Western European Community.

August 3, Sunday (June 13, by lunar calendar, 辛巳日 White Snake) Cloudy and Clear
771 Day of the War

War Situation
- A unit of the UN Forces retreats from the outpost in the western Yeoncheon briefly due to the Communist Forces' strong attacks on it and then removes the Communist Forces through hand-to-hand fighting.
- When the 114th main conference of the Armistice Conference resumes, both parties agree on a week recess again.
- The staff officer meeting continues to discuss the terms of the agreement.
- The liaison officer of the Communist Forces, Jang Chun-san, complains to the liaison officer of the UN Forces that the U.S. Army bombed the Armistice hall in Panmunjom on August 2.

At Home
- Various evasions of the law of the President election are exposed.
- The Government decides the detailed allocation principle of the Government dollars and the tungsten dollars.
- Two ships returned by the Japanese Government enter Busan Harbor.

Overseas
- The U.S. Naval Authority announces that they have researched a new way to construct a submarine which can set sail from a heavy aircraft carrier.

August 4, Monday (June 14, by lunar calendar, 壬午日 Black Horse) Cloudy and Clear
772 Day of the War

War Situation
- In the western Mundeungri valley, a search and attack of the enemy is repulsed by the UN Forces' outpost.
- The U.S. Naval Authority announces that two crewmen of a Mai Chin reconnaissance plane of the U.S. Navy were killed by the attack of two jet fighters with Chinese marks, but the reconnaissance plane returned at the west coast of Korea.
- A battalion of the British Royal Regiment of Fusiliers arrives in Busan Harbor to join the Korean War.
- The staff officers' meeting of the Armistice Conference cannot agree on the translation of the Korean and UN Forces.

At Home

- The Central Election Committee of the central division of the Liberal Party accuses the Prime Minister, Chang Taek-sang, the Vice Minister of the Home Affairs, Kim Tae-seon, and the chief of the Public Peace Agency, Yun Woo-gyeong of violating the election law of the President and Vice President and the National Public Service Law to the Supreme Prosecutors' Office.
- The Monetary Policy Committee decides to increase the minimum rate of the reserve requirement ratio.
- The Korean War-Bereaved Family Council announces to have Dr. Jeong Gi-won as the presidential candidate.

August 5, Tuesday (June 15, by lunar calendar, 癸未日 Black Sheep) Rainy and Cloudy
773 Day of the War

War Situation
- A unit of the UN Forces retreats from the outpost near the western Bukhan River due to two attacks of the Communist Forces.
- The staff officers' meeting of the Armistice Conference closes examining the wording of the Armistice agreement draft and completely agrees on the terms of the Armistice

Orphans welcoming the U.S. soldiers who visited an orphanage in Bupyeong (Aug. 3, 1952)

agreement draft.

- The UN Forces hand over the notification to accept the exchanges of relief supplies for POWs to the Communist Forces.

At Home

- The number of trading companies registered at the Ministry of Commerce and Industry reach 277 firms as of Aug 5 and 262 companies of them are of Korean nationality and 3 companies are American, while there are seven Chinese companies; and there are two Korea-China-India joint companies, while the Korean companies invested by Chinese capital are 30%~40% of them.
- The U.S. Ambassador to South Korea, Mucho, assesses the campaignes of the elections for President and Vice President in South Korea.

Overseas

- The presidential candidate of the Republicans, General Eisenhower, officially addresses the annual convention of the American Veterans' Committee after being nominated as the presidential candidate for the first time.
- In the International Red Cross Conference in Toronto, the Chinese delegate insists on the investigation of bacteriological warfare in Korea to the Canterbury Suffragan, Dr. Johnson.

August 6, Wednesday (June 16, by lunar calendar, 甲申日 Blue Monkey) Cloudy and Clear
774 Day of the War

War Situation

- The UN Forces' troops recapture the outpost in the western Bukhan River in the early morning which they retreated from last night.

At Home

- The dignity regulations of the police officers(the Ministry of Home Affairs' Instructions No. 42) are proclaimed.
- The UN Korea Committee dispatches its delegates to observe the President and Vice President election to each province.

Overseas

- The delegate of the U.K. to the UN states that the Armistice agreement of the Korean War is certain but needs a long time in a press conference.
- The U.K. Government announces that exporting goods to Tibet is prohibited without Government permission.

August 7, Thursday (June 17, by lunar calendar, 乙酉日 Blue Roster) Clear
775 Day of the War

War Situation

- An infantry unit of the ROK Army wipes out the night attack of the Communist Forces at the slope area for the outpost of the Capital Hill in the western Bukhan River.
- The ROK Reconnoitering Battalion conducts a search operation around the western area of Bukhan River but has no engagement with the Communist Forces.

At Home
- The Minister of Commerce and Industry, Lee Gyo-seon, states on strengthening the implementation of controlled economy.
- The Minister of Health and Social Affairs, Choe Chang-sun, has press conference on the problems of the Jeju Island refugees and labor wages.
- The Monetary Policy Committee decides to loan a fund of 38.1 billion won for four corporations including the Korea Coal Corporation.

Overseas
- The members of the Stahlhelm Veterans Association of the West Germany (134,000 members) nominate the former General of the Army, Kesselring who is in jail as a life sentenced war criminal, as their chairman.

August 8, Friday (June 18, by lunar calendar, 丙戌日 Red Dog) Clear
776 Day of the War

War Situation
- An aviation corps of the UN Forces attack the positions of the Chinese Communist Forces in the northern Capitol Hill.
- The representative of the UN Forces, Harrison, sends two letters to the Communist Forces through the liaison officer;
  (1) to request a detailed explanation on the indications of the POW camps in North Korea.
  (2) to refute the protest of the Communist Forces that a UN aircraft intruded into the neutral zone airspace.

At Home
- The Cabinet Meeting decides to hold the Presidential Inauguration Ceremony on August 15 in Seoul.
- The Korean Agricultural Rehabilitation Agency, Dr. Williams, has a meeting with the Vice Ministry of Agriculture and Forestry.
- The Geoje refugees protest against the decreasing rice distribution.

August 9, Saturday (June 19, by lunar calendar, 丁亥日 Red Pig) Clear
777 Day of the War

War Situation
- Battles on the Hill continued in the southwestern Bukhan River on the middle frontline.

- The Communist Forces implements the largest artillery fire since the outbreak of war with 21,600 shells fired over 24 hours before sunset.
- The UN Force heavily bombs the Sariwon airfield.

At Home
- The officials of the Ministry of Finance and the Ministry of Agriculture and Forestry states that the Government has financial difficulties in importing 700,000 tons of foreign grains.
- The Ministry of Education decides to send 300 students for study in foreign countries annually.
- *Radio Pyongyang* reports that the field investigation team of the International Scientist Committee comprising six bacteriologists of Britain, France, the Soviet Union, Sweden, and Oceania visited North Korea and depart after the field investigations on Aug. 15.

August 10, Sunday (June 20, by lunar calendar, 戊子日 Yellow Rat) Clear
778 Day of the War

War Situation
- The UN Forces engage in conflict at the Hill in eastern Panmunjom; The Communist Forces recapture it through a battle in the afternoon on Aug. 9.
- The U.S. Far East Air Forces plans to attack the military targets around Pyongyang again.

At Home

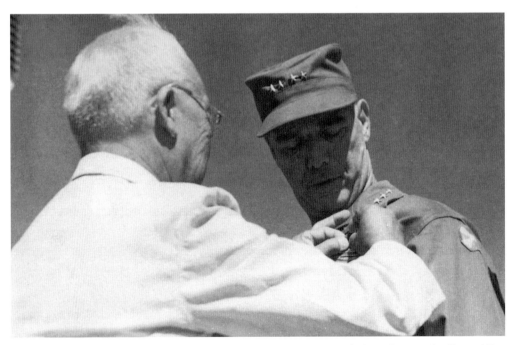

President Syngman Rhee awards an Order of Military Merit to the Eighth U.S. Army Commander, General Van Fleet (August 8, 1952)

- President Syngman Rhee attends the releasing ceremony of the civilian detainees (1,100 detainees) together with the Eighth U.S. Army Commander, General Van Fleet in Yeongdeungpo.
- Four Korean representatives of the International Free Legal Profession Conference in West Germany return home after the conference.
- The Ministry of Finance approves the financing plan for operating capitals of the Jeju-do Development of the Siksan Bank.

Overseas
- The public safety department of the Chinese Government declares the installation ordinance of the public safety and protection committee to strengthen the control of elements of revolution and domestic purge.
- The U.S. Secretary of Defense, Robert states that he discussed the struggle method of the Communist Forces and the military operation strategy in the Koran War at the ANZUS board of directors.

August 11, Monday (June 21, by lunar calendar, 己丑日 Yellow Ox) Clear
779 Day of the War

War Situation
- Battle situations on Bulmo Hill of the western frontline and in Capital Hill of the middle frontline are relatively calm.
- The guards of the UN Forces fire at the POWs of the Communist Forces in the 12th Geoje POW camp, and 38 people are wounded.
- The Armistice Conference, interrupted for the past three days, is resumed.
- The UN Forces requests the recess of the 115th main conference until Aug 19.

At Home
- Owners of media companies file a petition to request acquittal and discharge for the member of the National Assembly, Seo Min-ho.
- The National Tax Service establishes the period of emphasizing the tax season and warns of the punishment for failure to pay.
- The Ministry of Education decides to exhibit in the International Carving Competition in London on September 10.

Overseas
- The U.S. Assistant-secretary of State, Arison, states at the International Southeast Asian Affairs Committee in Washington that 10,000 Chinese volunteer soldiers in the Communist Forces in Indochina remain and the Allied Forces of Vietnam and France have 345,000 soldiers.
- The U.S. State Department announces the arms procurement program with Israel.

Firing a mortar on the enemy's position in Heungdeokri valley (August 10, 1952)

August 12, Tuesday (June 22, by lunar calendar, 庚寅日 White Tiger) Clear
780 Day of the War

War Situation
- The U.S. Marine Corps occupies the Siberia Hill after early recapturing the Bunker Hill in the eastern Panmunjom.
- The 1st Scottish battalion of the U.K. division leaves Korea for Hong Kong after finishing the 16-month term of service.
- The liaison officer of the UN Forces, Robinson, delivers a message to the liaison officer of the Communist Forces;
  They admit the fact that a UN air plane intruded into the neutral airspace and expresses the UN Forces´ regret.

At Home
- The Ministry of Social Affairs establishes a relief plan for 2,130,000 persons out of 9,300,000 persons who need relief goods.
- The South Gyeongsang Province recruiting district command calls up the draft of the front line workers at the request of the Eighth U.S. Army.
- The Commander of the UN Forces, General Clark, arrives in Seoul accompanied by his

wife to attend the inauguration ceremony of President Syngman Rhee.

August 13, Wednesday (June 23, by lunar calendar, 辛卯日 White Rabbit) Clear
781 Day of the War

War Situation

- The UN Air Force attacks the Chinese Communist Forces on Siberia Hill.
- The Commander of Geoje POW camp, Boatner, is appointed as the 4th U.S. Army Vice-Commander.
- The representative of the UN Forces of the Armistice Conference, Harrison, sends a letter to the Communist Forces in the liaison meeting;
  The Communist Forces must indicate site of new POW camps.

At Home

- The Ministry of Agriculture and Forestry evokes much criticism in the process of allocating the imported fertilizers with the tungsten exports dollars.
- A spreading rumor says that the former Minister of National Defense, Shin Sung-mo returned to Korea. He was involved in the National Defense Corps Incident and Geochang Incident.
- The Labor Standard Law is passed in the National Assembly.

Overseas

- The representatives of six European nations participating in the UN Forces do not agree on the issue of the service term of each country.

August 14, Thursday (June 24, by lunar calendar, 壬辰日Black Dragon) Clear
782 Day of the War

War Situation

- The UN Forces Commander, Clark, inspects the facilities of the UN Forces and the Headquarters of the ROK Army with the U.S. Army Commander, Van Fleet, in Daegu.

At Home

- President Syngman Rhee orders Yang Yu-chan the Korean Ambassador to the U.S. to launch an anti-Armistice Conference movement.
- The Foreign Exchange Subcommittee of the Korea-U.S. joint Economic Committee agrees on the Foreign Exchange Control Regulations.
- The International Club case is dropped and all the suspects are not prosecuted.

August 15, Friday (June 25, by lunar calendar, 癸巳日 Black Snake) Clear and Cloudy
783 Day of the War

War Situation

- The UN Air Force bombs the Communist Forces' supply base, Junghwa, as a warning in southern Pyongyang.
- The Communist Forces advise the UN Forces of the three locations of the newly established POW camps.

At Home
- "Commutation Command" (Presidential Decree No. 667) is declared and enforced.
- The Speaker of the House, Shin Ik-hee, demands three requirements to President Syngman Rhee in the congratulatory message of the National Liberation Day.
- The Seoul High Prosecutors' Office does not prosecute all the suspects of the International Club case.

Overseas
- The Chairman, Peng Dehuai, holds a military committee hearing a report on operation of the southeastern district troops from the Commander, Heoryong.

August 16, Saturday (June 26, by lunar calendar, 甲午日 Blue Horse) Cloudy, Clear and Cloudy
784 Day of the War

War Situation
- The 5th U.S. Air Forces bomb the Communist Forces Command and military assembly place in the northwestern Jinnampo.
- A squadron of fighter bombers of the UN Forces bombs the Communist Forces' positions Bunker Hill.

At Home
- The Seoul city is in conflict with the UN Korea Civil Affairs Department about the Seoul Rehabilitation Plan.
- The Horticulture Cooperative Association launches.

Overseas
- The UN Secretary-General, Trygve Lie, delivers an address in Oslo that it is difficult for any party to contend for the military victory in the Korean War.

August 17, Sunday (June 27, by lunar calendar, 乙未日 Blue Sheep) Cloudy
785 Day of the War

War Situation
- The Communist Forces halt the attack on the Bunker Hill.
- The U.S. Army Command announces a ban on reporting on the assigned troops of the UN Forces.

At Home
- The Former Minister of National Defense, Shin Sung-mo, returns from Japan.

- The Korean delegation of the 18th International Red Cross conference returns home.
- The representatives of the UN institutions visit Korea to inspect Korean situations.

August 18, Monday (June 28, by lunar calendar, 丙申日 Red Monkey) Rainy and Cloudy
786 Day of the War

War Situation
- All the activities in the frontline are minimized due to the bad weather.

At Home
- The Busan Municipal Assembly hears the report of administrating food.
- The Korea-U.S. Joint Economic Committee discusses 28 items such as Foreign Exchange Regulation.
- A strong typhoon hits the high grounds of the middle provinces.

Overseas
- The US rubber industry workers begin strikes to increase their wages.
- The South African Police arrest 362 people who participated in the Campaign against Racial Discrimination on charge of violation of the Segregation Laws of the South Africa Union.

August 19, Tuesday (June 29, by lunar calendar, 丁酉日 Red Rooster) Clear, Windy and Rainy
787 Day of the War

War Situation
- All the combats in the frontline are calm and come to a lull.
- The 116th main conference of the Armistice Conference resumes and decides a week recess.

At Home
- The Government submits the bill of the Industrial Recovery Bond Issue Law.
- The Cabinet Meeting decides to rend 200,000 seok of the Government´s holding rice to the poor and needy as an emergency food measure.
- The Ministry of Home Affairs establishes the Civil Defense Command and holds the first conference.

Overseas
- The Chief of Staff of the Greek Forces announces that the officers' meeting of Greek and Bulgaria on the border dispute was broken off due to the matter of responsibility.

August 20, Wednesday (June 30, by lunar calendar, 戊戌日Yellow Dog) Cloudy
788 Day of the War

War Situation

- Ground battles are sporadic and in small scales.
- The UN Air Forces attacks supply pools of the Communist Forces near Pyongyang.
- President Syngman Rhee inspects the middle frontline.

At Home
- The 17th National Assembly Plenary Session deliberates the bill of the Local Allocation Tax Law and so on.
- The Minister of National Defense, Sin Taeyeong, and the Army Chief of Staff, Paik Sun-yup, inspect Busan.(every military units, school and hospital)
- The Former Minister of National Defense, Shin Sung-mo, returns home after having fled to Japan on charges of the National Defense Corps Incident and the Geochang Incident.

August 21, Thursday (July 1, by lunar calendar, 己亥日 Yellow Pig) Cloudy
789 Day of the War

War Situation
- Ground combats show a relatively calm state.
- The Quartermaster General's office in the Headquarter of the Army establishes 16 accommodations for the soldiers who are on business trip in South Korea.

At Home
- The confidence vote on members of the Cabinet and ratifying the Prime Minister are becoming the main issues of the National Assembly.
- The Seoul city launches the arrangement project of war damaged areas.
- The Public Prosecutor General, Han Gyeong-man, announces that Shin Sung-mo, who would be involved in the Geochang Incident, was decided not to prosecute on July 17, due to the lack of evidence and an impossibility of any more investigation.
- The Government decides to loan 100,000 seok(1 seok is equivalent to 180 liters) of grains to farmers in a year.

August 22, Friday (July 2, by lunar calendar, 庚子日 White Rat) Rainy
790 Day of the War

War Situation
- All the combats in the frontline remain at the level of reconnoitering skirmishes.
- The U.S. Ambassador to Korea, Mucho, visits the flagship of the 7th U.S. Fleet and witnesses a scene of shelling by the fleet.

At Home
- The National Assembly Plenary Session passes the Local Allocation Tax Law.
- Representatives of each party in the National Assembly meet to discuss the Assembly by-election for the 27 members who are missing during the Korean War.

- The Cabinet Meeting introduces the bill of expansion of marine products (including grains and foodstuffs) in the military.
- The Ministry of Agriculture and Forestry decides to consult the Bank of Korea and the Financial Services Union about releasing 6 billion won as purchasing fund for 4,000 farming cows.
- The UN Reporter on the Korean rural economy interviews after inspecting drought damaged areas in North Gyeongsang Province.

Overseas
- The U.S. Naval Authorities announce the successful test of 4 kinds of new model Jet fighters on the aircraft carrier.

August 23, Saturday (July 3, by lunar calendar, 辛丑日 White Ox) Rainy
791 Day of the War

War Situation
- It rains in all the frontline. Combats are mostly reconnoitering skirmishes.
- The U.S. Eighth Army announces that 19 bodies out of 80 drowned soldiers are found dead due to the flood on August 18.

At Home
- President Syngman Rhee receives a petition to request a quantitative food rationing.
- The Government decides to loan 100,000 seok of wheat and barley to drought damaged farmers.
- The Ministry of Commerce and Industry pushes forward the Korea-Taiwan Friendship and Trade Treaty.

Overseas
- Radio Beijing gives a false report that the U.S. and ROK Army killed 170 POWs in the Geoje POW camp in January.

August 24, Sunday (July 4, by lunar calendar, 壬寅日 Black Tiger) Rainy and Cloudy
792 Day of the War

War Situation
- The frontline comes to a lull due to unfavorable weather.

At Home
- The Speaker of the National Assembly, Shin Ik-hee, visits Jang Myeon to have a short talk.
- The Ministry of Health cracks down unlicensed businesses and sales of baikban (boiled rice) and exposes 83 cases in the Busan city for 2 days.
- The Ministry of National Defense dissolves the Korean Disabled Veteran Association due to shortage of budget and sets a policy to establish the Special Disabled Veteran

Association with a minority of disabled veterans.
- The section chief meeting of district military affairs of the National Recruiting Command discusses the problems of simplifying military affairs and recognizing student status during the war.

August 25, Monday (July 5, by lunar calendar, 癸卯日 Black Rabbit) Rainy, Cloudy and Windy
793 Day of the War

War Situation
- Combats are lulled due to the heavy rain.

At Home
- In the 19th National Assembly Plenary Session, the special investigation team of the tungsten dollar case makes the second report.
  The Ministry of Agriculture and Forestry ignores the decision of the National Assembly of July 4 and then accepts the free disposition of 1,000 tons of fertilizer and 4,000 tons of wheat.
- The Police Station Organization (The Presidential Decree No. 680) and the regulations of Anti-aircraft Defense Unit (The Presidential Decree No. 681) are declared and implemented.
- Both the Korea and U.S. parties decide to dispatch the joint investigation team to every province due to the difference of the view on the expected amount of the rice crop.
- The residents' camps are built for the people evacuated for a time due to the order for the Geoje POW camps.

Overseas
- The UN Forces' Commander, Clark, reports to the Joint Chiefs of Staff the issues of releasing the POWs from South Korea rejecting the repatriation.
- President Truman appoints Ellis O. Briggs, U.S. Ambassador to Czechoslovakia as Ambassador to Korea.

August 26, Tuesday (July 6, by lunar calendar, 甲辰日 Blue Dragon) Clear
794 Day of the War

War Situation
- Fierce offensive and defensive battles between two sides occur in the Bunker Hill.

At Home
- In the 20th National Assembly Plenary Session, the interpellation session is held on the problems of the imported grains and fertilizers with the tungsten dollars and Korean Foreign Exchange and other goods processing;
  The Prime Minister promises a thorough investigation into the case of tungsten dollars by

organizing an investigation committee with the members of the Cabinet.
- President Syngman Rhee requests that the non-confidence resolution to the Minister concerned owing to the case of tungsten dollars should be stopped.

Overseas
- The representatives of India and Pakistan meet in Geneva to conclude the secret agreement to solve the Kashmir problem.

August 27, Wednesday (July 7, by lunar calendar, 乙巳日 Blue Snake) Clear and Rainy
795 Day of the War

War Situation
- An attack unit of the UN Forces engages the Chinese Communist Forces in the eastern Bukhan River.
- The 117th Armistice Conference decides a week recess and closes in 10 minutes from the beginning.
- The chief delegate of the Communist Forces, Nam Il, blames the UN Forces for the treatments of the POWs and requests the truth finding of the POW's riot between August 11 and 23.

At Home
- The joint meeting of the Government and the National Assembly Investigation Committee on the case of tungsten dollars is held in the Cabinet meeting room.
- The Legislation and Judiciary Committee passes the bill of the criminal law.
- The section chief meeting of district military affairs of the National Recruiting Command decides the regulations for the draft postponed student.

August 28, Thursday (July 8, by lunar calendar, 丙午日 Red Horse) Cloudy and Windy
796 Day of the War

War Situation
- A ship plane unit of the U.K. attacks Jinnampo on the west coast.
- The Commander of Geoje POW camp, Boatner, announces that the UN Forces observe the Geneva conventions.

At Home
- The representative of the surviving families of the dead soldiers calls on the President and delivers a massage requesting a special protection policy for them.

August 29, Friday (July 9, by lunar calendar, 丁未日 Red Sheep) Rainy and Cloudy
797 Day of the War

War Situation

- The UN Air Force heavily bombs the military targets in and around Pyongyang with 1400 planes in succession after pre-warning.

At Home
- The Cabinet Council passes 「the enforcement ordinance of the War time Better Living Law」.
- The Cabinet Council passes the plan to raise grain price submitted by the Ministry of Agriculture and Forestry.
- Experts of the land development insist on the need to unify the administrative organizations for irrigation works and developing farmland.

August 30, Saturday (July 10, by lunar calendar, 戊申日 Yellow Monkey) Cloudy
798 Day of the War

War Situation
- Prisoners in the Geoje POW camp resist the camp authority's order to work and come into conflict with the guards, resulting in 16 persons wounded.

At Home
- President Syngman Rhee makes statement on the departure of the US Ambassador, Mucho.
- The Ministry of Agriculture and Forestry requests the Ministry of Finance to finance 150 million dollars to import foreign grains(50,000 M/T).
- The Oriental Chemical Company in Samcheok pushes forward with the plan to be transfered into a fertilizer factory.

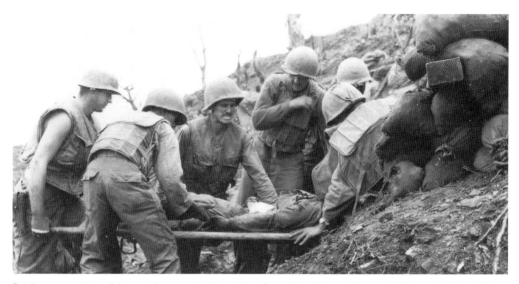

Soldiers evacuating a follow soldier wounded by artillery fires of the Chinese Communist Forces in Bulmo Hill.

August 31, Sunday (July 11, by lunar calendar, 己酉日 Yellow Rooster) Cloudy and Clear
799 Day of the War

War Situation

- The UN Forces repulse the Communist Forces which attacked the Bunker Hill in the eastern Panmunjom.
- The Far East Forces Command replaces the Commander of the UN POW camp with Colonel Cadwell.

At Home

- The Chief of Police Office, Kim Jong-won, denies the report that he ordered to torture suspects.
- *Radio Pyongyang* recommences its broadcasting which was stopped due to a heavy bombardment of the UN Air Forces on August 29.

September 1, Monday (July 12, by lunar calendar, 庚戌日 White Dog) Rainy
800 Day of the War

War Situation
- A unit of the UN Forces attacks the Communist Forces' positions south of Goseong.
- The Chinese Communist Forces launch a reconnoitering skirmish at Bunker Hill.

At Home
- The 23rd National Assembly Plenary Session passes the amendment bill of the local tax law.
- At the meeting of the Korea-U.S. Joint Economic Committee, the U.S. side insists that the poor grain harvest is due to the inappropriate application of fertilizers.

Overseas
- The UN Secretary-General, Trygve Lie, makes public the annual report to submit to the 7th Session of the UN General Assembly;
  - The UN furnishes U.S.$250 million as emergency assistance fund to South Korea, and furthermore prepares to provide U.S.$205 million for the Long-Term Plan to Rehabilitate Korea.

September 2, Tuesday (July 13, by lunar calendar, 辛亥日 White Pig) Rainy
801 Day of the War

War Situation
- A squadron of fighter bombers of the UN Force attacks the Sinuiju airfield.
- The chief delegate of the Communist Forces to the Armistice Conference, Nam Il, sends a message of complaint regarding the Geoje POW case (August 30).

At Home
- President Syngman Rhee instructs the rigid enforcement of regulations for stowaways to Japan.
- The Ministry of Social Affairs allocates 18,000 tons of relief grains for September to each province.

September 3, Wednesday (July 14, by lunar calendar, 壬子日 Black Rat) Rainy and Windy
802 Day of the War

War Situation
- The Communist Forces carry out a minor reconnoitering skirmish.

At Home

- The National Assembly Plenary Session passes a bill to dispatch a Korean delegate to the UN General Assembly and the Emigration Promotion Act.
- Via the Korean Ambassador to the USA, Yang Yu-chan, the Korean Government seeks the U.S. Administration's opinion about organizing a Pacific Alliance.
- The Ministry of Foreign Affairs instructs the Korean Mission in Japan to criticize the Japanese Government's policy on the repatriation of Koreans in Japan.
- In the final trial of the assasination attempt of the President case, the two accused, Kim Si-yeon and Ryu Si-tae are demanded death sentences.

Overseas
- The people´s Government of the Yenbin Korean Autonomous Region is established.
- A spokesperson of the U.K. Foreign Office announces British support for Japan's joining the United Nations.

September 4, Thursday (July 15, by lunar calendar, 癸丑日 Black Ox) Clear, Windy and Cloudy
803 Day of the War

War Situation
- The Chinese Communist Forces continue a reconnoitering skirmish for Bunker Hill in eastern Panmunjom.
- In the 118th main conference of the Armistice Conference, both parties stick to the original position on the POW exchange and a week recess is decided by the suggestion of the UN Forces again.

At Home
- The National Defense Committee in the National Assembly decides to dispatch a military observation mission to allied nations.

Overseas
- The Government of West Berlin city announces that East Germany has closed all the stores of West Germans and forfeited all their properties.

September 5, Friday (July 16, by lunar calendar, 甲寅日 Blue Tiger) Cloudy and Rainy
804 Day of the War

War Situation
- The UN Force repulses the attacks of the Chinese Communist Forces on the positions in western Yeoncheon.
- Eighth U.S. Army Commander, General Van Fleet, states that Communist guerrilla activities have declined significantly in South Korea.
- A security officer of the Communist Forces of the Armistice Conference runs through the neutral zone and surrenders to the UN Forces.

At Home

- The 25th National Assembly Plenary Session passes the bill of the Pension Act for families of dead soldiers and policemen and for wounded soldiers and policemen.
- The National Assembly passes the bill to strengthen the Navy and the Air Force.
- The Cabinet Meeting decides to submit the economic policy plan including food control.

Overseas

- The 23rd Army of the Chinese Communist Forces enters North Korea from Antung (present name is Dandong) and engages the Korean War.

  The 67th, 69th and 73rd Divisions under the command of Chinese Corps Commander, Jong Guochu, engages all the frontline in the summer attacking battle of the year 1953 after entering North Korea.

September 6, Saturday (July 17, by lunar calendar, 乙卯日 Blue Rabbit) Rainy and Clear
805 Day of the War

War Situation

- The Chinese Communist Forces attack the Capitol Hill on the western Bukhan River.
- The UN Forces withdraw from Bunker Hill.
- The Chief Delegate of the UN Forces to the Armistice Conference, Harrison, is promoted to lieutenant general and appointed as the U.S. Far East Army Commander but his duty as the chief delegate is to be continued for a while.

At Home

- The 26th National Assembly Plenary Session decides to postpone the consent on establishing the Constitution Research Committee.
- The first Joint Honorary Discharge ceremony of disabled veterans is held in the former 839th Unit.

September 7, Sunday (July 18, by lunar calendar, 丙辰日 Red Dragon) Rainy and Windy
806 Day of the War

War Situation

- UN Forces take over Capitol Hill after a fierce battle.
- West frontline, fierce battle at Bunker Hill.

At Home

- National Assembly decides to postpone the establishment of Constitution Amendment Research Committee (Minju Shinbo reports)
- The Ministry of Finance opposes the plan of the Ministry of Commerce and Industry to transfer the Oriental Chemical Company into a fertilizer factory.

Overseas

- *The Overseas Chinese Daily* in Hong Kong reports that the Chinese Communist Forces have engaged 8,000 soldiers of guerilla troops of the Chinese Nationalist Government in Fujian and Guangdong since mid-August.

September 8, Monday (July 19, by lunar calendar, 丁巳日 Red Snake) Rainy
807 Day of the War

War Situation
- The ROK Army engages the Communist Forces in a seesaw combat on Capitol Hill.

At Home
- The Chairman of the National Defense Committee of the National Assembly, Kim Jong-hoe, requests to expand the military assistance to the members of the U.S. Defense Committee of the House of Representatives visiting Korea.
- The Minister of Foreign Affairs, Byun Yung-tae, rejects the transfer of the Armistice Conference to the UN.

Overseas
- The Secretary of the U.S. Air Force interviews that the number of the U.S. Air Force planes increases up to 23%, compared to before-the-war and the improved Sabre jet fighters will be deployed in the Korean War soon.

September 9, Tuesday (July 20, by lunar calendar, 戊午日 Yellow Horse) Rainy, Cloudy and Clear
808 Day of the War

War Situation
- The UN Aviation Corps and Artillery Corps heavily bomb the Communist Forces' position on Capitol Hill.
- The UN Air Force attacks the Military Academy in Sakju again.

At Home
- The 28th National Assembly Plenary Session decides to dispatch an investigation team to typhoon-damaged areas of September 3.
- The National Assembly passes the amendment bill of the Farmland Reform Act for five years Extension of Payment Date for distributed farmland.
- Heated debate takes place over the foreign report that the management right of tungsten mines was transferred to an American.
- The Japanese ships' monopoly of marine transportation of the U.S. military supply and fishing operations heavily damages the Korean marine transport and fishing industry.

September 10, Wednesday (July 21, by lunar calendar, 己未日 Yellow Sheep) Cloudy and Rainy
809 Day of the War

War Situation

- The ROK Army repulses the attacks of the Communist Forces on Capitol Hill.
- A carrier-deck plane unit of the UN Forces attacks the power plant facilities in Bujeon and Changjin.

At Home

- The National Assembly passes the amendment bill of the National Assembly Law which allows a secret ballot for important agendas and constitutional amendment bills.
- The National Assembly resolves to decide the position of the National Assembly on the case of the tungsten exporting dollars in the next session after further investigations by the special investigation committee.

Overseas

- The United States, Britain, and France decide to provide support worth U.S.$99 million as economic and military assistance for Yugoslavia.
- The representative meeting of both India and Pakistan in Geneva on the Kashmir dispute ends in deadlock

September 11, Thursday (July 22, by lunar calendar, 庚申日 White Monkey) Rainy, Cloudy and Windy

810 Day of the War

War Situation

- The ROK Army repulses the Communist Forces attacking Capitol Hill through a fierce battle.
- The Vice Chief of Staff of the UN Forces, British Major General Shoesmith, visits Korea to inspect the frontline.

At Home

- The Government holds a relief measures meeting for disabled veterans attended by the U.S. authorities.
- The Cabinet Meeting decides to push forward with privatization programs of the state corporations facing management difficulties.

September 12, Friday (July 23, by lunar calendar, 辛酉日 White Rooster) Rainy and Windy
811 Day of the War

War Situation

- The ROK Army on Capitol Hill repulses five attacks of the Communist Forces.
- A squadron of light bombers of the UN Forces implements a warning strike on Seoheung.
- The 119th main conference of the Armistice Conference makes no progress and is held for 32 minutes and closed after agreeing on a week's recess.

At Home
- The Cabinet Meeting passes the regulation of the Examination and Deliberation Committee of the Local Government Act.
- The Minister of Foreign Affairs, Byun Yung-tae, states that the POWs who refused repatriation must be transferred to the third countries
- Disabled veterans accommodated in Dongnae and Geojeri Sanatorium visit the Ministry of Social Affairs requesting better treatment.
- A Coast patrol boat captures two Japanese fishing ships which violated the Korean territorial waters in the sea near Jeju Island.

September 13, Saturday (July 24, by lunar calendar, 壬戌日 Black Dog) Rainy
812 Day of the War

War Situation
- The Chinese Communist Forces reconnoiter the UN Forces' outpost in the northern Gorangpo.

At Home
- The out-of-National Assembly faction of the Liberty Party tries to win floor power groups in the National Assembly.

Overseas
- The NATO Forces start a huge military exercise and 160 warships of eight European nations leave the Clyde harbor in Scotland.

September 14, Sunday (July 25, by lunar calendar, 癸亥日 Black Pig) Rainy, Cloudy, Rainy and Cloudy
813 Day of the War

War Situation
- The battle for Capitol Hill continues.
- A squad of bombers of the UN Forces conducts nighttime bombing of Hongwon.

At Home
- A rumor of reshuffling of the ROK Cabinet is spreading.
- The Korea - U.S. Joint Committee for Relief Measure of Disabled Veterans is decided to set up.
- The chairman of the Australian Veterans Association, George Holland, arrives in Seoul to inspect the Australian Forces on the frontline.

September 15, Monday (July 26, by lunar calendar, 甲子日 Blue Rat) Cioudy
814 Day of the War

War Situation

- The Communist Forces launch a reconnoitering attack on Bunker Hill.

At Home

- The Ministry of Social Affairs establishes seven public food facilities in Jeonju and other areas for victims in the Suyeong area.
- The Ministry of Trade and Industry announces the total number of registered companies is 314.
- The authorities of educational affairs is criticized due to its support for the sales of a booklet which criticizes the Democratic Nationalist Party.

Overseas

- The criminal act exhibition of bacteriological warfare of the U.S. Army is held. Five showrooms are opened in the Beijing Palace Culture Exhibition. Five hundred specimens, photographs and official documents are displayed.
- The U.S. State Department opposes transferring the Armistice Conference to the UN General Assembly.

September 16, Tuesday (July 27, by lunar calendar, 乙丑日 Blue Ox) Clear
815 Day of the War

War Situation

- Attacks of the Communist Force are decreasing in all of the frontline.
- A POW committed suicide in the Geoje POW camp.

At Home

- The Commerce and Industry Committee of the National Assembly starts a nationwide inspection tour of the hydroelectric power generating facilities.

Overseas

- The UN Security Council rejects the bill of the UN membership of Libya by exercising the right of veto of the Soviet Union.
- The president of East Germany states that East Germany is establishing the national defense forces in the memorial services for Nazi victims.

September 17, Wednesday (July 28, by lunar calendar, 丙寅日 Red Tiger) Clear
816 Day of the War

War Situation

- The UN Air Force launches 16 attacks on the Communist Forces' base with napalm attacks on the Jihyeong Ridge.
- The U.S. Far East Command announces that six fighters of the Marine Corps crashed on the way while returning to the base.

- 17 POWs are wounded during a riot in the Geoje POW camp.

At Home
- President Syngman Rhee presents the Turkish and Philippine troops with medals after inspecting the eastern frontline.
- Shin Ik-hee discusses formation of the Democrats Association with the Prime Minister, Chang Taek-sang.
- The authorities of the Ministry of Agriculture and Forestry oppose the whole right of managing and polishing relief grains by the Monetary Cooperative Association.
- 12 persons are killed and 200 are wounded in a locomotive explosion on the Gyeongin Line.

Overseas
- The Bureau of Intelligence and Research of the U.S. State Department analyses the problems of the won-dollar exchange rate.
- The magazine France reports that the Soviet Union acquired the strategic bombing base and uranium mines in Tibet as a result of the China-Soviet Union meeting.

September 18, Thursday (July 29, by lunar calendar, 丁卯日 Red Rabbit) Clear and Cloudy
817 Day of the War

War Situation
- The ROK Army recaptures Jihyeong Ridge.
- Light combat occurs on the other frontline.
- A squadron of light bombers of the UN Forces destroys 150 vehicles of the Communist Forces moving southward of the frontline.

At Home
- The Government decides the Korean members of the Korea-U.S. Joint Committee of Measures for Disabled Veterans.
- Minister of Commerce and Industry, Lee Gyo-seon, opposes the use of the repayment dollars of UN loan to import grains.
- The new chief of the National Security Bureau, Mun Bong-je, expresses his inaugural words at a press conference.
- A mob violence incident of disabled veterans occurs in Waegwan;
  As many as 150 disabled veterans launch a surprise attack on a police station.

Overseas
- The UN Security Council rejects the motion on UN membership of Japan by the Soviet Union's veto.
- The U.S. State Department releases a white paper criticizing the slavery system in the Soviet Union.

September 19, Friday (August 1, by lunar calendar, 戊辰日 Yellow Dragon) Cloudy and Clear
818 Day of the War

War Situation
- The Communist Forces attack Bulmo Hill.
- The authorities of the UN Forces suppress a riot in the Bongamdo civilian detainee camps with 23 detainees wounded.

At Home
- The ROK Government decides to accede to the General Agreement on Tariffs and Trade.
- The Foreign Capital Management Administration takes a different position from the UN Korea Civil Affairs Department about the relief goods unloading business.
- The Ministry of Trade and Industry announces a new measure for the tungsten exporting dollars.
- The Minister of Foreign Affairs, Byun Yung-tae, releases a statement on the problem of Japanese ship's violation of the Korean territorial waters.
- The Navy Command announces the interception and arrest of a Japanese ship on September 12 by the coast patrol boat.

September 20, Saturday (August 2, by lunar calendar, 己巳日 Yellow Snake) Cloudy and Clear
819 Day of the War

War Situation
- Fierce battles take place on Bulmo Hill.
- The UN Forces attack Kelly Hill in northeast Yeoncheon at night.
- The 120th main conference of the Armistice Conference is held for 52 minutes and agrees on a week's recess.
- The Chief Delegate of the UN Forces, Harrison, refutes the fiction and tricks of the Communist Forces and strongly insists an exchange of lists of POWs.

At Home
- President Syngman Rhee receives a report on the situation of strike participants of the Electricity Labor Union.
- The Government repays the loan from the Bank of Korea with the sale money of relief goods.
- A disabled veterans' riot breaks out in the Busanjin station;
  About 350 disabled veterans get free rides on the train with a purpose to release 11 disabled veterans arrested for the case of a sudden attack on the Waegwan police station, but they are persuaded to disperse by the Vice-Minister of National Defense.

September 21, Sunday (August 3, by lunar calendar, 庚午日 White Horse) Clear, Cloudy and

President Syngman Rhee and the Eighth U.S. Army Commander, General Van Fleet, inspecting the U.S. Marine Forces (September 18, 1952)

Clear

820 Day of the War

War Situation
- The Capitol Division of the ROK Army repulses the attacks of the Communist Forces on the Jihyeong Ridge.
- The soldiers of the UN Forces collect U.S.$8,000 as relief aid for the Korean War orphans in a day.

At Home
- Seoul citizens have more difficulties in making a living due to rising prices and relief goods reduction.
- The Minister of Home Affairs, Jeon Heon-sik, makes a statement to the disabled veterans; The Government will establish permanent relief measures, rectifying social discrimination. He also requests orderly conduct by the disabled veterans.

Overseas
- *Xinhua News Agency* reports that the UN Forces used poison gas shelling 10 times on the frontline from July to August in the Korean War.

September 22, Monday (August 4, by lunar calendar, 辛未日 White Sheep) Clear
821 Day of the War

War Situation
- A company of the Chinese Communist Forces attacks outposts of the UN Forces by throwing stones in western Yeoncheon.
- The authority of the UN POW camp announces that four suicide cases have occurred since April, including one POW suicide in the Jeju Island POW camp.

At Home
- The Government decides to dispatch a delegation to the International Telecommunication Federation.
- The Minister of Justice, Seo Sang-hwan, makes a critical statement on the Japanese ship's patrol policy near Korean waters.

Overseas
- The Constitution Drafting Convention for the European Political Community is held in Strasbourg and elects the representative of West Germany, Brentano, as chairman.
- Up to 180,000 soldiers of the NATO Forces take part in joint military training for 10 days.

September 23, Tuesday (August 5, by lunar calendar, 壬申日 Black Monkey) Clear, Cloudy and Clear
822 Day of the War

War Situation
- Troops of the ROK Army heavily attack the North Korean Forces in a basin of the northeastern hill under the cover of the Artillery and the Tank Unit.
- Forty-nine POWs of the Chinese Communist Forces are injured in the riot in the Jeju Island POW camp.

At Home
- The Director of the Seoul District Prosecutors' Office, Min Bok-ki, announces that the police can arrest suspects only if they have an arrest warrant issued by a judge.

September 24, Wednesday (August 6, by lunar calendar, 癸酉日 Black Rooster) Clear
823 Day of the War

War Situation
- An Infantry Unit of the UN Forces attacks Kelly Hill under the cover of a tank unit in the northwestern Yeoncheon and withdraws due to the strong resistance by the Chinese Communist Forces.
- The UN Forces Commander, General Clark, visits Korea accompanied by the Navy Commander, Briscoe, to inspect the military situation of the frontline.

- The chief delegate of the Communist Forces of the Armistice Conference, Nam Il, delivers a protest letter against releasing 11,000 civilian detainees to the representative, Harrison, through the liaison officer.

At Home
- The Government provides new measure for carrying in the properties and donated goods.
- The Minister of Commerce and Industry, Lee Gyo-seon, arouses criticism on his arbitrary decision of personnel selection of the state corporation.
- The Ministry of Finance starts releasing the industrial fund with the repayment of the UN loan.

Overseas
- The mediator of the UN Kashmir Issue, Graham, submits a report about the failure of the 4th Kashmir disputes conciliation between India and Pakistan.

September 25, Thursday (August 7, by lunar calendar, 甲戌日 Blue Dog) Clear
824 Day of the War

War Situation
- A reconnaissance party of the UN Forces engages the Communist Forces near Gimhwa.
- The Chief Delegate of the Communist Forces of the Armistice Conference submits a memorandum through the liaison officer.

At Home
- The Liberty Party strengthens its political opposition to the Prime Minister, Chang Taek-sang.
- The Public Prosecutors' Office questions the Vice-Minister of Foreign Affairs due to the Japanese Furuichi entrance.
- The Ministry of Foreign Affairs instructs overseas students to return home after finishing their studies.

September 26, Friday (August 8, by lunar calendar, 乙亥日 Blue Pig) Rainy, Cloudy and Clear
825 Day of the War

War Situation
- A riot breaks out in the Jeju Island POW camp leaving five POWs of the Communist Forces wounded.
- The UN Forces Command announces that the Communist Forces secretly dispatch secret agents to Geoje and Jeju islands to provoke riots in the POW camps of the UN Forces.

At Home
- The Cabinet Meeting decides to establish the Integrated Industry Reconstruction Committee with the heads of six Ministries and Government Agencies.

- The Pension Act of War Dead Soldiers and Policemen Bereaved Family and Disabled Veterans (Law No. 256) is published.

Overseas
- The Burmese Government declares Martial Law in Shan State to prevent riots by the Communists.

September 27, Saturday (August 9, by lunar calendar, 丙子日 Red Rat) Clear
826 Day of the War

War Situation
- The UN Forces repulse the Chinese Communist Forces' attacks on Kelly Hill.
- The UN Forces Commander, General Clark, announces the Sea Defense Zone settlement around Korea.
  The goals of the settlement of the Sea Defense Zone is to block the Communist Forces' attacks from the Korean Coast, to prevent trespassing of a group of Communist spies into Korea, to prevent smuggling and to secure the safe passage of supply ships.
- The Chief Delegate of the Communist Forces to the Armistice Conference, Nam Il, sends a protest letter to Harrison through the liaison officer regarding the UN Forces' way of treating POWs.

At Home
- The Central Executive Committee of the Liberal Party adopts the amendment bill for the party organization by President Syngman Rhee.
- The Ministry of National Defense holds the special military affairs conference examining the problems of soldier's food supply and side dishes.
- A Notice for Drafting Young Men is published (The State Council No. 42);
  The Government drafts medical engineers aged from 28 to 39 and general engineers aged from 28 to 36 to cover the need of the military authorities during the period from October 1 of 1952 to August 31 of 1953.

September 28, Sunday (August 10, by lunar calendar, 丁丑日 Red Ox) Cloudy and Clear
827 Day of the War

War Situation
- The Communist Forces attack Capitol Hill at night under the cover of their Artillery and Tank Units.
- The Eighth U.S. Army Command announces that the UN Air Force mistakenly bombed Paengnori Hill held by Greek Forces.
- The 121st main conference of the Armistice Conference is held.
  The UN Forces offer alternative suggestions for the POW issues; the Chief Delegate,

A refugee village formed on a mountain slope in Paju. (September 26, 1952)

Harrison, offers a new suggestion about three ways to resolve POW problems.

At Home
• The Ministry of National Defense holds a round-table talk with war dead soldier families.

Overseas
• *Taipei Associated Press* reports that the Soviet Union completed construction of a hydrogen bomb plant.

September 29, Monday (August 11, by lunar calendar, 戊寅日 Yellow Tiger) Clear
828 Day of the War

War Situation
• The Chinese Communist Forces occupy two hills under the cover of the Tank Unit in eastern Geumseong.
• The Far East U.S. Navy announces that the destroyer, *SS Cunningham*, came under fire near Dancheon on September 19 and eight soldiers were wounded.

At Home
• The Cabinet Meeting decides to reject the amendment bill of the Farmland Reform Act passed by a majority vote of the National Assembly.

- The Ministry of Agriculture and Forestry establishes natural disaster restoration measures.
- Traffic restrictions in the areas where Communist guerrillas are infesting are proclaimed. (The Army Headquarters Instructions No. 234)

September 30, Tuesday (August 12, by lunar calendar, 己卯日 Yellow Rabbit) Clear
829 Day of the War

War Situation
- The UN Forces continue to attack two hills in the eastern Bukhan River.
- The spokesperson of the Eighth U.S. Army announces that the Soviet Union is taking part in the Korean War in support of North Korea.

At Home
- The Government decides to reject the amendment bill of the Farmland Reform Act.
- The Government submits a motion regarding the overseas exhibits of the national treasure art works.
- The Government decides to repair the Dongjin River bank at a cost of U.S.$ 49. 2 million.

Overseas
- The Second Buddhist Convention is held in Tokyo and adopts the declaration of peace based on Buddhism.
- Pakistan and France sign a trade agreement.

The completion ceremony of recruit training of the Korean Marine Corps (September 30, 1952)

October 1, Wednesday (August 13, by lunar calendar, 庚辰日 White Dragon) Clear
830 Day of the War

War Situation
- The 3rd Division of the ROK Army starts an attack to recapture Wire Hill in the eastern Bukhan River occupied by the Chinese Communist Forces.
- The Korean Rear Commander, Herren, arrives at Jeju Island to investigate the riot of POWs.
- The Secretary of the U.S. Air Force, Finletter, arrives in a Seoul suburb to inspect the frontline.

At Home
- The International Sanitary Regulation (World Health Organization Regulation No. 2) takes effect with the joining of Korea.
- The Ministry of National Defense reorganizes the first and second ordnance factory as its direct institutions.

Overseas
- The Korean Residents Veterans Association in Japan holds the first national meeting.
- The East German People's Assembly approves a bill to abolish the restrictions on all the former Nazis.

October 2, Thursday (August 14, lunar calendar, 辛巳日 White Snake) Clear
831 Day of the War

War Situation
- The ROK Army halts combat at Wire Hill in the eastern Bukhan River and withdraws.
- The authority of the UN Forces announces that a Chinese POW wounded in the Geoje POW camp riot (October 1) was airlifted to the Busan hospital and nine of those injured in the riot died.

At Home
- The Minister of Foreign Affairs, Byun Yung-tae, expresses his opposition to the three plans of exchanging POWs proposed by the U.S. Forces.
- The Korea-U.S. Joint Economic Committee agrees on an additional purchase for the revised relief program for disasters and flood damage.

October 3, Friday (August 15, by lunar calendar, 壬午日 Black Horse) Clear
832 Day of the War

War Situation

- The UN Forces recapture Nori Hill without any resistance after the withdrawal of the Chinese Communist Forces.
- The Vice Chief of Staff of the UN Forces, British Major General Shoesmith, visits the ROK Army Headquarters in Daegu and praises the great strides of the ROK Army in a short period in the conference with various levels of Commanders.

At Home

- A violent clash occurs between some soldiers of the Marine Corps and disabled veterans in the Busan city.
- A concrete plan of the Samcheok fertilizer plant is drawn up.

Overseas

- The first atomic test by Britain is conducted on Montebello Island in the Sea to the northeast of Australia.
- The UN announces that they will start the Korean Reconstruction Recovery Program regardless of the result of referral to the Armistice Conference.

October 4, Saturday (August 16, by lunar calendar, 癸未日 Black Sheep) Clear and Windy
833 Day of the War

War Situation

- An Infantry unit of the UN Forces continues to attack the Chinese Communist Forces' Hill in the southern Panmunjom.

A shoe repairman on a Seoul street. (October 2, 1952)

- The U.S. Far East Navy Command announces that a Canadian destroyer was hit by a shell in action and two soldiers were killed, while two soldiers were wounded in the sea near Seocheon.

At Home
- The Government promulgates of the establishment of the captured ships court and the captured ships high court. (Presidential Decree No. 707)
- The Government declares the Capture and Trial Decree for vessels violating the territorial waters.
- The Jeju Island combat police troops engage armed demonstrators at the outside of East Gate.

October 5, Sunday (August 17, by lunar calendar, 甲申日 Blue Monkey) Cloudy
834 Day of the War

War Situation
- The 3rd Division of the ROK Army repulses attacks by the Chinese Communist Forces on an outpost of the Bukhan River.
- The Chief Liaison Officer of the Communist Forces in the Armistice Conference, Colonel Jang Chun-san, protests against the violation of the skies of the meeting location by an Air Force plane on October 3.

At Home
- The U.K. Ambassador to Korea, G.C. Graham, arrives at Gimhae airfield.
- "The International Telecommunication" magazine is first published.

October 6, Monday (August 18, by lunar calendar, 乙酉日 Blue Rooster) Clear and Rainy
835 Day of the War

War Situation
- The 9th Division of the ROK Army engages in combat at White Horse Hill (Oct. 6~15).
- The Masan camp starts releasing civilian detainees and releases 500 detainees from North Gyeongsang Province for the first time.
- The Chief Delegate of the UN Forces in the Armistice Conference sends a letter to the Communist Forces via the liaison officer: to request a discussion for exchanging private parcels of POWs.

At Home
- The Minister of Social Affairs allocates 700 tons of powdered milk by a decision of the Joint Economic Committee to every province.

Overseas
- The Chinese Communist Forces starts the second counterattack. (10. 6~10. 31): A

counterattack operations is developed at the second frontline and begins in September 18. The Chinese Communist Forces have attempted 77 attacks on 66 military targets, while the UN Forces have counterattacked and repulsed 480 times and maintained 17 positions. Casualties and POWs number 25,000.

October 7, Tuesday (August 19, by lunar calendar, 丙戌日 Red Dog) Rainy and Clear
836 Day of the War

War Situation
- The UN Forces repulse the Communist Forces attacking White Horse Hill in northwestern Cheorwon.
- Sixteen POWs in the Geoje POW camp are wounded by contumacy of a POW.
- The liaison officer of the UN Forces, McCarthy, sends a message expressing the regret of the UN for the violation of the territorial skies by a UN aircraft on October 3.

At Home
- President Syngman Rhee emphasizes recruitments of Korean engineers instead of Japanese engineers in the Cabinet Meeting.
- The UN Committee on Unification and Reconstruction of Korea inspects Jeju Island to decide on a location for a power plant facility.

Overseas
- The U.S. delegate of the UN General Assembly responds to the President of Mexico that if the delegates of China and North Korea accept the voluntary repatriation proposal of the UN, they will consider the suggestion of Mexico.

October 8, Wednesday (August 20, by lunar calendar, 丁亥日 Red Pig) Cloudy and Clear
837 Day of the War

War Situation
- The 9th Division of the ROK Army and the French battalion continue hand-to-hand fights with the Chinese Communist Forces on the ridge of the White Horse and Arrow Head Hill.
- In the 122th main conference of the Armistice Conference, the Communist Forces reject the proposal of the UN Forces for exchanging POWs of September 28 and the Chief Delegate, Harrison, proposes an indefinite recess and stops the Conference.

At Home
- The Korea-U.S. Joint Economic Committee decides on the 1953 grain policy.
- The Korea-U.S. Joint Economic Committee agrees to transfer two chemical plants in Samcheok into ferrtilizer plants.
- The Ministry of National Defense, the Ministry of Home Affairs and the Ministry of Education discuss the ways of lowering illiterate rate of the draftable young men.

October 9, Thursday (August 21, by lunar calendar, 戊子日 Yellow Rat) Clear
838 Day of the War

War Situation
- A 9th Division Unit of the ROK Army continues to have a fierce hand-to-hand fight in the White Horse Hill.

At Home
- President Syngman Rhee appoints the Former Minister without portfolio, Lee Yun-yong, as Prime Minister and requests the approval of the National Assembly.

Overseas
- The U.S. Joint Chiefs of Staff requests President Truman to use a nuclear weapon in Korea.

October 10, Friday (August 22, by lunar calendar, 己丑日 Yellow Ox) Clear, Cloudy and Rainy
839 Day of the War

War Situation
- A Tank Unit of the ROK Army carries out operations against the Chinese Communist Forces around White Horse Hill.

At Home
- The Cabinet Meeting passes the bill for the academic credit approval during the wartime.
  - The 24,000 students out of 47,000 students in 65 universities who registered credits by the end of last May are recognized.
- The recruiting district command calls a roll for veterans.

Overseas
- The UN Security Council starts to discuss the Kashmir problems.
- A source of the Taiwan Nationalist Government states that the Chinese Communist Forces put the newly organized elite reserve corps, and the 3rd Army Corps to the Korean War to show off the Chinese Military Power before the UN General Assembly.

October 11, Saturday (August 23, by lunar calendar, 庚寅日 White Tiger) Rainy, Cloudy and Clear
840 Day of the War

War Situation
- The 9th Division of the ROK Army goes into the northern region to occupy the White Horse Hill and attacks it, surrounding it with other troops on three sides.
- The Chief Delegate of the Communist Forces in the Armistice Conference, Nam Il, sends a complaint letter to the Chief Delegate of the UN Force, Harrison who unilaterally declared indefinite recess of the Armistice Conference in October 8.

At Home
- The Minister of Health, Choe Jae-yu, announces that a presentation of the Korean Public

Health Nurse Training Fellowship is decided in the 3rd West Pacific Health Conference.
- The Ministry of Foreign Affairs states that the news collecting activities by japanese journalists in the rear areas will be definitely regulated and strictly cracked down.
- The Government agrees on the repatriation of Japanese harbor workers with the U.S. Forces authorities.

October 12, Sunday (August 24, by lunar calendar, 辛卯日 White Rabbit) Clear
841 Day of the War

War Situation
- The 9th Division of the ROK Army starts to attack at dawn and dominates White Horse Hill.
- The UN Navy authorities announce that the aircraft carrier, *U.S.S Los Angeles*, will join the Korean War again.
- Two POWs of the Chinese Communist Forces commit suicide in the Jeju POW camp.

At Home
- President Syngman Rhee praises the war exploit of the 9th Division of the ROK Army.
- The Minister of Social Affairs, Park Sureum, announces dispersed accommodations for disabled veterans.

October 13, Monday (August 25, by lunar calendar, 壬辰日 Black Dragon) Clear
842 Day of the War

War Situation
- All the ground combats are at reconnoitering skirmish level except the battle of White Horse Hill.
- The Eighth U.S. Army Commander, General Van Fleet, states after the frontline inspection
  : The battle of White Horse Hill is the fiercest position struggle in nearly a year and the 9th Division of the ROK Army has carried out great combat.

At Home
- The Ministry of Agriculture and Forestry, the UN Korea Civil Affairs Department, the Ministry of Social Affairs and the Monetary Cooperative Federation all agree on the unified management of imported grain and relief grains.
- *Pyongyang Broadcasting* reports that the North Korean Air Force bombed the UN Forces' base, Cho-do, for two hours on the night of Oct. 12.

Overseas
- The gliding training school opens in Stuttgart for the first time in the post-war period.

October 14, Tuesday (August 26, by lunar calendar, 癸巳日 Black Snake) Cloudy and Clear
843 Day of the War

War Situation

- The 2nd Division of the ROK Army and the 7th U.S. Division carry out a slowdown operation at Sniper Ridge and Samgak Hill. (Oct. 14~ Nov. 24)
- Fierce combat takes place in the Iron Triangle in the middle frontline.
- A contumacy by POWs for an order of guards happens in the Geoje POW camp and 15 prisoners are wounded.

At Home

- The National Assembly Plenary Session approves funding of 30 billion won to prevent pre-harvest sales of rice crops.
- The Cabinet Meeting introduces the General Election Act.
- The Anti-Limited Combat and Entire Attack Promoting Rally is held in Seoul.

October 15, Wednesday (August 27, by lunar calendar, 甲午日 Blue Horse) Rainy and Clear
844 Day of the War

War Situation

- A fierce hand-to-hand combat occures in the Jineung Ridge.
- The 9th Division recaptures the White Horse Hill.
- The Communist Forces protest that the UN Forces must take the responsibility for three wounded POWs of the Communist Forces on October 11.
- The UN Forces admit that a shell of the UN Force dropped in the Panmunjom Neutral Zone on October 8 and sends a message to express the regret of UN Forces.

At Home

- President Syngman Rhee pushes for an agreement for sending the national treasures abroad by the National Assembly.
- The Government makes protest against the infiltration of the territorial water by Japanese fishing boats.
- The Ministry of Health announces the establishment of ten relief hospitals all over the country to care for disabled veterans.
- The 2nd joint meeting of the Chief of Staff is held in the Navy Command.

Overseas

- The Steering Committee of the UN General Assembly requests adoption of the Korean Issue as the first agenda item.
- The Secretariat of the UN General Assembly adopts the suggestion of the Indian delegate to include the issue of South Africa in the General Assembly agenda.

October 16, Thursday (August 28, by lunar calendar, 乙未日 Blue Sheep) Clear
845 Day of the War

War Situation

- The Chinese Communist Forces search and attack Jihyeong Ridge three times.
- The Chief Delegate of the UN Forces, Harrison, sends a message to the chief delegate of the Communist Forces that the UN Forces are willing to resume the Armistice Conference in accordance with the good faith of the Communist Forces.
- Kim Il Sung and Peng Dehuai send a letter under joint signature to the UN Forces Commander, Clark.

At Home

- The Government declares the Capture and Trial of Ships Decree.
- The Minister of Social Affairs, Park Sur-eum, establishes the Vocational Training Agency for disabled veterans in Daejeon and 150 veterans are admitted first.

Overseas

- The North Vietnam Forces launch renewed attack an area between the Song Coi River and the Heihe River in the Indo-China War.

October 17, Friday (August 29, by lunar calendar, 丙申日 Red Monkey) Cloudy and Clear
846 Day of the War

War Situation

- The UN Forces repulse an attack by the Chinese Communist Forces on Jihyeong Ridge.
- The ROK Army withdraws from the summit of White Horse Hill due to the heavy artillery fire of the Communist Forces.

At Home

- The Director of the Public Information Office condemns the Japanese defamation against Korea and the violation of the Fishery Resources Protection Line.
- The U.S. Field Army Commander, Hodge, visits President Syngman Rhee under the guidance of the Eighth U.S. Army Commander, Van Fleet in Gyeongmudae.

October 18, Saturday (August 30, by lunar calendar, 丁酉日 Red Rooster) Clear
847 Day of the War

War Situation

- The ROK Army occupies two-thirds of Jeogyeo Ridge.
- The anti-aircraft artillery corps of the UN Army lands at Busan.
- The U.S. Field Army Commander, Hodge, visits the 9th Corps of the ROK Army with the Commander of the 9th Corps of the U.S. Army.

At Home

- The Minister of National Defense, Sin Tae-yeong, inspects the 9th Division of the ROK Army.

- Disabled veterans attack the official building in Waegwan in North Gyeongsang Province.
- Pyongyang Broadcasting announces that the North Korean Foreign Minister, Park Hon-yong, sent a message to the UN General Assembly and requested that North Korea representative be allowed to participate in the discussion of Korean Issue.

Overseas
- The 7th National Convention of the Taiwan Nationalist Party elects President Chiang Kai-shek as the next President by a unanimous vote.

October 19, Sunday (September 1, by lunar calendar, 戊戌日 Yellow Dog) Clear
848 Day of the War

War Situation
- The UN Forces defend positions on Jihyeong Ridge and White Horse Hill.
- The General Commander of the U.S. Field Army, Hodge, is interviewed in Seoul and says that the strategy of the Chinese Communist Forces is the same as the Japanese strategy in World War II.

At Home
- The National Assembly returns the year 1953 Reconstruction Plan to the Government.
- The Minister of Justice, Seo Sang-hwan, instructs crackdowns of pre-harvest sales of rice crops to every competent prosecution.

Overseas
- The U.S. Assistant Undersecretary of State addresses the UN General Assembly stating that the U.S. Government will strongly request the member nations of the UN which did not dispatch their military troops to fulfill their repsponsibility to block aggression.

October 20, Monday (September 2, by lunar calendar, 己亥日 Yellow Pig) Clear
849 Day of the War

War Situation
- The ROK Army repulses the Chinese Communist Forces at the main hill of the Sniper Ridge after fierce hand-to-hand combat.
- The UN Forces Commander, Clark, replies that if the Communist Forces want the Armistice Conference, the UN Forces are willing to resume the Armistice Conference.

At Home
- President Syngman Rhee orders the Minister of Foreign Affairs, Byeon Yeong-tae, who attended the UN General Assembly to return home.
- The National Assembly Plenary Session passes "the special motion of the interpellation for the disabled veteran treatment" and "the bill of the Amendment to the National Tax Collection Act."

- The Korea-U.S. Joint Economic Committee agrees to establish the management agency to operate the Korean Economic Revival and Relief Plan
- The advisory committee public reporting of national defense policies is established, composed of officials of the defense ministry and general managers and chief editors of newspapers and news agencies.

October 21, Tuesday (September 3, by lunar calendar, 庚子日 White Rat) Cloudy, Rainy and Windy
850 Day of the War

War Situation
- The 2nd Division of the ROK Army repulses nighttime attacks of the Chinese Communist Forces on Pinpoint Hill of Sniper Ridge.
- Light skirmishes occur in other parts of the frontline.

At Home
- President Syngman Rhee emphasizes that it is impossible to defend the entire frontline with only the ROK's defense capacity and he requests UN assistance.
- The National Assembly Plenary Session passes "the proposed amendment of the National Tax Collection Act," "the proposed amendment in the Special Imposition of Additional Taxes to the Tax Law Act," and "the proposed amendment in the Exceptions to Tax Laws Act."

October 22, Wednesday (September 4, by lunar calendar, 辛丑日 White Ox) Rainy, Clear and Windy
851 Day of the War

War Situation
- The ROK Army repulses continuous attacks of the Communist Forces for Jihyeong Ridge in the western Bukhan River.
- The ROK Army succeeds in recapturing Pinpoint Hill, which was captured by the Communist Forces after nine hours.
- A squadron of B-29 fighter bombers attacks the lead mine ral processing plant of the Communist Forces in eastern Antung.
- The UN Forces Command replaces the official spokesman of the UN Forces in the Armistice Conference.

At Home
- President Syngman Rhee states in a conference with foreign press that it is not possible to advance northward with only the Korean military power.
- U.S. Assistant Secretary of Defense, William Foster, visits Korea and inspects the military facilities in Busan and the United Nations' POW camps. He arrives in Seoul to inspect the frontline.

Battle of White Horse (October 20, 1952)

Overseas
• The French Cabinet decides to request parliament to ratify the Allied Command Europe Treaty.

October 23, Thursday (September 5, by lunar calendar, 壬寅日 Black Tiger) Clear, Cloudy and Windy

852 Day of the War

War Situation
• The 2nd Division of the ROK Army repulses a company's attack of the Communist Forces on Sniper Ridge.
• The 9th Division of the ROK Army recaptures the summit of White Horse Hill after hand-to-hand fighting.

At Home
• The Minister of Home Affairs, Jin Heon-sik, announces the relocation of public servants to renovate administrative works and to be fair in personnel administration.
• The Eighth U.S. Army Commander, General Van Fleet, states that it is impossible for the ROK Army to implement a great war with the Communist Forces by itself due to the

numerical inferiority.

October 24, Friday (September 6, by lunar calendar, 癸卯日 Black Rabbit) Clear and Windy
853 Day of the War

War Situation
- The ROK Army at White Horse Hill withdraws from the top of the mountain due to an attack of the Communist Forces.
- Troops of the British Commonwealth repulse the Chinese Communist Forces attacking Little Gibraltar Hill in western Yeoncheon.
- The Busan POW camp command announces that a riot occurred due to contumacy of POWs against the authorities in October 23, and 23 POWs are wounded.

At Home
- The anniversary of the United Nations Day is held in Busan.
- *Pyongyang Broadcasting* reports that the Foreign Secretary of North Korea, Pak Hon-yong, sent the chairman of the UN General Assembly a message that they would reject the decision of any issues related to Korea without the presence of the representative of North Korea.

October 25, Saturday (September 7, by lunar calendar, 甲辰日 Blue Dragon) Cloudy and Clear
854 Day of the War

War Situation
- The ROK Army recaptures Pinpoint Hill at the end of a fierce four-hour combat.
- The UN Forces repulse the Chinese Communist Forces searching and attacking Bunker Hill near Panmunjom.
- A Sabre fighter of the UN Forces shoots down two MIG fighters of the Communist Forces near Sinuiju.

At Home
- The National Assembly Plenary Session holds urgent meeting to discuss the convening, commandeering and labor draft of the Second Peoples' Force.
- The authority of the UN Forces returns the second pier of Busan Harbor to the Korea Government.
- The Namwon broadcasting station opens with the call sign HLKL and the output is 500w and the frequency is 1030kHz.

October 26, Sunday (September 8, by lunar calendar, 乙巳日 Blue Snake) Clear and Cloudy
855 Day of the War

War Situation

- The UN Forces repulse the North Korean Forces attacking Heartbreak Ridge on the eastern frontline.
- The UN Forces occupy Yoke Hill in the northern tip of the Sniper Ridge.
- An F-86 Saber fighter shoots down two MIG Jet fighters of the Communist Forces over North Korea.
- A squadron of B-29 fighter bombers attacks a supply center and a command center near Pyongyang.

At Home
- Two companies of the U.S. Army are deployed into the Jeju POW camp to stop the military training of POWs.

October 27, Monday (September 9, by lunar calendar, 丙午日 Red Horse) Cloudy and Clear
856 Day of the War

War Situation
- The UN Forces repulse the Communist Forces attacking Sniper Ridge and Triangle Hill.
- A fierce combat develops near Panmunjom on the western frontline.
- The U.S. Marine Corps recapture Hook Ridge overnight.

At Home
- The National Assembly Plenary Session approves a motion to request attendance of all members of the Cabinet and to question the overall Government affairs.
- The national convention to condemn marine transgressions of Japanese ships is held.
- The representatives convention of the National Fisheries Organizations declares a statement to maintain the sovereign power line of the sea.

October 28, Tuesday (September 10, by lunar calendar, 丁未日 Red Sheep) Cloudy and Clear
857 Day of the War

War Situation
- The UN Forces repulse all attacks of the Communist Forces to outposts near White Horse Hill and to outer covering positions of Sniper Ridge and Jihyeong Ridge in the middle frontline.
- The U.S. Marine Corps recaptures the outer covering positions captured by the Chinese Communist Forces in northeastern Panmunjom.
- A squad of fighters of the UN Forces attacks outposts and a supply center of the Communist Forces.
- The command of POW camps of the UN Forces announces that two companies of the U.S. Army are being deployed into the Geoje POW camp to stop the military training of POWs of the Communist Forces. A POW is killed and six POWs are wounded.

At Home

- The National Assembly constitutes a special investigation committee on the case of tungsten exporting dollar and receives the 4th report.
  : The entrepreneurs include the political funds and into the cost accounting inflicting damages of 40.05 billion won to farmers, the poor people in the cities.
- The National Assembly Plenary Session passes a resolution on organizing the members of the special investigation committee for the case of tungsten exporting dollars.
- The Korean Language Society publishes the 4th Grand Korean Dictionary.

Overseas

- The Taiwan Nationalist Government forces engage in a battle with three steamers and 15 warships of the Chinese communist forces for about 12 hours at the entrance of Zhu Jiang River (or Pearl River).

October 29, Wednesday (September 11, by lunar calendar, 戊申日 Yellow Monkey) Clear
858 Day of the War

War Situation

- UN Forces repulse the Communist Forces attacking the Triangle Hill.
- UN Forces recapture an outpost in the White Horse Hill in the western frontline.
- UN Forces Commander, Clark, and the U.S. Ambassador to Japan, Murphy, inspect the units on the frontline.

At Home

- The National Assembly Plenary Session announces a no-confidence resolution against the incumbent Cabinet members on September 26 according to the decision of the special committee to treat the tungsten exporting dollar case.
- The administrator of the Foreign Procurement Bureau announces that the Government will directly purchase foreign rice except for special cases.

October 30, Thursday (September 12, by lunar calendar, 己酉日 Yellow Rooster) Clear and Cloudy
859 Day of the War

War Situation

- The Chinese Communist Forces attack three outposts of the UN Forces west of Triangle Hill.
- 2,000 soldiers of the Chinese Communist Forces launch a nighttime attack on Triangle Hill held by the UN Forces.
- A squadron of B-29 fighter bombers of the UN Forces attacks a supply center of the Communist Forces-in Unpari in the west coast and Songsari in Wonsan.

At Home

- The National Assembly Plenary Session passes the resolution for the quorum of the non-confidence resolution of the Cabinet members.
- The Integrated Elementary School in Seoul is dissolved and every elementary school has been restored to the original state.
- A group of armed spies make a sudden attack on the Seogwipo hydroelectric power plant and destroy generating facilities.

Overseas
- The U.S. State Department releases confidential information.
  : The Eighth U.S. Army Commander, General Van Fleet, suggested in April to increase the South Korean military Forces to 20 divisions but then the U.S. Forces Commander Ridgway opposed it.

October 31, Friday (September 13, by lunar calendar, 庚戌日 White Dog) Rainy and Clear
860 Day of the War

War Situation
- The POW Command of the UN Forces announces that 178 POWs are injured due to riots in four locations in the Geoje POW camp.
- The liaison officer of the Communist Forces delivers a letter notifying the map indicating the locations of the POW camps and the revised names and ranges of the POW camps in North Korea.

At Home
- The Ministry of National Defense and the Ministry of Social Affairs announce a plan to establish a return-to-the-soil foundation for disabled veterans.
- The Bank of Korea announces that the amount of currency in circulation is 845 billion won.

November 1, Saturday (September 14, by lunar calendar, 辛亥日 White Pig) Clear, Cloudy, Clear and Windy
861 Day of the War

War Situation
- An attack unit of the UN Forces attacks the Chinese Communist Forces' Hill at the Sacheon River at night.
- The British aircraft carrier, HMS Ocean, returns home after completing its term of duty in the seas off Korea.
- A squadron of fighters of the UN Forces destroys 90 artillery units behind Jeogyeog Hill and Triangle Hill.

At Home
- The Cabinet Meeting decides on a construction bill of a plate glass plant and to loan 18.9 billion won from the Government .
- The Minister of National Defense, Sin Tae-yeong, states on Air Force Chief of Staff Maj. Gen. Kim Jung-ryul was transfered to the dean of the Air Force Academy at his own wish and the Maj. Gen. Choe Yong-deok, is nominated for the replacement.

November 2, Sunday (September 15, by lunar calendar, 壬子日 Black Rat) Clear
862 Day of the War

War Situation
- A seesaw combat continues at Sniper Ridge and Triangle Ridge.
- An F-86 jet fighter shoots down a MIG Jet fighter and destroys two MIG fighters over North Korea.
- A squad of B-86 fighter bombers air-attacks supply areas and military facilities near Pyongyang.

At Home
- The police report that 135 Koreans out of 250 Koreans who attempted illegal entries to Japan were forcibly returned to Korea on October 23 to face summary trials.
- The representative of Korea, Paik Nak-jun, leaves Korea to attend the session of the UNESCO General Assembly.

Overseas
- The delegate of Mexico to the UN General Assembly submits a new resolution for transferring POWs.
- The representative of France emphasizes free repatriation of the POWs.

- The UN Forces Command announces that the *U.S.S Oriskany* of Task Force 77 has entered the Korean War.

November 3, Monday (September 16, by lunar calendar, 癸丑日 Black Ox) Clear
863 Day of the War

War Situation
- The UN Forces repulse the Communist Forces searching and attacking positions of eastern Heartbreak Ridge on the eastern frontline.
- The ROK Army repulses the Chinese Communist Forces attacking Sniper Ridge.
- B-29 planes attack supply bases of the Communist Forces in Anju and Seopo-ri in northern Pyongyang.

At Home
- The Minister of Agriculture and Forestry, Sin Jung-mok, announces the control of the rice-polishing mills.
- The ROK Army establishes the 71st and 72nd chemical duty company military unit for the first time.
- A group of armed spies penetrate into Chungju and sets fire to the district office.
- The UN Forces repulse a company of the Chinese Communist Forces for the Sniper Ridge.

November 4, Tuesday (September 17, by lunar calendar, 甲寅日 Blue Tiger) Clear
864 Day of the War

War Situation
- The entire frontline is experiencing a lull in the fighting.

At Home
- The Vice-Secretary of State of Italy visits President Syngman Rhee.
- The Government appoints Jin Seung-nok as Chairman of the Higher Civil Service Examination Board.
- The Commander of the Marine Corps of the Pacific Ocean Area, General Hart, visits Korea.

November 5, Wednesday (September 18, by lunar calendar, 乙卯日 Blue Rabbit) Clear
865 Day of the War

War Situation
- Combat starts at Gimhwa Ridge.
- Combat continues in the Sniper Ridge and the Triangle Hill.
- A squadron of B-29 bombers attacks a supply area of the Communist Forces 54.7 km east

of Pyongyang.

At Home

- The Public Information Office denies the rumor that has been spreading recently that the Government is evacuating Chuncheon Citizens.
- The security department and the Provost Marshal headquarters of the Eighth U.S. Army agree that the Korean National Police will in be charge of supervising the U.S. military supplies owned by Koreans.

Overseas

- The representative of India submits a draft resolution to resolve a stalemate in the Armistice Conference of the Korean War.
- The outcome of the U.S. Presidential Election is that the General of the Army, Eisenhower, is elected with overwhelmingly votes exceeding the majority votes of 266 and Nixon, the Republicans candidate, is elected as Vice-President.

November 6, Thursday (September 19, by lunar calendar, 丙辰日 Red Dragon) Clear
866 Day of the War

War Situation

- A unit of the UN Forces repulses the Chinese Communist Forces attacking Jackson Hill in northeastern Cheorwon.
- A squadron of fighter bombers of the UN Forces destroys five bridges in Cheongcheon River.

At Home

- President Syngman Rhee formally invites the president-elect, Eisenhower, to Korea via the Embassy of the Republic of Korea in Washington.
- The Minister of Justice, Seo Sang-hwan, announces the findings on the investigation of the case of tungsten exporting dollars by the prosecution authorities
  : The trader illegally charged 230,000 won per sack, higher than the official price set by the Government in the free disposition of wheat flour and fertilizer.

November 7, Friday (September 20, by lunar calendar, 丁巳日 Red Snake) Clear and Windy
867 Day of the War

War Situation

- The U.S.S Missouri attacks military facilities of the Communist Forces in Seocheon in the east coast.
- A squadron of Sabre jet fighters of the UN Forces shoots down a MIG jet fighter and four MIG Jet fighters in the skies between Jeongju and the Yalu River.

At Home

- U.S. Assistant Undersecretary of State, Rosenberg, visits Korea.
- The Minister of Agriculture and Forestry, Sin Jung-mok, states at the National Assembly that the 1953 food shortage will be 6,230,000 seok, but the Government will receive 4,500,000 seok of food foreign countries.

Overseas
- The delegate of Israel in the UN General Assembly suggests immediate cessation of the Korean War and resumption of the Armistice Conference.
- The delegate of Egypt in the UN Political Committee informally suggests release of POWs in the neutral zone.

November 8, Saturday (September 21, by lunar calendar, 戊午日 Yellow Horse) Clear and Windy
868 Day of the War

War Situation
- The UN Forces repulse the Chinese Communist Forces attacking the Jihyeong Ridge.
- A squadron of B-29 bombers of the UN Forces attacks Jinnampo, Hwangju, and Supung at dawn.

At Home
- The National Assembly plenary session decides a motion to examine the contents of the speech by the National Assembly lawmaker Yun Chi-yeong.
- Daejeon Broadcasting holds the building dedication ceremony of its high-power broadcasting facility.

November 9, Sunday (September 22, by lunar calendar, 己未日 Yellow Sheep) Clear and Cloudy
869 Day of the War

War Situation
- The UN Forces repulse the Communist Forces conducting reconnoitering attacks a few times for outposts in the Jihyeong Ridge and Gorangpo.
- U.S. Assistant Secretary of Defense, Rosenberg, inspects the frontline.

At Home
- The Cabinet Meeting decides to release 50 billion won to purchase the rice to curb a rice price hike.
- A group of armed spies invade an area between the Mulgum station and the Wondong Station and engage the railroad police for two hours.

Overseas
- The U.S. State Department approves the bill to expand the Korean Army.
- The U.S. Assistant Secretary of Defense, Rosenberg, visits Korea and has an important meeting with President Syngman Rhee.

November 10, Monday (September 23, by lunar calendar, 庚申日 White Monkey) Clear and Cloudy
870 Day of the War

War Situation
- The UN Forces repulse an attack on Sniper Ridge by a company of the Chinese Communist Forces.
- An Infantry unit of the Chinese Communist Force penetrates into Pork Chop Hill between the Bulmo Hill and the T-type Hill in western Cheorwon.
- A squadron of B-29 fighter bombers attacks a collecting point of military troops and a supply base in Sinanju and Gangdong.

At Home
- The National Assembly Plenary Session passes the "Amendment Bill to the Registration Tax Act," "the amendment bill to the Inheritance Tax Law" and "the motion for the pledge to observe the UNESCO Charter."
- The Minister of Transport, Kim Seok-kwan, organizes the Maritime Commission under the direct control of the President to inspect vessels and to examine the qualification of sailors.

November 11, Tuesday (September 24, by lunar calendar, 辛酉日 White Rooster) Rainy, Clear and Windy

871 Day of the War

War Situation
- UN Forces repulse the Communist Forces' attack Three Hills in the eastern frontline.
- UN Forces repulse the Chinese Communist Forces attacking Pork Chop Hill in western Cheorwon.
- A B-29 squadron attacks Sinuiju and Sinanju.

At Home
- The National Assembly Plenary Session passes the approval of the financial and economic emergency action to increase resale prices of government monopoly items.
- The Ministry of National Defense postpones the draft of 5,000 teachers of all the primary schools.

November 12, Wednesday (September 25, by lunar calendar, 壬戌日 Black Dog) Rainy and Windy

872 Day of the War

War Situation
- The ROK Army recaptures Pinpoint Hill on Sniper Ridge.
- A squadron of B-29 fighter bombers attacks the Daedonggang Bridge in Pyongyang.

At Home

Soldiers of the 9th Division of the ROK Army injured in combat. (November 10, 1952)

- The Government decides to redeem the bonds issued by Europe and the U.S. council of the Republic of Korea in 1919.
- The representative of the 7th UNESCO General Assembly, Paik Nak-jun, is dispatched
- The ROK Army gains control over Pinpoint Hill after fierce combat.

Overseas
- The UN representative of Korea issues a statement on request of the release of POWs and the unity of territory.
- 275 U.S. Airplanes have violated the border of Liaotung 61 times. (Nov. 12-27)

November 13, Thursday (September 26, by lunar calendar, 癸亥日 Black Pig) Rainy, Cloudy and Windy

873 Day of the War

War Situation
- The Chinese Communist Forces attack the UN Forces in the Sniper Ridge at night.
- A squadron of B-29 fighter bombers attacks the Cheolsan military facility and a supply center of the Communist Forces in Seopori, north of Pyongyang.
- A squadron of B-26 bombers conducts a nighttime attack on the Communist forces' supply center and supply route.

At Home
- The National Assembly Plenary Session passes "the bill of the Chambers of Commerce and Industry Act" and "the resolution to organize the special committee for preparing the visit of the next U.S. President, the General of the Army Eisenhower."
- The Minister of Agriculture and Forestry, Sin Jung-mok, states on the organization of the

Refugees reaching out their hands to get the relief goods handed out by soldiers of the U.S. Forces.(November 15, 1952)

Farmers Association.

November 14, Friday (September 27, by lunar calendar, 甲子日 Blue Rat) Rainy, Cloudy and Windy
874 Day of the War

War Situation
- A U.S. boxcar transport plane carrying 44 soldiers and crew collides with a mountain about 29km northeast of Seoul and all people aboard are killed.
- The liaison officers of both the UN Forces and the Communist Forces investigate the case of the death of an American nurse killed by a bullet of the Communist Forces on the road between Munsan and Panmunjom on November 12.

At Home
- President Syngman Rhee requests approval of Lee Gap-seong, after designating him as Prime Minister.
- The Cabinet Meeting decides on the fall-harvested grain sales and selling price.

Overseas
- The France and Vietnam allied Forces repulse the North Vietnamese Forces' attacks at

Phat Diem in the southeastern triangle zone of the Song Koi River.

November 15, Saturday (September 28, by lunar calendar, 乙丑日 Blue Ox) Clear, Cloudy and Clear
875 Day of the War

War Situation
- A troop of the UN Forces repulses a reconnaissance attack by a company of the North Korean Communist Forces in the southern Goseong at dawn.
- A troop of the ROK Army occupies Pinpoint Hill on Sniper Ridge again.
- The UN Navy with the U.S.S Missouri as the flagship resumes bombard the Wonsan Harbor.
- A squadron of B-29 fighter bombers attacks Hamheung.

At Home
- The Ministry of Foreign Affairs orders tighter enforcement on curtailing naturalization of of Koreans to foreign countries to all the diplomatic and consular offices.
- The head office of the Federation of Korean Residents in Japan requests the Ministry of Foreign Affairs to dispatch an Education Attaché to the Korean Mission in Japan.

November 16, Sunday (September 29, by lunar calendar, 丙寅日 Red Tiger) Clear, Cloudy and Windy
876 Day of the War

War Situation
- A troop of the UN Forces repulses attacks by two companies of the Chinese Communist Forces for the Pinpoint Hill on Sniper Ridge.
- A troop of the Chinese Communist Forces attacks the Hook Hill near the Imjin River on the western frontline.

At Home
- The Cabinet Meeting decides to establish Central Preparation Committee for Welcoming the president-elect, Eisenhower.
  The composition of the Central Preparattion Committee includes a wide range of civilians, the legislature, the judiciary and the administration.
- The Ministry of Trade and Industry Ministry suspends all import permits for the preferential foreign exchange according to Announcement No. 67.

Overseas
- The U.S. Atomic Energy Commission announces the successful test of the hydrogen bomb on Eniwetok Island.

November 17, Monday (October 1, by lunar calendar, 丁卯日 Red Rabbit) Clear

877 Day of the War

War Situation

- The UN Forces repulse a reconnoitering skirmish of the Chinese Communist Forces seeking to capture Sniper Hill.
- A squadron of B-29 fighter bombers attacks an ammunition dump in Pyongyang and a smelter near the Yalu River.

At Home

- The Liberal Party outside the Assembly submits the list of 67 members including Bae Eun-hui and completes the registration of a parliamentary negotiation body.
- The Ministry of Trade and Industry requests foreign traders to actively use Korean ships for exports and imports.

November 18, Tuesday (October 2, by lunar calendar, 戊辰日 Yellow Dragon) Clear and Windy

878 Day of the War

War Situation

- The Chinese Communist Forces occupy the Rocky Point Hill of Sojiyeong Ridge.
- The Black Watch troop of the British Forces repulse attacks of the Chinese Communist Forces for the Hook Hill in the western frontline at night.
- Three Phantom fighters which made sorties from the U.S. aircraft carrier, U.S.S Oriskany, shoot down two MIG 15 fighters and damage one MIG 15 fighter over the east coast.

At Home

- The Minister of Home Affairs, Jin Heon-sik, denies the rumor of the return of the evacuated Government;
  The government declares that the news of the partial return of the Government to Seoul from Busan is no more than a strengthening the branch offices in Seoul, and spreading such rumors may well be punishable.
- The Ministry of Foreign Affairs states that the U.S. Government approved entry permits for 100 migrants from Korea every year.

Overseas

- The representatives of the United States, the UK and France show their positions toward the compromise proposal of India;
- The U.S. has a high probability of opposition and the U.K. will review prudentially and France will agree in principle.

November 19, Wednesday (October 3, by lunar calendar, 己巳日 Yellow Snake) Cloudy, Clear and Windy

879 Day of the War

War Situation

- The UN Forces repulse continuous searches and attacks by the Chinese Communist Forces.
- The U.S. Far East Air Force strongly attacks the Communist Forces' dominating area up to 32.1 km south of the Yalu River.

At Home

- The newly appointed U.S. Ambassador to Korea Briggo arrives at Gimpo airport.
- The Chief of Staff of the U.S. Air Force, General Vandenberg, states that if the attack order to Manchuria is given, the UN Air Force will immediately carry it out.

November 20, Thursday (October 4, by lunar calendar, 庚午日 White Horse) Clear and Windy
880 Day of the War

War Situation

- The ROK Army repulses a battalion attack by the Communist Forces for Pinpoint Hill of the Sniper Ridge after hand-to-hand fighting.
- A squadron of F-86 Sabre fighters of the U.S. Air Force shoots down five MIG-15 Jet fighters of the Communist Forces and destroys one MIG-15 Jet fighter of the Communist Forces over North Korea.
- A squadron of B-28 fighter bombers attacks Gunuri and Seoncheon.

At Home

- The National Assembly Plenary Session rejects the approval of the appointment of the Prime Minister, Lee Gap-seong by 76 votes to 94.
- The Monetary Policy Committee advises government to enact "the law for money lending business and profit."
recommends to the Government to enact "the law on money lending business and interest regulation.

November 21, Friday (October 5, by lunar calendar, 辛未日 White Sheep) Clear, Cloudy and Clear
881 Day of the War

War Situation

- A small unit of the Chinese Communist Forces attacks the UN Forces' position on Russell Hill in the northern Triangle Hill and Pinpoint Hill of Sniper Ridge at night.
- A squadron of B-29 fighter bombers attacks the military assembly place and supply base near Wonsan and the south Huicheon railroad bridge.
- A squadron of F-86 Sabre fighters shoots down a MIG jet fighter over North Korea.

At Home

- Seven Ministers of the Ministry of Agriculture and Forestry, the Ministry of Finance, the

Ministry of National Defense, etc. issue an order for the Grain Saving with co-signing to every city and province.

- The Director of Public Information Office states the prohibition of reporting on the visit of the U.S. President Eisenhower except the official announcement of the Public Information Office.

Overseas

- The Australian representative of the UN Political Committee suggests discussion of the Indian proposal first.
- The representatives of 21 countries which supported the U.S. proposal for exchanging POWs meet to decide their position on the Indian proposal.

November 22, Saturday (October 6, by lunar calendar, 壬申日 Black Monkey) Clear, Cloudy and Rainy
882 Day of the War

War Situation

- The ROK Army repulses attacks of the Chinese Communist Forces for possession of Rocky Point Hill on Sniper Ridge.
- A reconnaissance party of the UN Forces engages the enemy on the road between Geumseong and Gimhwa.
- A squadron of B-29 fighter bombers attacks Haeju and Pyongyang.

At Home

- The National Assembly Plenary Session passes "the amendment bill of the License Tax Law," and, "the amendment bill of the Corporate Tax Act" and "the Examination of the Question of Approval and the Legal Basis for the Agreement on Economic Coordination."

November 23, Sunday (October 7, by lunar calendar, 癸酉日 Black Rooster) Cloudy and Rainy
883 Day of the War

War Situation

- The Chinese Communist Forces attacks Pinpoint Hill on Sniper Ridge.
- A squadron of F-86 Sabre fighters shoots down a MIG-15 fighter of the Communist Forces over the Yalu River.
- A squadron of B-26 fighter bombers destroys 200 cargo trucks of the Communist Forces with bombing of the North Korean supply route at night.

November 24, Monday (October 8, by lunar calendar, 甲戌日 Blue Dog) Rainy and Windy
884 Day of the War

War Situation

- Troops of the UN Forces repulse a dawn attack by the Chinese Communist Forces on the UN Forces' positions on Sniper Ridge.
- A squadron of B-26 light bombers destroys 80 supply vehicles in Wonsan, Yangdok and Pyongyang.

At Home
- The National Assembly Plenary Session passes "the bill of the Economic Coordination

Children getting inoculated in the Munsan refugee camp (Nov. 22, 1952. 11. 22)

Special Accounts Law," "the amendment bill of the Sessional Indemnity for the member of the National Assembly," "the amendment bill of the Foreign Capital Special Account Law" and "the resolution on the representative on Korean resident in Japan for attending the National Assembly."

- The Five Country Committee approves U.S.$70 million of the Korea Rebuilding Expenses and promises to continue to offer U.S.$250 million.
- The Seoul Metropolitan City Mayor announces the city's readiness of security measures for the visit to Korea by U.S. President Eisenhower.

November 25, Tuesday (October 9, by lunar calendar, 乙亥日 Blue Pig) Cloudy, Clear and Windy
885 Day of the War

War Situation
- The Australian and British Forces on the western frontline return to base after heavily damaging the Communist Forces' positions.
- A squadron of B-26 fighter bombers destroys 155 supply vehicles of the Communist Forces with night bombing.

At Home
- The National Assembly Plenary Session approves the resolution on sending a message to President Eisenhower to request reinforcement of the Korean Army, Navy and Air Forces.
- The Hwacheon Power Plant holds the building dedication ceremony of restoration work in the presence of the U.S. President.

November 26, Wednesday (October 10, by lunar calendar, 丙子日 Red Rat) Clear and Cloudy
886 Day of the War

War Situation
- A light reconnoitering skirmish happens near Ganseong and the northwestern basin on the eastern frontline.
- The UN Forces repulse the Chinese Communist Forces attacking Jackson Hill in northeastern Cheorwon.
- Allied aircraft comprising 140 F-80 and F-84 fighters of the UN Forces heavily bomb the Wonsan military assembly point.
- A squadron of B-29 fighter bombers attacks the Haeju and Pyongyang supply area.

At Home
- The National Assembly Plenary Session passes "the motion of the amount of pension according to the Families of the War Dead and the Disabled Veterans' Pension Act" and agrees on 600,000 won of the Government proposal as the amount of pension according to the Families of the War Dead and the Disabled Veterans' Pension Act.

- The National Assembly passes "the bill of the National Life Insurances Law" and "the Post-Office Annuity Law."

Overseas
- The U.S. Air Force bombs four detached garrison buildings of the 11th POW camps of the Chinese Communist Forces.

November 27, Thursday (October 11, by lunar calendar, 丁丑日 Red Ox) Cloudy and Rainy
887 Day of the War

War Situation
- A clash occurs at Sniper Hill.
- A squadron of B-29 fighter bombers attacks the Haeju supply base and a railroad near Pyongyang.

At Home
- The National Assembly Plenary Session passes "the legislative bill for elevating the Geoje-eup to a county."
- The Minister of Home Affairs, Jin Heon-sik, and the Minister of Justice, Seo Sang-hwan issue a joint statement urging to write the name and address when sending complaints or proposals on Government policy.

Overseas
- In the UN Political Committee, the representatives of 11 countries including Canada, France, Australia, etc., makes supportive comments on the Indian proposal.
- The spokesman of the U.S. Representative states that the U.S. Government supports the amendment proposed by India.

November 28, Friday (October 12, by lunar calendar, 戊寅日 Yellow Tiger) Rainy, Windy, Clear and Windy
888 Day of the War

War Situation
- Minor clashes occur in Yeoncheon and western Mundeung-ri of the eastern frontline.
- 49 B-29 fighter bombers attack the traffic and supply center and the airfield of the Communist Forces in Uijuro and Sinuiju.

At Home
- The National Assembly passes the amendment bill of the National Assembly Law.

Overseas
- The Foreign Minister of North Korea, Pak Hon Yong, states the November 23 proposal of the Soviet Union in the UN Political Committee to peacefully resolve the Korean issues is accepted, Pyongyang Broadcasting Service reports.

- The Chinese Foreign Minister, Zhou Enlai, states that the only way to resolve the Korean issue is through the proposal by the Soviet Union.

November 29, Saturday (October 13, by lunar calendar, 己卯日 Yellow Rabbit) Clear
889 Day of the War

War Situation
- The UN Forces repulse the Communist Forces attacking Pinpoint Hill on Sniper Ridge.
- The National Assembly passes "the bill of the Customs Law" without any amendment.

At Home
- The National Assembly Plenary Session passes the proposal for organizing the special accounting of relief budget for the War Dead Soldiers and Policemen and military expenses.
- 20 independent assemblymen including Gwak Sang-hun register a negotiation body as an independent group.

November 30, Sunday (October 14, by lunar calendar, 庚辰日 White Dragon) Cloudy and Rainy
890 Day of the War

Soldiers of the Eighth U.S. Army eating a Thanksgiving turkey dish in a bunker (1952. 11. 27).

War Situation

• The UN Air Force has made 930 sorties and has bombed supply places of the Communist Forces in Haeju, Sariwon and Gowon, etc.

• A squadron of B-29 fighter bombers attacks the Hawasalli supply area of the Communist Forces in southern Wonsan.

At Home

• The National Assembly approves the Accession to the International Civil Aviation Agreement (the Chicago Convention).

• The Government revises "the Regulations on the Division of Duties of the Ministry of Postal Service" and "the Job Assignment of the Communication Office."

• The theater company, Geukyeop, is founded and performs the first play, "Wailing," written by Yu Chi-jin.

December 1, Monday (October 15, by lunar calendar, 辛巳日 White Snake) Rainy, Cloudy and Windy

891 Day of the War

War Situation
- A squadron of Shooting Star fighters of the UN Air Force heavily attacks a supply center of the Communist Forces in the western frontline.
- The liaison officer of the Communist Forces hands over a letter to the liaison officer of the UN Forces to complain that a UN airplane bombed the 9th Suncheon POW camps.

At Home
- The National Assembly Plenary Session passes "the amendment bill of the Commodity Tax" which is drastically increasing the luxury goods taxes and the license tax.
- The Ministry of Postal Service begins to receive the International telecommunication service bills in U.S. dollars only.
- A state of emergency is declared in the three southern provinces.

December 2, Tuesday (October 16, by lunar calendar, 壬午日 Black Horse) Rainy, Clear and Rainy

892 Day of the War

War Situation
- The UN Forces repulse the Communist Forces' attack on Rocky Hill.
- The Communist Forces attack the ROK Army's position in the middle frontline and exchange artillery duels between their artillery corps.

At Home
- President Syngman Rhee is interviewed by foreign journalists.
  He opposes the Armistice compromise of India and insists on driving the Communist Forces back to the border.
- The National Assembly decides to dispatch the consolation party in the frontline.

Overseas
- The U.S. Secretary of Defense, Robert, approves rejection of the compulsory repatriation of POWs at a press conference.
- The Chinese Government suggests repatriating 30,000 Japanese in China if the Japanese Government provides ships to transport them.

December 3, Wednesday (October 17, by lunar calendar, 癸未日 Black Sheep) Clear and Cloudy

War Situation
- The ROK Army recaptures Pinpoint Hill in the middle frontline.
- Brig. Gen. D.A. Kendrew is appointed as brigade Commander of the first Division of the British Commonwealth Forces.

At Home
- President Syngman Rhee has a summit conference with U.S. President-elect, Eisenhower.
- The National Assembly Plenary Session passes "the first supplementary revised budget bill for 1952" and "the proposition for ceasing the demolition order for illegal structures."

December 4, Thursday (October 18, by lunar calendar, 甲申日 Blue Monkey) Clear
894 Day of the War

War Situation
- The ROK Army completely recaptures all the positions which were held by the Communist Forces on Sniper Ridge.
- The representative of the UN Forces in the Armistice Conference notifies the liaison officer of the Communist Forces of the establishment of a POW camp for the Communist Forces.

At Home
- The National Assembly Plenary Session passes "the motion of the Government Loan Guarantees for the salvage work fund of the ship, *Purudo*, in the Korea Shipbuilding Corporation."
- The UN Forces command issues permits to go out fishing north of the 38th parallel.

Overseas
- The representative of the Soviet Union, Vyshinsky, requests to clarify the exact definition of "Act

The president-elect of the United States, General Eisenhower visits Korea. (December 2, 1952)

451

Orphans in the orphanage are pleased as they received shoes (1952. 12. 3)

of Aggression"to the judiciary committee.

December 5, Friday (October 19, by lunar calendar, 乙酉日 Blue Rooster) Clear
895 Day of the War

War Situation
- The ROK Army repulses the Chinese Communist Forces attacking Pinpoint Hill.
- 11 fighter planes of the Communist Forces try to attack Seoul at night but are repulsed by anti-aircraft batteries of the UN Forces.

At Home
- U.S. President-elect Eisenhower visits Gyeongmudae to call on President Syngman Rhee and has an 30-minute meeting.
- The Air Force Chief of Staff, Choe Yong-deok, has a meeting with Eisenhower and requests reinforcement of Korea's Air Force.
- The National Assembly Plenary Session passes "the proposition for releasing the Korean War criminals."

December 6, Saturday (October 20, by lunar calendar, 丙戌日 Red Dog) Clear
896 Day of the War

War Situation

- The ROK Army repulses the Communist Forces' attack on Sniper Ridge.
- The UN airplanes make sorties and destroy military assembly points and supply bases of the Communist Forces in North Korea.

December 7, Sunday (October 21, by lunar calendar, 丁亥日 Red Pig) Clear
897 Day of the War

War Situation
- The Far East Air Force Command lifts the flight prohibition order to the UN cargo planes which was issued during the visit of President-elect Eisenhower.
- The UN POW camp command announces that Communists tried to stir up a riot in the Geoje POW camp but were quelled and a POW who tried to escape was killed and a POW was wounded.

At Home
- The Seoul Police Bureau installs two-way radios to police station jeeps.

Overseas
- The British and Japanese Government start to negotiate an Aviation Agreement between both countries.
- The French Forces Command in Indochina announces that the largest offensive and defensive battle is developing in Nha San in six years.
- President Truman appeals to the people for strengthening of the national defense in the 11th memorial day of the attack on Pearl Harbor.

December 8, Monday (October 22, by lunar calendar, 戊子日 Yellow Rat) Cloudy and Rainy
898 Day of the War

War Situation
- A squadron of fighter bombers of the UN Air Force attacks the supply network of the Communist Forces in North Korea.
- A POW is killed and a POW wounded in a secret meeting in the Geoje POW camp.

At Home
- Pyongyang Broadcasting in North Korea blames that the visit to Korea of U.S. President-elect Eisenhower would enlarge the war.

December 9, Tuesday (October 23, by lunar calendar, 己丑日 Yellow Ox) Cloudy and Rainy
899 Day of the War

War Situation
- The ROK Army repulses the Communist Forces' nine nighttime attacks and holds Sniper Ridge.

- Aircraft carrier planes of the UN Task Fleet have made 352 sorties and bomb two points on the main railhead near the border between China and North Korea, Najin and Hoeryong classification yards in eastern North Korea.

At Home
- President Syngman Rhee requests unity to solidify the national sovereignty.
- The Pacific Sugar Manufacturing Company in Chicago remits $30 mil. of relief funds for injured soldiers to President Syngman Rhee.

December 10, Wednesday (October 24, by lunar calendar, 庚寅日 White Tiger) Rainy, Clear and Windy

900 Day of the War

War Situation
- The Communist Forces hand over a complaint memorandum regarding a wounded POW and a killed POW who tried to escape to the UN Forces.

At Home
- A three man committee comprising the Minister of Finance, Maj. Gen. Heron and the representative of the UN Korean Reconstruction Agency, is established to promote the Korean Industrial Rehabilitation Work.
- The UN Korea Committee approves the Recovery Program of U.S.$70 million submitted by the UN Korean Reconstruction Agency and notifies the UN General Assembly.
- The whole electric power transmission is completely cut off as distribution lines, power cables, and electric poles in all over the country broke down due to the high snowfall for 9 days.

Overseas
- The UN Political Committee rejects the invitation for the delegate of Tunisia submitted by the delegate of Pakistan. (24 vs. 26)
- The NATO Military Committee decides that the goal of the Western Europe Defensive Strength is 98 Divisions.

December 11, Thursday (October 25, by lunar calendar, 辛卯日 White Rabbit) Clear, Cloudy, Clear and Windy

901 Day of the War

War Situation
- A 1st Division of the ROK Army engages near the Imjin River. (Nori and Betty high ground battle, December 11~13)

At Home
- The Army Chief of Staff, Paik Sun-yup, states that he handed over a long petition for

strengthening the fighting capacity of the ROK Army when Eisenhower visited Korea.
- The National University President Meeting is held by the Ministry of Education.

December 12, Friday (October 26, by lunar calendar, 壬辰日 Black Dragon) Clear and Windy
902 Day of the War

War Situation
- The ROK Army withdraws from Large and Small Nori Hill after inflicting heavy damage on the Communist Forces.
- The Eighth U.S. Army Commander, General Van Fleet, states that the UN Forces are fully prepared for the winter attacks by the Communist Forces.
  He implies that two divisions of the ROK Army will join the war soon.

At Home
- The National Assembly Plenary Session adopts "the propositions of the extension of return-to-the-soil areas and the transfer of administrative authority in reclaimed areas."
- The representatives of 85 countries hold the public peace rally in Vienna and request ending of the Korean War.

December 13, Saturday (October 27, by lunar calendar, 癸巳日 Black Snake) Clear
903 Day of the War

War Situation
- The ROK Army completely recaptures Small-Nori Hill after 10 attacks and attacks the Large-Nori Hill.

At Home
- The Cabinet Meeting decides the Presidential Decree for dispatching Military Attachés to the Korean Missions abroad.
- The International Federation of Red Cross decides to urge exchanging POWs and the Armistice.
- The Eighth U.S. Army Commander, General Van Fleet, announces the reinforcement of three divisions of the ROK Army.

Overseas
- The UN Special Political Committee discusses the UN membership and the representative of Poland addresses the dissent from enlisting Korea and Japan.
- The executive committee of the International Red Cross approves the resolution of India about the POW issues. (15 vs. 2)

December 14, Sunday (October 28, by lunar calendar, 甲午日 Blue Horse) Clear, Cloudy and Clear

904 Day of the War

War Situation

- The ROK Army repulses the Chinese Communist Forces' attacks on Pinpoint Hill and Small-Nori Hill.
- The representative of the Communist Forces complains to the Armistice representative of the UN Forces that the UN airplanes attacked supply vehicles of the Communist Forces on December 13.

At Home

- The Agreement on Economic Cooperation between Korea and the United States is signed.
- The Ambassador of Korea to the United States reports to the acting Prime Minister that they have received U.S.$8,552,225.92 of the fourth UN repayments from the U.S. Government.

December 15, Monday (October 29, by lunar calendar, 乙未日 Blue Sheep) Clear, Cloudy, Clear and Windy

905 Day of the War

War Situation

- The Korean Army repulses the Meeting Communist Forces' nighttime attack on Rocky Hill and Triangle Hill on December 14.

At Home

- The Special Cabinet Meeting suggests to the President the rapid designation of the Prime Minister.
- Kim Il Sung announces that the systematic and ideological reinforcement of the Communist Party is the basis of its victory in the 5th Plenary Session of the Party's Central Committee.

December 16, Tuesday (October 30, by lunar calendar, 丙申日 Red Monkey) Clear and Windy

906 Day of the War

War Situation

- The ROK Army repulses the Communist Forces' attacks on Pinpoint Hill of the Sniper Ridge.
- An F-86 Sabre jet fighter shoots down a MIG-15 fighter over the Yalu River.
- The UN Air Force engages 180 aircraft of the Communist Forces north of the Cheongcheon River and shoots down four of them.
- The representative of the Communist Forces hands over a written protest for the Bongamdo POW case.

At Home

- The Ministry of Finance and the Ministry of Agriculture and Forestry agree to release 30 billion won of debt clearance fund of pre-harvest sales of rice crop.

December 17, Wednesday (November 1, by lunar calendar, 丁酉日 Red Rooster) Clear and Windy
907 Day of the War

War Situation

- Small attacks and reconnaissance attacks occur all over the frontline.
- The authority of the UN POW camp announces that the death toll of the Bongamdo POW incident reached 87.

At Home

- The Minister of National Defense, Sin Tae-yeong, announces the reinforcement policy of the ROK Army.
- North Korea rejects the UN proposal for the exchange of POWs.

December 18, Thursday (November 2, by lunar calendar, 戊戌日 Yellow Dog) Clear, Cloudy, Clear and Windy
908 Day of the War

War Situation

- Ground combats are light all along the frontline.
- The UN Force hands over a letter to admit the violation of a neutral zone and explains to the liaison officer that it was a contingent event.

At Home

- The members of the U.S. Foreign Relations Committee visit the President in Gyeongmudae.

Overseas

- The Iranian Government extends the period of the Martial Law which is till December 20 for two months.

December 19, Friday (November 3, by lunar calendar, 己亥日 Yellow Pig) Clear
909 Day of the War

War Situation

- A squadron of fighter bombers of the UN Air Force carries out the largest attack in a week to supply vehicles of the Communist Forces.
- The UN postal officer and the security officer of the Communist Forces exchange postal matters of POWs.

At Home

- The Rockefeller Foundation decides to give assistance to the Korean Language Society.
- "The Newspaper of the College of Liberal Arts and Sciences" (the representative: Kim Sang-gi) is registered.

Overseas

- The Special Political Committee of the UN General Assembly passes the U.S. draft resolution on the UN membership of Japan.(48 vs. 5)
- 13, 000 Japanese workers in the British Commonwealth Base in Japan enter strike at midnight.

December 20, Saturday (November 4, by lunar calendar, 庚子日 White Rat) Clear, Cloudy and Windy

910 Day of the War

War Situation

- Ground combats continue to dwindle.
- The UN POW camp Commander in Korea, Thomas W. Heren denies some domestic press reports that the Government is planning to take over the jurisdiction over POWs.

At Home

- The 15th National Assembly Plenary Session goes into session.
- The Government proclaims "the Chambers of Commerce and Industry Act."

December 21, Sunday (November 5, by lunar calendar, 辛丑日 White Ox) Clear

911 Day of the War

War Situation

- The UN Forces repulse the Communist Forces' attack on Bulmo Hill.

At Home

- The Government and the U.S. Army agree on the release of the anti-Communist POWs.
- The Foreign Minister of North Korea, Pak Hon-yong, notifies to the Chairman of the UN General Assembly, Pearson, that the U.S. Army killed 82 POWs of the Communist Forces in the Bongamdo POW camp.

Overseas

- The UN Rules Committee decides to introduce the condemnation of the Soviet Union for the Bongamdo POW incident as an official agenda.

December 22, Monday (November 6, by lunar calendar, 壬寅日 Black Tiger) Clear

912 Day of the War

War Situation

- Combats are light and propaganda wars continue.
- The armed Communist guerrillas disguising themselves as ROK soldiers attack the Gijang Station in the Donghae Nambu Line at 8 p.m.
- The UN Forces Commander, Clark, states that the Bongamdo POW case had been meticulously planned by the leader of POWs of the Communist Force.

At Home
- The Government declares "the amendment bill of the National Assembly law."
- The UN Korean Reconstruction Agency reveals that it has approved relief projects by 25 relief organizations since the outbreak of the Korean War.
- The standing committee of the Supreme People's Assembly of North Korea decides to reorganize administrative districts and abolishes 'myeon' and establishes laborer's district.

December 23, Tuesday (November 7, by lunar calendar, 癸卯日 Black Rabbit) Clear and Cloudy
913 Day of the War

War Situation
- Ground combats remain calm.
- A squadron of fighter bombers of the UN Forces attacks a military assembly point of the North Korean Forces and an airfield near Pyongyang.

At Home
- The National Assembly decides to dispatch a delegation to the U.S. President's inauguration in Washington.
- The National Assembly Plenary Session passes the bill of organizing the special committee for covering the 1953 budget deficit.
- The Gunsan post office starts the service of coastal shortwave radio work and wireless work.

December 24, Wednesday (November 8, by lunar calendar, 甲辰日 Blue Dragon) Clear and Windy
914 Day of the War

War Situation
- The UN Forces repulse the Chinese Communist Forces attacking outposts on the T-type Hill on the western frontline.
- A POW is killed due to the contumacy of order to dissolve illegal night assembly in the Geoje POW camp.

At Home
- President Syngman Rhee delivers a Christmas message to soldiers in Korea.
- The Public Information Office announces the decision of unconstitutionality by the

Constitutional Court of the 9th Special Measures Decree on dealing with crime under a state of emergency.

Overseas

- Pravda newspaper of the Soviet Union blames that the Bongamdo POW case is the result of the U.S. policy to continue the Korean War.

December 25, Thursday (November 9 by lunar calendar, 乙巳日 Blue Snake) Clear, Cloudy and Windy

915 Day of the War

War Situation

- 41 MIG-15 Jet fighters of the Communist Forces attempt to approach Seoul failed due to sorties of Sabre Jet fighters.
- Four MIG jet fighters launch air raids on Seoul.

At Home

- The Monetary Policy Committee decides to increase the retention rate of Bank of Korea bill in the deposit reserve of financial institutions.
- Pyongyang Broadcasting reports that Premier Kim Il Sung, stated that the military supplies of North Korea, such as ammunition, weapons and so on, had drastically increased due to the support of Communist countries.

December 26, Friday (November 10, by lunar calendar, 丙午日 Red Horse) Clear and Windy

916 Day of the War

War Situation

- Ground battles remain in a calm state.
- A squadron of B-29 bombers conduct a night bombardment on Jeongju, 32.1km north of Sinanju.
- One POW of the Communist Army is killed in the Geojedo POW camp.

At Home

- The Ministry of Health announces that total amount of the UN imported medicines reaches U.S.$2,050,000 excluding the quarnatine materials.
- A big fire breaks out in the Seomun Market, Daegu.

December 27, Saturday (November 11, by lunar calendar, 丁未日 Red Sheep) Clear, Cloudy, Clear and Windy

917 Day of the War

War Situation

- The Communist Forces continue to broadcast propaganda.

• A Greek transport plane which took off from the Korean base crushed killing all 14 passengers and crew.

At Home

• The Minister of Home Affairs, Jin Heon-sik, states the organization of the independent combatant police unit to make a full defensive preparation for sweeping Communist guerrillas.

Overseas

• The U.S. Department of Defense announces that 58,000 young men of conscription age will be called up for military service in the following February due to a rotating policy of the U.S. Forces.

December 28, Sunday (November 12, by lunar calendar, 戊申日 Yellow Monkey) Clear and Windy

918 Day of the War

War Situation

• 200 aircraft of the U.S. Air Force bomb the Communist Forces' assembly place in Pyongyang.
• A squadron of F-86 Sabre Jet fighters shoots down a MIG-15 fighter over Pyongyang.

At Home

• 200 bombers of the U.S. Air Force bomb the Communist Forces' assembly place in Pyongyang.

December 29, Monday (November 13, by lunar calendar, 己酉日 Yellow Rooster) Clear

919 Day of the War

War Situation

• The Communist Forces broadcast propaganda to start a full-scale attack on the UN Forces in Gimhwa in the middle frontline in January 4.
• The Chinese Communist Forces carry out a small-scale attack on Sniper Ridge and Triangle Hill.

At Home

• The Minister of Agriculture and Forestry, Sin Jung-mok, issues orders to every provincial governor to ration 30,000 seok of year-end grains for war victims and poor peoples.

Overseas

• The Foreign Minister of Japan signs the U.K.-Japan Aviation Agreement with the Ambassador of Great Britain to Japan
• The Ho Chi Minh Forces withdraw from northwestern Hanoi.

December 30, Tuesday (November 14, by lunar calendar, 庚戌日 White Dog) Clear and Cloudy
920 Day of the War

War Situation
- The U.S. battleship, U.S.S Missouri, bombards Cheongjin.
- B-29 fighter bombers drop 200 tons of bombs in Anju and Uijuro.

At Home
- The Director of the Public Information Office, states that President Syngman Rhee will not reject a meeting with any Japanese leaders if the UN Force Commander, General Clark, arranges it.
- The reverted forests and fields are to be nationalized.
- The Chief of Naval Operations, Son Won-il, states that the U.S. Navy expresses its policy to help the ROK Navy on request.

December 31, Wednesday (November 15, by lunar calendar, 辛亥日 White Pig) Clear and Windy
921 Day of the War

War Situation
- All the frontline is calm.

At Home
- The Ministry of Agriculture and Forestry announces that the grain production of the year is 15,523,514 *seok*.
- The census of the population is taken at midnight.
- The target of the relief activities is 9,128,351 persons.
- In the refugee area, the number of middle schools and high schools is 52 and the number of students is 28,000.
- The Federation of Red Cross appeals that the first step of the exchange of POWs is to exchange sick and wounded POWs.

I will oppose an international treaty that does not specify the unification of

Korea.

- President Syngman Rhee

1953

The Year of Black Snake Dangi 4286

January 1, Thursday (November 16, by lunar calendar, 壬子日 Black Rat) Clear and Windy
922 Day of the War

War Situation
- The UN Artillery Unit marks New Year's Day by launching a nighttime attack.
- The ROK Night Unit beats off the Communist Army's reconnoitering skirmish on the Sniper Ridge.

At Home
- President Syngman Rhee makes a New Year's statement stressing the need for accomplishment of the reunification of Korea.
- Kim Du-bong, Chairman of North Korean Supreme Committee releases a New Year's message.

Overseas
- The Governments of China and the USSR make a joint statement announcing that the U.S.S.R will transfer the operating rights of the Jangchun railroad to the Chinese Government.
- Hungary withdraws from UNESCO.

January 2, Friday (November 17, by lunar calendar, 癸丑日 Black Ox) Cloudy, Clear and Windy
923 Day of the War

War Situation
- The UN Forces repulse the assault of a company of Communist troops on the western front and repel several minor reconnoitering attacks of the enemy.
- The UN Forces severely bombard the seacoast of North Korea.
- The UN Air Forces drop 100 tons of high-yield bombs on the supply zones of the Communist Army in the southern part of Pyongyang.

At Home
- The Speaker of the National Assembly, Shin Ik-hee leaves Busan to make a consolidating visit to the ROK Army.
- A freight train of the U.S. Army overturns on the Second Geum River Bridge between Iwon and Simcheon on the Gyeongbu line.

January 3, Saturday (November 18, by lunar calendar, 甲寅日 Blue Tiger) Clear and Windy
924 Day of the War

War Situation

- The ROK Army repels an attack by the Communist troops who penetrated into the Sniper Ridge.
- A U.S. B-29 bomber squadron attacks military targets of the Communist troops around Sinuiju and Sinanju and destroys more than 200 buildings.
- The Eighth U.S. Army announces that the casualties of the Korean War for the year 1952 reached 159,000 persons.

At Home
- A train collision occurs on the Gyeongbu line between Iwon and Sincheon, leaving 26 people dead and more than 30 wounded.

January 4, Sunday (November 19, by lunar calendar, 乙卯日 Blue Rabbit) Cloudy and Clear
925 Day of the War

War Situation
- Calm situation on the western front, small-scale reconnoitering operations on the other fronts.
- The UN Air Forces conduct night attacks on the trains and trucks of the Communist troops.
- F-84 and F-80 fighter planes attack hard the supply lines of the Communist troops and destroy 32 buildings.

At Home
- The Korean Government announces that President Syngman Rhee will visit Tokyo for talks

Artillery Units of UN Forces located near DMZ (1953).

with General Mark W. Clark, Commander of the UN Forces on Jan. 5.
- The inspection commission starts to investigate the suspicious case of South Gyeongsang District military administration.

Overseas
- The U.S. Civil Defense Center discloses a part of its future plan for a nuclear attack and biological warfare.

January 5, Monday (November 20 by lunar calendar, 丙辰日 Red Dragon) Cloudy, Snowy, Windy and Clear
926 Day of the War

War Situation
- The ROK Army repels the Communist Forces who had invaded the Jane Russell Position.
- The Australian Air Forces records 15,000 sorties since the beginning of the war.
- The UN Forces dismiss Colonel McCarthy from the position of head liaison officer, and appoint Colonel Carlock as his replacement.

At Home
- President Syngman Rhee leaves for Japan to have a talk with General Mark W. Clark, accompanied by the First Lady, Mdm. Francesca, Chief of General Staff, General Baek Seon-yeop, Navy Chief of Staff, Admiral Son Won-il and several other assistants on the UN Forces Commander's plane.

January 6, Tuesday (November 21 by lunar calendar, 丁巳日 Red Snake) Clear, Cloudy and Windy
927 Day of the War

War Situation
- The UN Forces repulse four enemy platoons who had penetrated into the central front line in the eastern part of the Bukhan River after a hard battle.
- The U.S.S Missouri, a battleship, Birmingham, a British cruiser and an aircraft carrier,glory attack the positions of the Communist Forces on the Haeju peninsula.

At Home
- President Syngman Rhee holds talks with General Mark W. Clark, Commander of the UN Forces and has another talk with Japanese Prime Minister Yoshida.
- The Korean Government formulates a draft bill on a special account Act for the agricultural financing.

Overseas
- President Syngman Rhee visits the United Nations Command to have a talk with General Clark, Commander of the UN Forces.
- A West German spokesperson announces that the United States pledged to supply

weapons for the 12 Divisions of West German Forces which would join the NATO Forces.

January 7, Wednesday (November 22 by lunar calendar, 戊午日 Yellow Horse) Snowy, Clear and Windy

928 Day of the War

War Situation
- The UN Forces repelled the Communist troops who attacked at dawn the Pinpoint position and the Russell position in the Sniper Ridge.
- A Sabre jet fighter squadron shoots down a MIG fighter in an air battle in North Korea.
- The fighter-bomber of U.S. Marine Corps bombs the railways near Pyongyang, Jinnampo, Gangdong, and Haeju.

At Home
- President Syngman Rhee returns from Japan.
- U.S. President Dwight D. Eisenhower and British Prime Minister Winston Churchill hold discussions on the issue of expanding the Korean front.

January 8, Thursday (November 23, by lunar calendar, 己未日 Yellow Sheep) Clear and Windy

929 Day of the War

War Situation
- The UN Forces attack and sweep up the Communist Forces concealed in the fortress near Panmunjom.
- More than 1,000 UN Forces from the Netherlands, Greece, Thailand and Belgium arrive in Korea.

Injured soldier is transferred to Navy hospital ship using mechanized LCM (early 1953)

At Home

- The Ministry of Agriculture and Forestry organizes the Korean Committee of the UN Food and Agriculture organization.
- The Korea-U.S. Joint Economic Committee agrees to raise retroactively the unloading charges for grain.

Overseas

- The Federation of Korean Residents in Japan holds a central board meeting and decides to dispatch six observers to the Korea National Assembly and raise four issues.
- The U.S. Secretary of Defense Robert A. Lovett gives testimony before the House Armed Services Committee.

January 9, Friday (November 24 by lunar calendar 庚申日 White Monkey) Clear and Windy
930 Day of the War

War Situation

- The ROK Army destroys nine underground fortresses on the eastern frontline.
- 300 bombers of the UN Forces launch a fierce attack on the railroad intersection on the border of Manchuria.

At Home

- Provincial governors' conference was held in the assembly hall of South Gyeongsang Province after three years' adjournment.

January 10, Saturday (November 25, by lunar calendar, 辛酉日 White Rooster) Clear and Windy

The scene of a fire at Gukje Market in Busan (1953. 1. 10)

931 Day of the War

War Situation

- Ground warfare with small-scale reconnoitering skirmishes for 5 times.
- 300 UN bombers attack Onechon, Anju, and Naewonsan key transportation routes between Manchuria and North Korea, including nighttime bombings.
- B-29 bomber squadron drops 50 of 110-ton-bombs on Seoncheon train switchyard.

At Home

- The Ministry of Defense establishes a Committee for Rank Evaluation of Military Officers.
- Korea receives two LSSL vessels from the U.S. Navy and holds a naming ceremony in Jinhae.
- The Standing Committee of the Supreme People's Assembly of North Korea adopts "The Code of People's Income Tax."

January 11, Sunday (November 26 by lunar calendar, 壬戌日 Black Dog) Clear and Rainy
932 Day of the War

War Situation

- The ROK Air Force blows up 10 concealed supply centers of the Communist Army in the northern part of the eastern frontline.
- The UN Command announces Korea received U.S$590 million in financial assistance from the allied nations from the start of the Korean War to November 1952.

At Home

- The third trial regarding the case of assassination attempt of President Syngman Rhee is held in the Daegu High Court.
- The U.S.-Korea Combined Economic Board decides to distribute 1,500,000 Korean seok (about 60,000 ton) of relief grain to the drought-stricken areas.

Overseas

- French troops in Vietnam retreat from the Fondo outpost located within 8km from the China-Vietnam border line, which is 322 km away from Hanoi in a northwest direction.

January 12, Monday (November 27, by lunar calendar, 癸亥日 Black Pig) Windy and Clear
933 Day of the War

War Situation

- The UN Forces repel the Communist Forces from the Sudo mountain position by concentrated firing of mortars and field-guns.
- A B-29 bomber squadron bombs the railway facilities of the Communist Forces near Sinanju.

At Home

- The National Assembly plenary session passed a resolution to constitute a special committee for the investigation of the case of the sinking of the Changgyeong-ho.
- A large fire breaks out in Chungmuro Street, Busan, at 3 p.m., and 250 buildings are destroyed by the fire.

Overseas
- The Chinese Air Force shoots down a U.S. B-29 bomber, which flew into the north-east region of China by mistake.
- The Chinese Communist Army secures a victory over the UN Smack operations. (1.12~1.20)
- Ho Chi Minh's troops show up even in the southern part of Saigon, Vietnam.

January 13, Tuesday (November 28, by lunar calendar, 甲子日 Blue Rat) Clear and Windy
934 Day of the War

War Situation
- The Eighth U.S. Army Command announces that Chairman Mao Zedong has posted the 47th Army and the 37th Army as his royal guards unit and the replaced troops were deployed at the western frontline.

At Home
- The Ministry of Transportation decides to spend 100 million won as condolence money for the wrecked ship, Changgyeong-ho.
- Central Education Committee holds a meeting in the South Gyeongsang Province Local Assembly hall.
- Four Korean ice skaters depart to participate in the Helsinki Winter Olympic Games in late January.

January 14, Wednesday (November 29, by lunar calendar 乙丑日 Blue Ox) Clear and Windy
935 Day of the War

War Situation
- Small-scale close battles in the Mundeungri valleys on the mid-eastern frontline.
- B29 bomber squadron bombs the switchyard of Eastern Sinanju and Gunwuri with 110 ton of bombs.
- Colonel Lumage, Chief of Engineers of the Eighth U.S. Army inspects the Korean Corps of Engineers.

At Home
- The spokesman of the Korean Government announces that President Syngman Rhee has no intention to reopen Korea-Japan talks without a sincere attitude by Japan.
- The National Assembly plenary session passes a resolution on the Korea's accession to

the Red Cross.

- Ulleungdo Island suffers a severe natural disaster due to heavy snow from the January 11, and 15,000 people undergo hardship without food.

January 15, Thursday (December 1, by lunar calendar, 丙寅日 Red Tiger) Clear
936 Day of the War

War Situation

- The UN Forces attack the Communist Army on a small scale near Panmunjom.
- A Sabre jet-fighter squadron clashes with 38 MIG fighters in the southern part of the Yalu River.
- The UN Command sends to the Communist Army an official letter advising the restriction of transport of supplies for the use of representatives between Kaesong and Pyongyang.

At Home

- President Syngman Rhee holds discussions on the issue of strengthening the ROK Forces with the United Nations Forces Commander, General Mark W. Clark and the Eighth U.S. Army Commander, General James A. Van Fleet.
- The National Assembly plenary session passed a revised bill of the National Assembly Law.

January 16, Friday (December 2, by lunar calendar, 丁卯日 Red Rabbit) Clear and Windy
937 Day of the War

War Situation

- The UN Tank Unit and Artillery Battalion heavily bombard the positions of the Communist Forces from Cheorwon and Gimhwa.
- The Commander of the U.S. Far-East Air Force, Lieutenant General Wayland confirms that the U.S. Air Forces were completely prepared to make a bombardment on Mainland China under the orders of President Eisenhower.

At Home

- The Cabinet Meeting passes a bill for establishing a combat police Unit in the southeastern district.
- The Central Education Committee adopts a proposition for abolishing the system of national examinations for entering middle school.

Overseas

- The Polish Government submits a memorandum to the U.S. Embassy in Poland blaming the United States for large-scale espionage activities.

January 17, Saturday (December 3, by lunar calendar, 戊辰日 Yellow Dragon) Clear, Snowy,

Rainy and Windy

938 Day of the War

War Situation

- B29 bomber squadron bombards Pyongyang at night with 90 tons of high explosive bombs
- The UN Forces POW Command announces one North Korean POW was killed in the Sangmudae camp.

At Home

- The Minister of Home Affairs Jin Heon-sik announces that the Government is to transfer the power of appointment of public officials under third grade to the local governors.
- 33rd Korea National Winter Sports Festival is held in Cheongju.

January 18, Sunday (December 4, by lunar calendar, 己巳日 Yellow Snake) Snowy, Rainy, Clear and Windy

939 Day of the War

War Situation

- The UN Forces reconnaissance party advances to the northern part of Gorangpo to conduct reconnoitering activities.
- The UN Forces repulses the attack of the Communist Forces battalion from the northern Gimhwa, and destroys 5 tanks.

At Home

- The Relief Works Committee for Korea of the International Chamber of Commerce issues a statement before their leaving Korea wishing for the victory and reunification of Korea.
- The Armistice talks representative of the Communist Forces, Nam Il calls upon the UN Forces party to account for the killing of POWs.

Overseas

- The Polish Broadcasting Agency blames the U.S for large-scale espionage.

January 19, Monday (December 5, by lunar calendar, 庚午日 White Horse) Clear and Cloudy

940 Day of the War

War Situation

- Reconnoitering skirmishes occur in the eastern part of the eastern frontline.
- The UN Tank Unit demolishes 74 bunkers of the Chinese Communist Army in the northeastern part of Cheorwon.
- A B29 bomber squadrons bombs two supply points in the North Korea with 110 tons of bombs.

At Home

- President Syngman Rhee declares he has hopes for amicable consultations on the relations between Korea and Japan.
- The National Assembly Plenary Session passes a bill of parliamentary inspection of Government offices and a law of testimony and appraisal in the National Assembly.

Overseas
- The French Forces in Indochina announce that they have defeated Ho Chi Minh's troops in the vicinity of Hanoi after a fierce battle in a point 9.7 km away from Thai Binh.
- The French Forces retreated to An-teh due to the heavy attacks of the North Vietnamese troops.

January 20, Tuesday (December 6, by lunar calendar, 辛未日 White Sheep) Cloudy, Windy and Clear
941 Day of the War

War Situation
- UN Forces repulse the attacks of the Chinese Communist Army at Heartbreak Ridge.
- The UN Tank Unit bombards for 5 days the camps of the Communist Army, from Cheorwon to Gimhwa.

At Home
- The patriotic youth from Yangsan district set up a volunteer Unit named Bolt Troop.
- North Korea made an announcement blaming the U.S. Air Force for bombing Hamheung city.

January 21, Wednesday (December 7, by lunar calendar, 壬申日 Black Monkey) Clear and Windy
942 Day of the War

War Situation
- The UN reconnaissance Unit battles with the Communist Army, killing many enemy troops in the northwest part of Ganseong and northeast part of Mundeungri.
- The UN Tank Unit continues to bombard the enemy in the central frontline.

At Home
- President Syngman Rhee sends a congratulatory message on the inauguration ceremony of President Dwight D. Eisenhower.
- The Korean Government asks Japan to liberate Korean War criminals.
- The ROK Army decides to rename the first Army recruit training center as the Strong Army Center (Gangbyeong-dae).

January 22, Thursday (December 8, by lunar calendar, 癸酉日 Black Rooster) Clear
943 Day of the War

War Situation

ROK soldiers on watch in the frontline (1953. 1. 22)

- Communist Forces who had penetrated the east frontline retreat, leaving behind bodies 60 of their troops.
- F-84 Thunder jet fighter squadron advances to the 64.4 km point from the Korea-Manchuria border and heavily bombard the supply line of the Communist Army.
- The ROK Air Force heavily bombards the Communist Army's camps and destroys several ammunition depots.

At Home
- The Korean Government promulgates the Revised National Assembly Law.
- The Korean Government asks the Japanese Government to liberate 29 Korean War criminals who were imprisoned in Sugamo prison, Japan.
- The head of the United Nations Korean Reconstruction Agency declares that U.S.$ 1 billion would be needed for the reconstruction of Korea.
- The North Korean Military Committee adopts a resolution for strengthening the counterespionage struggle and people's self-defense works in the wartime.

January 23, Friday (December 9, by lunar calendar, 甲戌日 Blue Dog) Clear and Windy
944 Day of the War
War Situation
- The UN Forces in the mid-eastern front repulse the attacks of the Communist Army.
- The ROK Army launches an attack on the Nori Mountain position and kills 85 enemy troops with the support of the UN Air Force and heavy artillery.
- The Sabre jet fighter squadron shoots down four MIG fighters in an air battle in North Korea.

At Home

- The National Assembly plenary session passes a Labor Union Bill.
- Minister of Education, Kim Beop-rin declares the entrance examination of middle and high school is to be carried out by a national examination.

January 24, Saturday (December 10, by lunar calendar, 乙亥日 Blue Pig) Clear and Windy
945 Day of the War

War Situation

- The UN tank troops heavily bombard the Communist Forces in the central frontline all day long.
- The UN Forces light bomber squadron heavily bombs key supply bases in North Korea day and night.

At Home

- The Liberal Party calls a general meeting of the Assembly members and nominates 13 official candidates for chairman of the standing committees.
- The joint meeting of the Korea-U.S. electricity workers agrees to restore mainly first the distribution facilities of electricity.

Overseas

- The U.S. Forces Far East Command appoints Lieutenant General Maxwell Taylor, the U.S. Army Vice-Chief of Staff, as the Eighth U.S. Army Commander in replacement of General Van Fleet.

January 25, Sunday (December 11, by lunar calendar, 丙子日 Red Rat) Clear
946 Day of the War

War Situation

- The UN Forces conduct a violent assault for four hours on Potato Hill in the western part of Cheorwon with the support of 40 bombers and scores of tanks.
- A heavy cruiser Rochester bombards the supply facilities and bunkers in the southern part of Goseong and destroys 21 bunkers.

At Home

- More than 20 armed espionage agents penetrate into Jungmunri, Jeju Island and flee after being defeated.
- An international goodwill football game is held in Dongrae, Busan to celebrate the inauguration of President Eisenhower.

Overseas

- The first free election is held in Vietnam.
- Senator McCarthy makes a public speech on TV.

January 26, Monday (December 12, by lunar calendar, 丁丑日 Red Ox) Windy and Cloudy
947 Day of the War

War Situation

- The UN tank troops conduct fierce bombardments on the fortresses of the Communist Army in the central front.
- The UN Forces launch a surprise attack on the T-type fortress and Bulmo Hill in the western part of Cheorwon.
- The ROK Air Forces heavily bomb all the frontline areas with the U.S. Marine Attack Squadron.

At Home

- The National Assembly plenary session passes a resolution about sending a message on the replacement of the Eighth U.S. Army Commander.
- Minister of Finance Baek Du-jin announces that the Korean Government will maintain an exchange rate of 6,000 won to one U.S. dollar and crack down on the illegal dealers of currency.

January 27, Tuesday (December 13, by lunar calendar, 戊寅日 Yellow Tiger) Cloudy, Windy and Clear
948 Day of the War

War Situation

- The UN Tank troops continue to bombard the positions of the Communist Army in the central frontline.
- U.S.S Missouri bombards Cheongjin port for three hours with 21.6cm and 50cm cannons.

At Home

- Korea and Japan hold preliminary talks in Tokyo.
- The Finance Subcommittee of the Korea-U.S. Combined Economic Board passes a resolution to backdate the raising of processing wages of the imported grains.

January 28, Wednesday (December 14, by lunar calendar, 己卯日 Yellow Rabbit) Clear and Windy
949 Day of the War

War Situation

- The fighters and bombers of the UN Air Force blow up 50 railroad facilities on the west coast of North Korea.
- B29 bomber squadron drop 110 tons of high explosive bombs on the Communist Army's camps 19.3 km south of Pyongyang.

At Home

- The National Assembly plenary session passes a resolution for investigation into the case of a vessel sinking in the sea near Gunsan, and another case of a grain carrier sinking in the sea near Pohang.

Overseas
- The UN headquarters announces that West Germany decided to dispatch to Korea 10 Units of Medical Corps.
- The UN Command declares that the leader of POW riots in the Geoje camp proved to be North Korean General Nam II.

January 29, Thursday (December 15, by lunar calendar, 庚辰日 White Dragon) Clear
950 Day of the War

War Situation
- No noteworthy battles take place anywhere on the frontline.
- B29 bomber squadron bombs the supply bases near Pyongyang.

At Home
- The chairmen of Standing Committees and a Committee of the Whole are elected in the National Assembly.
- The Ministry of Commerce and Industry takes emergency measures to restore the Yeongwol Power Plant to promote the production of tungsten.

January 30, Friday (December 16, by lunar calendar, 辛巳日 White Snake) Cloudy and Clear
951 Day of the War

War Situation
- Light reconnoitering battles take place in the frontlines.
- Sabre jet fighter squadron shoots down a Soviet bomber in Jinnampo and another MIG in an air battle of the southern part of Yalu River.

At Home
- The Minister of Finance Baik Du-jin signs an accord with the UN Civil Investigation Group on the case of backdated raising of unloading wages of the imported grains.

Overseas
- Spain formally joins the United Nations.
- Chinese Communist Forces Command announces military drills for a counter amphibious operation.

January 31, Saturday (December 17, by lunar calendar, 壬午日 Black Horse) Cloudy, Clear and Windy
952 Day of the War

War Situation
- The UN Navy and Air Force conduct day-long attacks on Wonsan seaport together with USS Missouri.

- The UN Air Force Mustang squadron bomb all along the front line and destroy 15 Tochkca positions.

At Home
- The National Assembly plenary session passes a resolution for sending a message on requesting military and economic assistance and another bill on the labor dispute.
- The Rescue Headquarters announces that 1,903 houses were burnt down and the number of sufferers reaches 10,214 persons in the disastrous fire of Busan.

February 1, Sunday (December 18, by lunar calendar, 癸未日 Black Sheep) Clear
953 Day of the War

War Situation

- The attacks of two platoons of Chinese Communist Forces on the outpost positions of the UN Forces in the northern part of Gimhwa are repelled.
- A Reconnoitering Unit of Communist troops launches two times' attacks to the position of UN Forces south of Pyeonggang.
- Two platoons of the Chinese Communist Forces launch a night time attack on the UN Forces' outside positions near the Bulmo(bare mountain) Hill.

At Home

- Korea Aviation College is established.
- Japanese Delegation of Marine Products visits President Syngman Rhee to discuss the fishery problems between Korea and Japan.

February 2, Monday (December 19, by lunar calendar, 甲申日 Blue Monkey) Cloudy and Clear
954 Day of the War

War Situation

- The UN Forces recapture Bulmo Hill under the covering bombardment of rearguard Units that had retreated provisionally from the outpost positions near Bulmo Hill.
- The UN Tank troops continue to attack ceaselessly the bunkers of the Communist Army for 16 days.

At Home

- Twenty-nine members of National Assembly including Lee Jong-yeong propose a no-confidence motion in Minister of Home Affairs Jin Heon-sik.
- The ROK Air Force Intelligence School is established in Seoul.

Overseas

- President Eisenhower delivers the State of the Union Message to Congress:
  A declaration of the cancellation of neutralization of Taiwan and speedy strengthening of ROK Armed Forces.

February 3, Tuesday (December 20, by lunar calendar, 乙酉日 Blue Rooster) Clear, Windy and Cloudy
955 Day of the War

War Situation

- The UN Infantry troops and the Infantry units under the cover of an air squadron launch a surprise attack on the positions of the Communist troops in the west Gorangpo and kill about 400 Chinese Communist enemies.
- Newly appointed Eighth U.S. Army Commander, General Taylor arrives in Seoul with UN Forces Commander General Clark and pays a courtesy call on President Syngman Rhee.

At Home
- The National Assembly plenary session passes a bill for setting up a special investigation committee to probe the violation of human rights.
- The National Assembly passes a resolution to collect relief fund for the victims of a big fire in the Gukje market, Busan.

February 4, Wednesday (December 21, by lunar calendar, 丙戌日 Red Dog) Cloudy
956 Day of the War

War Situation
- Only reconnoitering skirmishes occur in the ground warfare.
- The UN B-26 fighter-bomber squadron conducts continuous sorties for 13 days and attacks the supply vehicles of the Communist troops.

At Home
- The National Assembly plenary session passes a motion to defer a resolution of no confidence in the Minister of Home Affairs by the time of completion of the parliamentary inspection of the administration.
- The 'Daichi Dairou Maru (第一大邦丸)' accident occurs in the open waters near Jeju Island.

February 5, Thursday (December 22, by lunar calendar, 丁亥日 Red Pig) Cloudy and Clear
957 Day of the War

War Situation
- The Chinese Communist Army conducts six reconnoitering attacks against the UN Forces camps.
- The U.S. 5th Air Forces Shooting Star bomber destroys a Communist ship anchored in Jinnampo port.

At Home
- The National Assembly plenary session passes a resolution to conduct 1953 general inspections of Government offices and another resolution to carry out a national movement to comfort soldiers and policemen fighting in the frontlines.

February 6, Friday (December 23, by lunar calendar, 戊子日 Yellow Rat) Clear

Refugees in Geumchon, Paju are receiving relief goods from the U.S. soldiers. (1953. 2. 5)

958 Day of the War

War Situation

- The UN Infantry troops battles against two platoons of the Communist Army and kills 15 enemy soldiers in the western part of Cheorwon.
- The U.S. 5th Air Force announces that the newest all-weather night fighters (P94B type) will be deployed in the Korean War from March.
- The UN Forces POW camp announces one POW of the Chinese Communist Army was killed on Jeju Island after he threw a stone at a camp guard.

At Home
- The National Assembly plenary session adopts a resolution to constitute a special committee for reorganization of Government systems and another resolution to improve the salaries of Government officials.
- The National Assembly plenary session adopts a resolution about the education of disabled soldiers and policemen.

February 7, Saturday (December 24, by lunar calendar, 己丑日 Yellow Ox) Clear and Windy
959 Day of the War

War Situation
- The UN Forces repel the Communist Army's reconnoitering attacks five times from the main line of resistance in the east side of the Sniper Ridge.
- The UN Forces attack the main positions near the White Horse Hill in the central frontline and kill 17 Chinese Communist enemy soldiers.

At Home
- The National Assembly plenary session passes a revised bill of the court organization law.
- A special committee of investigation of the National Assembly presents a report to the general meeting about the causes and damages of the sinking of the Changgyeongho, blaming the shortcomings in the vessel administration of the authorities of Marine affairs.

Mortar is fired at the enemy position in the west of Cheorwon. (1952. 2. 7)

February 8, Sunday (December 25, by lunar calendar, 庚寅日 White Tiger) Clear and Windy
960 Day of the War

War Situation
- The UN Forces repulse attacks by a company of the Communist Army in the main line of resistance between the basin of the eastern front line and Sandbag Hill.
- General Clark, Commander in Chief of the UN Command declares that two Divisions would be reinforced for the ROK Army to comprise a total 14 Divisions.

At Home
- The People's Daily of North Korea published a lead editorial titled "Commemorating the fifth anniversary of the North Korean People's Army."

February 9, Monday (December 26, by lunar calendar, 辛卯日 White Rabbit) Clear
961 Day of the War

War Situation
- Small-scale reconnoitering skirmishes occur in several frontline areas.
- The UN Forces retreat from the northern Yeoncheon after being attacked by small Units of the Communist Forces.
- The UN Air Force bomber squadron launches four attacks in waves on the industrial area of Gyeomipo.

At Home
- The National Assembly conducts inspections of Government offices.
- The representatives of five non Governmental organizations launch a national conference including the Korean National Association, the Korean Peasants League, the Korean Labor Union, the Korean Young Men's Association, and the Korean Women's Society.

Overseas
- Pravda, the Russian Communist newspaper allude to the issue of the cancellation of neutralization of Taiwan claiming, "The United States aims to prolong the Korean War and enlarge the war in the Far East Asia."

February 10, Tuesday (December 27, by lunar calendar, 壬辰日 Black Dragon) Clear and Rainy
962 Day of the War

War Situation
- No decisive battles occur in the frontlines.
- The U.S. 77th Task Fleet bombers bombs the supply base and railroad facilities of the Communist Forces.
- The UN Command announces that one POW was killed and 38 were injured in the course of suppressing the riots of Geoje P.O.W. camp on Feb. 9.

At Home
- The Student National Defense Corps and Headquarters of Recruiting Districts promote a movement of enlightening propaganda to recruit student volunteers.

Overseas
- Mao Zedong sends Joseph V. Stalin a telegram congratulating the U.S.S.R on the 3rd anniversary of the Sino-Soviet Treaty of Friendship, Alliance and Mutual Assistance.

February 11, Wednesday (December 28, by lunar calendar, 癸巳日 Black Snake) Clear and Windy
963 Day of the War

War Situation
- All the frontlines remain silent.
- The UN Tank troops attack the positions of the Communist Army in the western front line.

At Home
- President Syngman Rhee issues a statement demanding a blockade of the Chinese coast.
- Eight passengers are killed and 62 injured in a bus accident in the Wanju-gun district.

February 12, Thursday (December 29, by lunar calendar, 甲午日 Blue Horse) Rainy and Cloudy
964 Day of the War

War Situation
- The UN Forces launch a small-scale attack in the eastern frontline.
- The UN Reconnaissance Party clashes with a platoon of the Communist Army for 40 minutes near the Mundeungri Valley.
- The Commander of the British Commonwealth of Nations Forces declares that 1,000 soldiers of the ROK Army are enrolled in the British Armed Forces.

At Home
- The ROK Armed Forces Information and Education Division holds a lecture meeting in Busan for the recruitment of military cadets.
- The medical officers of the U.S. 21st Army Hospital in Busan donate medical textbooks to the Medical College of Seoul National University.

Overseas
- The Government authorities of Thailand announce a military reinforcement plan for the national defense including the purchase of 20 jet fighters, four warships and a considerable number of tanks.

February 13, Friday (December 30, by lunar calendar, 乙未日 Blue Sheep) Rainy and Cloudy
965 Day of the War

War Situation
- The ROK Army repulses the attacks by two platoons of Communist troops and kills 73 Communist soldiers.
- The UN Forces repel the attacks of Communist troops near Bunker Hill and Kelly Hill.
- The Commander of the British Commonwealth of Nations Forces is replaced.

At Home
- An incident is reported regarding the chasing of a Japanese fishing boat by a Korean patrol boat.

Overseas
- 87 former Nazi Royal guards accused of massacre were all sentenced to death by a default judgment in the French military tribunal.

February 14, Saturday (January 1, by lunar calendar, 丙申日 Red Monkey) Clear, Cloudy, Windy and Clear
966 Day of the War

War Situation
- The UN Forces repel a small-scale attack by Communist troops from an outpost position in the southwest of Pyongyang.
- The UN Forces Artillery Unit repulses Communist troops who were advancing southward in the valley near the Bulmo Hill of the mid-western frontline.
- A UN Navy destroyer bombards the Communist troops who had attacked the ground troops of the UN Forces on the island off Wonsan port.

At Home
- The Ministry of Agriculture and Forestry amends the price of Government-owned grain by-product retrospectively from Feb. 1.

Overseas
- Bandung general meeting of ECAFE (Economic Commission for Asia and the Far East) passes a motion of Pakistan advising ECOSOC (United Nations Economic and Social Council) to grant seven countries including Korea qualifications for full membership instead of associate membership.

February 15, Sunday (January 2, by lunar calendar, 丁酉日 Red Rooster) Clear and Windy
967 Day of the War

War Situation
- The UN Forces Reconnoitering Unit engages in a small Unit combat in the western and northern part of the eastern frontline.
- The UN Tank troops bombard the targets of the Communist troops in the mid-western

frontline.

- The UN Air Forces bomb the Supung power plant and the railroads of Sinanju and Jaeryeong.

At Home

- The Korean Government imposes "emergency measures on currency" at 6 a.m. by issuing the emergency order No.13. The value of Korean currency is devaluated to one hundredth. The Unit of currency is changed from Won to Hwan, The Hwan-dollar exchange rate is fixed at 60 Hwan per one dollar.
- President Syngman Rhee issues a special statement about the emergency measures on currency.
- Minister of Finance Baik du-jin makes an announcement asking for national cooperation to prevent inflation and stabilize the value of currency.

February 16, Monday (January 3 by lunar calendar, 戊戌日 Yellow Dog) Clear and Windy
968 Day of the War

War Situation

- Sporadic reconnoitering combats continue in the ground warfare.
- The search and attack of a squad of Communist troops is repelled in the northwest of Gorangpo and Cheorwon.

At Home

- Cabinet Meeting resolves to set up countermeasures for the emergency measures on currency including restriction of deposit payments.
- The countermeasure center for emergency currency orders all the banks and financial institutions to extend the office hours for money exchanges.

Overseas

- American congressman Call proposes a bill to hand over six American destroyers to the Nationalist Chinese Forces to set up a blockade along the Chinese coast.

February 17, Tuesday (January 4, by lunar calendar, 己亥日 Yellow Pig) Cloudy and Clear
969 Day of the War

War Situation

- The ROK Army engages in nine battles with the Communist enemies just from midnight to morning in the eastern front.
- The UN carrier-based bombers make more than 300 sorties continuously to strike the military facilities of the Communist troops around Wonsan and East coast.

At Home

- President Syngman Rhee sets out his dissenting opinion about the Nationalist Chinese

Exchange of old currency into new currency (1953. 2. 17)

Troop's participation in the Korean War.
- The regulations of war-time wages and benefits (Presidential Order No. 752) was released on Feb. 15 and retrospectively from Nov. 1, 1951.

February 18, Wednesday (January 5, by lunar calendar, 庚子日 White Rat) Windy and Clear
970 Day of the War

War Situation
- The U.S. Air Force denies the Communist Army's report that a U.S. jet fighter was shot down in the skies over Manchuria.
- The UN POW camp announces that one Chinese Communist POW was found hanged on Feb. 16 in the 3rd camp of Geoje.

At Home
- The Korean Government publishes the enforcement decree of the Customs Law.
- The Minister of Finance Baik Du-jin and the president of the Bank of Korea announce on Feb. 17 that the U.S. sale of U.S$3.5 million to the Bank of Korea is done as a means of Korean money procurement for the UN Forces.

February 19, Thursday (January 6, by lunar calendar, 辛丑日 White Ox) Clear, Windy and Cloudy
971 Day of the War

War Situation

- A UN Reconnoitering Unit kills 15 Communist soldiers near the Namgang River in the eastern front.
- Close battles continue in the Mundeungri valleys.
- The UN Tank troops and Artillery Units continue to bombard the bunkers of the Communist troops in the eastern frontline.
- The UN POW Command announces that one civilian detainee, trying to escape, was shot and injured by a guard on Feb. 18.

At Home

- Minister of Finance Baik Du-jin explains the basic necessities for the emergency measures on currency in the National Assembly plenary session.
- The Headquarters of the National Police instructs the provincial police bureaus to follow the guidelines of the emergency measures on currency, including advices to open grocery stores and the prevention of old currency circulation.

Overseas

- The Ministry of Foreign Affairs of the Taiwan Nationalist Chinese Government announces that it concluded a treaty of friendship with Spain.
- The Minister of Defense of the United Kingdom Alexander declares in a news conference with the U.S. Press Corps that the only military solution for the Korean War will be to advance to the Pyongyang to Wonsan line.

February 20, Friday (January 7, by lunar calendar, 壬寅日 Black Tiger) Clear, Windy and Cloudy
972 Day of the War

War Situation

- The UN Tank troops continue to bombard the positions of the Communist Forces.
- The UN Forces repel the attacks of the Communist Forces from the outpost position near the Bunker Hill.

At Home

- The headquarters of emergency measures on currency announces the reduction of the flour ratio and an additional release of U.S$ 1 million foreign currency.

Overseas

- Pyongyang Broadcasting accuses the U.S. Forces of trying to break the agreement on establishing Panmunjom as a neutral zone and disregarding the existence of the Armistice talks venue.

February 21, Saturday (January 8, by lunar calendar, 癸卯日 Black Rabbit) Clear, Cloudy and Windy

973 Day of the War

War Situation

- The Air Force authority announces that 33 pilots had made more than one hundred sorties as of Jan. 16.

At Home

- The National Assembly plenary session passes a motion approving the emergency measures on currency.

Overseas

- Mao Zedong, Zhou Enlai, and Zhu De sent a congratulatory telegram on the 35th anniversary of the founding of the Soviet Army.

February 22, Sunday (January 9, by lunar calendar, 甲辰日 Blue Dragon) Windy, Clear and Cloudy

974 Day of the War

War Situation

- The UN Forces repel the attacks of the Communist Chinese troops in the east of the Hantan River and Sniper Ridge.
- The UN Reconnoitering Unit attacks the Communist Chinese troops and killed 18 enemies in the west of Gorangpo.

At Home

- The UN Forces Commander General Mark W. Clark proposes to the Communist troops' Commander in Chief a prompt exchange of injured POWs.
- The Commander of Land Forces of NATO visits Korea.

Overseas

- The Government of the People's Republic of China and North Korea proposes an overall solution of the POW problem (Feb. 22-March 28).
- The U.S. Ministry of Defense announces its plan to conduct an atomic bomb test in the spring of 1953 with the joint mobilization of 20,000 soldiers of Army, Navy and Air Forces in the State of Nevada, U.S.

February 23, Monday (January 10, by lunar calendar, 乙巳日 Blue Snake) Cloudy, Windy and Clear

975 Day of the War

War Situation

- The ROK Army launches a surprise attack the Communist troops and kills 96 enemies on the eastern frontline.
- The UN Tank Units attack the frontline positions of the Communist troops in the central frontline and in a part of the eastern frontline.

At Home

• A total of 931 anti-Communist POWs from North Korea who had been in detention in Busan file a petition written in blood to the speaker of the National Assembly, in which they ask their early release and participation in the warfare advancing northward.

February 24, Tuesday (January 11, by lunar calendar, 丙午日 Red Horse) Cloudy and Rainy
976 Day of the War

War Situation

• Only small-scale reconnoitering skirmishes continue on all the fronts.
• The UN Forces in the western front completely repel the Communist troops who have attack the outpost position after five hour battle.

At Home

• Minister of Home Affairs Jin Heon-sik declares that any foreign fishing ship violating the territorial waters of Korea be captured and also be fired upon if necessary.
• Minister of Agriculture and Forestry Sin Jung-mok demands the cooperation of relevant agencies and businessmen in the process of executing grain policy under the situation of emergency measures on currency.

February 25, Wednesday (January 12, by lunar calendar, 丁未日 Red Sheep) Rainy
977 Day of the War

War Situation

• The UN Forces repulse a company of the Communist troops which have attacked the positions of the UN Forces from the northwest of Gimhwa.
• The UN Forces repel the attacks of the Communist troops and kill 50 enemies in the west of Cheorwon.
• The UN Tank Units shell at dawn the positions of the Communist troops in the southeast of Panmunjom.
• The UN warships including USS Missouri destroy 15 military facilities of the Communist troops.

At Home

• President Syngman Rhee declares that a Japanese vessel's sailing through Korean waters will be regarded as a hostile act.
• The Commander of the UN Forces Mark W. Clark announces that the U.S. Government agrees to pay U.S$85.8 million, an unadjusted amount from the UN Forces loan before Feb. 7, 1953, to the Korean Government.

Overseas

• The UN General Assembly Political Committee decides to consider the Korean problem as the first item on the agenda and Russia's motion to invite the North Korean delegate to the UN is rejected by 36 to 16.

- The Korean mission to Japan issues an announcement about the accident of Dairou Maru according to the direction of President Syngman Rhee.

February 26, Thursday (January 13, by lunar calendar, 戊申日 Yellow Monkey) Clear
978 Day of the War

War Situation

- The U.S. Far Eastern Air Forces announces that the UN Forces discovered a Russian-made twin-engine light jet bomber, IL-28, on the Korean frontlines.
- The UN POW Command announces that one POW was killed and two were injured as they tried a surprise attack on an American officer on patrol on February 24.

At Home

- Minister of Defense Sin Tae-young issues an announcement, "Korea is now in need of the support from the friendly nations as the food supply for the ROK Army is in a bad situation."

February 27, Friday (January 14, by lunar calendar, 己酉日 Yellow Rooster) Clear
979 Day of the War

War Situation

- The ROK Army repels an attack by 200 Communist troops on the eastern frontline.
- Just one squad of UN troops attacks more than a company of Communist troops and kills 45 enemy troops.
- The UN Forces repulse an attack by Communist troops on the Kelly Hill in the west of Yeoncheon.
- The Thunder jet bomber squadron attacks the training camp of the Communist troops in Chosan.

At Home

- The Korean Government officially declares, "The dominium of Dokdo Island belongs to the Republic of Korea."
- The Korean Government promulgates the act of emergency measures on currency and enforces it.
- The financial agencies are closed due to the delay of the promulgation of the emergency measures act.

February 28, Saturday (January 15, by lunar calendar, 庚戌日 White Dog) Clear and Rainy
980 Day of the War

War Situation
- The UN Infantry troops kill about 100 enemy troops in six days of small-scale battles.
- The UN Tank troops continue to bombard the enemy troops' positions.

At Home
- The National Assembly plenary session enters its temporary recess from March 2 to 14, but decides to conduct continuous inspections of the Government offices.
- The Ministry of Education designates Daegu Munhwa Theater as the National Theater of Korea and reopens it to give a stage to "Field Flowers(Yahwa)" written by Yoon Baik-nam and directed by Seo Hyang-seok as an opening performance.

Overseas
- The U.S. Department of Commerce announces the total amount of trading to Asian countries in 1952 is U.S$ 1.91 billion in exports and U.S$ 1.57 billion in imports.

March 1, Sunday (January 16, by lunar calendar, 辛亥日 White Pig) Cloudy and Clear
981 Day of the War

War Situation
- The UN troops repulse the attacks of a company of Chinese Communist troops after a 45-minute battle, conducted on an outpost position of the UN Forces.
- The UN troops repel the attacks of a platoon of the Chinese Communist troops in the west of Kelly Hill.

At Home
- The 34th anniversary of the March 1 Independence Movement, The national convention for "the Unification of Korea through military operations" was held in the Capitol building in Seoul.
- The Ministry of Communications starts to use long distance calls for military uses including linking the military police, the quartermaster corps and the other major Units.

March 2, Monday (January 17, by lunar calendar, 壬子日 Black Rat) Rainy, Windy and Clear
982 Day of the War

War Situation
- The ROK Army repels an attack by a company of Communist troops on Capitol Hill.

At Home
- Minister of National Defense Sin Tae-young announces the deadline of application for the military cadet is postponed to the 7th of this month.
- The Korea Chamber of Commerce and Industry discusses the emergency measures on currency and issues an announcement asking for the protection of industries.

Overseas
- The UN Security Council resumes the discussion on the Korean problem. Andrei Yanuarievich Vyshinsky, representative of the USSR, strongly pushes his proposal to set up an international commission to deal with the Korean problem.

March 3, Tuesday (January 18, by lunar calendar, 癸丑日 Black Ox) Cloudy, Clear and Windy
983 Day of the War

War Situation
- The UN Forces repel a platoon of the Communist troops which has attacked from the northwest of Geumsung.
- The ROK Army repulses two squads of the Communist troops from Sniper Ridge and

Amseok Peak after a hard battle.

At Home
- The Cabinet Meeting sets up the "Seven principles of economic reconstruction."
- The Cabinet Meeting approves a loan of 48 billion Korean Hwan as grain purchase capital for the Korean Central Grain Market to control the grain price.

March 4, Wednesday (January 19, by lunar calendar, 甲寅日 Blue Tiger) Clear, Cloudy and Windy
984 Day of the War

War Situation
- The ROK Army repulses an attack by a battalion of the Communist Forces in the afternoon after temporary occupation, following a frontal attack on Mall Hill, and killed 180 enemy soldiers.
- The Eighth U.S. Army Public Information Officer (PIO) announces that the casualties of the Communist Forces during March reached 7,500, the smallest number since the beginning of the war.

At Home
- CINC, UN Command, General Clark arrives in Seoul and holds talks with the Commander, Eighth U.S. Army General Taylor and President Syngman Rhee.

Overseas
- The UN representatives of the 15 Asian and African nations hold lengthy discussions on the Korean problem.
- U.S. President Eisenhower holds a nighttime talk, which has been scheduled to be held the following day and they agree on matters after the death of Stalin.

March 5, Thursday (January 20, by lunar calendar, 乙卯日 Blue Rabbit) Cloudy and Clear
985 Day of the War

War Situation
- USS Missouri bombards the seashores of Weonsan port.
- A UN Navy carrier-based aircraft squadron destroys Jangjin the first power plant

At Home
- The spokesman of the Government declares its decisive measures including direct firing at ships which invade the peace line (the Syngman Rhee line).
- The Ministry of Agriculture and Forestry issues the mix proportion guidelines on fertilizer for barley crops to the Provincial administrators and decides to execute the regulations for foreign currency loans for preferential allocation of grains.

March 6, Friday (January 21, by lunar calendar, 丙辰日 Red Dragon) Clear and Windy

986 Day of the War

War Situation
- UN Forces attack Rocky Point Hill to the north of Gimhwa, killing 85 Communist soldiers and injuring 55 after a 24-hour battle.
- 300 civilian detainees stir up sedition in Bongamdo POW camp and two POWs are injured.

At Home
- President Syngman Rhee issues a statement on the death of Stalin, leader of the Soviet Union saying "It is regretful for me to hear the news of Stalin's death but I hope his successors to build cooperative relations between our two nations."

Overseas
- The Korean Ambassador to the UN Im Byeong-jik delivers an address in the UN General Assembly Special Political and Decolonization Committee (Fourth Committee).
- The national convention of the French Communist Party ends earlier than scheduled.

March 7, Saturday (January 22, by lunar calendar, 丁巳日 Red Snake) Cloudy, Windy and Clear
987 Day of the War

War Situation
- The UN Forces Reconnoitering Unit repels the Communist troops from Bulmo Hill in the west of Cheorwon after 30 minutes' close battle.
- The UN Forces repel the Chinese Communist troops in the northeast of Gimhwa after two hours' battle and kill or injure 70 enemy troops.

At Home
- The Government disbands the Center for Currency Management, which was established on February 25 to conduct emergency measures for currency.
- North Korea dispatches to Moscow an official condolence delegation headed by Park Jeong-ae for Stalin's funeral.

March 8, Sunday (January 23 by lunar calendar, 戊午日 Yellow Horse) Clear and Windy
988 Day of the War

War Situation
- Commander in Chief UN Command (CINC, UNC) General Taylor conducts an inspection of the war situation all along the eastern fronts for two days on March 6~7 and calls up Commanders under his command to hold a secret joint meeting.

At Home
- President Syngman Rhee issues a message about returning to the capital, saying "It is now being prepared but wait for the time being until the proclamation of the Government is published."

- The Korean Government proclaims the Labor Union Law, Labor Dispute Mediation Law and Labor Relations Commission Law.

Overseas
- Radio Pyongyang reports that the North Korean Government dispatched to Moscow an official condolence delegation consisted of four persons including deputy prime minister for the Stalin's funeral.
- Ex-Commander of the Eighth U.S. Army Van Fleet gave testimony in the Senate Armed Service Committee to use atomic weapons in the Korean War.

March 9, Monday (January 24, by lunar calendar, 己未日 Yellow Sheep) Clear and Windy
989 Day of the War

War Situation
- The ROK Army repulses two platoons of the Communist troops in a one-hour close-quarters battle after an invasion of four positions in the west of Ganseong.
- The ROK Army Reconnoitering Unit has a brief close quarters battle and killed 36 enemy troops in the northwest of Cheorwon.

At Home
- The Korean Government proclaims the Law of the Marine Products Industry.
- The Ministry of Education refers to the National Education Committee the authorization for establishing four colleges including Busan Medical College, Masan Pharmacy College, Dongyang College and Gyelim College and two universities including Jungang and Chosun University.

March 10, Tuesday (January 25, by lunar calendar, 庚申日 White Monkey) Clear, Cloudy and Rainy
990 Day of the War

War Situation
- 300 Communist troops attack the UN Forces Hill in the west of the Imjin River on the western front, but they retreat with 45 casualties.
- Nam Il, representative of the Communist Forces asks to reopen the Panmunjom truce talks.

At Home
- The Korean Government proclaims the revised Decree on the Student Military Drill.
- The National Education Committee passes a resolution to establish a National University in Busan, rejects another resolution to establish Dongyang and Gyelim College and decides to increase doctoral courses to 10 majors.

Overseas
- The Egyptian Government signs an agreement to barter wheat and cotton with the Soviet

Union, Poland, and Bulgaria.

March 11, Wednesday (January 26, by lunar calendar, 辛酉日 White Rooster) Rainy, Windy and Cloudy
991 Day of the War

War Situation
- The ROK Army has a close battle with a platoon of the Communist Forces which had attacked the Sniper Ridge in reconnaissance.
- The ROK Army Reconnoitering Unit which has advanced to the northwest of Mundeungri has a close battle with two squads of the Communist troops and killed 14 enemies.

At Home
- The headquarters of the Recruiting District make an announcement that the requisition age of military work service will be raised to 50.

March 12, Thursday (January 27, by lunar calendar, 壬戌日 Black Dog) Rainy, Windy and Clear
992 Day of the War

War Situation
- The UN Forces Reconnoitering Unit has a close battle with 50-80 Communist troops in the south of Pyeonggang on the central front.
- Royal Thai Armed Forces(RTAF) delegation visits RTAF camp Korea on their way back home after a tour of surveying the U.S. military facilities.

At Home
- President Syngman Rhee issues an announcement asking for military advancing to the Korean-Manchurian border.
- Two police deputy commissioners including Hwang Hak-seong leave to survey the American police system.

March 13, Friday (January 28, by lunar calendar, 癸亥日 Black Pig) Clear
993 Day of the War

War Situation
- UN Air Force jet fighters shoot down four MIG jet fighters in the North Korean skies.

At Home
- The headquarters of the National Police announce that the number of Communist guerrillas decreased to 1,000 which were 500 less than the previous winter.

Overseas
- Japanese manufacturers prepare to produce bazookas according to the order of the U.S. Army.

March 14, Saturday (January 29, by lunar calendar, 甲子日 Blue Rat) Clear
994 Day of the War

War Situation
- The Ministry of Communication begins to construct the facilities for a radio regulatory monitoring bureau.
- Geoje POW camp declares that it intends to reject repatriation of injured POWs from North Korea.

Overseas
- A no-confidence motion in the Yoshida cabinet proposed by three factions of the opposition party is passed in the National Diet due to the separation of the Japanese Liberal Party and the House of Representatives. It is dissolved as a result, and a general election is to be held on April 19.
- A senior official in Washington discloses a vision that the U.S. Government is to implement a long-term plan to increase the armed Forces of the East Asian free nations.
- General Douglas MacArthur stresses in the commemoration ceremony of the U.S. Military Academy Foundation, that "The only solution to the Korean war is a UN Forces' victory."

March 15, Sunday (February1, by lunar calendar, 乙丑日 Blue Ox) Cloudy
995 Day of the War

War Situation
- Ground warfare is almost ceased due to heavy rain and snow.

At Home
- The Korea-Japan talks reopen in Tokyo.
- The Ministry of National Defense transfers the operation of the armory to the Army.

March 16, Monday (February 2, by lunar calendar, 丙寅日 Red Tiger) Clear, Cloudy, Windy and Clear
996 Day of the War

War Situation
- The Chinese Communist Forces fiercely attack Gibraltar Hill but are repelled through hand to hand fighting by the UN Forces.

At Home
- The Korean Government proclaims the registration order of the persons with an academic or artistic career.
- The Ministry of Transportation sets up the Railroad Construction Bureau.
- The Chinese Communist Forces take the offensive against the UN Forces on Gibraltar Hill.

March 17, Tuesday (February 3, by lunar calendar, 丁卯日 Red Rabbit) Cloudy and Clear

War Situation

• Nam Il, the chief representative of Communist Forces blames the UN Forces for aerial bombardment on Kaesong and criticizes that they were compelled to adopt a motion to hand over the problem of the POW camps to the UN General Assembly.

At Home

• The National Assembly Plenary Session passes a motion about the annuity by the pension law for the families of the war dead soldiers and policemen and injured soldiers and policemen, deciding the annuity will be increased from 6,000 won to 12,000 won.

• The Korean Government welcomes the Dominican Republic's suggestion to dispatch its troops to Korea.

March 18, Wednesday (February 4, by lunar calendar, 戊辰日 Yellow Dragon) Clear
998 Day of the War

War Situation

• The ROK Army repulses the reconnoitering attacks of the Communist Forces by delivering concentrated fire in the northwest of Ganseong.

At Home

• The Korean Government promulgates the Labor Union Act, Labor Dispute Act and Labor Relations Commission Act.

• North Korea makes an ungrounded claim that the U.S. Army scattered poison gas bombs around the Pyeonggang district in Gangwon Province.

March 19, Thursday (February 5, by lunar calendar, 己巳日 Yellow Snake) Cloudy, Rainy and Windy
999 Day of the War

War Situation

• The UN Forces reconnoitering Unit advances to the outpost positions of the Communist Forces 16 times throughout the night on all eastern fronts and kills 47 enemy combatants through close battles.

• The U.S. Marine Corps attack the positions and bunkers of the Communist Forces in the northwest of Gorangpo and return after 10 minutes' hand-to-hand combat.

At Home

• The Ministry of Social Affairs discloses the reality of the case that 20 persons starved to death in Sunchang-gun, North Jeolla Province.

• The death sentence is demanded for Kim Si-hyeon and Ryu Si-tae who are accused of attempted assassination of President Syngman Rhee in the 7th arraignment trial.

March 20, Friday (February 6, by lunar calendar, 庚午日 White Horse) Rainy, Windy, Clear and Cloudy

1,000 Day of the War

War Situation

- The UN Forces artillery Unit repulses the attack of the Chinese Communist Forces on small Nori Hill on the western front.
- The exchange of the injured POWs begins.

At Home

- The National Assembly Plenary Session passes a motion to maintain the exchange rate as 60 Hwan to a dollar.
- The Acting Prime Minister, Baek Du-jin, makes an administrative speech about the second revised supplementary budget bill of the 1952 fiscal year in the National Assembly.

Chinese Communist POWs at Geoje POW camp enjoying warm spring sun. (1953. 3. 20)

• Son Won-il, the chief of Navy Operations of the ROK Navy (CNOROKN) declares that it will maintain the sovereign line of the Korean waters.

Overseas

• The President of the Philippines, Elpidio Quirino, formally receives a transfer document from Raymond A. Spruance, the U.S. Ambassador, according to the U.S.-Philippine mutual defense agreement, concerning the provision of four PBY-type amphibious planes, and 700 cars of various models.

March 21, Saturday (February 7, by lunar calendar, 辛未日 White Sheep) Clear and Windy
1,001 Day of the War

War Situation

• The ROK Marine Corps guarding the west coast, north of the 38th parallel reply to the fierce bombardments of the coast batteries of the Communist Forces and destroy three enemy positions.

At Home

• The National Assembly Plenary Session passes the Public Educational Officials bill for the teachers' certificate and guarantee of status.
• The National Assembly passes a resolution opposing the Armistice.
• Baek Du-jin is nominated as the Prime Minister and the Cabinet Meeting passes the election law for the upper House.

March 22, Sunday (February 8, by lunar calendar, 壬申日 Black Monkey) Clear and Rainy
1,002 Day of the War

War Situation

• The U.S. Marine Corps repulse the attacks of the 800 soldiers of Chinese Communist Forces on the Bunker Hill, killing 112 enemy troops.
• The aircraft carrier USS Missouri, the cruiser USS Los Angeles, and the destroyer, USS Helsay Powell, bomb Wonsan all morning.

At Home

• The National Assembly makes a decision on the legal number of the member of the upper House to be 72.
• The Ministry of Industry and Commerce allots six hundred and sixty million (660,000,000) Hwan as industrial funds.

March 23, Monday (February 9, by lunar calendar, 癸酉日 Black Rooster) Clear
1,003 Day of the War

War Situation

- The reconnoitering Unit of ROK Army begins to use napalm bombs for the first time as the ROK Army repels two platoons of the Communist Forces.
- The UN Forces' light bombers attack the parking lots and locomotives of the Communist Forces supply lines all over North Korea.

At Home
- The National Assembly Plenary Session passes a motion to introduce an urgent bill for the criminal law.
- The National Assembly organizes a special committee on the movement for unification by adcance north.

March 24, Tuesday (February 10, by lunar calendar, 甲戌日 Blue Dog) Cloudy, Clear and Windy
1,004 Day of the War

War Situation
- The UN Forces repulse two companies of the Communist Forces after two hours of battles, after attacking White Horse Hill at dawn.
- Both the United States and Communist China increase their troops for the battle of Bulmo Hill.
- The ROK Army has a battle with a company of the Communist Forces in the northwest of Yeoncheon and kill 22 enemy combatants.
- The POWs raise disturbance in the Geoje POW camp and three POWs are injured by the firing of Korean guards.

At Home
- The Korea-U.S. Joint Economic Committee determines the Hwan-dollar exchange rate as sixty Hwan to one dollar the same as before.

Overseas
- Taiwan's leader, Chiang Kai-shek, asserts emphatically to a U.S. reporter "It is essential for the free Asian nations to set up an Anti-Communist Military Federation in order to be unified against Communism."

March 25, Wednesday (February 11, by lunar calendar, 乙亥日 Blue Pig) Cloudy, Clear and Windy
1,005 Day of the War

War Situation
- The ROK Army reconnoitering Unit advances to the north of Sataeri west of Ganseong and has a battle with a platoon and two squads of the Communist Forces, killing and injuring 16 enemy combatants.
- The ROK Army repels the Communist Forces which attacked the Jihyeong Ridge.
- The Eighth U.S. Army Commander, Maxwell D. Taylor, makes a reconnoitering flight in

The U.S. Marine Forces marching in review.(March 25,1953)

person over the Bulmo Hill battlefield.

At Home
- The Ministry of Industry and Commerce makes an urgent request for food rations to the Ministry of Agriculture and Forestry as the major mining production is about to be closed due to the food shortage.
- The South Gyeongsang Province Local Police Bureau declares a special guard over its province.

March 26, Thursday (February 12, by lunar calendar, 丙子日 Red Rat) Clear and Windy
1,006 Day of the War

War Situation
- The 1st Division of the U.S. Marine Corps succeeds in defending the Vegas Hill.(March 26-30)
- The ROK Army Unit repels the reconnoitering Unit of the Communist Forces in the north of Sataeri and the east of the Bukhan River.

At Home

A war orphan being presented with clothes by a U.S. marine. (March 26, 1953)

- The Korean Government submits to the National Assembly a revised and strengthened the Military Veterans Support Law.
- The Monetary Policy Committee makes a decision to loan 7.7 billion Hwan to the Joseon Electric Power Corporation.

March 27, Friday (February 13, by lunar calendar, 丁丑日 Red Ox) Cloudy
1,007 Day of the War

War Situation
- The U.S. Marine Corps succeed in recapturing one outpost position on Bulmo Hill under the cover of heavy artillery.
- Two POWs trying to escape are killed in the Geoje POW camp.

At Home
- President Syngman Rhee advises to reorganize the Korean Farmers League as the Central Farmers Commission considering the conflicts of the Peasant League.
- The Cabinet Meeting passes the militia order.

Overseas
- The UN Political Committee rejects a motion of the Soviet Union to invite North Korea and the People's Republic of China to discuss germ warfare.

March 28, Saturday (February 14, by lunar calendar, 戊寅日 Yellow Tiger) Rainy and Windy
1,008 Day of the War

War Situation

- The U.S. 5th Air Force announces that the improved F-86 fighter-bombers are deployed in the U.S. bomber squadron in Korea, which are able to carry atomic bombs.
- The Commander of the Communist Forces accepts the proposal to exchange injured POWs.

At Home

- The National Assembly Legislation and Judiciary Committee passes a bill to establish the South-west Police Forces.
- The Minister of Home Affairs, Jin Heon-sik, expels the Japanese laborers from Korea after they landed illegally in Incheon through the employment by the UN Forces.

Overseas

- Gromyko, the Soviet Ambassador to the UK returns to England after acting for the representative of the Soviet Union to the UN, Vyshinsky.
- Stevenson, the Secretary of the Army, leave for East Asia to survey the ammunition supply for the Korean War.

March 29, Sunday (February 15, by lunar calendar, 己卯日 Yellow Rabbit) Cloudy, Rainy and Windy
1,009 Day of the War

War Situation

- The U.S. Marine Corps attack and repel the Chinese Communist Forces on Vegas Hill and kill or injure 457 enemy combatants.
- The UN Forces Command makes an important announcement.

Overseas

- The Prime Ministers of India and Burma have a surveying tour on the border of the two nations.

March 30, Monday (February 16, by lunar calendar, 庚辰日 White Dragon) Clear, Rainy, Windy and Clear
1,010 Day of the War

- A heavy bomber squadron of the UN Air Force fiercely bombs the Communist Forces' position near Bulmo Hill.
- The National Assembly Plenary Session passes a resolution about the special accounts law for recovering the war situation and the 5th issue of Government bonds for National Foundation.

March 31, Tuesday (February 17, by lunar calendar, 辛巳日 White Snake) Clear and Cloudy

1,011 Day of the War

War Situation

- The ROK Army battles for two hours with the Chinese Communist Forces who attacked Christmas Hill on the eastern front and kill more than 100 before repelling them.
- The liaison officers of the UN Forces and the Communist Forces have a meeting in Panmunjom to adjust the exchange problem of the heavily injured POWs.

At Home

- An advisor for President Syngman Rhee declares that the five conditions for the Armistice of the Korean War insisted by the President will not be changed.
- Stevenson, the Secretary of the U.S. Army visits Korea to survey the fronts and has a pleasant talk with President Syngman Rhee together with General Clark, the Commander of the UN Forces.

April 1, Wednesday (February 18, by lunar calendar, 壬午日 Black Horse) Cloudy
1,012 Day of the War

War Situation
- In the liaison officers meeting of both sides, the UN Forces ask for the locations of POW camps of the Communist Forces.

At Home
- The Special Cabinet Meeting is held in Busan.
- The Cabinet Meeting passes "the bill to establish the National Busan University" and "the bill to dispatch education attache to the foreign missions."

Overseas
- The delegate of India to the UN, Menon, proposes to discuss the new Chinese Armistice agreement project.

April 2, Thursday (February 19, by lunar calendar, 癸未日 Black Sheep) Clear
1,013 Day of the War

War Situation
- An Armored Regiment of the ROK Army engages the Chinese Communist Forces in Gimhwa in the middle frontline.
- Troops of the ROK Marine Corps engage the Chinese Communist Forces in the southern uninhabited region of Panmunjom.
- The liaison officer of the Communist Forces hands over a message from Kim Il Sung and Peng Dehuai to the UN Forces Commander, Clark.

At Home
- The National Assembly passes "a resolution to oppose the statement of China for the Armistice."

April 3, Friday (February 20, by lunar calendar, 甲申日 Blue Monkey) Clear, Cloudy, Windy and Clear
1,014 Day of the War

War Situation
- Troops of the U.S. Forces repulse the Chinese Communist Forces attacking outposts in the middle frontline after two hour battle.
- The liaison officer of the UN Forces receives the discretion of the date for resuming the Armistice talks from the UN Forces Commander, Clark.

At Home

Flyers distributed in the Korean War.

- The Ministry of Finance decides the tax base wheat flour imported by the grain company as 695 hwan per sack.
- The Ministry of Agriculture and Forestry holds the directors' meeting of industrial department in every province and city and it decides a detailed plan for tidal damage farmers, especially for the food prolbem farmers.

Overseas
- The Yugoslav Government expresses support for the complaints of the Burmese Government to the UN against the Taiwan Government.
- The Foreign Ministry spokesman of France announces that 14 Frenchmen detained in North Korea (including the former French deputy minister to South Korea) were released and he notifies that they will arrive in Moscow according to information received from the Government of the Soviet Union.

April 4, Saturday (February 21, by lunar calendar, 乙酉日 Blue Rooster) Clear and Windy

1,015 Day of the War

War Situation

- The UN Forces repulse the Communist Forces attacking outposts in the eastern Bukhan River.
- The UN Forces on Christmas Hill engage a company of the Communist Forces under cover of the artillery unit and repulse them overnight.

At Home

- President Syngman Rhee approves to release $10 million with the April special loan of the Korean Foreign Exchange as stabilization policy.

April 5, Sunday (February 22, by lunar calendar, 丙戌日 Red Dog) Cloudy, Clear, windy and Cloudy
1,016 Day of the War

War Situation

- The ROK Army engages the Communist Forces in the Mundeungri Valley.
- The UN Forces Command agrees on the proposal of the Communist Forces to exchange sick and wounded POWs.

At Home

- President Syngman Rhee expresses his opposition to the Armistice in the inauguration ceremony of the second Corps of the ROK Army.
- Ministry of Home Affairs plants and protects roadside trees nationwide and installs police model forest.

Overseas

- The new railroad between China and North Korea connecting Guseong, Guyang and Deokcheon is completed and an opening ceremony is held.
- Tokyo Broadcasting System reports that Commander in chief of the Vietnam National Forces, Nguyen Van Hinh, is planning to visit Korea to inspect the ROK Army.

April 6, Monday (February 23, by lunar calendar, 丁亥日 Red Pig) Clear
1,017 Day of the War

War Situation

- The liaison officer of the UN Forces suggests nine principles for the exchange of sick and wounded POWs.
- The UN Forces practice an receiving drill for the sick and wounded POWs with helicopters and doctors in the Munsan Freedom Village.

At Home

- The National Assembly Plenary Session passes the bill of "the time shifting of the National Assembly Plenary Session" and "the bill to establish the Combat Police to force the

Southwest district."

April 7, Tuesday (February 24, by lunar calendar, 戊子日 Yellow Rat) Cloudy and Clear
1,018 Day of the War

War Situation
- An infantry troops of the ROK Army recapture a hill between Christmas Hill and Capitol Hill after four counterattack operations but withdraws due to a major offensive of the Chinese Communist Forces.
- The officer meeting of both sides agrees on five items in the agreement.

At Home
- The ceremony of the World Health Day is held in the Busan City Theater.
- The Chief of police office of South Gyeongsang Province states that the Special Task Force will act to suppress hulligan on a street at night.

Overseas
- The UN Political Committee decides to immediately deliberate the complaint of Myanmar for the Nationalist Government Forces which still remain in Myanmar.

April 8, Wednesday (February 25, by lunar calendar, 己丑日 Yellow Ox) Clear
1,019 Day of the War

War Situation
- The Chinese Communist Forces attack an outpost of the UN Forces on Bunker Hill of the western frontline.

At Home
- The National Assembly reports the investigation of damages by storms and the Government declares 'the supporting order for victims.'
- The Minister of Education, Kim Beop-rin, requests adherence to the declared limitation of freshman tuition in middle schools and high schools.

Overseas
- The UN General Assembly Plenary Session adopts the disarmament resolution supported by Western Europe.

April 9, Thursday (February 26, by lunar calendar, 庚寅日 White Tiger) Clear and Cloudy
1,020 Day of the War

War Situation
- In the 4th liaison officers meeting, the Communist Forces suggest repatriating 100 sick and wounded POWs a day but the UN Forces suggest 500 sick and wounded POWs a day.

At Home

- The Ministry of Agriculture and Forestry decides to release 3,000 hwan to 500,000 families from 163 million hwan of Farming funds from May.
- "The World of Thought" is published by representative Chang Chun-ha.

April 10, Friday (February 27, by lunar calendar, 辛卯日 White Rabbit) Rainy and Clear
1,021 Day of the War

War Situation

A classification practice to repatriate POWs in the Geoje POW camp. (November 4, 1953)

512

- The Chinese Communist Forces broadcast propaganda to the U.S. Marine Corps' position near Panmunjom that the war ended.
- In the liaison officer meeting, the Communist Forces suggest a detailed plan to the UN Forces to exchange POWs.
- The UN Forces Commander, Clark, approves a draft of the agreement to exchange sick and wounded POWs.

At Home
- The National Assembly Plenary Session passes "the request to repatriate the kidnapped members of the National Assembly" and "the dispatch of the resolution to exchange sick and wounded POWs."
- Mass public rallies against the Armistice without the unification of Korea are held in Seoul and Busan.
- The representative of the Armistice talks of the Communist Forces, Nam Il, requests official talks.
- President Syngman Rhee attends the graduation ceremony of the Military Staff College.

Overseas
- The Propaganda Department of the Communist Party of China announces a notice regarding the propaganda on the Armistice Negotiation question of the Korean Peninsula. The UN Forces Commander, Clark approves the draft agreement to exchange sick and wounded POWs agreed by both the UN Forces and the Communist Forces.

April 11, Saturday (February 28, by lunar calendar, 壬辰日 Black Dragon) Cloudy and Windy
1,022 Day of the War

War Situation
- A squadron of U.S, Sabre fighters shoots down three MIG fighters and destroys three fighters.
- The liaison officer meeting of both the UN Forces and the Communist Forces formally signs the agreement to exchange sick and wounded POWs.

At Home
- President Syngman Rhee announces his statement to independently advance north and to oppose the Armistice; He states that the ROK Army will advance north unilaterally.

April 12, Sunday (February 29, by lunar calendar, 癸巳日 Black Snake) Clear and Windy
1,023 Day of the War

War Situation
- The third Division of the ROK Army recaptures Texas Hill in the middle frontline for the fifth time.

- The ROK Army concentrates fires on the Communist Forces' position in the northwestern Gorangpo.
- The liaison officer meeting agrees to begin the repatriation of sick and wounded POWs on April 20.

At Home
- President Syngman Rhee announces the statement to request an advance into the border between Korea and Manchuria.
- The Ministry of Agriculture and Forestry plans to distribute the free seed grain of millet and bean for the area of 443,343 Jeongbo (町步=9,917.4㎡) to prevent rural exodus.
- The UN Korean Reconstruction Agency establishes the 1954 reconstruction plan and appropriates $130 million.

April 13, Monday (February 30, by lunar calendar, 甲午日 Blue Horse) Clear, Windy and Cloudy
1,024 Day of the War

War Situation
- The ROK Army repulses a reconnaissance party of the Communist Forces in western Ganseong and in northern Sataeri.
- The staff officers meeting of both the UN Forces and the Communist Forces completely agree on the details of the exchange of sick and wounded POWs.
- Soldiers and medics of the UN Forces practice the retrograde transport and the exchange of transition.

At Home
- The Ministry of Trade and Industry plans to clean up abandoned mines and requests it to the Privatization Projects Agency of the state operated mining industry.
- The headquarters of the reception of sick and wounded POWs is established.

Overseas
- The authorities of the French Forces in Hanoi announce that the Allied Forces of France and Laos withdraw from Sam Nuea in northern Laos due to the pressure of two Divisions of the Ho Chi Minh Forces.
- The Ho Chi Minh Communist Forces occupy a position in the southern area of the Tourane harbor and 13 soldiers of the French Forces are killed and 25 soldiers are missing.
- The Minister of Defense of France, Pleven, states that if they fail in the Indo-China War, the Middle East and Africa will be in danger.

April 14, Tuesday (March 1, by lunar calendar, 乙未日 Blue Sheep) Clear, Cloudy and Clear
1,025 Day of the War

War Situation

- The UN Forces engage the Communist Forces three times in outposts of the southern Panmunjom.
- A Shooting Star jet-fighter squad of the U.S. flies over North Korea to protect 20 vehicles of the transportation unit which departed from the Cheonma POW camp to Kaesong in North Korea.

At Home
- The Finance and Economy Committee of the National Assembly passes "the legislative amendment bill of the Liquor Tax Law" after revisions.
- The Daegu high court of justice bails Seo Sang-il, Baeng Nam-hun and Kim Seong-gyu who are sentenced with provation as the persons involved in the sniping the president.

Overseas
- A person who is close to the UN Forces Commander states that the Communist Forces completed the final defense line highly modernized on the opposite side of the Yalu River.

April 15, Wednesday (March 2, by lunar calendar, 丙申日 Red Monkey) Cloudy
1,026 Day of the War

War Situation
- A North Korean Army Unit consisting of 150~200 soldiers attacks a position of the UN Forces in the west of Heartbreak Ridge; The U.S. Army kills 30 soldiers of the Communist Forces with 25 casualties.

At Home
- The National Assembly Plenary Session passes "the bill of the Labor Standards Law" and "the motion to stick the present price of raw cotton."
- The Ministry of Agriculture and Forestry announces that the amount of importing grains on April 13 is 1,870,000 seok which are 37% of the amount planned to import.

April 16, Thursday (March 3, by lunar calendar, 丁酉日 Red Rooster) Clear and Windy
1,027 Day of the War

War Situation
- The UN Forces Command requests to meet at Panmunjom on April 17 to hand over the letter of the Chief Representative of the UN Forces, Harrison, to resume the Armistice talks.

At Home
- The National Assembly introduces the bill of the Criminal Law legislated for the first time after the Government formation in the 55th National Assembly Plenary Session and it finishes the first reading.

Overseas
- The Taipei Associated Press reports that the former 24th Division Commander in Korea,

Maj. Gen. Dean, is transported from a POW camp near Pyongyang to Beijing.

April 17, Friday (March 4, by lunar calendar, 戊戌日 Yellow Dog) Clear, Windy, Cloudy and Clear
1,028 Day of the War

War Situation
• UN Forces Commander Clark orders to notify to the Communist Forces side that the UN Forces hope to meet on April 18 to discuss the main conference of the Armistice talks.

At Home
• The former vice president, Lee Si-yeong, dies.
• The National Assembly Plenary Session passes a bill of the expression of condolence for the death of the former vice president, Lee Si-yeong.
• The delegation of the U.S. presidential envoy, Taskar, visits Korea to inspect the economic conditions of Korea and forms the three-year plan for Korea aid.

April 18, Saturday (March 5, by lunar calendar, 己亥日 Yellow Pig) Cloudy and Clear
1,029 Day of the War

War Situation
• The UN Forces recapture Porkchop Hill in the western frontline after a fierce battle.
• The staff officers meeting of both parties discusses the handover time of exchanging sick and wounded POWs which will be carried out on April 20.

At Home
• The Government proclaims "the Public Educational Officials Law" stipulating eligibility and guarantee of status of the officials.
• The Ministry of Agriculture and Forestry decides to organize inspection teams in every province and to monitor the distribution situation of wheat flour for preparing against disaster.

Overseas
• The 6th atomic bomb tests in the year of 1953 are conducted in Nevada.
• The Armed Services Committee of NATO (the North Atlantic Treaty Organization) is held in Paris.

April 19, Sunday (March 6, by lunar calendar, 庚子日 White Rat) Cloudy and Clear
1,030 Day of the War

War Situation
• The UN Forces Command announces that the UN Forces Commander, Clark orders the Eighth U.S. Army Commander, Taylor, to establish two more Divisions in the ROK Army.
• The UN Forces Commander, Clark, arrives at Munsan and states that the possibility of the

The representative of the Communist Forces, Lee Sang-jo, and the representative of the UN Forces, Admiral John Daniel, signing the agreement for exchange of POWs at Panmunjom. (1953. 4. 17)

Armistice is much higher than before.

At Home
- The wives' party of 12 Ministries and four Offices of the Government visit and pay their respects at the National Cemetery laying a flower bouquet in front of the graves.

April 20, Monday (March 7, by lunar calendar, 辛丑日 White Ox) Clear and Windy
1,031 Day of the War

War Situation
- The exchange of sick and wounded POWs starts in Panmunjom. (April 20-May 3)
- The UN Forces receive 50 Koreans and 50 other POWs and send 400 North Korean POWs and 100 Chinese POWs.

At Home
- President Syngman Rhee announces plans to establish two Divisions of the ROK Army (the 22nd and the 25th infantry Divisions) and he hopes that the two established Divisions will carry out their duty to the fullest and assist the U.S. Army.

Overseas
- The Philippine Air Force announces that the Philippine Government will dispatch two

companies of the Air Force.
- U.S. Secretary of State Dulles explains the Korean issues in a press conference.

April 21, Tuesday (March 8, by lunar calendar, 壬寅日 Black Tiger) Clear, Cloudy and Windy 1,032 Day of the War

War Situation
- In the second exchange of sick and wounded POWs, the UN Forces receives 35 U.S. soldiers, 12 U.K. soldiers, 3 Turkish soldiers and 50 ROK soldiers in the total of 100.

At Home
- The National Assembly Plenary Session listens to a report of the inspection of the administration conducted by the National Assembly.
- The Government appoints the Director of the Railway Bureau of Seoul, Lee Jong-nim, as the Vice-Minister of Transportation.

Overseas
- Six Britons released in North Korea depart from Moscow for Berlin on a British airplane.

April 22, Wednesday (March 9, by lunar calendar, 癸卯日 Black Rabbit) Cloudy, Windy and Clear 1,033 Day of the War

War Situation

General Clark visiting the Freedom Village to welcome the POWs.(April 20, 1953) 100 POWs of the UN Forces arrive at Panmunjom in the day.

The exchange of sick and wounded POWs in Panmunjom.(April 22,1953)

- A Marine Unit of the ROK Army repulses the Chinese Communist Forces attacking the area near Panmunjom after 4 hours of battle.
- A squad of fighter bombers of the UN Air Forces bombs a supply center of the Communist Forces in Sariwon.

At Home
- The National Assembly Plenary Session adopts a resolution on carrying out a national movement for unification by marching north.
- The central headquarters of the Student National Defense Corps hold the general rally of the Student National Defense Corps for unification by marching north in celebration of the 4th anniversary of the founding in the Chungmuro square in Busan.

April 23, Thursday (March 10, by lunar calendar, 甲辰日 Blue Dragon) Clear and Windy
1,034 Day of the War

War Situation

- Shock troops of the ROK Army ambush the Communist Forces in southern Panmunjom and kill 20 soldiers.
- Maj. Gen. Daniel announces that the Communist Forces promised a repatriation of all the sick and wounded POWs.

At Home
- President Syngman Rhee laments the death of Lee Si-yeong and consoles the bereaved family.
- The National Assembly organizes a special committee on the movement for unification by marching north.
- The Government submits "the bill of the Upper House Election Law" to the National Assembly.
- The public general rally of unification by marching north opposes the Armistice dividing Korean territory and holds a mass meeting exclaiming the advance to the north in Busan.

Overseas
- The UN General Assembly agrees to set up a special international committee to investigate the Communist Forces' denunciation of bacteriological warfare in Korea. (51 in favor, 5 against and 4 abstentions)
- The Korean Residents Union in Japan issues the letter of confidence to the delegate sending to the Korean National Assembly, Kim Jae-hwa(金華載), Kim Gwang-nam, Kim Young-jun, Won Sim-chang and Kim Jae-hwa(金在和).
- The Japanese Government requests the release of three criminals out of in 12 war criminals of A-class who are over 70 years old in the Sugamo prison.
- U.S. President Eisenhower mentions the Korean Armistice in a press conference.

April 24, Friday (March 11, by lunar calendar, 乙巳日 Blue Snake) Clear and Cloudy
1,035 Day of the War

War Situation
- In the liaison officer meeting, the representative of the UN Forces, Maj. Gen. Daniel, promises that the UN Forces will increase the number of sick and wounded POWs of the Communist Forces to respond to the measures stated by the Communist Forces on April 23.

At Home
- The National Assembly approves the appointment of the Prime Minister, Baek Du-jin.
- President Syngman Rhee officially orders the Prime Minister, Baek Du-jin to also serve as the Minister of Finance and the administrator of the Ministry of Planning.
- The Tasca delegation listens to the actual circumstances of the Korean Commerce and Industry from the representative of Korea Chamber of Commerce at the Prime Minister's

Office.

- The headquarters of the Korean Residents Association in Japan announces the opposition of the Armistice without the unification.

April 25, Saturday (March 12, by lunar calendar, 丙午日 Red Horse) Clear
1,036 Day of the War

War Situation

- In the 6ᵗʰ exchange of sick and wounded POWs, the UN Forces receive 100 sick and wounded POWs of the UN Forces. (17 soldiers of the U.S. Army, four soldiers of the U.K., four soldiers of the Turkish Forces, 75 soldiers of the ROK Army)

At Home

- The Prime Minister, Baek Du-jin, assumes his office in front of the National Assembly building.
- In the 5th day, the Tasca talks discusses issues of importing raw material and supply mechanical material to promote the production and to resolve the difficulties of the fishing industry and the iron industry.

April 26, Sunday (March 13, by lunar calendar, 丁未日 Red Sheep) Rainy and Cloudy
1,037 Day of the War

War Situation

- The main conference of the Armistice talks resumes in six months.
  The representative of the Armistice talks in the Communist Forces, Nam Il, opposes the appointment of Switzerland as the Neutral Nation for supervising and managing the release of POWs.
- The 7th exchange of sick and wounded POWs takes place.

At Home

- The authorities of military affairs in the Ministry of National Defense decide to conscript all the young men of draft age under 25 who are working in the vital organs and institutions of the Government.
- The Korea-U.S. Economic conference opens.

April 27, Monday (March 14, by lunar calendar, 戊申日 Yellow Monkey) Clear
1,038 Day of the War

War Situation

- In the main conference of the Armistice talks, the chief delegate of the UN Forces makes a counterargument against the six-item suggestion on the POW issues which was submitted by the Communist Forces on April 26.

- In the 8th exchange of sick and wounded POWs, the UN Forces repatriate 500 soldiers of the North Korean Communist Forces and finish repatriating 4,000 sick and wounded POWs of the UN Forces.

At Home

- The Ministry of Commerce and Industry suggests the five-year industry plan to the Tasca delegation.
- The Government abolishes the current Hangeul orthography and instructs to use the old type Hangul orthography.
- The Korean Language Society states its views on opposing the abolishment of the current Hangeul orthography.

April 28, Tuesday (March 15, by lunar calendar, 己酉日 Yellow Rooster) Clear and Windy
1,039 Day of the War

War Situation

- Shock troops of the ROK Army attack two positions of the Communist Forces near the Myohyeong Hill on the eastern frontline.
- The representative of the UN Forces warns that the UN Forces will adjourn the Armistice talks if the Communist Forces do not suggest a constructive proposal.

At Home

- The National Assembly Plenary Session passes "the bill of the Old Imperial Court Property Law."
- The National Assembly passes "the amendment bill of the Liquor Tax Law."
- The Budget and Accounts Committee of the National Assembly completes the comprehensive audit of the 1953 Government revenue and expenditure budget.

Overseas

- The advance Units of the Ho Chi Minh Army raiding Laos approach within 20 km of the capital town of Luang Prabang.

April 29, Wednesday (March 16, by lunar calendar, 庚戌日 White Dog) Cloudy, Rainy and Windy
1,040 Day of the War

War Situation

- The UN Forces Command announces an official statement on the issues of POW exchange that the foreign transfer of the POWs who rejected the repatriation means deportation.
- The UN Forces repatriate 500 Communist POWs to the Communist Forces.

At Home

- The Five-year economic reconstruction plan is materialized and the Government appropriates $600 million. (40 billion hwan in the Korean currency)
- The Director of the Security Department, Mun Bong-je, announces that two Communist guerrillas who tried to visit Japan in a smuggling vessel are arrested.

April 30, Thursday (March 17, by lunar calendar, 辛亥日 White Pig) Rainy, Clear and Windy
1,041 Day of the War

War Situation
- A Sabre jet fighter squad of the UN Forces engages in an air battle with MIG fighters of the Communist Forces over North Korea and shoots down 3jet fighters and destroys 2 jet fighters.
- In the main conference of the Armistice talks, the representative of the UN Forces, Harrison, rejects Asian countries as the Neutral Nation to supervise the exchange of POWs and he requests the Communists Forces side to designate the Neutral Nation to supervise the exchange of POWs.

At Home
- The National Assembly Plenary Session passes "the resolution of the investigation for the Sancheong's state of public security" and "the 1953 budget bill."
- The 15th regular session of the National Assembly decides to extend the National Assembly by May 30 for a month.

Overseas
- The French Forces of Indochina announces that the Ho Chi Minh Forces occupy Nam Bak after the hard fought battle 80km of Luang Prabang, the capital of Laos.

May 1, Friday (March 18, by lunar calendar, 壬子日 Black Rat) Cloudy and Windy
1,042 Day of the War

War Situation

- Ground battles are calm.
- Thunder jet fighters bomb a collecting point of the Communist Forces on the western frontline.

At Home

- The National Assembly Plenary Session passes "the amendment bill of the Korea Minting and Security Printing Corporation Law" and "the bill of issuing 2 billion hwan of national bonds."
- The National Assembly passes the national budget bill - The general accounting is 28,420,860,000 hwan, the cost of settlement of the war is 57.7 billion hwan, and the special account is 149,712,780,000 hwan.

Overseas

- The U.S. State Department announces that 48,000 POWs of the Communist Forces do not want to be repatriated.

May 2, Saturday (March 19, by lunar calendar, 癸丑日 Black Ox) Cloudy, Clear and Windy
1,043 Day of the War

War Situation

- A company of the Chinese Communist Force attacks the UN Forces' position within 4.8 km of eastern Gimhwa at night.
- The Chinese Communist Forces attacks the resistance line of the UN Forces in northeastern Gorangpo.

At Home

- The committee of inspection of state administration, the National Assembly selects the member of the National Assembly, Oh Seong-hwan, as the chairman.
- The Ministry of Health establishes free milk porridge posts in many rural areas which are in a food-short state for the spring season.

May 3, Sunday (March 20, by lunar calendar, 甲寅日 Blue Tiger) Clear
1,044 Day of the War

War Situation

- Companies of the Chinese Communist Forces attack the UN Forces' positions in the

Mundeungri Valley and near Panmunjom.

- The Chinese Communist Forces attack Units of the Australian Army and the British Army in Gorangpo on the western frontline.

At Home

- The chairman of the Armed Services Committee the U.S. House of Representatives states the necessity to uphold the insistence on unification about the Korean War.
- The French Government requests the U.K. Government to transfer 50 cargo planes to be used in the Laos War.

May 4, Monday (March 21, by lunar calendar, 乙卯日 Blue Rabbit) Clear, Cloudy and Rainy
1,045 Day of the War

War Situation

- The representative of the UN Forces, Harrison, designates Pakistan as the Neutral Nation for supervising the repatriation of POWs.
- The representative of the UN Forces, Harrison, warns that if the Communist Forces do not engage in the Armistice Conference with a constructive attitude, the talks will be stopped.

At Home

- The National Assembly Plenary Session passes "the amendment bill of Korea Coal Corporation Law"
- The central council of the National Social Organizations dissolves itself due to establishing

President Syngman Rhee and his wife and Cabinet Member (May 2, 1953)

the struggle council of unification by marching north.

Overseas

• The French Forces and Laos Forces intensify their defense positions to protect the capital of Laos.

May 5, Tuesday (March 22, by lunar calendar, 丙辰日 Red Dragon) Cloudy and Rainy
1,046 Day of the War

War Situation

• All of the frontline is calm.
• Task fleets of the U.S. Navy bombard military targets of the Communist Forces in the Wonsan port of the east coast.
• The representative of the UN Forces, Harrison, states an opposition to transferring the POWs who do not want the repatriation to foreign countries as it is not practical.

At Home

• The foreign affairs subcommittee of the National Assembly adopts "the bill of the Foreign Study Law" after a preliminary examination with partial amendments.
• The 17th, 604th, 611th and 614th troops districts of Imsil, Jangsu, Sunchang, Namwon, in

U.S. Soldiers unloading presents to be given to children in an orphanage. (May 5, 1953)

526

"North Jeolla Province" handed over its authority to the Southwest district combat police force.

Overseas
- The French Union Minister, Letourneau, announces that France will not abandon any part of Indochina.

May 6, Wednesday (March 23, by lunar calendar, 丁巳日 Red Snake) Cloudy and Rainy
1,047 Day of the War

War Situation
- All of the frontline enters a lull.
- The U.S. battleship, USS New Jersey, bombs Wonsan Port and a Thunder jet fighter squad bombs the Kanggye reservoir.
- The Chief Representative, Harrison proposes the release of Korean POWs and then to send them home when the Armistice Agreement is signed.

At Home
- The National Assembly Plenary Session approves the dispatch of a telegram to the chairman of the House Armed Services Committee, Mr. Shot.
- The Ministry of National Defense establishes the permanent censorship for military affair organizations and forms the inspection team of military affairs with civil officials and soldiers over lieutenant colonel rank.

May 7, Thursday (March 24, by lunar calendar, 戊午日 Yellow Horse) Rainy and Windy
1,048 Day of the War

War Situation
- The U.S. battleship, USS New Jersey and the cruiser, USS Bremerton, dash into Wonsan Port and then bombard intensively the coast-batteries of the Communist Forces.
- The Communist Forces agrees on the proposal of the UN Forces that the POWs who do not want to be repatriated will stay in Korea and suggests eight new items such as establishing the repatriation committee of five nations.

At Home
- The National Assembly Plenary Session passes "the bill of the Mobilization of Labor Force in Time of War Law" and "the amendment bill of the Families of the War Dead and Disabled Veterans' Pension Act."
- The National Assembly passes "the bill of increasing capital for the Korea Shipbuilding Corporation."
- The members of the appointments committee and the classification committee of service status for dishonorable discharged soldiers are appointed.

- The spokesman of the Indochina French Forces states that the Laos evacuation of the Ho Chi Minh Forces is an invasion abandonment concerning the rains which will start on May 15.

May 8, Friday (March 25, by lunar calendar, 己未日 Yellow Sheep) Rainy
1,049 Day of the War

War Situation

- Ground battles continue to be calm.
- A Navy vessel of the UN Forces dashes into the fog-shrouded Wonsan Port with a radio detection and bombs military facilities and coast-batteries of the Communist Forces.

At Home

- President Syngman Rhee notifies the U.S. Government that he does not recognize the Armistice.
- The agreement of transferring Bando Hotel and Samjeong Building between Korea and the United States is signed and takes effect.

May 9, Saturday (March 26, by lunar calendar, 庚申日 White Monkey) Clear
1,050 Day of the War

War Situation

- A Thunder jet fighter squad of the UN Forces attacks a assemble place of the Communist Forces near the Yalu River.
- The chief delegate of the UN Forces, Harrison, expresses that they are willing to discuss the eight-item proposal of the Communist Forces as the base plan.

At Home

- The Ministry of Home Affairs requests to prevent electric accidents to the Ministry of Commerce and Industry.
- A General Rally for Unification by marching north is held in Chungmuro square in Busan.
- The Changsin Welfare Establishment for Mothers and Children opens.

Overseas

- Radio Beijing criticizes the chief delegate of the UN Forces, Harrison, for questioning whether the Communist Forces are trying to sabotage the completion of the Prisoners of War Exchange Pact.
- The U.S. Secretary of State, Dulles, expresses that they will adjust parts of the eight items of the Communist Forces after discussing it with other troop dispatching countries of the Korean War.

May 10, Sunday (March 27, by lunar calendar, 辛酉日 White Rooster) Clear
1,051 Day of the War

War Situation

- Ground combats are calm.
- A Thunder jet fighter squad of the UN Forces bombs the Supung power plant on the Yalu River.

At Home

- The Liberal Party holds the National Convention in Daejeon.
- The Government decrees "the appeal evaluating regulation for the military disciplinary punishment."

May 11, Monday (March 28, by lunar calendar, 壬戌日 Black Dog) Clear, Cloudy, Rainy and Windy
1,052 Day of the War

War Situation

- Ground combats and air battles are calm due to the heavy rain.
- The representative of the Communist Forces, Nam Il, insists that issues of the POWs who do not want to be repatriated must be discussed in a political conference.

Overseas

- Zhou Enlai announces a statement for strictly complaining about the violation of the Chinese territorial skies by U.S. aircraft.
- The Korean-Japanese Conference discusses property rights of former Japanese residents in Korea.

May 12, Tuesday (March 29, by lunar calendar, 癸亥日 Black Pig) Rainy, Cloudy and Clear
1,053 Day of the War

War Situation

- The UN Forces Commander, Clark, arrives at Munsan with a new alternative proposal of the UN Forces about the eight-item proposal of the Communist Forces.

At Home

- President Syngman Rhee has a meeting with the UN Forces Commander, Clark, under tightest secrecy.
- The Navy enrolls civil servants in the navy as soldier who are under the age of the conscription.

Overseas

- The UN Secretary General, Hammarskjold, appoints the retired lieutenant general of the U.S. Army, John Coulter, as the UN representative of the UN Korean Reconstruction Agency for the next two-year term from May 16.

- The personnel of the leading members of the U.S. Forces transfer.

May 13, Wednesday (April 1, by lunar calendar, 甲子日 Blue Rat) Cloudy, Clear and Cloudy
1,054 Day of the War

War Situation
- The ROK Army repulses 1,000 soldiers of the Chinese Communist Forces attacking Texas Hill of the central eastern frontline after a fierce ten-hour battle.
- The UN Forces suggests that they will be released as civilians and will be transported to the central committee when they refuse repatriation after 60 days, they will be released and the Contral Committee will be disclued. The Communist Side rejected this proposal on the spot.

At Home
- The Aggregate Corporation of the Federation of the Korea Knitted Fabrics Industry Association is founded. (President: Kim Hang-bok)

May 14, Thursday (April 2, by lunar calendar, 乙丑日 Blue Ox) Cloudy, Clear and Windy
1,055 Day of the War

War Situation
- The ROK Army repulses a company of the Chinese Communist Forces attacking in northern Gimhwa of the central eastern frontline.
- The Chief delegate, Harrison, attacks the Communist Forces for transferring some of the Korean POWs in the Communist Forces and forcing them to do compulsory labor.

At Home
- Anti-Communist POWs present a release petition to President Syngman Rhee.
- Brigadier General, Rogers proceeds to his post as the director of the ROK Army Advisory Group in succession to the director, Lyon.
- Gwangmyeongwon teaches blind veterans in Braille education.

Overseas
- The U.S. Pacific Ocean Security Conference (Honolulu) is closed.

May 15, Friday (April 3, by lunar calendar, 丙寅日 Red Tiger) Clear and Windy
1,056 Day of the War

War Situation
- The Chinese Communist Forces attack the Turkish Troops in Panmunjom.
- The representative of the Communist Forces, Nam Il, blames that the new suggestion of the UN Forces is a self-contradiction.

At Home

- The Speaker of the National Assembly, Shin Ik-hee, holds an Oriental painting exhibition to be presented to the Queen of England in the office of the Speaker of the National Assembly.
- The National Association of the Korea Young Men and the Labor Union with joint name announce a critical statement on the Liberal Party Convention held in May 10.

May 16, Saturday (April 4, by lunar calendar, 丁卯日 Red Rabbit) Cloudy and Clear
1,057 Day of the War

War Situation
- The Communist Forces heavily attack the UN Forces' position in every frontline including the middle frontline.
- The ROK Army in the middle frontline repulses the Chinese Communist Forces attacking with a Regiment after a fierce battle.

At Home
- The ministerial meeting decides to shorten the term of a college graduation by four months.

Overseas
- The Xinua News Agency of China reports that the new suggestion of the UN is to try to prevent the compulsory repatriation of POWs.
- The U.S. Mutual Security Agency announces the cessation of economic aid for Iceland.

May 17, Sunday (April 5, by lunar calendar, 戊辰日 Yellow Dragon) Clear
1,058 Day of the War

War Situation
- An Infantry Unit of the ROK Army mounts a counterattack against the Chinese Communist Forces which has occupied the outpost of the ROK Army in the central east frontline.
- The chief delegate, Harrison, departs for Tokyo to discuss the Armistice issues with the UN Forces Commander, Clark.

At Home
- The national arts contest is held in North Korea.

Overseas
- The Japanese Socialist Party blames that the Prime Minister, Yoshida, has cooperated with the U.S. to delay the Armistice conclusion of the Korean War.
- The NATO Forces Commander, Ridgway, arrives at Washington to present the final report to the Congress and President Eisenhower.

May 18, Monday (April 6, by lunar calendar, 己巳日 Yellow Snake) Clear and Windy

1,059 Day of the War

War Situation

- The ROK Army has repulsed the Communist Forces' attacks four times on Heartbreak Ridge.
- A Sabre jet fighter squad shoots down 12 MIG jet fighters in the air battles over North Korea.

At Home

- The Speaker of the National Assembly, Shin Ik-hee, and the member of the National Assembly, Kim Dong-sung, visit Europe and Britain to visit allied combatant nations and attend the coronation ceremony of the Queen of England.
- The spokesman of the Government emphasizes that the request of the chief delegate of the UN Forces in the Armistice talks, Harrison, for releasing Korean POWs at the Armistice completion is correct and does not need any amendment.

May 19, Tuesday (April 7, by lunar calendar, 庚午日 White Horse) Clear
1,060 Day of the War

War Situation

- The ROK Army repulses the Chinese Communist Forces attacking Christmas Hill and Sniper Ridge on the central eastern frontline.
- The Armistice talks which is planned to resume on May 20 is postponed till May 25.

At Home

- The Ministry of Education issues the decision that the educational expense for the posterity of patriotic martyrs for the country and surviving patriots is exempt.
- The Government Administration Ministery returns to Seoul.
- The Foreign Ministry of North Korea announces an denounciation statement on bombing the Suncheon and Sunan reservoirs.

Overseas

- The Korean delegates of the Korean-Japanese Conference submit the list of property claims to Japan in the subcommittee meeting of property claims.

May 20, Wednesday (April 8, by lunar calendar, 辛未日 White Sheep) Clear, Cloudy and Clear
1,061 Day of the War

War Situation

- The Chinese Communist Forces attacks the UN Forces' outpost on Hook Hill of the western frontline.

At Home

- The Ministry of Social Affairs decides to recruit 1,400 office workers according to the sudden increase of the relief office works of the military and police.

Overseas
- The authorities of the Indochina French Forces announce that the Ho Chi Minh Forces occupy Muang Khua 140 km north of the capital of Laos, Luang Prabang.

May 21, Thursday (April 9, by lunar calendar, 壬申日 Black Monkey) Cloudy
1,062 Day of the War

War Situation
- The ROK Army repulses the Chinese Communist Forces attacking the UN Forces' position in the eastern frontline after 12 hour bloody battle.

At Home
- The Hwacheon power plant is restored.
- Canadian Brigadier General, Nell Burton, visits Korea to inspect the Korean Military Academy and pays a courtesy call on the headquarters of the ROK Army.

Overseas
- The U.K. Prime Minister, Winston Churchill, states that it is possible to make a new proposal to realize the Armistice completion of the Korean War.

May 22, Friday (April 10, by lunar calendar, 癸酉日 Black Rooster) Rainy and Windy
1,063 Day of the War

War Situation
- The UN Forces repulse the Chinese Communist Forces after several clashes in the Midwestern frontline.
- The representative of the UN Forces, Harrison, states that they will try to realize repatriation of kidnapped South Korean persons.

At Home
- The Ministry of National Defense states that the physical examination of strong young men under 32 years old is not for extending the age of military force mobilization but only for assessing the number of young men available for service.

May 23, Saturday (April 11, by lunar calendar, 甲戌日 Blue Dog) Cloudy and Clear
1,064 Day of the War

War Situation
- All of the frontline is calm.
- The U.S. Forces engage a company of Chinese Communist Forces.
- The delegation of Korea is enforced in the Armistice talks.

At Home

- The National Assembly decides to review treating problems of the Korean Service Corps (KSC) in the four subcommittees of National Defense, Home Affairs, Health and Social Affairs, and Finance and Economy.
- The special envoy, Tasca, attends a citizen's rally in Gwangju and states that Korea has a lot of mineral resources and it is possible to become an industrial country, depending on the exploition of them.

Overseas
- French and Vietnamese allied Forces take the initiative in the Song Koi delta combat and northern Laos.

May 24, Sunday (April 12, by lunar calendar, 乙亥日 Blue Pig) Clear
1,065 Day of the War

War Situation
- The Chinese Communist Forces attack two positions of the ROK Army with heavy artillery between Geumseong and Gimhwa.
- Two U.S. cruisers (Bremerton, Manchester) bomb coast-batteries of the Communist Forces, dashing into Wonsan Port.

At Home
- The Minister of Foreign Affairs, Byeon Yeong-tae states that he absolutely opposes the Armistice completion neglecting the Division of Korea.
- The North Material Cultural Heritage Conservation Commission and the Ancient Relic Expedition discovers bronze potter´s wheels in the Naknang tomb in southeastern Pyongyang.

May 25, Monday (April 13, by lunar calendar, 丙子日 Red Rat) Clear and Windy
1,066 Day of the War

War Situation
- The U.S. battleship, USS New Jersey, heavily attacks coast-batteries of the Communist Forces near the Daedong River.
- A fighter bomber squad of the U.S. Marine Corps drops 29,500 kg of high explosive bombs on an assembly point of the Communist Forces in Sinmak.
- The UN Forces hold a secret meeting for new suggestions.

At Home
- The delegation of the Korean Women´s Association in Japan visits Korea to encourage the Korean War refugees and hands over 46 boxes of clothes and blankets.
- The Daegu Daily News publishes its first issue.

May 26, Tuesday (April 14, by lunar calendar, 丁丑日 Red Ox) Clear and Windy
1,067 Day of the War

War Situation
- A squadron of Sabre jet fighters in the U.S. Air Force shoots down twelve MIG jet fighters: five in the morning and seven in the afternoon.

At Home
- The Vice-Speaker of the National Assembly, Jo Bong-am, insists that ignoring opinions of Korea in the Armistice talks is an infringement of sovereignty.
- The Canadian Mission visits Gwangmyeongwon to meet blind veterans and donates 45 Braille writers.

May 27, Wednesday (April 15, by lunar calendar, 戊寅日 Yellow Tiger) Cloudy
1,068 Day of the War

War Situation
- The liaison officers of both parties hold a meeting by request of the Communist Forces and discuss the complaint that two ROK soldiers in North Korean Army military uniforms invaded the neutral zone.

At Home
- The Board of Education and the Education District are organized and the normal compulsory education starts.
- An anti-Armistice demonstration is held in Seoul.

Overseas
- The Chinese Communist Forces and the North Korean Army develop the second phase of the summer offensives.(May 27~ June 16)

May 28, Thursday (April 16, by lunar calendar, 己卯日 Yellow Rabbit) Cloudy, Rainy and Windy
1,069 Day of the War

War Situation
- The representative of the ROK Army, Choe Deok-sin, hands over a letter expressing the view of Korea for the Armistice talks to the representative, Harrison.
- The liaison officers of both parties hold a meeting by request of the UN Forces and discuss administrative problems.

At Home
- The delegation of the National Assembly has an interview with the representative of the UN Forces in the Armistice talks, Harrison and requests to immediately consider a new proposal.
- The Struggle Committee for Unification by marching north rejects humiliating new armistce

proposal of the UN Forces.

May 29, Friday (April 17, by lunar calendar, 庚辰日 White Dragon) Rainy, Cloudy and Windy
1,070 Day of the War

War Situation
- The 25th Division (the Turkish brigade) loses the Nevada outpost.
- The 1st Division of the British Commonwealth defends Hook Hill.

At Home
- President Syngman Rhee departs for Jinhae to attend the Cabinet Meeting to discuss the Armistice.
- The National Assembly passes a bill to investige the press article that the President approved the Armistice Proposal of the UN Forces unofficially.
- The Korean Youth Association states that they oppose the Armistice talks ignoring the opinions of South Korean people.

May 30, Saturday (April 18, by lunar calendar, 辛巳日 White Snake) Cloudy
1,071 Day of the War

War Situation
- The UN Forces on the western frontline develop hand-to-hand fighting with the Chinese Communist Forces.

At Home
- President Syngman Rhee hands over an official letter for the Armistice to the U.S. President, Eisenhower.
- The National Assembly Plenary Session decides to form a Special Investigation Team, to investigate grain administration and to punish the person in charge.
- The 15th regular session of the National Assembly is closed.

Overseas
- Radio Beijing blames the Japanese Government for intentionally delaying repatriation of Chinese in Japan to the mainland China.
- Saran, the former Commander of the French Forces in Indochina, states to the Press Corps that if aid is provided, the victory of the allied Forces in the Indochina War will be certain.

May 31, Sunday (April 19, by lunar calendar, 壬午日 Black Horse) Cloudy and Rainy
1,072 Day of the War

War Situation
- The Chinese Communist Forces attack the UN Forces' outpost in northern Gimhwa.

- The representative of the ROK Army in the Armistice talks, Maj. Gen. Choe Deok-sin, interviews a Press Corps in Seoul, and states that if the new suggestion of the UN Forces in May 25 is not withdrawn or amended, the Armistice talks will continuously be rejected.

At Home
- President Syngman Rhee emphasizes no concession in the Armistice talks and states that if provision for the unity of Korean territory is not written, he will reject any international agreement.

Overseas
- The Ambassador of Korea to Washington, Yang Yu-chan, states that if the UN Forces do not complete the unification of Korea and do not withdraw after the Armistice talks, the ROK Army will continue to fight for the unification.

June 1, Monday (April 20, by lunar calendar, 癸未日 Black Sheep) Cloudy and Rainy
1,073 Day of the War

War Situation

- The Communist Forces attack the UN Forces' position on Myohyeong Hill in the western frontline.
- The ROK Army repulses the Communist Forces attacking Sniper Ridge in the mid-frontline.
- A reconnaissance party of the UN Forces engages the Chinese Communist Forces near Large Nori Hill in the western frontline.

At Home

- President Syngman Rhee hands over a compromise proposal to the United States.
- Korean products are exhibitted at the international trade fair in Canada.
- The Air Force reforms a training center of facility noncommissioned officers and moves it into the airman school.

Overseas

- The presidential candidate of the Democratic Party in the Philippines, Romulo, and the presidential candidate of the Nationalist Party, Magsaysay agree to cooperate in preventing the schemes of supporters of the President in office, Quirino.

An elementary school in Seoul giving lessons in the schoolyard as its classrooms have been burnt down. (June 5, 1953)

June 2, Tuesday(April 21, by lunar calendar, 甲申日 Blue Monkey) Cloudy
1,074 Day of the War

War Situation
- Combat continues on Luke Castle Hill in the eastern frontline.
- The Chinese Communist Forces attack Porkchop Hill and T-type Hill in the western frontline.
- The UN Air Force launches 226,800 kg of high explosive bombs at the Communist Forces' positions in the eastern frontline.

At Home
- President Syngman Rhee hands over a proposition to withdraw foreign troops after concluding the Korea-U.S. Mutual Defense Agreement to the U.S. President.
- The U.S. Secretary of the Army, Stephenson, states at the Appropriations Subcommittee of the Senate that the cost of the Korean War has reached US$15 billion.

June 3, Wednesday (April 22, by lunar calendar, 乙酉日 Blue Rooster) Clear and Windy
1,075 Day of the War

War Situation
- The ROK Army mounts fierce counterattacks and repulses the Communist Forces on Luke Castle Hill.

At Home
- President Syngman Rhee proposes to conclude conclude the Korea-U.S. Mutual Defense Agreement before the Armistice.
- The Minister of Foreign Affairs, Byeon Yeong-tae, hands over four conditions for the Armistice including a Korea-U.S. Mutual Defense Agreement to the U.S. President.
- The joint memorial ceremony of the Army, Navy and Air Forces is held.
- The Federation of Korea Cultural Organization agrees on a registration problem of culture persons with the Education Ministry.

Overseas
- The U.S. Senate unanimously approves an active objection to the UN membership of China.

June 4, Thursday (April 23, by lunar calendar, 丙戌日 Red Dog) Cloudy and Rainy
1,076 Day of the War

War Situation
- Infantry Units of the ROK Army develop recapturing battles for seven outposts lost on the May 27 in the eastern frontline and mid frontline.
- The representative, Choe Deok-sin, refuses to attend the Armistice talks in succession and

only the liaison officer, Colonel Lee Soo-young, attends.

At Home
- The National Assembly Plenary Session decides to organize the Armistice Measures Special Commission.
- The Director of the Public Information Office warns that if the Chinese Communist Forces do not withdraw their troops from Korea, there will be no Armistice.

June 5, Friday (April 24, by lunar calendar, 丁亥日 Red Pig) Rainy, Cloudy and Windy
1,077 Day of the War

War Situation
- Combat continues on Myohyeong Hill in the eastern frontline.
- The authority of the UN POW camp announces that 2,000 anti-Communist POWs demonstrated against the Armistice proposal of the UN Forces in the Masan POW camp.

At Home
- The UN Forces Commander, General Clark, visits Korea and has a talk with President Syngman Rhee.
- A combat police unit launches in Namwon in North Jeolla Province.

June 6, Saturday (April 25, by lunar calendar, 戊子日 Yellow Rat) Rainy
1,078 Day of the War

War Situation
- The Communist Forces penetrate into the eastern side of the Luke Castle Hill in the eastern frontline.
- The main conference of the Armistice talks is held at the request of the Communist Forces and is adjourned within 19 minutes. The representative of Korea does not attend.

At Home
- President Syngman Rhee announces the Government's intention to fight to the bitter end even without U.S. support.
- The Ministry of Commerce and Industry establishes a checking regulation of exported ores.
- The Ministry of Agriculture and Forestry signs an aid agreement for farming equipment and raw materials with the UN Korean Reconstruction Agency.

June 7, Sunday (April 26, by lunar calendar, 己丑日 Yellow Ox) Rainy
1,079 Day of the War

War Situation
- Troops of the UN Forces fail a recapturing operation for Luke Castle Hill in the eastern

frontline.

- The main conference of the Armistice talks is held at 11 a.m. and has taken two recesses at the request of the Communist Forces.

At Home

- The UN Forces Commander, Clark, arrives in Seoul and returns to Tokyo after two emergency consultations with President Syngman Rhee.
- The Acting Prime Minister, Byeon Yeong-tae, states that the U.S. President, Eisenhower, expressed his objection to conclude the Korea-U.S. Mutual Defense Agreement after the Armistice.
- A Semi-Emergency Martial Law is declared in all over the country.

June 8, Monday (April 27, by lunar calendar, 庚寅日 White Tiger) Rainy, Clear and Cloudy
1,080 Day of the War

War Situation

- The staff officer meeting of both parties has held two secret talks and had discussed details of exchanging POWs.

At Home

- President Syngman Rhee reasserts his decision to continue combat operations.
- The National Assembly Plenary Session passes a motion on the standby for the Armistice and suspension of bill consideration.
- The standing committee of supreme people's assembly in North Korea organizes the national construction committee and renames the city construction ministry as the city management ministry.

Overseas

- Both representatives of the Korean Armistice Negotiation sign the agreement on the scope of power of the Neutral Nation Repatriation Committee.
- The U.S. Ambassador of Korea, Yang Yu-chan states in a press conference that if the Armistice is completed in present state, the ROK Army will continue to fight.

June 9, Tuesday (April 28, by lunar calendar, 辛卯日 White Rabbit) Cloudy and Clear
1,081 Day of the War

War Situation

- The main conference of the Armistice talks is held, but adjourned in 12 minutes at the request of the Communist Forces side.

At Home

- The Commander of the Eighth U.S. Army, General Maxwell Taylor, pays a visit to President Syngman Rhee and holds a 30-minute secret discussion.

- The National Assembly makes a decision to send a message objecting the Armistice Talks to the UN General Assembly, the President of the United States, U.S. Senate, U.S. House of Representatives and the British Prime Minister.
- The police bureau of Seoul Metropolitan City issues an emergency order as a warning for the demonstration against the Armistice.

Overseas

- Radio Beijing reports that both parties of Panmunjom Armistice talks reached a complete and final agreement on the exchange of the war prisoners.
- The U.S. Secretary of National Defense, Charles E. Wilson declares in his testimony to the United States Senate that the withdrawal of U.S. Armed Forces will be conducted at least after six months.

June 10, Wednesday (April 29, by lunar calendar, 壬辰日 Black Dragon) Cloudy, Clear and Cloudy
1,082 Day of the War

War Situation

- The North Korean Army increases its pressure for control of Christmas Hill in the eastern frontline.
- Seven thousand soldiers of the Chinese Communist Forces start an attack in the mid-eastern frontline at night.
- The Chinese Communist Forces attack Harry Hill in northwestern Cheorwon.

At Home

- The National Assembly Plenary Session passes a bill against raising the military exchange rates
- The Army Chief of Staff, Baek Seon-yeop, returns from the United States to Seoul and immediately visits Gyeongmudae to meet President Syngman Rhee.
- The Minister of Foreign Affairs, Byeon Yeong-tae, and the Minister of National Defense, Sin Tae-yeong, testify on the Armistice negotiation in the National Assembly.
- Stores in Seoul are closed to demonstrate opposition to the Armistice.

Overseas

- The Korean Ambassador to the UN, Im Bong-jik, announces that progress in the Armistice talks made Korean distrust of Western nations.
- The Swiss Government notifies its participation in the Neutral Nations' Commission for the repatriation of POWs in the Korean War to the U.S. Government.

June 11, Thursday (May 1, by lunar calendar, 癸巳日 Black Snake) Cloudy and Clear
1,083 Day of the War

War Situation

- The UN Forces recapture Christmas Hill which has been lost to the Communist Forces.
- The U.S. 3rd Division repulses several attacks of the Chinese Communist Forces with 1,000 soldiers for Harry Hill in northwestern Cheorwon.
- The UN Air Force heavily bombs the Communist Forces' positions at the frontline under cover of its ground Forces.

At Home
- President Syngman Rhee states that the Armistice under the current conditions means death to Koreans.
- The National Assembly Plenary Session adopts "a recommendation for forming a Korea-U.S. alliance" and "the suggestion for developing a national movement against the Armistice."
- The citizens' rally to support the Government's stance is held in Busan.

June 12, Friday (May 2, by lunar calendar, 甲午日 Blue Horse) Clear, Cloudy and Clear
1,084 Day of the War

War Situation
- Offensive and Defensive battles on hills in the middle frontline are aggravated.
- The UN Force repulses 600 soldiers of the Communist Forces attacking the Sniper Ridge in northwestern Gimhwa.
- A Sabre jet fighter squad of the UN Forces attacks the northwestern part of Jinnampo and an airfield of northwestern Sariwon.

At Home
- The Ministry of National Defense establishes the Armistice Task Force constituted with the Army, Navy and Air Forces.
- Anti-Armistice protests are held in Seoul and Busan every day.

June 13, Saturday (May 3, by lunar calendar, 乙未日 Blue Sheep) Cloudy, Clear and Cloudy
1,085 Day of the War

War Situation
- The Communist Forces attack the vicinity of Capitol Hill under fierce artillery cover.
- A Sabre jet fighter squad of the UN Forces shoots down two MIG jet fighters and smashes a MIG jet fighter of the Communist Forces.
- The staff officer meeting of both parties reviews the finial detail of the Armistice agreement and the Military Demarcation Line.

At Home
- The National Assembly Plenary Session passes a motion for opening the Plenary Committee.

- The Ministry of Commerce and Industry appropriates $1,623,000 for the 1953 Small and Medium Industry Recovery Program.
- Communist airplanes drop flare bombs on Incheon and Gimpo Airport. An air-raid warning is sounded in Seoul.

June 14, Sunday (May 4, by lunar calendar, 丙申日 Red Monkey) Cloudy
1,086 Day of the War

War Situation
- The Communist Forces launch a huge nighttime attack in the mid-eastern frontline and eastern frontline.
- The U.S. battleship, USS New Jersey, gives converging fires from its board to the Communist Forces' bases to support the UN ground Forces at Myohyeong Hill on the east coast.

At Home
- The National Assembly holds closed session of the member committee of the to establish counter measures for the Armistice issue.
- The Cabinet Meeting passes "the legislative bill to establish the Korean UNESCO Committee."

Overseas
- The King of Cambodia flees to Thailand as an exile and protest against French Government's breaching its promise to allow Cambodia's full independence from France.

June 15, Monday (May 5, by lunar calendar, 丁酉日 Red Rooster) Cloudy and Clear
1,087 Day of the War

War Situation
- The Communist Forces heavily attack the UN Forces' positions with 30,000 soldiers in the mid-frontline and eastern frontline.
- The UN Navy attacks coastal targets of the Communist Forces under cover of the ground Forces.
- The UN Air Fleet sallies into the Communist Forces' outposts with 2,115 sorties, the highest since the outbreak of war.

At Home
- President Syngman Rhee warns that he will not ignore the activities of journalists who have been reporting unfavorable articles on Korea.

Overseas
- The U.S. State Department announces that Sweden, Switzerland, India, Poland, and Czechoslovakia officially notified to the U.S. Government their participations in the Neutral

Nations Commission for exchanging POWs of the Korean War.
- The Ministry of National Defense of Switzerland announces that 50 Swiss representatives of the Neutral Nations Commission for exchanging POWs will arrive in Korea within two months after the Armistice agreement and they will stay for about six months.

June 16, Tuesday (May 6, by lunar calendar, 戊戌日 Yellow Dog) Cloudy, Clear and Windy
1,088 Day of the War

War Situation
- The 5th and 8th Divisions of the ROK Army develop a new defense line in the Jihyeong Ridge in the upper area of the Bukhan River.
- The UN aircraft continues to cover ground troops.

At Home
- The leading members' meeting of the Korea-U.S. military is held with the attendance of President Syngman Rhee in the middle frontline.
- The Ministry of Finance states that the Seoul branch office of the Ministry of Finance will deal with the nation's annual expenditure funds from June 15 to prepare for returning to the capital.

June 17, Wednesday (May 7, by lunar calendar, 己亥日 Yellow Pig) Rainy and Windy
1,089 Day of the War

War Situation
- The UN Forces Commander, Clark, appoints Maj. Gen. Bryan as the representative of the UN Forces for the Joint Military Armistice Committee which will be established after the Armistice Agreement.
- The main conference of the Armistice talks resumes and takes a recess at the UN Forces' request 20 minutes later;
  The representative of Korea, Maj. Gen. Choe Deok-sin, undauntedly continues to refuse to attend the Armistice talks.

At Home
- President Syngman Rhee replies to a letter(June 6) from U.S. President Eisenhower saying that Korea cannot allow the Armistice.
- The Minister of Home Affairs, Jin Heon-sik, declares a state of air defense emergency and enforces it in Seoul, Gyeonggi Province and Gangwon Province.

June 18, Thursday (May 8, by lunar calendar, 庚子日 White Rat) Rainy, Clear, Rainy and Windy
1,090 Day of the War

War Situation

- The UN Forces repulse the Chinese Communist Forces' attack after a fierce battle on Harry Hill in northwestern Cheorwon.
- The staff officers meeting of the Armistice talks is held for an hour and a half from 11 a.m. and then takes a recess indefinitely. And then, official translator's meeting is subsequently held.

At Home
- President Syngman Rhee orders the release of 27,000 anti-Communist POWs in the UN POW camps.
- The Monetary Policy Committee decides the bid rate of dollar for won (60 to 1) and the selling rate of dollar for won (61 to 1).
- The Provost Marshal, Won Yong-deok, announces that all patriotic POWs in the UN POW camps in Korea are released at 5 a.m. on June 18.

Overseas
- The President of the UN General Assembly, Pearson, states that it is very serious situation for the Korean Government to release anti-Communist POWs from North Korea.

June 19, Friday (May 9, by lunar calendar, 辛丑日 White Ox) Cloudy, Rainy and Windy
1,091 Day of the War

War Situation
- The UN Air Force develops the biggest star shell operation since the outbreak of the Korea War in the upriver Bukhan, the southern Geumseong frontline.
- The Command of the UN POW camps announces that 494 anti-Communist POWs escaped the 10th Bupyeong POW camp at dawn in the June 19 and 30 were killed and 114 were injured.
- The representatives of troops dispatching nations in the Korean War discuss beforehand about the release of anti-Communist POWs.

At Home
- President Syngman Rhee discloses his letter to U.S. President Eisenhower in which he wrote that he could not accept the conditions of the Armistice.
- Kim Il Sung and Peng Dehuai send a complaint letter about releasing POWs to the UN Forces Commander, Clark.

June 20, Saturday (May 10, by lunar calendar, 壬寅日 Black Tiger) Rainy
1,092 Day of the War

War Situation
- The 5th U.S. Air Force announces that the UN Force lost 19 airplanes due to anti-aircraft firing by the Chinese Communist Forces in the week.

- The Chief delegate of the Communist Forces hands over to the representative of the UN Forces the complaint letter about the case of releasing POWs which Kim Il Sung and Peng Dehuai sent to the UN Forces Commander, Clark.

At Home
- The Ministry of Health orders to cure anti-Communist POWs for free to every provincial hospital.
- The Provost Marshal Won Yong-deok states that the ROK Military Police will release the entire Korean anti-Communist POWs at any price.
- The Communist Forces request to reaccommodate the released POWs in the Armistice talks.

Overseas
- The UN Forces Commander, Clark, sends a complaint letter to President Syngman Rhee that it is not possible to predict what kind of results would aeise by releasing anti-Communist POWs.

June 21, Sunday (May 11, by lunar calendar, 癸卯日 Black Rabbit) Rainy, Clear and Cloudy
1,093 Day of the War

War Situation
- The ROK Army repulses the Chinese Communist Forces' attack on Christmas Hill in the eastern frontline.

At Home
- Anti-Communist POWs escape in the Daegu POW camp in a mass.
- The U.S. Airborne Troops monitor POW camps.

Overseas
- The UN Forces Commander, Clark, states that the Korean Government is totally responsible for releasing anti-Communist POWs.
- India, Switzerland, and Sweden notify the U.S. Government that they are ready to join the Neutral Nations Commission for the repatriation of POWs in the Korean War.

June 22, Monday (May 12, by lunar calendar, 甲辰日 Blue Dragon) Rainy and Windy
1,094 Day of the War

War Situation
- A UN Navy destroyer bombards the Wonsan coast-batteries.

At Home
- President Syngman Rhee suggests three conditions for the Armistice to the UN Forces Commander, General Clark.
- The spokesman of the UN POW camps' command states that 107 POWs of the Chinese

Communist Forces escaped on June 21 and that it arrested 57 and extradited them to the UN Forces and 50 were detained by the Korean Police.

June 23, Tuesday (May 13, by lunar calendar, 乙巳日 Blue Snake) Rainy, Clear, Windy and Cloudy 1,095 Day of the War

War Situation
- The Chinese Communist Forces attacks the UN Forces' position near Gimhwa in the mid-frontline.
- The UN POW camp command announces that a strangled corpse of an anti-Communist prisoner was found near the Busan POW camp on June 22.
- The UN Forces' delegation of the Military Armistice Commission which will be the highest organization after the Armistice agreement establishes its head office in Munsan.

At Home
- President Syngman Rhee suggests three conditions for agreeing on the Armistice completion; (1) The Chinese Communist Forces' evacuation or both the Chinese Communist Forces and the UN Forces withdraw together; (2) Before the evacuation, the Korea-U.S. Mutual Defense Agreement must be signed; (3) Political talks will be held within three months of the time limit after the Armistice Agreement. If the political talks fail to agree on peace settlement, the war will continue.

Overseas
- The President of the UN General Assembly, Pearson, hands over a complaint letter

the U.S. officers meeting the North Korean officers to discuss the Armistice agreement in Panmunjom. (June 23 1953)

548

blaming President Syngman Rhee for releasing anti-Communist POWs.

June 24, Wednesday (May 14, by lunar calendar, 丙午日 Red Horse) Clear, Cloudy and Windy
1,096 Day of the War

War Situation
- The Security Commander of the southern area, Lee Yong-moon, Brig. Gen, dies by an air plane accident.

At Home
- President Syngman Rhee notifies that if the Armistice completes in the current conditions, the ROK Army will leave the command of the UN Forces Commander.
- Radio Pyongyang announces the total wartime accomplishments for three years since the outbreak of the Korean War as announced by the Communist Forces' Command of North Korea.

June 25, Thursday (May 15, by lunar calendar, 丁未日 Red Sheep) Rainy and Windy
1,097 Day of the War

War Situation
- The Communist Forces continue to attack Sniper Ridge in northwestern Gimhwa.
- A B-29 fighter bomber squad of the UN Forces bombs the North Korean airfield for five days.

At Home
- The Military Police Command detained Cho Byung-ok who blamed the release of anti-Communist POWs and arrested Kim Seong-ju.
- The Provost Marshal, Won Yong-deok, states that there will not be any more releases of POWs and the security of POW camps is transferred to the U.S. Army.
- The Korea Musician Association is founded (the chairman: Hyun Jae-myung).

June 26, Friday (May 16, by lunar calendar, 戊申日 Yellow Monkey) Rainy
1,098 Day of the War

War Situation
- The ROK Army withdraws from Capitol Hill due to the Communist Forces' attack in the mid-eastern frontline.
- A squadron of Sabre jet fighters shoots down two MIG jet fighters over the Yalu River.

At Home
- The Military Manpower Administration of Ministry of National Defense lifts the identity reporting period of the Second Peoples' Force;
  They overlook past evading actions and lift the regulation of evading inducing declarations

freely.

Overseas
- The Chief delegate of the UN Forces in the Armistice talks, Harrison, leaves Munsan and arrives at Tokyo to have a talk with the UN Forces Commander, Clark.
- Radio Beijing blames that the insistence of President Syngman Rhee for the withdrawal of foreign troops before the Armistice completion is to continue the war.

June 27, Saturday (May 17, by lunar calendar, 己酉日 Yellow Rooster) Rainy
1,099 Day of the War

War Situation
- The 3rd Division of the ROK Army recaptures the Lockout summit on the southern Capitol Hill.
- A combat continues in Sniper Ridge in the mid-eastern frontline.

At Home
- President Syngman Rhee and the Assistant Secretary of State, Robertson, hold the second talks.
- The Central Executive Committee of the Democratic Nationalist Party decides to support the release of POWs and the opposition to the Armistice completion.

Overseas
- UN Secretary-General Hammarskjold, expresses his opposition to President Syngman Rhee's insistence to continue the Korean War for unification in a radio broadcast.
- The President of the Philippines, Quirino, signs the act of amnesty for the Japanese war criminals to commute all death sentenced criminal to a life imprisonment.

June 28, Sunday (May 18, by lunar calendar, 庚戌日 White Dog) Cloudy, Rainy and Windy
1,100 Day of the War

War Situation
- The ROK Army in the Gwanmang Mountain of the southern Capitol Hill in the mid eastern frontline withdraws due to the Communist Forces' attack at night.
- ROK Army repulses from 2 outpost positions Small Nori Hill on the western frontline due to the Communist Forces' attack.
- The UN Forces Commander, Clark, notifies the Communist Forces that it is impossible to reaccomodate POWs.

At Home
- The U.S. presidential envoy, Robertson, holds the 3rd round of secret talks with President Syngman Rhee.
- The section chief meeting of public information in every province and city is held in the

conference room of the Capitol building.

- The Radio Pyongyang blames President Syngman Rhee and U.S. supporters of the Korea-U.S. Mutual Defense Agreement and accuse that the Defense Agreement will interrupt the political talks.

June 29, Monday (May 19, by lunar calendar, 辛亥日 White Pig) Rainy and Cloudy
1,101 Day of the War

War Situation

- The 3rd Division of the ROK Army recaptures Gwanmang Mountain in the south of Capitol Hill after a fierce five-hour battle.
- The liaison officer of the UN Forces holds a meeting in Panmunjom and hands over the reply of the UN Forces Commander, Clark, for the letter of the Communist Forces which requested to reaccomodate anti-Communist POWs.

At Home

- President Syngman Rhee has the 4th round of talks with the UN Forces Commander, Clark.
- The Ministry of Commerce and Industry changes the standard of the price of cotton cloth from 14 su (手, thread) to 16 su.

June 30, Tuesday (May 20, by lunar calendar, 壬子日 Black Rat) Cloudy and Clear
1,102 Day of the War

War Situation

- A fierce combat in the Virginia Hill between Christmas Hill and the Bukhan River in the eastern frontline.
- The U.S. envoy, Robertson, inspects the frontline with the political advisor, Murphy and the Assistant Secretary of State, McAdoo, and visits the U.S. Division in the western frontline.
- The Supreme Allied Commander of the NATO, Ridgway, requests to hold the Armistice talks on the Dutch hospital ship in the Wonsan Port.

At Home

- The U.S. presidential envoy, Robertson (the Assistant Secretary of State), has the 5th round of talks for 55 minutes with President Syngman Rhee.
- The National Assembly Plenary Session passes the bill for the investigation of Gwangju and Yeosu spies and Sin Hyeong-sik case.
- The Central Radio Station returns from Busan to Seoul and broadcasts 14 hours per day.
- The Radio Pyongyang claims that the reply of the UN Forces Commander, Clark in June 29 is an unfaithful indication for the Armistice of the U.S. Government.

July 1, Wednesday (May 21, by lunar calendar, 癸丑日 Black Ox) Clear, Cloudy and Clear
1,103 Day of the War

War Situation

- The ROK Army recaptures the Virginia Hill in the east of Bukhan River and withdraws due to a counterattack of the Chinese Communist Forces.
- A hand-to-hand fight occurs at Gwanmang Mountain of the western Capitol Hill.
- The UN fighters and bombers have made 1,535 sorties and attacked supply targets and troops of the Communist Forces.

At Home

- The Minister of Foreign Affairs, Byeon Yeong-tae, hands over the letter of President Syngman Rhee describing his position on the current situation he faces to the U.S. Presidential Envoy, Robertson.
- The Korean Trade Association establishes a lapse rate of collecting special dues.
- The UN Civil Agency in Korea is dissolved and starts again as the UN Civil Assistance Command in Korea.

Overseas

- The General Assembly of UNESCO elects Evans as the secretary-general.
- The UN Forces Commander, Clark, holds a top-level meeting of the Army, Navy, and Air Force with the chief of staff of the U.S. Army, Collins, in the UN Forces Command in Tokyo.

July 2, Thursday (May 22, by lunar calendar, 甲寅日 Blue Tiger) Cloudy and Rainy
1,104 Day of the War

War Situation

- The Eighth U.S. Army Commander, Taylor, holds a series of secret talks with Commanders of the Army, Navy, and Air Force in Korea.

At Home

- The Minister of Foreign Affairs, Byeon Yeong-tae, says in an interview that he does not refuse the U.S. President's promise of peaceful unification but insist on a time limit.
- The Minister of National Defense, Son Won-il, stresses an enforcement of conscription to strengthen the ROK Army and the impossibility of the Armistice Agreement without Korea.

July 3, Friday (May 23, by lunar calendar, 乙卯日 Blue Rabbit) Rainy and Windy
1,105 Day of the War

War Situation

- The ROK Army recaptures Gwanmang Mountain in the mid-eastern frontline around daybreak.
- Ship planes of the UN attack the Communist Forces' positions, taking a risk of rainfall and heavy cloud.

At Home
- The National Assembly Plenary Session has the second reading for the bill of the Criminal Law and debates clause by clause from the Article 174 to the Article 258 and passes it with a partial amendment.
- The U.S. presidential envoy, Robertson, visits President Syngman Rhee with Ambassador Briggs and Advisor Murphy and hands over the reply for his previous letter to him.
- The North Korean Broadcasting blames the reply of the UN Forces Commander, Clark, on June 29.

Overseas
- The President of the General Assembly, Hammarskjold, decides to convene the UN General Assembly on June 15 if it is not possible to finalize the Armistice Agreement of the Korean War in 10 days.

July 4, Saturday (May 24, by lunar calendar, 丙辰日 Red Dragon) Cloudy and Clear
1,106 Day of the War

War Situation
- The ROK Army kills 130 soldiers of the Chinese Communist Forces by a gunfight in the Sniper Ridge.
- The authorities of the UN Forces announce that 8,000 remaining POWs after the release of anti-Communist POWs moved to Busan and Nonsan.

At Home
- President Syngman Rhee declares U.S. Independence Day as the Peace Prayer Day.
- The North Korea Government appoints Choi Yong-kun as the deputy prime minister.

July 5, Sunday (May 25, by lunar calendar, 丁巳日 Red Snake) Rainy and Windy
1,107 Day of the War

War Situation
- Ground combats are calm.
- The Southern District Garrison Command announces the June wartime accomplishment: 96 Communist guerrillas are killed, four are captured, and six defect.

At Home
- President Syngman Rhee states, "I have tried to get rid of misunderstanding each other in the present meeting with the U.S. presidential envoy, Robertson but it is not possible to

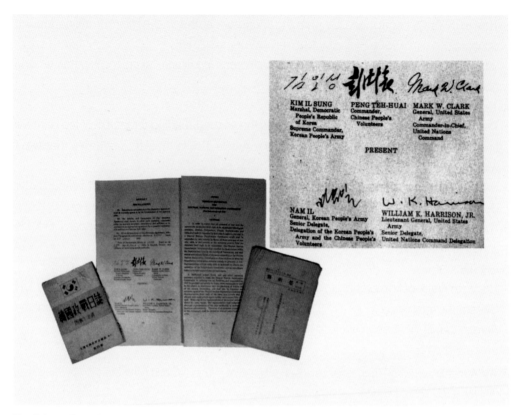

The Original Text of the Armistice agreement.

predict the result of the meeting."

July 6, Monday (May 26, by lunar calendar, 戊午日 Yellow Horse) Rainy and Windy
1,108 Day of the War

War Situation
- Ground combats are calm due to the heavy rain.
- The 7th U.S. Division loses control of Porkchop Hill.(July 6~10)
- The Eighth U.S. Army Commander calls his brains of the Armed Forces such as Corps Commanders under the supervision.

At Home
- President Syngman Rhee has talks with the U.S. presidential envoy, Robertson and Ambassador Briggs for an hour.
- The Ministry of Commerce and Industry returns to Seoul.
- The Decree on the Establishment of the UNESCO in Korea is declared and the Korean branch of UNESCO is established.

Overseas

- The representatives of 16 combatant nations in the Korean War agree to support the Armistice of the Korean War; they support a policy of the UN Forces Commander, Clark, to complete the Armistice in his way.

July 7, Tuesday (May 27, by lunar calendar, 己未日 Yellow Sheep) Clear, Cloudy and Windy
1,109 Day of the War

War Situation

- A combat in the eastern Berlin Hill and northern Berlin Hill of Gorangpo continues.

At Home

- The National Assembly Plenary Session passes a bill to send the encouragement for struggles against Communists in the other areas of East Germany.
- The Minister of Home Affairs, Jin Heon-sik, establishes a dedicated intelligence section in the security agency to prevent the activities of spies and Communist remnants.

July 8, Wednesday (May 28, by lunar calendar, 庚申日 White Monkey) Rainy and Cloudy
1,110 Day of the War

War Situation

- The liaison officer of the Communist Forces hands over the reply of the Communist Forces' Commander on July 7 for the letter of the UN Forces Commander, General Clark, on June 29 in the liaison officers meeting.

At Home

- President Syngman Rhee has the 10th talks with the U.S. presidential envoy, Robertson.
- The National Assembly Plenary Session passes a recommendation on the illegal occupation of Dokdo Island by the Japanese Government officials.

July 9, Thursday (May 29, by lunar calendar, 辛酉日 White Rooster) Cloudy
1,111 Day of the War

War Situation

- The Communist Forces' attack on Kim Il Sung Hill in the eastern frontline is repulsed.
- Outposts in the northern Berlin Hill and the eastern Berlin Hill of the Gorangpo and outposts in the Arrow Head Hill and the Pork Chop Hill in the western frontline are surrounded and fierce clashes occur.

At Home

- President Syngman Rhee has talks with the advisor, Murphy, the Ambassador, Briggs, the U.S. president envoy, Robertson and the UN Forces Commander, Clark.
- The National Assembly Plenary Session passes "the bill of the criminal law" and "the bill

for improving the treatment of disabled veterans."

July 10, Friday (May 30, by lunar calendar, 壬戌日 Black Dog) Cloudy and Clear
1112 Day of the War

War Situation
- The main conference of the Armistice Conference resumes in 20 days and it is held as secret talks for 29 minutes and then closes.
- The last procedure of the Armistice is discussed at the main meeting of the Armistice Conference.

At Home
- The National Assembly Plenary Session passes "the amendment bill of the Farmland Reform Law."
- The Ministry of National Defense appoints the Chief of Staff of Naval Operations, Park Ok-kyu, as the Chief of Naval Operations according to the order of the Minister of National Defense, Son Won-il.

July 11, Saturday (June 1, by lunar calendar, 癸亥日 Black Pig) Clear, Cloudy, Clear and Windy
1113 Day of the War

War Situation
- The ROK Army repulses 4,000 soldiers of the Chinese Communist Forces in the mid-eastern frontline.
- President Syngman Rhee confers Presidential Citation on the Eighth U.S. Army.

At Home
- President Syngman Rhee closes the Korea-U.S. talks with the Assistant Secretary of State, Robertson, which has been opened 14 times since June 26.
- President Syngman Rhee warns in the award ceremony of the Eighth U.S. Army that if Korea does not achieve the unification, South Korea will continue to be in danger.

July 12, Sunday (June 2, by lunar calendar, 甲子日 Blue Rat) Clear, Cloudy and Clear
1114 Day of the War

War Situation
- The UN Navy and Air Force hit the Wonsan Port all day long.
- A Sabre jet fighter squad of the UN Forces shoots down seven MIG fighters and smashes a MIG fighter.
- The Communist Forces broadcasts in the western frontline the propaganda that peace will come to the U.S. Army in a few days.

At Home

- Envoy Robertson feels disconcerted by a report by a U.S. media correspondent that President Syngman Rhee stated that the Korean Government had not agreed on the Armistice but they would not oppose it for three months, and Robertson refuses to comment.
- The ship of the Japanese Maritime Safety Agency which invaded Dokdo Island is fired upon.

Overseas
- The chairman of the UN General Assembly expresses the intention to convene the General Assembly after the Armistice Agreement of the Korean War.
- The Assistant Secretary of State, Robertson, arrives at Haneda Airport in Tokyo and states to a press briefing that the result of the talks with President Syngman Rhee is satisfactory.

July 13, Monday (June 3, by lunar calendar, 乙丑日 Blue Ox) Cloudy and Clear
1115 Day of the War

War Situation
- The final attack of the Chinese Communist Forces starts. (July Main Attack)
- Fighter-bombers and light bombers of the UN Forces attack the Communist Forces' positions in the frontline.
- The Black Watch Troops of the U.K. depart from Korea after paying their respects at the UN Cemetery.

At Home
- The Public Information Office announces a statement about the Korea-U.S. talks; President Syngman Rhee emphasizes that the goal of Korea unification will not change.
- North Korea appoints Park Ui-wan as the deputy prime minister of Cabinet.

July 14, Tuesday (June 4, by lunar calendar, 丙寅日 Red Tiger) Cloudy and Windy
1116 Day of the War

War Situation
- Three Divisions of the ROK Army withdraw from the Sniper Ridge to the southern shore of the Kumsong stream.
- A fighter bomber squad of the UN Forces launches more than 181,400 kg of bombs on the Chinese Communist Forces in the mid-eastern frontline.

At Home
- The National Assembly hears an investigation report for the case of the Gwangju and Yeoju spies and the case of Sin Hyeong-sik's treacherous words and actions.
- Four persons, including the secretary-general of the Democratic Nationalist Party, Cho Byung-ok and so on are taken to police custody in the Seoul District Public Prosecutors'

Office for violating "the National Security Law" and "the National Guards Law"

July 15, Wednesday (June 5, by lunar calendar, 丁卯日 Red Rabbit) Rainy and Windy
1117 Day of the War

War Situation
- Two companies of the Communist Forces attack the U.S. Army's position in the western Mundeungri and occupy it at dawn.
- The Chinese Communist Forces input its reinforcing Units to a perimeter in the mid-eastern frontline, under cover of heavy rain and continue to attack.

At Home
- The National Assembly Plenary Session passes "the amendment bill of the Remuneration Law for members to the National Assembly."
- The Prime Minister, Baek Du-jin, announces that the U.S. presidential envoy already advised the U.S. Government to support the Korean Economic Assistance Three-Year Plan.

July 16, Thursday (June 6, by lunar calendar, 戊辰日 Yellow Dragon) Rainy, Cloudy, Clear and Windy
1,118 Day of the War

War Situation
- The Communist Forces deploy 16 T-34 type tanks of the Soviet Union to support attacks on the UN Forces in the mid-eastern frontline.
- The main conference of the Armistice talks adjourns in 25 minutes.
- The spokesman of the UN Forces, Colonel Här, states that the talks still are secret talks.

At Home
- President Syngman Rhee encourages soldiers of the second Corps of ROK Army in the mid-eastern frontline.
- The UN Forces Commander, General Clark, arrives in Seoul and visits Gyeongmudae and has a talk with President Syngman Rhee.

Overseas
- The People's Liberation Army of China repulses amphibious operations of the nationalist Army of Taiwan for Fukien Dongshandao.
- Riots break out in various parts of India. The armed Forces move out to put down demonstrations in Calcutta.

July 17, Friday (June 7, by lunar calendar, 己巳日 Yellow Snake) Cloudy
1119 Day of the War

War Situation

- The North Korean Communist Forces invade the UN Forces' positions in the eastern and western Luke Castle Hill on the eastern frontline.
- President Syngman Rhee inspects the mid-frontline which is under battle conditions with the Army Chief of Staff, Baek Seon-yeop.
- The UN Forces Commander, General Clark, consults with the representative of the UN Forces in Munsan for three hours.

At Home
- The Government holds a celebration for the Constitution Day in the Capitol plaza.
- The Communist Forces accepts the Armistice Agreement.

July 18, Saturday (June 8, by lunar calendar, 庚午日 White Horse) Cloudy
1120 Day of the War

War Situation
- The ROK Army advances slowly in the mid-eastern frontline. An area of 8.8km of the occupied zone is recaptured but stubborn resistance of the Communist Force blocks it gradually.
- A fight bomber squad of the UN Forces has made 375 sorties to 4 p.m. and covers Ground Forces.
- The Chinese Communist Forces propagates that the Armistice agreement will be signed on July 19 in the western frontline in English.

At Home
- The Cabinet Meeting reviews the Dokdo issues and the details for concluding the Korea-U.S. Mutual Defense Treaty in the Syngman Rhee-Robertson Joint Communique.

Overseas
- The Public Information Division of the Nationalist Army of Taiwan announces that shock troops of the Nationalist Army of Taiwan attack Dongshandao between Shantou and Xiamen on June 16.

July 19, Sunday (June 9, by lunar calendar, 辛未日 White Sheep) Rainy, Cloudy and Rainy
1,121 Day of the War

War Situation
- The ROK Army fiercely attacks Samwon Hill in the eastern frontline and captures it.
- An Artillery Unit of the UN Forces finds out a Regiment of the Chinese Communist Forces reaching Kumsong River under cover of darkness and attacks it.
- The main conference of the Armistice talks resumes at 2 p.m. and repeats recessing and resuming and then it is adjourned at 5:47.

Overseas

- Pravda in the Soviet Union accuses the United States of being responsible for the delay of the Armistice Agreement as they have overlooked the activity of President Syngman Rhee.

July 20, Monday (June 10, by lunar calendar, 壬申日 Black Monkey) Rainy
1122 Day of the War

War Situation
- Ground combats are alleviated in the mid-eastern frontline.
- An official translators meeting of the Armistice talks is held.

At Home
- President Syngman Rhee instructs the outline of holding a national convention of the National Association to the members of the central committee of the Liberal Party and all of the representatives in every branch of the National Association.
- The Government appoints Sin Tae-yeong as the Commander before declaring "The Citizen Armed Forces Decree."
- The Minister of Foreign Affairs, Byeon Yeong-tae, states that Korea will not attend the signing ceremony of the Armistice agreement.

July 21, Tuesday (June 11, by lunar calendar, 癸酉日 Black Rooster) Cloudy and Rainy
1123 Day of the War

War Situation
- Ground combats are relatively calm.
- The ROK Army repulses attacks with more than a company Force of the Communist Forces in five Hills from the night of July 20 to the morning of July 21 in the mid-eastern frontline.

At Home
- A senior-level official of the Government states that President Syngman Rhee is looking forward to a reply from Washington on the issues that could not be resolved when the U.S. presidential envoy visited Korea.

July 22, Wednesday (June 12, by lunar calendar, 甲戌日 Blue Dog) Cloudy, Rainy and Cloudy
1124 Day of the War

War Situation
- The North Korean Communist Forces searches and attacks lightly for the Luke position and Cook position in the eastern frontline.
- The UN Navy shoots down three MIG jet fighters over the Yalu River.

At Home
- President Syngman Rhee announces a statement in the form of a reply letter for the

question submitted by foreign press reporters;

"We Koreans will postpone our determination while the UN Force persuades the Chinese Communist Force to withdraw but if the Armistice fails, we will act freely."

- Gyeongchanhoe is formed to protect the collections of 80,000 sacred writings of Buddhism in the Haeinsa Temple.

July 23, Thursday (June 13, by lunar calendar, 乙亥日 Blue Pig) Rainy, Clear and Cloudy
1,125 Day of the War

War Situation

- A fierce combat is carried out in the Samwon Hill of mid-eastern frontline and the ROK Army captures it under cover of artillery a 10 a.m. but withdraws from it after two hours.
- The staff officer meeting of both parties is held at 11 a.m. for 2 hours and 42 minutes.

At Home

- The Radio Pyongyang reports that the preparation for signing the Armistice agreement is reaching the final stage.

Overseas

- U.S. President Eisenhower agrees on the Korea Economic Aid Six-Year Plan.

The Military Demarcation Line defined in the Armistice agreement on July 27, 1953. The Demilitarized Zone is established 2km from the Military Demarcation Line on both sides.

- U.S. Secretary of State, Dulles, proposes a Korea-U.S. summit conference be held after the signing of the Armistice Agreement.

July 24, Friday (June 14, by lunar calendar, 丙子日 Red Rat) Cloudy and Clear
1,126 Day of the War

War Situation

- An attack Unit of the ROK Army starts counterattack in Kumsong in the mid-eastern frontline and captures a hill.
- The UN Forces and the Communist Forces are advancing and retreating in the battle around the Going North Hill in a perimeter of Kumsong.
- The Communist Forces complete the construction work for the signing ceremony hall of the Armistice agreement.
- The Armistice Inspection Commission of the Communist Forces arrives in North Korea.

At Home

- President Syngman Rhee states that he understands that the United States agreed on the time limit for the political talks and reaffirming the position of South Korea for the Armistice.
- The Korea Government and the United States agree on the draft Armistice agreement.

July 25, Saturday (June 15, by lunar calendar, 丁丑日 Red Ox) Cloudy and Clear
1,127 Day of the War

War Situation

- The 1st U.S. Marine Division repulses the Chinese Communist Forces' attack for the Berlin Hill in the eastern frontline.
- The liaison officers in the Armistice Conference hold the 5th secret talks.

At Home

- The National Assembly Plenary Session passes "the bill for attending international conferences of members of the National Assembly."
- The Minister of Foreign Affairs, Byeon Yeong-tae, states that President Syngman Rhee will refuse the invitation for dispatching the delegate of Korea in the signing ceremony of the Armistice agreement.

Overseas

- The Senate Appropriations Committee of the U.S. rejects a suggestion of Senator McCarthy to suspend aid allocations for the allied nation which continues trading with China.
- The East German Guard establishes a 3km barbed-wire entanglement between the Occupied Western Berlin and the Eastern Berlin to prevent importing foodstuffs from West Germany.

July 26, Sunday (June 16, by lunar calendar, 戊寅日 Yellow Tiger) Clear and Windy
1128 Day of the War

War Situation

- All of the frontline enters a lull.
- The liaison officer meeting of both parties has been held until the night.
- The UN Forces Commander, General Clark, makes a statement in Tokyo at 4 p.m.

At Home

- The UN Forces Commander, Clark, arrives in Seoul by plane at 6:50 p.m. and states that the Armistice Agreement will be a foothold for permanent world peace.

The UN Forces Commander, General Clark, signing the Armistice agreement in Munsan.(July 27,1953)

- The Prime Minister, Baek Du-jin, instructs that the Government agency which didn't return to Seoul must complete returning by July 31 and must sit at their desks in Seoul on August 1.
- The Minister of National Defense, Son Won-il, states that in the current situation, Korea will not interrupt the Armistice but will not cooperate either.

Overseas

Representatives of both sides signing the Armistice agreement in Panmunjom. (1953. 7. 27)

- The UN Secretary-General, Hammarskjold, decides that the UN Special General Assembly will be held on August 17 and send invitations to all member countries.
- Radio Beijing comments that the first touchstone of the United States which shows the will for the Armistice will be that the ROK Army and the UN Forces withdraw from the DMZ within the prescribed time limit after the Armistice agreement.
- The Commander of the French Ground Forces of the North French-Indochina, Maj. Gen Corgni, warns that after the Armistice agreement of Korea, if China enforces its military aid for the Vietminh Forces, it will be an international problem.
- The spokesman of the department of state of India states that if the Armistice agreement is signed, 4,000 Indian soldiers who have been dispatched in Korea will start to leave for India.

July 27, Monday (June 17, by lunar calendar, 己卯日 Yellow Rabbit) Clear
1129 Day of the War

War Situation
- All of the frontline stops battles at 10 p.m.

U.S. soldiers being delivered news of the Armistice completion in the field trenches. (July 27, 1953)

- The UN Forces Commander announces the Military Demarcation Line officially decided according to the Armistice agreement.
- The Armistice agreement is signed.
- The Supreme Commander of the North Korean Army, Kim Il Sung, officially signs the Preamble to the Armistice agreement in Pyongyang at 10 p.m.

At Home
- President Syngman Rhee announces on the occasion of the signing of the Armistice agreement that "We Koreans must achieve the goal of unification without fail."
- The UN Commission for the Rehabilitation of Korea announces on the Armistice completion that the UN Korea Committee will try to support Korea to achieve the United Independent Democratic Korea peacefully.

Overseas
- U.S. President Eisenhower requests the U.S. Congress to approve US$200 million for the first installment of the Korea Relief Fund.
- Moscow Broadcasting reports that the Moscow Government guarantees the efforts of the North Korean Government to unify and recover.

Korea's Long-Existing Military Demarcation Line Becomes Increasingly Fortified

Lee, Joong Keun 李重根

The 38th parallel "disappeared" as a fixed meridian line after the signing of the Armistice agreement on July 27, 1953. It was replaced by a flexible Military Demarcation Line (MDL). The line has been separating the South and North for over six decades, leaving painful hearts of dispersed families and heavy casualties and wasted mountains and rivers destroyed by firing and bombing. It has remained an eternal tragedy to the Korean people.

The three-year war left a massive loss of lives and properties. The war victims now known number 620,000 soldiers of the ROK Army; 160,000 soldiers of the UN forces; 930,000 soldiers of the North Korean Army; 1,000,000 soldiers of the Chinese Communist Forces; 2,500,000 civilians; 3,700,000 refugees; 300,000 war widows; 100,000 war orphans; and 10,000,000 separated families. As many as 19,000,000 people suffered damages, which was over half of South Korea's total population of 30,000,000 persons.

After the Armistice agreement, the United States, China, the Soviet Union and other nations concerned agreed to hold political negotiations to conclude the Korean War politically. It was held in Geneva on April 26, 1954 and was attended by 15 nations out of the 16 UN participating countries, except South Africa, and the Soviet Union and China from the Communist Forces. In the two month-long Geneva talks, important issues were discussed such as an election for unification under the observation of the international community and withdrawal of foreign troops from Korea. But the talks were closed without any conclusion on June 15, 1954. It was nothing more than acknowledging internationally of the Armistice system to stop the war as it was. As a result, the United States and the Soviet Union came to possess nuclear bombs, while a new type of international order was created to enable the maintenance of a world peace system equipped with nuclear weapons.

The Korean War became another international war. It has caused a great change of the international order. The Armistice agreement divided the international order after the Second World War into two blocs by ideology. And a fierce system competition was brought about between the capitalist and socialist countries which were reorganized in blocs. The United States established the North Atlantic Treaty Organization (NATO) and has constructed a security system for the Asia-Pacific region. Meanwhile, the Soviet Union established the Warsaw Treaty Organization to strengthen the defense of Eastern Europe as the Communist power in the Western Europe gradually weakened. Japan functioned as a military supply base for the Korean War. Due to the war, Japan could recover its depleted economic power as a defeated nation of the Pacific War and emerged as a key nation of East Asia.

The Korean War affected the Third World. Even though they achieved independence, Third World nations became well aware of the reality that participating either in the

U.S. camp or in the Soviet Union camp could be dangerous, so the apprehension of war has been amplified among them. China, making the most of the opportunity, has emerged as a leading power of the Third World. The Nations of the Third World adopted a powerful resolution to maintain their solid territorial rights and to respect their sovereignty through the Bandung Conference and the NAM (Non-Aligned Movement) and developed them into a Group of 77 Nations.

South Korea and North Korea have grown apart from each other, developing different systems and different social structures after the Armistice agreement. However, a war without the sounds of gunfire continues between the two. Their military power development was prioritized before the social structures and systems. The competitive efforts to strengthen the military power have caused the South-North confrontations and continuous tensions between the two parties. The flexible Military Demarcation Line has sometimes created opportunities for them to exchange conciliatory gestures, but the confrontational nature of the conflict on the Korean Peninsula has not changed in over 60 years. Both sides' supreme goals seem to be a peaceful unification, but they cannot find a way to attain it.

The South Korean have produced 11 Presidents – from the first President, Syngman Rhee, who had led the nation through the Korean War, to the 18th President, Park Geun-hye until now – while North Korea has been led by Premier Kim Il Sung, his son, Kim Jong Il, and now by his grandson, Kim Jong Un.

After North Korea's severing electric power transmission to South Korea on May 14, 1948, South Korea and North Korean underwent the War, thereafter they respectively developed their economies. However, the 2012 statistical data reveal a big difference between the economic performances of the two Koreas.

1) Population as one of the most important economic resources, South Korea: 49,770,000, North Korea: 24,308,000

2) GDP (gross domestic product): South Korea KRW 1,235 trillion vs. North Korea KRW 32.4 trillion

3) Total volume of trade (export and import): South Korea US$1.0796 trillion vs. North Korea US$6.3 billion.

4) Capacity of Power Generation (electricity), South Korea 79,342,000 KWatt vs. North Korea, KWatt 6,920,000.

5) Actual generation of power (electricity): South Korea 496,900,000 KWatt vs. North Korea 21,100,000 KWatt.

6) Import volume of crude oil: South Korea 926,763,000 barrels vs. North Korea 3,840,000 barrels.

7) Total length of roads: South Korea 105,931 km vs. North Korea 26,110 km

8) Per Capita Income (GNI): South Korea KRW24,920,000 vs. North Korea
KRW1,330,000

The MDL is neither a international line drawn by the world, nor a border line. It is important for us to change the MDL to a peace line through the efforts of both South and North Korea. The 38th parallel is a fixed line but the MDL is a flexible line. We have to treat the flexible line as a "starting line" for unification.

After the Armistice signing we have overcome a number of crises and have achieved the dream of an economic power shining on the global stage. Now, following the celebration of the 60th anniversary of the Armistice, South Korea and North Korea have to eliminate hostility, slander, and provocations toward each other based upon true cooperation, and try to clear the disgrace of the only country left divided in the world.

Now South Korea and North Korea face a difficult situation to assimilate each other in economy, politics, society and culture due to the stereotypes that have developed over the past 60 years. After the Second World War, soldiers of the Soviet Union said bitterly to themselves, "If we go to the United States to earn a living, we have to provide meals every morning by ourselves." After the unification of Germany, East Germans said, "There was no jobless person during the East German era but now we are worried about getting a job." All of us South Koreans should take the North Korean defectors into consideration to be assimilated with us in all the fields of the economy, society and culture as our South Korean family members.

If we recover our ethnic homogeneity with time, both South and North Koreans, must gather our thoughts to reach unification through the reform of consciousness. It will need time and patience. And also we should solve every problem through communication and compromise. In the economy, we should restore the trust process on the Korean Peninsula for the sake of our common prosperity. We must accomplish peaceful unification in the interests of achieving mutual prosperity through the cooperation of South and North Korea.

1950. 6. 25 ~ 1953. 7. 27

Korean War 1129
[Abridgment]

Editor in Chief	Lee, Joong Keun
Executive Editor	Kim, Myong Ho
Publisher	Lee, Joong Keun

Responsible Supervisor for Translation Chang, Myung Kwan

Printing Date | 7, May 2015
Publishing Date | 10, May 2015
Publisher | Lee, Joong Keun
Published by | WooJung Publishing Co.
Address | 120-23 Booyoung Bldg. Seosomun-dong Jung-gu Seoul, Korea
Telephone | 82-02-3774-5500   Fax | 82-02-3789-5333
http://www.booyoung.co.kr

ISBN   979-11-86233-13-9 03300   (Not for sale)